The Employment Trib

The Employment Tribunals Handbook

Practice, procedure and strategies for success

3rd Edition

by
Alan Payne
Barrister
5 Essex Court

John Paul Waite
Barrister
5 Essex Court

Jonathan Dixey
Barrister
5 Essex Court

Bloomsbury Professional

Bloomsbury Professional Ltd, Maxwelton House, 41–43 Boltro Road, Haywards Heath, West Sussex, RH16 1BJ

Bloomsbury Professional, an imprint of Bloomsbury Publishing Plc

A CIP Catalogue record for this book is available from the British Library.

ISBN: 978 1 84766 672 7

Typeset by Phoenix Photosetting, Chatham, Kent
Printed and bound in Great Britain by Martins the Printers
Berwick-upon-Tweed, Northumberland

Acknowledgements

The 3rd edition is dedicated to Luca Amaan Payne, born on 22 September 2010.

Special thanks are extended to John Waite, father of John-Paul Waite, and Jane Richards for their extensive work on the original draft of this book and for the many helpful suggestions which they made.

In addition, thanks are extended to Farrah Mauladad of Crown Office Chambers, wife of Alan Payne, for her patience in helping complete the subsequent editions of this book.

Finally, the authors would also like to thank all the members of the Employment Team at 5 Essex Court for their help with this edition.

About the Authors and Co-authors

Alan Payne

Alan Payne is a barrister and a member of the specialist employment law team at 5 Essex Court. He has extensive experience, both in the employment tribunal and Employment Appeal Tribunal, acting primarily for employers, in a wide variety of claims involving discrimination (all types), unlawful deduction of wages, unfair dismissal, equal pay, WTR and TUPE. He has also acted in a number of cases focusing on post termination restraints (both obtaining and resisting injunctions). He is develop vetted and has been a member of the panel of Treasury Counsel since 2003 and, in 2011, was appointed to the A panel. He is fluent in French and Italian. Prior to joining the Bar in 1996, he worked for a number of years as a lawyer for Heinz plc.

John-Paul Waite

John-Paul Waite is a practising barrister and member of the specialist employment law team at 5 Essex Court. He has extensive experience acting for individuals, public and private companies and Government Departments in all areas of employment law. He has been a member of the panel of Treasury Counsel since 2002.

Jonathan Dixey

Jonathan Dixey was called to the Bar in 2007. Following pupillage at 5 Essex Court he is now a member of the employment law team with a wide range of experience acting for both employees and employers involving claims for unfair dismissal, discrimination, breach of contract, redundancy and TUPE. Prior to joining the Bar Jonathan advised at the Citizens' Advice Bureau offering a particular focus on employment disputes.

Glossary

ACAS	Advisory, Conciliation and Arbitration Service
All ER	All England Law Reports
CA	Court of Appeal
CBI	Confederation of British Industry
CPR	Civil Procedure Rules
DDA	Disability Discrimination Act 1995
EAT	Employment Appeal Tribunal
ECJ	European Court of Justice
EDT	Effective date of termination
EPCA	Employment Protection (Consolidation) Act 1978
ERA	Employment Rights Act 1996
ET1	Employee's originating application, including grounds of complaint
ET3	Employer's notice of appearance, including grounds of resistance
ETA	Employment Tribunals Act 1996
ETS	Employment Tribunals Service
FRU	Free Representation Unit
HL	House of Lords
ICR	Industrial Cases Reports
IRLR	Industrial Relations Law Reports
NIRC	National Industrial Relations Court
PHD form	Preliminary Hearing Directions form (EAT)
PHR	Pre-hearing review
RRA	Race Relations Act 1976
SDA	Sex Discrimination Act 1975
TUC	Trades Union Congress
TULR(C)A	Trade Union and Labour Relations (Consolidation) Act 1992

Contents

Table of statutes

References are to paragraph number

Table of statutory instruments

References are to paragraph number

Table of EC Material

References are to paragraph number

Table of cases

References are to paragraph number

C

D

T

U

Chapter 1

Tribunals Today

Introduction

[1.1] If popularity is a test of success, employment tribunals (formerly called industrial tribunals) have passed with flying colours. Since their creation in 1964 the number of applications made to tribunals has increased dramatically such that in 2009/10 employment tribunals received 236,100 claims over an ever increasing range of jurisdictions.

At the heart of the employment tribunals' popularity lie a number of factors:

- the limited circumstances in which an unsuccessful party can have a costs award made against it
- the relative informality of proceedings;
- the lifting of the maximum cap on compensation in unfair dismissal cases, and its removal altogether in discrimination cases;
- the increased number of claims which the tribunal has jurisdiction to hear;
- the restricted avenues of appeal from a tribunal's factual findings; and
- the growing consciousness of workplace rights and obligations.

The popularity of tribunals, and the massive administrative burden which that popularity imposes on the system, is a factor that parties should bear in mind when conducting their case. Employment Judges are usually inundated with letters and applications from parties ranging from such matters as applications for postponement, further particulars, disclosure, preliminary hearings, pre-hearing reviews and strike outs. A party who displays an accurate knowledge of practice and procedure, and sets out its position in a clear and persuasive way, has a head start when communicating with the tribunal, whether orally or in writing. This book is intended to assist in that process. It is a guide to how employment tribunals operate and the powers at their disposal.

Tribunals: the industrial jury

[1.2] Tribunals have often been described by the higher courts as 'Industrial Juries' (see, for example *Sutcliffe v Big C's Marine Ltd* [1998] IRLR 428). This reflects:

- Their composition (see **1.3**).
- Their knowledge and practical experience of the workplace – normally from the first-hand experience of the two lay members, sometimes also from Employment Judges whose careers may have included periods in industry and commerce.
- The extensive latitude that they are afforded, provided they properly apply the law, to decide issues of fact.

Different tribunals may well take contrasting views of the same factual situation. This introduces an element of unpredictability into tribunal proceedings. At the same time, however, most tribunals are likely to be knowledgeable about what constitutes good working practices and procedures and (in terms of the lay members) themselves experienced in the reality of putting such practices and procedures into effect.

The importance that tribunals attach to good practice and procedure by the employer is one of the keys to understanding the way in which they operate.

Composition of tribunals

[1.3] A full tribunal consists of an Employment Judge and two lay members. The Employment Judge must be a solicitor or barrister of at least five years standing who is appointed by the Lord Chancellor. One of the lay members will have experience acting for and representing the interests of employees, and the other for employers; thereby ensuring that the composition of the Tribunal is as balanced as possible.

[1.4] The role of the Employment Judge is to preside over (or chair) proceedings. This means that, during the course of a hearing, he/she will:

- be the person (other than where the witnesses are asked questions by the lay members) who speaks to the parties;
- introduce the parties to the tribunal at the outset of the case;
- actively manage the hearing to ensure that it is conducted in accordance with the rules of natural justice;
- if a decision of the tribunal is given orally, deliver that decision;

- draft the written reasons of the tribunal;
- advise the lay members of the tribunal on the law, although a decision on a legal issue remains one for the tribunal as a whole.

In a three-person tribunal, the Employment Judge's vote carries no greater weight than that of either of the lay members.

The role of the lay members

[1.5] The lay members will usually not speak during a hearing other than to ask questions of witnesses upon completion of their evidence. The lay members' role is not, however, confined to deciding issues of fact. Whilst, on matters of law, they may be reluctant to depart from guidance they are given by the Employment Judge, they have a right to do so and sometimes their practical knowledge will be relevant in deciding such issues. This is demonstrated most vividly by the fact that appeals from employment tribunals are heard by the Employment Appeal Tribunal (EAT), which is *solely* concerned with issues of law, but which still consists of a lawyer and two or four lay members. As Mr Justice Wood, a former President of the EAT, remarked lay members 'sit not as assessors but as full members of the court…'.

Does the tribunal need to be unanimous?

[1.6] The answer to this question is 'no'. A 2:1 majority decision is sufficient. Where there is a majority decision, the written reasons for the decision, drafted by the Employment Judge, should set out both the majority and the minority view (*Parkers Bakeries v R E Palmer* [1977] IRLR 215). This requires the Employment Judge, in drafting his/her decision, to accurately reflect both his/her own view and the view of the member(s) with whom he/she is in disagreement.

Employment Judge sitting alone

[1.7] The vast majority of claims which a tribunal has jurisdiction to hear must be determined by a three-person tribunal. An Employment Judge may, however, sit alone in a number of situations:

- When dealing with matters of procedure and the management of proceedings at case management discussions under *rule 10* of the *Employment Tribunals Rules of Procedure 2004* (the *2004 Rules*) (see **chapter 12**);

- When conducting pre-hearing reviews under *rule 18* of the *2004 Rules* (see **chapter 13**);
- In the event of non-compliance, when striking out a claim under rule 13(1)(b) or when making a costs or preparation of time order under *rule 13(1)(a)* of the *2004 Rules;*
- When considering whether to grant an extension of time in which to present a response in accordance with *rule 4(4)* of the *2004 Rules* (see **chapter 7**);

In addition, there are a number of specific claims which can actually be determined by an Employment Judge sitting alone (see *section 4(2)* and *(3)* of the *Employment Tribunals Act 1996* (*ETA 1996*)). These include claims for unauthorised deduction of wages, redundancy payments and claims for holiday pay. They do not, however, include claims for unfair dismissal or discrimination.

Note that, in the case of a pre-hearing review, *rule 18(3)(a)* gives one or more of the parties the right to insist upon a case being heard by a full tribunal, but only if the request is made no less than ten days before the date of the hearing. *Rule 18(3)(b)* also gives the Employment Judge the power, of his/her own motion, to insist upon a full tribunal hearing the case.

Two-member tribunals

[1.8] The need for a two member tribunal usually arises when one of the lay members falls ill or is otherwise indisposed. It is important to emphasise that both parties have an absolute right to object and insist upon three members hearing the case.

An Employment Judge may sit with one member only if all of the parties agree (*regulation 9(3)* of the *Employment Tribunals (Constitution and Rules of Procedure) Regulations 2004* – the *2004 Regulations*). A decision to proceed without first obtaining such consent will render the decision liable to be set aside upon appeal (*Quenchers Ltd v McShane* (1993) The Times, 8 February. Where the tribunal proposes sitting with only one lay member it must inform the parties from which panel the lay member is taken from. If this information is not provided to the parties their consent is vitiated and the proceedings are rendered a nullity (*Rabahallah v BT Group plc* [2005] IRLR 184)).

Where a two-member tribunal sits, and each is in disagreement, the Employment Judge will carry the casting vote (*rule 17(1)* of the *2004*

Regulations). In other words, a two-member tribunal potentially gives considerably more power to the Employment Judge.

The rules under which tribunals operate

[1.9] Unlike the civil courts, tribunals are 'creatures of statute'. This means that they were created by an Act of Parliament, and that all the powers they have derive from legislation (whether acts of Parliament or Statutory Instruments). The current Act (superseding previous Acts) under which the tribunals derive their power is the *Employment Tribunal Act 1996* (*ETA 1996*). *Section 1(1)* of the *ETA 1996* provides:

> 'The Secretary of State may by regulations make provision for the establishment of tribunals to be known as employment tribunals.'

Within those words can be seen the key importance of regulations in tribunal proceedings. The Act, apart from dealing with the composition of tribunals and issues of jurisdiction, highlights the various areas in which regulations can be made. It is the regulations themselves that govern how tribunals operate. The current regulations in place are the *Employment Tribunals (Constitution and Rules of Procedure) Regulations 2004 (SI 2004/1861).* Most of the relevant rules of procedure are contained in *Schedule 1* to those Regulations, although there are a number of important provisions (including the overriding objective) contained in the main body of the Regulations.

Reference to 'the Rules' in this book means the rules contained in *Schedule 1* to the *2004 Regulations*.

The overriding objective

[1.10] *Regulation 3* of the *2004 Regulations* requires tribunals and Employment Judges to give effect to 'the overriding objective' when exercising any of their powers under the regulations. This is a provision which came into effect for the first time with the *2001 Regulations*, and which is sufficiently important to justify a chapter of its own in this book (see **chapter 8 – fairness: the overriding objective**). The overriding objective will be a familiar concept to those experienced in the civil courts and the provisions of the *Civil Procedure Rules*. It provides a consistent set of principles to which the tribunals must seek to give effect when exercising their procedural powers. The overriding objective of the rules is to enable tribunals and Employment Judges 'to deal with cases justly'. This includes, so far as practicable:

- ensuring that the parties are on an equal footing;
- dealing with cases in a way which is proportionate to the complexity or importance of the issues;
- ensuring that cases are dealt with expeditiously and fairly; and
- saving expense.

In addition, the parties are required to 'assist the tribunal or the Employment Judge to further the overriding objective' (*regulation 3(4)*).

Claims a tribunal can hear

[1.11] The *types* of claim a tribunal has the power (or 'jurisdiction') to hear are *not* set out in the *2004 Regulations* or the *ETA 1996*. Instead they are contained in the individual statutes which create the particular right to pursue that claim in the first place. So, for example, the right at law not to be unfairly dismissed is contained in *section 94* of the *Employment Rights Act 1996* (*ERA 1996*), whilst the right to bring a claim of unfair dismissal to a tribunal is contained in *section 111* of the same Act. Similarly, the prohibition against discrimination on the grounds of a protected characteristic, for example, age, disability, sex or race (in an employment context) is contained in *section 39* of the *Equality Act 2010*, whilst *section 120* of the Act provides for the right to complain of discrimination to a tribunal.

It is worth noting that employment tribunals also have jurisdiction to hear certain claims which were previously the sole domain of the civil courts. Notable amongst them are claims for breach of contract arising from or being outstanding upon the termination of the employment of the employee. The right to bring such a claim before a tribunal is, however, still created by statute, in this case *section 3* of the *ETA 1996*, and the *Employment Tribunals Extension of Jurisdiction (England and Wales) Order 1994*. Most people associate tribunals with claims for unfair dismissal and discrimination, matters that still dominate their workload. There are, however, numerous other claims that a tribunal can determine.

A full list of the ever increasing number of claims that employment tribunals in England and Wales have jurisdiction to consider are contained in **appendix I: claims a tribunal can hear**. For ease of reference, the table also sets out:

- the length of employment an employee is required to have before they are entitled to bring a specific claim ('the qualifying period'); and
- the time limits within which a claim needs to be brought before the tribunal.

The tribunal's discretion to extend the prescribed time limits, referred to only briefly in footnotes, is discussed in more depth in **chapter 5 – time limits**.

Since tribunals derive their jurisdiction entirely from statute, they have no powers other than those conferred on them by Parliament. In practical terms, this means that, unless a statutory provision specifically permits a claim to be brought before a tribunal, a tribunal simply has no power to hear the matter. Even where a tribunal has discretion as to whether or not it can hear a case, the criteria that it must apply in reaching its decision will be provided for by statute or by rules created pursuant to powers granted by statute. Tribunals, in fact, have no inherent or residual jurisdiction.

Any decision of a tribunal acting outside its jurisdiction is null and void, irrespective of whether or not lack of jurisdiction was raised as an issue during the proceedings. So, for example, where, due to lack of available space, a tribunal held a hearing in a room marked 'private' and with a door that could not be opened from the outside, the Court of Appeal held that the tribunal had no jurisdiction to hear the case (*Storer v British Gas plc* [2000] ICR 603). The Court of Appeal was of the view that, since the rules require any hearing to take place in public (except in a number of limited circumstances, none of which were applicable on the facts of this case), the tribunal had no jurisdiction to hold a hearing in private. The case was therefore sent back to be reheard in public.

Jurisdiction to hear contractual claims

[1.12] Tribunals have jurisdiction to hear a breach of contract claim if it arises or is outstanding on the termination of employment (*Employment Tribunals Extension of Jurisdiction (England and Wales) Order 1994*). This means that an employee can bring claims for damages for, amongst other things, wrongful dismissal, arrears of pay and benefits. However, only certain breaches of contract can be dealt with by the tribunal (claims relating to intellectual property rights and claims for damages due in respect of personal injury are for example specifically excluded). It is important to note that tribunals only have jurisdiction to hear a breach of contract claim if the contract or the employment in which the employee worked has been terminated (*Capek v Lincolnshire County Council* [2000] ICR 878). This was recently confirmed in *Southern Cross Healthcare v Perkins and Others* [2010] EWCA Civ 1442 in which the Court of Appeal emphasised that the tribunal had no general power of contractual interpretation outside the context of breach of contract claims raised on or after the termination of employment.

Territorial jurisdiction

[1.13] Pursuant to *regulation 19(1)* of the *2004 Regulations* tribunals in England and Wales only have jurisdiction to hear cases where:

- the respondent or one of the respondents resides or carries on business in England and Wales;
- had the remedy been by way of action in the county court, the cause of action would have arisen wholly or partly in England and Wales;
- the proceedings are to determine a question which has been referred to the tribunal by a court in England and Wales; or
- in the case of proceedings to which *Schedules 3, 4* or *5* to the *2004 Regulations* applies, the proceedings relate to matters arising in England and Wales.

For the purposes of these regulations a company is considered to 'reside' in England or Wales where it has a registered office in either region.). Hence, where a company had its operational base outside of England but its registered office in London, as confirmed by the records at Companies House, it was held to reside in the United Kingdom ((*Odeco (UK) Inc v Peacham* [1979] ICR 823). If there is doubt as to whether a company is registered in the England and Wales, a list of all companies with registered offices in England is held at Companies House.

Similarly, companies have been held to 'reside' in England and Wales where it can be established that a company 'carries on business' in England or Wales (*Knulty v Eloc Electro-Optiek and Communicatie BV* [1979] ICR 827).

Tribunals will often look at matters beyond the issue of where a company is registered; hence in *Jackson v Ghost Ltd* [2003] IRLR 824, the EAT held that even where a company is registered and carried on business abroad, it may still 'reside' in England if the majority of its directors and its major shareholders, who control the company, live in England. Another recent example of where a tribunal accepted jurisdiction on the basis that a company carried on business in England, was a claim involving cabin personnel employed in Hon Kong by British Airways, who flew to and from England. Despite the fact that the employee lived in Hong Kong, the Court of Appeal concluded that a tribunal had jurisdiction to hear race and age discrimination claims provided the employee does his or her work 'partly' in Great Britain (*British Airways Plc v Ms Eliza Mak & Ors* [2011] EWCA Civ 184).

The status of case law in tribunal proceedings

[1.14] A tribunal's place in the court hierarchy can be summarised as follows:

Employment tribunals > Employment Appeal Tribunal > Court of Appeal > Supreme Court > European Court of Justice.

Each court in this chain is bound by the decision of the court(s) above it. Where there is a conflict between the decision of a lower and higher court, the decision of the latter always takes precedence. Thus a tribunal is bound to follow a decision of the Court of Appeal who in turn must follow a decision of the Supreme Court (or its predecessor the House of Lords). Where there is a conflict between the decision of the EAT and a higher court, for example the Court of Appeal, the latter takes precedence. Where two decisions in the same court (whether EAT, Court of Appeal or Supreme Court) conflict with each other, tribunals have a choice as to which one to follow. Note, however, that the EAT, Court of Appeal and Supreme Court will strive to avoid such conflicts occurring.

In an employment context, case law is predominately concerned with interpreting and construing legislation in circumstances where there is doubt as to what it means. So, for example, there is an enormous volume of case law that interprets the unfair dismissal provisions contained in *section 94* of the *ERA 1996*. Tribunals are bound by this case law. Note, however, that Parliament is entitled to introduce new legislation reversing, revising or superseding that interpretation. There are also areas, for example in relation to the requirements of natural justice, where the rules are silent, and the parties will have to look to case law to extract the relevant principles.

How to obtain and search for relevant case law and legislation

[1.15] For those who are not qualified lawyers, this can be a daunting process. A sensible first port of call is to obtain a relevant textbook. So, for practice and procedure, this book can be used as a starting point, pointing the reader in the direction of relevant statutes and cases. On the substantive law, a reader might have regard to *Tolley's Employment Handbook,* which is regularly updated. The textbooks will give appropriate references for the authority relied upon. Where for, example, a reference to a case is given as [1979] IRLR 415, this refers to page 415 of the Industrial Relations Law Reports for 1979. A list of the relevant abbreviations will be given, usually at the beginning of the book. To obtain any piece of legislation, one of the simplest means, if the reader has Internet access, is to access one of a number of websites such as www.legislation.gov.uk, or www.opsi.gov.uk. It is important to bear in mind that legislation can and very often is amended. This means that the text of an Act or statutory instrument is frequently different from that which was originally drafted (for example, the *ERA 1996* has undergone considerable amendment since its enactment in 1996).With case law, there are two choices: either to buy the relevant reports, usually at considerable expense, or to access them via a public library or other relevant source. It may be that a local service, such as a Citizens Advice Bureau, or ACAS, will be able to advise on how to obtain such material (see **chapter 2 – getting advice**). In referring to authorities in the tribunal, parties can reasonably expect the tribunal to have the relevant statutory authorities available to them. In terms of cases, it is good practice to have copies of authorities for each member of the tribunal and the other side. If this is not possible, the tribunal should at least be given the name and reference for the authority.

The nature of tribunal proceedings today

Public or private?

[1.16] The vast majority of tribunal proceedings are required to be held in public. The exceptions are dealt with in **chapter 21 – private hearings and restricted reporting orders**. This means that any member of the public can observe a tribunal hearing taking place, and indeed doing so is one of the best means of becoming familiar with proceedings. There is no restriction, other than in the limited circumstances described in **chapter 21**, upon proceedings being reported, and there is frequently at least one reporter at a particular centre obtaining details of the cases being heard.

Formal or informal?

[1.17] The absence of wigs and gowns, the fact that everyone is seated at all times (save for when the Employment Judge and lay members enter and/or leave the room) and the right of any person to appear (either on behalf of themselves or someone else) in tribunal proceedings all contribute to an atmosphere of informality. In other respects, however, tribunals are quite like civil courts. Hearings follow a similar structure (see **chapter 18 – hearing I: order of proceedings**), with members of the tribunal asking testing questions of witnesses, and Employment Judges sometimes stopping parties (or their representatives) in the course of final submissions in order to deal with specific points.

Rule 14(2) of the *2004 Rules* requires the tribunal to, so far as it appears appropriate, seek to avoid formality in its proceedings. It further states that tribunals are not bound by the formal rules of evidence which apply to civil courts (for an explanation of the tribunal's approach to evidence, see **chapter 19 – hearing II: the conduct of proceedings by the tribunal**).

Tribunals strive to avoid an intimidating atmosphere and will generally assist unrepresented parties in understanding the law and in developing their case. Employment Judges will often, for example, assist un-represented parties by cross examining the witnesses of the other side. The presence of un-represented parties is not uncommon given that legal aid is not available for representation before employment tribunals.

At the same time, they have a wide range of procedural powers which parties must comply with. Further, they are not allowed to let informality undermine the principles of natural justice, such as giving each party a sufficient opportunity to prepare for the case it has to meet and to put its case (see **chapter 19**).

Checklist – tribunals today

- If possible, go and observe tribunal proceedings taking place; they are open to the public and it is an invaluable way of getting familiar with how they operate.
- Recognise the importance of good practice and procedure in the workplace in most tribunal proceedings, including the requirement to follow statutory grievance and disciplinary procedures (see **chapter 4**).
- Research the substantive law in the area in which the claim is brought.
- Consider whether there are any pre-claim requests for information which can be obtained from the other side (see **chapter 3 – pre-claim requests for information**).
- Have regard to whether the tribunal has jurisdiction to hear the type of claim in question (see **appendix I**).
- Consider whether there are any other jurisdictional requirements (for example, 12 months' qualifying service in most non-discriminatory unfair dismissal claims).
- Keep in mind the short time limits for bringing claims (see **chapter 5** and **appendix I**).
- Think about the directions which the tribunal has the power to make before the full hearing (see **chapter 12 – case management orders**).
- Prepare thoroughly for the full hearing (including preparing and serving sufficient copies of all documents relevant to the claim or application on the Tribunal and the other party well before the hearing).
- Familiarise yourself with how the full hearing will be conducted (see **chapters 18–20)**.

Chapter 2

Getting advice

Introduction

[2.1] Three questions may spring to mind when it comes to the seeking of advice and representation. Do I need it? Where can I get it? How much will it cost? This chapter looks at the options both in terms of seeking general advice and securing representation in tribunal proceedings.

Do I really need advice?

[2.2] Employment tribunals are *intended* to be a forum which is accessible to parties (both employers and employees) representing themselves. Indeed, the *Employment Tribunals (Constitution and Rules of Procedure) Regulations 2004* require tribunals to adjudicate on cases in a way that (as far as possible) places the parties on an equal footing. This means that if one side has a professional representative, the tribunal will strive to ensure that the other side is not put at a disadvantage. Nevertheless, employment law is a growing and ever more complex area, with a large body of case law. Despite the fact that costs are generally not recoverable by the successful party, many feel that they need the reassurance and security of professional representation and advice (which can sometimes be available without charge).

Even if a decision is made not to engage a representative at the hearing, it is important to be as well informed as possible when approaching tribunal proceedings. There are a number of organisations, listed below, which can provide free, general advice. It can be advantageous, both for employers and employees, to seek dispassionate advice at an early stage as to prospects of success. It is usually necessary to instruct a solicitor, barrister, consultant or Citizens Advice Bureau (CAB) to obtain an opinion specific to your case as the organisations offering general advice will usually not do so. This initial outlay *may* in the long run end up saving costs.

Emotions tend to run high in employment disputes. The hard truth is that the tribunal is required to decide the case objectively and according to the law, not according to an individual's perception of justice. In an unfair dismissal case, for example, the tribunal is not permitted to ask 'what would it have done in that situation?' It must confine itself to issues such as the procedure adopted by the employer (the soundness of which is an area ripe for seeking advice upon) and whether dismissal fell within 'the range of reasonable responses' available to that employer. It may be that a potentially fair dismissal is rendered unfair by the procedure adopted. Or it may be that an employee who is outstanding and appreciated in certain areas has been fairly dismissed for the particular reason relied upon by the employer (ie redundancy). For both employers and employees, it is important to listen to well-informed objective advice, despite the fact that the advice may not be what the party wants to hear or thinks is fair. Parties should bear in mind that tribunal proceedings can be very demanding, both in terms of time and expense, and it is best to embark upon them with a realistic view as to the likely outcome.

When should advice be sought?

[2.3] Advice and/or representation can be sought at any stage, from before a claim is brought to after proceedings have concluded (for example in relation to the potential to appeal or enforcement of awards). A representative does not have to be retained from the beginning to the end of a case. It is important to remember, however, that the advisor or representative needs to be given sufficient time and information to carry out the task entrusted to them. In order to maximise the opportunity of saving costs it is often sensible to obtain advice at an early stage to avoid bringing a misconceived claim or adopting an unsustainable position.

When seeking representation at a full hearing, the earlier a representative is instructed the better. As this book demonstrates, there are often a number of essential preliminary matters relating to the preparation of a case for full hearing, for example preparation of statements and evidence, disclosure of documents, seeking of directions etc which need to be done. Instructing a representative from the outset of a case has the advantage of enabling that person to develop a coherent strategy for the best possible presentation of the claim/defence before the tribunal. It is also important to keep in mind time limits. So, if an employee is contemplating bringing a claim but needs advice, the earlier they seek it the better, since ordinarily they have just three months to bring most of the more common claims.

From whom should advice be sought?

[2.4] This depends upon individual requirements, such as the complexity of the case, and resources available. HR managers may seek advice from ACAS (the Advice, Conciliation and Arbitration Service), their professional or trade associations, employment law consultants, solicitors or barristers. Individual employees may approach ACAS, a CAB, an advice centre, a solicitor or barrister or their trade union. Solicitors will generally seek advice either from other practitioners in their firm or from a barrister. There are also a number of lay employment advisors and it is always possible that knowledgeable friends, such as HR specialists or others who have previously been involved in employment cases, may be able to assist – even if only to the extent of advising where to go next. Finally, all parties should be aware of the benefits of seeking general advice from the organisations below. All the contact details of these organisations are listed at the end of this chapter.

Organisations offering free general advice

ACAS

[2.5] The Advice, Conciliation and Arbitration Service (better known as ACAS) is a publicly funded, free advisory and information service open to employers, employees and their representatives (it also has a well-known conciliation role discussed elsewhere). It does not provide a representation service. It is an experienced organisation which offers general advice on employment law matters although its advisors are unlikely to be qualified lawyers. Crucially, ACAS will also advise on the setting up of procedures and on other means of resolving disputes in the workplace. As stated in **chapter 1 – tribunals today**, tribunals are required (in relevant cases) to have regard to the ACAS codes of practice in deciding whether a fair procedure has been adopted, a fact which underlines the organisation's importance.

ACAS seeks to promote high standards in the workplace by providing extensive advice to employers and employees. In addition, it publishes booklets, leaflets and handbooks which are available on its website (see **2.17**). ACAS also runs a telephone helpline offering advice and support (see **2.17**).

A word of warning: ACAS is a general advisor, not a representative. You cannot 'retain' it to act on your behalf. It will not look at documentation personal to your case or carry out a thorough investigation into the circumstances of your individual claim. It is effectively a question and answer service open to employers and employees, giving general advice to both sides. For this reason, if a member of ACAS gives wrong advice, it is difficult to sue it or hold it to account. ACAS, as its name suggests, also has a strong conciliation and mediation role.

Equality and Human Rights Commission (EHRC)

[2.6] The EHRC has responsibility for the promotion and enforcement of equality and non-discrimination laws. In October 2007 it took over the responsibilities of the Equal Opportunities Commission, the Commission for Racial Equality and the Disability Rights Commission. The EHRC offers advice to employers, employees and others on all aspects of equality laws and human rights and in particular on the *Equality Act 2010*. As with ACAS, the EHRC can advise on matters such as the formulation and implementation of equal opportunities policies in the workplace.

Organisations offering advice and representation

Citizens Advice Bureaux (CAB) and Law Centres

[2.7] CABs and Law Centres are a free service open to employees and small employers. It is possible to retain them to act as a representative in employment disputes, though whether they have staff or volunteers available to do so will vary. In some cases, due to lack of resources they may not be able to assist beyond an early stage in the proceedings.

CABs and Law Centres retain both paid staff and volunteers who have a basic training in employment law. These people may, or may not, have a professional legal qualification. Some also utilise barristers and solicitors, who are either employed by them, or, more usually, provide their time as volunteers. Two organisations used by CABs and Law Centres are the Free Representation Unit (FRU) and the Bar Pro Bono Unit. FRU provide trainee and newly qualified lawyers for free. The Bar Pro Bono Unit may be able to offer a more experienced barrister also for free. Both organisations are designed for people who lack the means to afford representation, but can only provide representation subject to availability of a lawyer willing to take on the case. If your priority is to receive the advice and/or representation of a professional lawyer through a CAB or Law Centre, the best option is to speak to the particular centre concerned and see what it can offer.

Solicitors

[2.8] Solicitors are professional lawyers regulated by the Law Society who offer both advice and representation (see **2.13–2.16**). The Law Society (for address and website see **2.18**) provides an easily searchable database of solicitors who hold themselves out as specialising in employment law in particular geographical areas. It is often useful to take further steps to ascertain the quality of a firm or individual. This can be done by word of mouth or by asking the solicitor questions about the extent of their experience in the area. The specialist associations, for example the Employment Lawyers Association or the Employment Law Bar Association, do not publish a list of their members for use by the public.

Barristers

[2.9] The Bar provides a specialist advocacy and advisory service. Generally speaking, it is not possible to approach a barrister directly – you must first retain a solicitor, who then instructs a barrister (counsel). Barristers are instructed for a number of reasons, for example to appear as advocate at the hearing, to provide an independent view on the prospects of success in a case or to give advice on a particular issue.

In certain circumstances it may be possible for individuals or organisations to instruct barristers directly under schemes known as 'Public Access' and 'Licensed Access'. For further details of how this can be done contact the Bar Council (for address and website see page 23).

Employment law consultants

[2.10] Unlike the civil courts, there is no requirement for a person to be a professional lawyer in order to represent a person in an employment tribunal. Various individuals and consultancy firms offer advice and/or representation services to both individuals and smaller employers. Some advertise their services in professional journals, local newspapers and on websites.

Whilst a consultant may, or may not, have a legal qualification, he is obliged to be registered with the Secretary of State for Justice in order to represent a party before an employment tribunal. Indeed, a consultant who represents a person before an employment tribunal without being duly registered commits a criminal offence.

Despite these changes, both the range and the quality of consultants' advice continue to show considerable variation. It may, therefore be helpful to 'ask around' for recommendations based on personal knowledge. It also remains important, to enquire as to experience and qualifications before instructing a consultant great care should be taken when agreeing terms of payment, including carefully reading any conditional fee agreement. Many consultants provide free initial consultations. In view of the fact that consultants do not have to belong to a professional body, (see **2.13–2.16**).

How much will it cost?

[2.11] CABs, Law Centres, ACAS, the EHRC and FRU are free.

Solicitors and barristers

[2.12] Rates vary enormously from firm to firm and barrister to barrister. The amount charged will usually be dependent upon such matters as: (a) degree of experience; (b) the extent of specialisation in the area; (c) standing in the profession; and (d) importance of the case (this usually, though not always, relates to the amount of money at stake). Neither the Law Society nor the Bar Council publishes guidance figures on appropriate levels of fees. *Chambers UK: A Client's Guide to the Legal Profession,* available at a number of public libraries, includes a survey of typical charge out rates for solicitors and barristers.

Note: with barristers there is usually a significant difference between their fees for advisory work (which can often be lower than that of a solicitor of equivalent experience) and their fee for appearing as an advocate in the tribunal – to which there is sometimes a premium attached, known as the 'brief fee'. Seeking preliminary written advice from counsel can often be a cost-effective way, both for the solicitor and lay client, of working out whether there exists a viable claim or defence, which in turn enables the party to develop a coherent settlement strategy.

Fees should be discussed and agreed with the solicitor at the outset. It may be that the solicitor will offer an initial free consultation, although this is less likely with the more sizeable firms.

Most firms require, if the case is not to be done on a 'conditional fee basis' (see **2.15**), payment on account from the client before they start work.

No win, no fee

[2.13] Some solicitors (and barristers) and employment law consultants accept work on a conditional fee basis. This means that the client pays nothing unless they are successful in the case. On the face of it, this is an attractive option, and indeed is often the only means by which many people, predominately employees, can obtain legal representation in tribunals. What is the drawback? Whilst, if you lose, you pay nothing, if you win the lawyer is entitled to an enhanced payment of up to twice his normal fee. In employment tribunals each side usually pays their own costs – so, if you are an employee, the legal fees will be taken out of the compensation you receive.

How does it work? The client enters in to a conditional fee agreement (CFA) with the solicitor. In the agreement, the solicitor will state their normal hourly rate and then indicate the uplift (up to a maximum of 100%) which will be applied to that rate in the event of success. The extent of the uplift will normally be dictated by that solicitor's opinion as to the prospects of success. If, for example, the prospects are only 50%, the uplift will frequently be 100% on his normal fee. The agreement will also usually specify that, if the case settles, the solicitor will recover his fees for the work done at an enhanced rate. It is also likely to contain provisions for payment to the solicitor where the client refuses to take his advice to accept a reasonable settlement from the other side, and provisions for insurance. Where a barrister is engaged, a separate CFA will be concluded between the barrister, the solicitor and the client.

Do's and Don't's

Do:

- Ask about the qualifications and experience of a proposed representative.
- Ensure that terms and conditions of payment (including conditional fees) are agreed beforehand.
- Decide whether you want preliminary advice or representation to the conclusion of a case, and ensure that what is agreed is recorded.
- Try, if at all possible, to seek the advice of a person who specialises in employment law.
- Balance the costs of seeking advice (if there are any) against what is at stake in the particular dispute.
- If you disagree, or do not understand advice, challenge it and ask further questions.
- Use ACAS for general advice on what tribunals regard as good practice in the workplace and take thorough notes of the advice you receive.
- Instruct a representative if you feel you do not have: (a) the expertise to do the case yourself; or (b) the time to give it the attention it needs.
- Remember, if you are representing yourself, do not be intimidated by the opposition, or be afraid to seek the tribunal's assistance – tribunals are intended to be open to non-lawyers.
- Always give a representative the full story, so that they can properly assess the strength of the case against you.
- Remember that the costs of running a case are not only financial – time and, possibly, emotional stress also come into the equation.

Don't:

- Use an unqualified representative unless you are satisfied as to their experience and expertise.
- Ignore clear advice given to you by a representative.
- Launch a case purely for vindictiveness or just to 'get your day in court'.

Useful addresses

ACAS

[2.14]

Website: www.acas.co.uk
Helpline: 08457 47 47 47

Head Office and ACAS London

- Euston Tower
  286 Euston Road
  London
  NW1 3JJ

ACAS East Midlands

- Lancaster House
  10 Sherwood Rise
  Nottingham
  NG7 6JE

ACAS East of England

- ACAS House
  Kempson Way
  Suffolk Business Park
  Bury St Edmunds
  Suffolk
  IP32 7AR

ACAS North East

- Cross House
  Westgate Road
  Newcastle upon Tyne
  NE1 4XX

ACAS North West

- Commercial Union House
  2–10 Albert Square
  Manchester
  M60 8AD
- Pavilion 1
  The Matchworks
  Speke Road
  Speke
  Liverpool
  L19 2PH

ACAS South East

- Suites 3–5
  Business Centre
  1–7 Commercial Road
  Paddock Wood
  Kent
  TN12 6EN
- Cygnus House
  Ground Floor
  Waterfront Business Park
  Fleet
  Hampshire
  GU51 3QT

ACAS South West

- The Waterfront
  Welsh Back
  Bristol
  BS1 4SB

ACAS West Midlands

- Apex House
  3 Embassy Drive
  Calthorpe Road
  Edgbaston
  Birmingham
  B15

ACAS Yorkshire and Humber

- The Cube
  123 Albion Street
  Leeds
  LS2 8ER

ACAS Scotland

- 151 West George Street
  Glasgow
  G2 2JJ

ACAS Wales

- Third Floor
  Fusion Point 2
  Dumballs Road
  Cardiff
  CF10 5BF

The Law Society

[2.15]

Website: www.lawsociety.org.uk

Address

- The Law Society's Hall
  113 Chancery Lane
  London
  WC2A 1PL

Telephone: 020 7242 1222
Fax: 020 7831 0344

The Bar Council

[2.16]

Website: www.barcouncil.org.uk

Address

- 289–293 High Holborn
  London
  WC1V 7HZ

Telephone: 020 7242 0082

The Legal Ombudsman

[2.17] The Legal Ombudsman is an independent and free service which has responsibility for handling and investigating complaints about lawyers.

Website: www.legalombudsman.org.uk

Address

- PO Box 15870
  Birmingham B30 9EB

Telephone: 0300 555 0333
Email: enquiries@legalombudsman.org.uk

Equality and Human Rights Commission

[2.18]

Website: www.equalityhumanrights.com

Helpline (England):	0845 604 6610
Helpline (Scotland):	0845 604 5510
Helpline (Wales):	0845 604 8810

Address (Manchester)

- Arndale House
  The Arndale Centre
  Manchester
  M4 3AQ

Address (London)

- 3 More London
  Riverside Tooley Street
  London
  SE1 2RG

Address (Cardiff)

- 3rd Floor
  3 Callaghan Square
  Cardiff
  CF10 5BT

Address (Glasgow)

- The Optima Building
  58 Robertson Street
  Glasgow
  G2 8DU

National Association of Citizens Advice Bureaux

[2.19]

Website: www.citizensadvice.org.uk

Address

- Myddleton House
  115–123 Pentonville Road
  London
  N1 9LZ

Telephone: 020 7833 2181
Fax: 020 7833 4371

Free Representation Unit

[2.20]

Website: www.thefru.org.uk

Address

- 6th Floor
  289–293 High Holborn
  London
  WC1V 7HZ

Telephone: 020 7611 9555

Law Centres Federation

[2.21]

Website: www.lawcentres.org.uk

Address

- 22 Tudor Street
  London
  EC4Y 0AYTelephone: 020 7842 0720

Fax: 020 7842 0721

Chapter 3

Pre-claim correspondence & requests for information

Introduction

[3.1] Where a dispute arises in the workplace both employees and employers are expected to seek to resolve their differences before commencing proceedings in an employment tribunal. Where the parties are unable or unwilling to resolve such disputes, communicating in writing with the other side before proceedings are issued can prove to be vitally important. It provides the background against which the subsequent litigation is viewed and it is therefore important that parties adopt a sensible attitude in correspondence so as not to risk subsequently alienating the Tribunal.

Pre-claim correspondence has the following principal benefits:

- It enables each party to gain an understanding of the other's case;
- It may therefore facilitate settlement at an early stage, avoiding the time, expense and anxiety of proceeding to tribunal; and
- In the case of exceptionally weak claims or defences, it may be adduced at the conclusion of the proceedings as evidence of the losing party's unreasonableness in bringing, contesting or proceeding with the claim.

[3.2] There are two main types of pre-action correspondence: first there are letters which set out the factual and legal basis of a proposed claim/defence, secondly there are written offers to 'settle' a claim. The former can and should be placed before the tribunal, the latter (ie offers to settle) should not be shown to the tribunal until after the substantive dispute has been determined. The relevance of offers to settle is in relation to costs – so for example where at the end of a hearing an employee recovers less than the amount he was offered by the employer, before he issued the proceedings, the employer is then able to argue that the employee's refusal of the offer to settle was unreasonable and that the employee should pay some or all of the costs associated with the employment proceedings (for a fuller discussion on costs, see **chapter 24**).

Employee's letter before claim

[3.3] The stronger and more persuasive the letter, the more likely it is to have the desired effect on the employer. The contents should be accurate, particularly in open correspondence (ie correspondence not involving the settling or compromise of the claim), as the letter may be used as evidence in any subsequent proceedings. There is nothing to prevent the employee writing an open letter setting out their case, and accompanying this with a separate 'without prejudice' letter giving proposals for settlement. The advantage of this approach is that the open letter goes 'on the record', and can be evidence of a consistent position adopted by the employee throughout the dispute, whereas the latter provides the employee with the option of seeking his costs in the event that the Tribunal awards the employee a greater award than contained in the offer to settle.

[3.4] The letter before claim should:

- be headed 'Letter before claim';
- where containing an offer to settle, be headed 'without prejudice' (this very important since a failure to include this heading leads to a significant risk of the letter being adduced in evidence before the Tribunal and thereby undermining the employee's position);
- identify the type of claim/s that the employee intends to bring;
- set out, in outline form, the factual basis of the claim;
- state (in without prejudice letters) what is required from the employer (ie the level of compensation or other remedy sought) in order for the claim not to proceed, giving the basis of any calculation;
- give the employer a reasonable deadline for responding;
- state the name of the intended respondent in the action;
- state that any necessary pre-condition of bringing the claim, the GP (Grievance Procedure: see **chapter 4: the new compulsory disciplinary and grievance procedures** for a full discussion), has been complied with.

Example of letter before claim

[Without prejudice save as to costs (see below)].

Dear [...]

We act for Bill Smith who intends to bring proceedings against Jones and Co for unfair dismissal.

The circumstances of his dismissal were as follows: On 5 December 2010 Mr Smith was invited to attend the office of Steve Martin, the managing director. He was informed at the meeting that, due to 'a few cash flow problems', the company would be making him redundant, and that his last day of work would be 8 December 2010. He was further informed that he would receive one month's pay in lieu of notice, together with his statutory redundancy pay.

His dismissal was plainly unfair for the following reasons:
(a) a true redundancy situation did not exist; and
(b) in any event, an unfair procedure was carried out, including a total absence of consultation, fair selection criteria or attempts to find our client alternative work.

In relation to (a), our client will assert that he was told by Steve Martin, a week before his dismissal, that he 'would have to improve or the company would get rid of him'. There is compelling evidence that this was a disguised capability dismissal. He will further rely upon the fact that another person has since been employed to carry out his job on similar pay.

In addition, you failed to follow the ACAS Code on Disciplinary and Grievance Procedures. Specifically, you failed to set out in writing, prior to the meeting on 5 December 2010, Mr Smith's alleged conduct or characteristics, or other circumstances, which led to you contemplating his dismissal. In accordance with his statutory rights, our client appealed on 5 January 2011 but your client decided to maintain its decision.

[The following paragraph can, if desired, be contained in a separate without prejudice letter, with the paragraphs above forming part of an open letter.]

We ask you to pay our client the sum of £22,000 within 21 days, or we will commence proceedings on his behalf in an employment tribunal. This sum is calculated on the basis of six months' loss of earnings, which is the period our client reasonably estimates will be necessary to find alternative work of a similar level. We urge you to recognise that this figure may well increase if the case is brought to tribunal and our client has failed, by that stage, to secure alternative work. We expressly reserve the right to draw this offer to the Tribunal's attention when considering the issue of costs, should proceedings subsequently culminate in the Tribunal making a greater award than this offer of settlement.

We look forward to hearing from you within 21 days of the date of this letter

Responding to the letter before claim

[3.5] If the letter before claim contains an offer of settlement, the response to that will be without prejudice, and not for disclosure to the tribunal. The extent to which the employer is able to provide a detailed response to the allegations made will vary from case to case. A strong and persuasive reply may have the effect of deterring the employee from proceeding or inducing them to settle. Such letters should generally include:

- a response to the legal points raised by the employee;
- a response to the factual assertions made by the employee;
- where appropriate, a request for further information from the employee, for example in relation to any new position that they have taken up, or as to how their alleged loss is calculated or information concerning the steps that they are taking to try and find new employment; and
- a response (in a without prejudice letter) to any financial offer of the employee, either accepting it, rejecting it or making a counter offer.

[3.6] Where the employee has sent an open letter setting out their claim, in which no offer of settlement is made, the employer should respond in kind, since both may then be evidence in tribunal proceedings.

Example of response

Thank you for your letter of [...]. Your client was dismissed on [...] by reason of redundancy. The version of events recited in your letter is inaccurate and misleading. In particular we reject the implication in your letter that your client was unaware of any redundancy situation existing until the date of his dismissal and your assertion that a genuine redundancy situation did not exist.

Your client was employed as a sales officer in the West Midlands region. At a meeting on [...] the company decided that, in order to reduce overheads, it would cease to operate in that area. Two days later, your client was informed of this decision. His response was: 'well, sales have not been that great so as long as I get a decent package I don't really mind'. He was offered, at this meeting, the position of junior sales officer in the South East with no loss of pay. He declined this offer for personal reasons. He made no suggestions as to suitable alternative positions.

On [...], the board of the company decided that, in view of your client's rejection of the offer which had been made to him, it should give active consideration to making him redundant, since there were no other positions which he could occupy in the organisation. A meeting was arranged with your client on 5 December 2010. Your assertion that your client was, prior to this meeting, not given any information as to the purpose of that meeting is denied. He was informed in writing that the meeting would be to decide whether, in the light of current economic circumstances, he was redundant. At the meeting on 5 December 2010 your client could advance no basis for asserting that he was not redundant. Accordingly at the conclusion of the meeting he was informed that he was being made redundant. He received his contractual notice period and his statutory redundancy pay. It is expressly denied that any additional employee has been employed since your client's departure. In the circumstances, he was fairly dismissed by reason of redundancy and any claim against the company will be strenuously defended. If, which is denied, there is held to be any procedural flaw, the company will assert that it is inevitable that the dismissal would have taken place in any event, and that your client's loss is nil.

Use of questionnaires in discrimination cases

[3.7] Questionnaires can be a useful tool for applicants in discrimination cases, who often face significant difficulties in otherwise obtaining sufficient information to assess the potential merits of their claim. Essentially, they provide the applicant, within the prescribed format of the questionnaire, with the opportunity to ask questions of the employer, at an early stage, with a view to establishing whether they have been discriminated against. This is an additional facility in discrimination cases which can be used in conjunction with obtaining disclosure from the employer after proceedings have begun (see **chapter 11 – disclosure**). The questionnaire and answers are admissible as evidence in proceedings. Employees are required to state the basis upon which they consider they may have been discriminated against and the requests for information should be restricted to these issues. There is rarely direct evidence of discrimination, which places the onus on the employee to seek evidence upon which the tribunal could draw an inference of discrimination.

[3.8] The use of questionnaires will often assist both parties in deciding whether to bring or resist a claim for unlawful discrimination. It is important the parties bear in mind that tribunals will seek to give effect to the spirit rather than the form of these provisions: so that even where the questions put by the employee are not put to the employer using the correct form, a tribunal may still draw an adverse inference of discrimination from evasive, incorrect or nil replies (see, for example, *Dattani v Chief Constable of West Mercia Police* [2005] IRLR 327 in the context of an inference in a race discrimination claim under the *Race Relations Act 1976, s 65*).

[3.9] The remainder of this chapter sets out the law as it currently relates to discrimination cases brought under the *Equality Act 2010*. For the position in respect of claims arising before October 2010 the reader should refer to the 2nd edition of this book.

Time limits

[3.10] In order to be admissible under the *Equality Act 2010, s 138(3)* a question must be served:

- before proceedings are commenced; or

- where proceedings have been commenced, within 28 days beginning with the presentation of the complaint (or later with the permission of the tribunal).

As the time limit for bringing a claim before an employment tribunal is usually three months from the date of the act complained of (see **chapter 6 – time limits**) it is possible that a response may not be received before the expiry of the limitation period. An applicant should not delay making a claim whilst awaiting a response from the employer because time will continue to run the applicant runs the risk of finding himself time-barred.

[3.11] Whilst a strict time limit is not imposed for an employer to respond to questions put to it, if the employer fails to answer a question within eight weeks of being served with the questions the tribunal may draw an inference from that failure (the *Equality Act 2010, s 138(4)*; see **3.14**).

Prescribed forms

[3.12] The Questions and Answers Forms come in a form prescribed by the Secretary of State (the *Equality Act 2010 (Obtaining Information) Order 2010*). The Questions and Answers Forms to be used for obtaining information on prohibited conduct can be found in **appendix II – questions and answers forms**. Separate Questions and Answers Forms are provided for applicants seeking information on equality of terms. Copies of the various forms can be found on the Government Equalities Office website at www.equalities.gov.uk.

[3.13] Each form provides scope for the employee to add additional questions themselves. Frequently, an employee will ask questions relating to such matters as:

- the qualifications/gender/race of a successful candidate for a job;
- the reasons for the selection of that other candidate;
- the gender or racial composition of the workforce or those with disabilities;
- an analysis of how such groups have been treated by the company in specific factual situations, for example promotion or dismissal; and
- equal opportunities training carried out by the employer.

Remember that there is no 'rule' as to what questions should be asked, provided they are relevant and not oppressive in the amount of information they seek from the respondent. The applicant should think carefully about what questions are most likely to assist them. In a given case, there may well be a number of questions specific to the particular circumstances of the applicant that should be answered. For example: 'Is it accepted that I was told on [...] by [...] that I was almost certain to be promoted to the job in question?' Employees are strongly advised to seek the assistance of organisations such as the Equality and Human Rights Commission (www.equalityhumanrights.com).

Responding to the questionnaire

[3.14] Employers are advised to take the questionnaire seriously since their answers will stand as evidence in the case. By virtue of the *Equality Act 2010, s 138(4)* a tribunal may draw an adverse inference from an employer's failure to answer a question within eight weeks of being served with the questions or if the answer is considered to be evasive or equivocal. A failure to answer a question, however, does not give rise to an automatic inference of discrimination. The tribunal must consider whether the failure has any evidential value in relation to the actual discrimination being alleged (*D'Silva v NATFHE* [2008] IRLR 412).

[3.15] An employer will usually be justified in refusing to provide information if a request is irrelevant to the alleged act of discrimination or if the query is oppressive or disproportionate. An example of both might be where a request is made for the details of all applications for employment made to the company in the last ten years. Where an employer refuses to provide information it should include, in the form, the basis upon which it is doing so in order to protect its position. Alternatively, prior to completing the form, the employer should write to the employee asking the relevance of the request or seeking to narrow down the issues. Simply leaving the section blank or worse refusing to respond at all is very inadvisable. The tribunal's power to draw an inference from a failure to answer or to answer in a specific manner is expressly excluded where the employer reasonably refuses to answer a question in circumstances where to give an answer could prejudice criminal proceedings.

[3.16] As with Questions Form, there is a prescribed Answers Form for responding. This can be found in **appendix II**. The questionnaire need not purely benefit the employee. It can also give the employer a crucial insight into the case of the employee and allow it to formulate a response.

Do's and Don'ts

Do:

- Decide whether pre-claim correspondence should be with or without prejudice – all offers to settle claims (and responses to such offers) automatically fall into the latter category and should be marked 'without prejudice' and should not be disclosed to the tribunal, save in relation to the issue of costs.
- Consider making use of and/or responding to a questionnaire in discrimination cases.
- Use pre-claim correspondence as a means of facilitating settlement and saving costs.

Don't:

- Allow pre-claim correspondence or questionnaires to take precedence over complying with time limits for bringing a claim.
- Make factual assertions in open correspondence, which you later go back on.
- Adopt an unreasonable tone or make unreasonable demands; particularly in open correspondence which is likely to be considered by the tribunal.

Chapter 4

Dispute resolution

Introduction

[4.1] In an attempt to reduce the number of complaints being registered with employment tribunals, the *Employment Act 2002* introduced mandatory dispute resolution procedures. These procedures were brought into effect on 1 October 2004 by the *Employment Act 2002 (Dispute Resolution) Regulations 2004* ('the *EA(DR)R 2004*'). In the same month ACAS issued an updated Code of Practice: Disciplinary and Grievance Procedures so as to take into account the statutory procedures and provide guidance as to how the new procedures applied. The statutory dispute resolution procedures were however widely considered to be too prescriptive and insufficiently flexible. They also resulted in a considerable amount of satellite litigation, thus further undermining their stated aim of encouraging employers and employees to resolve disputes without recourse to costly and complex litigation. As a result the unpopular statutory 2004 dispute resolution procedures were repealed by the *Employment Act 2008* and, as of 6 April 2009, were replaced by a more flexible regime.

[4.2] Most claims brought after 6 April 2009 will be subject to the new regime, however it is likely to be some time before all claims under the old regime are resolved. In addition, the *Employment Act 2008 (Commencement No 1, Transitional Provisions and Savings) Order 2008* provides that certain claims may yet still fall to be considered under the old regime. As the vast majority of current claims will be subject to the new regime ('the 2009 regime'), this book will focus on the 2009 regime.

Given, however, that there will be an ever diminishing number of claims which will still be subject to the old regime ('the 2004 regime'), a summary of the 2004 regime is provided. It is important to emphasise that this summary is not intended to provide an exhaustive assessment of the considerable amount of case law relating to the 2009 regime.

Which regime applies?

[4.3] As indicated above the new regime came into force on 6 April 2009. Whilst it is clear that the more time which, the fewer the cases to which the old regime applies, there will however unfortunately remain for some time a not insignificant number of cases to which the 2004 regime continues to apply (especially the grievance procedure requirements).

In relation to dismissal and disciplinary cases the 2004 regime applies to situations where the employer has commenced dismissal and disciplinary action prior to 5 April 2009 (including notifying the employee in writing of the act which is may result in dismissal and disciplinary).

In relation to grievances the 2004 regime continues to apply where:

- The action complained of by the employee took place before 5 April 2009; or
- The action complained of by the employee began on or before 5 April 2009 and continued beyond that date, and the employee has submitted a written grievance or a tribunal claim:
  - On or before 4 July 2009 if it relates to a claim which has a three-month jurisdiction period (ie unfair dismissal etc);
  - On or before 4 October 2009 if it relates to a claim which has a 6 month jurisdiction period (ie redundancy payment, or equal pay etc).

Unless the circumstances surrounding a complaint fall within one of the categories set out above, the more flexible 2009 regime will apply. This new regime, as will be explained below, aims to maintain the incentive on parties to try and resolve their differences without recourse to the employment tribunals, whilst removing some of the draconian consequences of non-compliance. Consequently, both employers and employees should still make every effort to resolve disputes in the work setting since tribunals are unlikely to have sympathy for unreasonable failures to comply with principles underlying the new regime.

Dispute resolution: statutory disciplinary and grievance procedures under the 2004 regime

[4.4] *Schedule 2* to the *Employment Act 2002* set out the general framework for the compulsory system of dispute resolution in the workplace. This procedure applied to all employers irrespective of their size and to all 'employees' as defined in the *Employment Rights Act 1996 (ERA 1996)*. These statutory procedures, like the 2009 regime, amounted to a *minimum* standard which applied to employers and employees. Hence, any in-house disciplinary/grievance procedures, in so far as they are not inconsistent with the requirements of the statutory procedures, remained lawful and unaffected by the statutory procedure (*Employment Act 2002, s 30(2)*). On the other hand any term in an employment contract that purported to limit the operation of the statutory procedures was deemed to be void.

[4.5] The statutory procedures consist of:
- Dismissal and Disciplinary Procedures ('DDP'); and
- Grievance Procedures ('GP').

In relation to both the DDP and GP there are 'standard' and 'modified' procedures which apply depending on the circumstances of the case (see **4.8** and **4.14**).

[4.6] The statutory provisions sought to ensure that all employees (save in exceptional cases of misconduct) had access to a minimum standard formal dispute resolution process *before* they are dismissed. They also reflected a desire to change the growing perception that an application to the employment tribunals was an automatic step in dispute resolution. The *Employment Act 2002* therefore aimed to shift the initial obligation of dispute resolution from the tribunals back to the employers, the employees and the work place. The 2004 regime envisaged that an application to the employment tribunal would only be made after the parties have attempted (unsuccessfully) to settle their differences through the statutory dispute resolution procedures. It aimed to ensure compliance with the procedures by penalising the party at fault. Employees who failed to comply with the procedures risked having their awards being reduced by up to 50%, or even being *denied* access to the employment tribunals. Employers, who are at fault, on the other hand, were liable to find any award payable to the employee being increased by up to 50%, and were also at risk of an *automatic* finding of dismissal.

The 2004 regime: dismissal and disciplinary procedures

[4.7] The DDP applies when an employer contemplates dismissing' or 'taking relevant disciplinary action against an employee' (*EA(DR)*

R 2004, reg 3(1)). In this context, 'relevant disciplinary action' means 'action, short of dismissal, which the employer asserts to be based wholly or mainly on the employee's conduct or capability, other than the suspension on full pay or the issuing of warnings (whether oral or written)'.

[4.8] The DDP does not apply (*EA(DR)R 2004, reg 4(1)*) in the following circumstances:

- all an employer's employees of a particular description or category to which the employee belongs are dismissed, provided that the employer offers to re-engage all those employees so dismissed either on or before the termination of their contracts;
- the dismissal is one of a number of dismissals in respect of which the duty to consult representatives applies (*Trade Union and Labour Relations (Consolidation) Act 1992, s 188*);
- at the time of dismissal the employee is participating in industrial action which is unofficial or unprotected by the *1992 Act*;
- the (principal) reason for dismissal is that the employee took protected industrial action and the dismissal would therefore be unfair;
- the employer's business suddenly ceases to function due to unforeseen events so that it is impractical to employ any employees;
- the (principal) reason for the dismissal is that the employee could not continue to work in his position without contravening a statutory enactment;
- there is an applicable dismissal procedures agreement designated by an order under the *ERA 1996, s 110*; or
- the (principal) reason for the dismissal is retirement of the employee.

Other exceptions include circumstances where the parties will be treated as having complied with the procedures: for example when an employee applies to the tribunal for interim relief under the *ERA 1996, s 128* and the initial stages of the relevant procedure have been followed but the appeal has not yet taken place (*EA(DR)R 2004, regulation 5(1)*). Similarly, the parties will be treated as having complied with the procedures when an appropriate alternative appeal procedure exists and the employee uses it. Such a procedure has to operate by virtue of a collective agreement made between two or more employers or an employer's association and one or more independent trades unions (*EA(DR)R 2004, reg 5(2)*).

In addition, the DDP will not apply where there are reasonable grounds for believing that commencing the procedure or complying with the subsequent requirement would result in a significant threat to a person or their property, further harassment or it is not practicable to commence or comply within a reasonable period (*EA(DR)R 2004, reg 11(3)*).

[4.9] Two alternative forms of DDP are provided for – the 'standard' procedure and the abbreviated and much simpler 'modified' procedure. The standard procedure applies in all cases other than the limited exceptional circumstances where the modified procedure applies.

The standard procedure

[4.10] The 'standard' procedure, which is used in most cases, involves three basic steps:

- a written statement of complaint given to the employee setting out the matters which cause the employer to consider dismissing or taking other disciplinary action, and inviting the employee to a meeting to discuss these concerns;
- a meeting to discuss the complaint, and
- a right of appeal against the employer's decision.

[4.11] The standard procedure must be used in *all* dismissal situations, even ones unrelated to conduct (ie redundancy or non-renewal of a fixed term contract), save:

- Where an employee has been summarily dismissed (ie dismissed without notice or payment in lieu) for gross misconduct at the time the employer becomes aware of the misconduct, *and*
- where the employer was entitled to (ie acted reasonably in) summarily dismissing the employee without making additional enquiries into the circumstances in which the conduct took place.

In a number of exceptional situations such as where an employee is dismissed whilst carrying out an unofficial strike, or where a legal impediment has arisen preventing the employment lawfully continuing (ie an asylum seeker who has no right to work or whose work permit has been withdrawn).

The modified procedure

[4.12] In broad terms the modified procedure applies to situations which justify summary dismissal. *Regulation 3(2)* states that it applies where:

- there is a dismissal without notice by reason of the employee's conduct;

- the dismissal took place at the time the employer became aware of the conduct or immediately thereafter;
- the employer was entitled in the circumstances to dismiss without notice or payment in lieu of notice; and
- it was reasonable in the circumstances to dismiss before enquiring into the circumstances in which the conduct took place.

[4.13] The modified procedure simply requires the employer to provide an employee with a written statement as to the reasons for dismissal and a right of appeal. As can be seen from the bullet points above it mainly applies to situations where an employer, acting reasonably, reacts to an act of gross misconduct by dismissing *immediately* and asking questions later. The need for 'immediacy' was underlined by the EAT in *O'Neil v Wooldridge Ecotech Ltd* [2008] All ER(D) 34; where the dismissal of an employee the day after the act of misconduct was not deemed to be sufficiently 'immediate' to justify the use of the modified procedure. From an employer's perspective the key issue will be establishing that his reaction was 'reasonable', which ordinarily will require an employer to show that any investigation would have been futile.

The 2004 regime: grievance procedures

[4.14] Under the GP an employee is required to raise a grievance concerning any action which:

(i) his employer has taken or is contemplating taking against him (*EA(DR)R 2004, reg 2(1)*); and
(ii) which could form the basis of a complaint to an employment tribunal of a type set out at *Schedule 3* or *4* to the *Employment Act 2002* (*EA(DR)R 2004, reg 6(1)*).

Particularly common actions which are routinely raised under the GP are claims for unfair dismissal, discrimination and equal pay claims. In addition, complaints culpable failures to act can and should be raised under the GP (*Edebi v Canary Wharf Management Ltd* [2006] ICR 719).

[4.15] The GP does not apply in circumstances where:

- an employee who has ceased being employed wishes to raise a grievance and compliance with procedures is no longer practicable (*EA(DR)R 2004, reg 6(4)*);
- the grievance is about an actual or contemplated dismissal (but not

a constructive dismissal) (*reg 6(5)*). Where an employee wishes to complain against his dismissal he must appeal under the DDP;
- the grievance is about relevant disciplinary action which the employer has or might take unless one of the reasons for the grievance is that:
  - the employee complains that the disciplinary action is discriminatory;
  - the employee wishes to assert that grounds on which the employer took or is contemplating taking the action are unrelated to the grounds on which the employer is asserting that the action was or is being taken;
- there are reasonable grounds for believing that commencing the procedure or complying with the subsequent requirement would result in a significant threat to a person or their property, further harassment or it is not practicable to commence or comply within a reasonable period (*EA(DR)R 2004, reg 11(3)*).

[4.16] As with the DDP, the *Employment Act 2002*, provides for a 'standard' procedure and a simplified 'modified' procedure, the former being used for all grievances save where:
- the employee has ceased to be employed by the employer,
- the employer was
  - — unaware of the grievance before the employment had ended, or
  - — aware of the grievance but the standard grievance procedure had not been commenced or completed before the last day of employment, or
- the parties have agreed in writing in relation to a particular grievance, after it has come to the employer's knowledge, that the modified procedure should apply.

The standard procedure

[4.17] The standard GP involves three basic steps:
- the employee is required to set out the grievance in writing and send his employer a copy of this written grievance;
- the employer must then hold a meeting, at a reasonable time, to discuss the grievance with the employee (who must take reasonable steps to attend the meeting);
- the employer must inform the employee of the right of appeal against the first instance decision on his grievance and, if the

employee exercises the right of appeal the employer must hold a further meeting.

The modified procedure

[4.18] The modified procedure provides for a similar process but without any meetings: in effect the parties aim to resolve the grievance through written correspondence. The employee sets out the grievance and the basis for it, and the employer sets out his response.

Practical implications of the statutory procedures

[4.19] The statutory procedures (DDP and GP) have important consequences for employment tribunal procedure. Some impact on the employer and some on the employee:

- Sanctions for non-compliance by the employer include:
  - automatic findings of unfair dismissal and a statutory award reflecting this (see **4.20** below);
  - increased awards at the conclusion of tribunal hearings (see **4.22** below).
- Sanctions for non-compliance by the employee include:
  - denial of access to the tribunal (see **4.19** below);
  - reduced awards at the conclusion of tribunal hearings (see **4.22** below).
- Modification of the statutory time limits for bringing tribunal proceedings (see **4.25** below).

It should be noted that, under the *EA(DR)R 2004, reg 12* non-compliance with a relevant statutory procedure by either party has the effect that the non-completion of the procedure will be attributable to that party and neither party shall be under any obligation to comply with any further requirement of the procedure. The first party at fault cannot therefore seek to justify its failure to follow a relevant procedure by relying on any subsequent failure by the other party to comply with the procedures. Effectively, the first person to fail or refuse to engage in the relevant procedure will be treated as having caused all further non-compliance, and the relevant sanctions will apply accordingly. This is of course subject to the various provisions which allow for the parties to be treated as having complied in certain circumstances.

Compliance as a pre-condition to bringing a claim

[4.20] Under *the Employment Act 2002, s 33(2)* an employee who does not comply with the first step of the GP (ie who fails to send his employer a written grievance in a case to which the GP apply) is precluded from bringing a claim before an employment tribunal. In addition, an employee will be unable to present a complaint to an employment tribunal where less than 28 days have elapsed since the date when he lodged his written grievance with his employer. In practice this means that an employee cannot issue tribunal proceedings until his employer has had 28 days to comply with the GP. If, within this period, the employer complies with his obligations under the procedure (eg invites the employee to employee to attend a meeting or requests further information concerning the grievance to assist him in responding etc) a tribunal is likely to stay any application to allow the internal procedure to run its course.

Section 32(4) also provides that an employee will not be able to present a complaint to a tribunal where he has lodged his grievance more than one month after the end of the original time limit for making a complaint to the tribunal. So, for example, an employee who completes his statement of grievance, alleging an unlawful deduction of wages, four and half months after the date of the deduction would be time barred from presenting a complaint. The time limit for bringing a claim for unlawful deduction from wages is three months from date of deduction (*ERA 1996, section 23*).

For obvious reasons, it was this draconian aspect of the 2004 regime which produced a considerable amount of litigation by claimants who were barred from bringing claims.

Automatically unfair dismissal

[4.21] Any failure by an employer to comply with the DDP renders a dismissal 'automatically' procedurally unfair (*section 98A* of the *ERA 1996, s 98A* which was inserted by the *Employment Act 2002*). So, for example, the dismissal of an employee who has not been given the opportunity of attending a meeting accompanied by a representative of his choice will be automatically unfair. In these circumstances, whether or not the dismissal is unfair for any other reason, an employee will be entitled to a minimum award equivalent to four weeks' pay; save if this would result in injustice to the employer (*ERA 1996, s 120(1A)* and *(1B)*).

[4.22] Under the *Employment Act 2002* even where an employer's decision to dismiss is substantively reasonable, an employee can still succeed in his claim for unfair dismissal, solely on the grounds of a procedural breach of the DDP, albeit that it is likely that any award in such circumstances would be restricted to the statutory minimum (ie four weeks' salary).

It is also important to understand that procedural compliance with the DDP does not necessarily render a dismissal fair. The fact that the DDP was followed merely enables the employer to seek to justify the fairness of the dismissal on the ordinary grounds of reasonableness as set out in the *ERA 1996, s 98*.

Adjustment of awards

[4.23] In order to encourage parties to comply with and to use the statutory procedures, tribunals have the power to increase or decrease awards by between 10–50%, depending on which party has failed to comply with the procedures and the extent of any non-compliance (*Employment Act 2002, s 31*). Tribunals will determine which party is 'wholly or mainly' to blame for the failure to comply with a requirement of the procedure and reduce or increase an award accordingly. Conduct during subsequent tribunal proceedings is not, however, relevant in determining the appropriate uplift or reduction (*McKindless Group v McLaughlin* [2008] IRLR 678).

[4.24] A finding of procedural non-compliance will normally result in a 10% increase or decrease of an award in favour of the innocent party. In appropriate cases, where a tribunal considers that it is 'just and equitable' to do so, the award may be further reduced or increased up to a maximum of 50%. In exceptional circumstances, a tribunal has the discretion not to adjust the award. So for example, an employee who has failed on two occasions, without good reason, to attend the meeting required under the DDP, is likely to find his award reduced by between 10% and 50%; the extent of the reduction depending on the circumstances surrounding his failure to attend. Conversely, an employer who in similar circumstances, fails to attend the disciplinary meeting, or fails to invite an employee to a meeting under the GP, is likely to find any award increased by between 10 and 50%.

[4.25] In addition where an employer has failed to comply with the DDP the employee is entitled to an award equivalent to four weeks' pay and a declaration that he has been unfairly dismissed (*ERA 1996, section 120(1A)*).

Time limits

[4.26] Time limits for bringing claims are set out in detail in **chapter 5.** For the present purposes, however, it is sufficient to flag up the fact that, where the statutory procedures continue to apply the time limit for bringing a claim (ie the time within which a claim must be presented to a tribunal) are extended in order to give the parties a realistic opportunity to resolve their dispute utilising the statutory dispute resolution procedures. The *EA(DR)R 2004, reg 15* provides that wherever either the DDP or the GP apply the normal time limit for presenting a complaint is extended by three months, starting from the day after the normal time limit would have expired. It is important to note that this extension only applies where the statutory procedures were being followed (or where the employee has reasonable grounds for believing that they were being followed) before the expiry of the normal statutory time limit applicable to the type of complaint. This means that where an employee neither raises a grievance nor seeks to lodge a complaint with the employment tribunal within the normal time limit there will be no automatic extension of time.

Dispute resolution: the revised disciplinary and grievance procedures under the 2009 regime

[4.27] As explained in **4.2** above, for most claims which arise after 6 April 2009 the 2009 regime will apply. The relevant transitional arrangements can be found in the *Employment Act 2008 (Commencement No 1, Transitional Provisions and Savings) Order 2008*. In short, the 2009 replaces the inflexible old 2004 statutory procedures with a revised ACASS Code of Practice entitled 'Disciplinary and grievance procedures'. Whilst this revised code is less technical and more flexible the previous statutory dispute resolution procedures, the steps it envisages employers and employees taking remain broadly similar

The ACAS Code of Practice 'Disciplinary and grievance procedures'

[4.28] The Code was published in April 2009. It provides basic practical guidance to employers, employees and their representatives and sets out the principles for handling disciplinary and grievance situations in the workplace. The Code is supplemented by a non-statutory guide 'Discipline and grievances at work: the ACAS guide' which is available on the ACAS website (www.acas.org.uk) and by the ACAS helpline.

[4.29] The foreword to the Code advises that employers and employees should always seek to resolve disciplinary and grievance issues in the workplace. Where this is not possible, seeking the assistance of a third party may be appropriate: this might be an independent third party or an internal mediator who has not had prior involvement in the disciplinary or grievance issue. The Code sets out 'the basic requirements of fairness that will be applicable in most cases' and emphasises that 'it is intended to provide the standard of reasonable behaviour in most instances'.

[4.30] The Code, which is *not* applicable to apply to dismissals due to redundancy or the non-renewal of fixed term contracts, applies to:

- Disciplinary situations including misconduct and/or poor performance. .
- Grievances relating to concerns, problems or complaints that employees raise with their employers.

Whilst a failure by an employer or employee to observe any provision of the Code does not of itself render him liable to any proceedings (*Trade Union and Labour Relations (Consolidation) Act 1992, s 207(1)*), such a failure does, however, have two significant consequences:

- Firstly, the Code is admissible in evidence in proceedings before an employment tribunal and any provision of the Code which appears to the tribunal to be relevant to any question arising in those proceedings shall be taken into account in determining that question (*Trade Union and Labour Relations (Consolidation) Act 1992, s 207(2)*); and
- Secondly, in appropriate cases tribunals may also adjust any awards by up to 25% for any unreasonable failure to comply with any provision of the Code (*Trade Union and Labour Relations (Consolidation) Act 1992, s 207A*) (see **4.34** below).

General principles

[4.31] Employers are encouraged to act fairly and transparently. This means that rules and procedures for handling disciplinary and grievance situations should be developed and used. These rules and procedures should be set down in writing, and be specific and clear. Employees and/or their representatives should be involved in the development of the rules and procedures. Steps should be taken to help employees and managers should understand what the rules and procedures are, where they can be found and how they are used.

[4.32] Whenever a disciplinary or grievance process is being followed 'it is important to deal with issues fairly'. This is a key principle underlying the Code. In practical terms it means:

1 Issues should be raised and dealt with promptly. Meetings, decisions and confirmation of those decisions should not be unreasonably delayed.
2 Employers and employees should act consistently.
3 Employers should carry out necessary investigations to establish the facts of the case.
4 Employers should inform employees of the basis of the problem and give them an opportunity to put their case before any decisions are made.
5 Employers should allow employees to be accompanied at any formal disciplinary or grievance meeting.
6 Employers should allow an employee the right of appeal against any formal decision made.

Keys to handling disciplinary issues

[4.33] In handling disciplinary issues, employers are required to:

- Establish the facts of each case by carrying out, without unreasonable delay, necessary investigations of potential disciplinary matters.
- Inform the employee in writing of the problem, providing sufficient information about the alleged misconduct or poor performance and its consequences to enable the employee to answer the case at a disciplinary meeting.
- Hold a meeting with the employee to discuss the problem.
- Allow the employee to be accompanied at the meeting.
- Decide on appropriate action and inform the employee in writing.

- Provide the employee with an opportunity to appeal against any adverse decision.

As can be seen, whilst the rigid three stage process of the 2004 regime has been replaced, the basic nature of the procedure and the need for fairness remain broadly similar.

Keys to handling grievances

[4.34] If it is not possible to resolve the grievance informally, employees are required to raise the matter formally without unreasonable delay with a manager who is not the subject of the grievance. This should be done in writing and should set out the nature of the grievance. Where the employer receives such a grievance they should:

- Hold a meeting with the employee within a reasonable period of time to discuss the grievance.
- Allow the employee to be accompanied at the meeting.
- Decide on appropriate action and inform the employee in writing. Where appropriate, the employer should set out what action it proposes to take to resolve the grievance. The employee should be informed of his right of appeal.
- Allow the employee to take the grievance further if it is not resolved.

Consequences of non-compliance

[4.35] In any proceedings before an employment tribunal the Code tice is admissible in evidence and any provision of the Code which appears to the tribunal to be relevant to any question arising in those proceedings should be taken into account in determining that question (*Trade Union and Labour Relations (Consolidation) Act 1992, s 207(2)*).

[4.36] In proceedings before an employment tribunal relating to a claim by an employee under any of the jurisdictions listed in *Schedule A2* to the *Trade Union and Labour Relations (Consolidation) Act 1992* applies. The jurisdictions listed in *Schedule A2* are:

(a) the *Trade Union and Labour Relations (Consolidation) Act 1992, s 145A* (inducements relating to union membership or activities);
(b) *section 145B* of that Act (inducements relating to collective bargaining);

(c) *section 146* of that Act (detriment in relation to union membership and activities);
(d) *paragraph 156* of *Schedule A1* to that Act (detriment in relation to union recognition rights);
(e) the *ERA 1996, s 23* (unauthorised deductions and payments);
(f) *section 48* of that Act (detriment in employment);
(g) *section 111* of that Act (unfair dismissal);
(h) *section 163* of that Act (redundancy payments);
(i) *the National Minimum Wage Act 1998, s 24* (detriment in relation to national minimum wage);
(j) the *Equality Act 2010, ss 120* and *127* (discrimination etc in work cases);
(k) the *Employment Tribunal Extension of Jurisdiction (England and Wales) Order 1994 (SI 1994/1623)* (breach of employment contract and termination);
(l) the *Employment Tribunal Extension of Jurisdiction (Scotland) Order 1994 (SI 1994/1624)* (corresponding provision for Scotland);
(m) the *Working Time Regulations 1998 (SI 1998/1833), reg 30* (breach of regulations);
(n) the *Transnational Information and Consultation of Employees Regulations 1999 (SI 1999/3323), reg 32* (detriment relating to European Works Councils);
(o) the *European Public Limited-Liability Company Regulations 2004 (SI 2004/2326), reg 45* (detriment in employment);
(p) the *Information and Consultation of Employees Regulations 2004 (SI 2004/3426), reg 33* (detriment in employment);
(q) the *Occupational and Personal Pension Schemes (Consultation by Employers and Miscellaneous Amendment) Regulations 2006 (SI 2006/349), Sch, para 8* (detriment in employment);
(r) the *European Cooperative Society (Involvement of Employees) Regulations 2006 (SI 2006/2059), reg 34* (detriment in relation to involvement in a European Cooperative Society);
(s) the *Cross-border Railway Services (Working Time) Regulations 2008 (SI 2008/1660), reg 17* (breach of regulations); and
(t) the *Employment Relations Act 1999 (Blacklists) Regulations 2010 (SI 2010/493), reg 9* (detriment connected with prohibited list).

[4.37] In proceedings to which *s 207A* applies, if it appears to the tribunal that:
(a) the claim to which the proceedings relate concerns a matter to which a relevant Code of Practice applies,

(b) the employer has failed to comply with that Code in relation to that matter, and
(c) that failure was unreasonable

the employment tribunal may, if it considers it just and equitable in all the circumstances to do so, increase any award it makes to the employee by no more than 25% (*section 207A(2)*).

[4.38] Similarly, in proceedings to which *section 207A* applies, where an employee unreasonably fails to comply with the Code of Practice the tribunal may, if it considers it just and equitable in all the circumstances to do so, reduce any award it makes to the employee by no more than 25% (*s 207A(3)*). Where an award falls to be adjusted under *section 207A* and under the *Employment Act 2002, s 38* (Failure to give statement of employment particulars, etc) the adjustment under *s 207A* is to be made before the adjustment under that section.

[4.39] As can be seen from the above, the changes introduced by the *Employment Act 2008* have not radically altered the steps which need to be taken by employers and employees. On the contrary, the Code of Practice maintains in broad terms the three step approach that previously existed under the 2004 regime. What has changed, however, are the consequences of non-compliance: employees who, under the 2004 regime, would have found themselves barred from bringing proceedings before an employment tribunal due to their failure, for example, to comply with the GP, are now able to bring proceedings; albeit with the risk of having any award of damages reduced by up to 25%. Likewise, an employer who fails to comply with the disciplinary procedure will no longer be subject to an automatic finding of unfair dismissal, although the risk remains of an increase by up to 25% of any damages that awarded to the employee. It remains to be seen whether the 2009 procedures result in a reduction in the number of claims being registered.

Chapter 5

Time limits

Introduction

[5.1] In general, tribunals only have the jurisdiction (ie the power) to hear claims that are brought within the relevant statutory time limits. These time limits are normally set out in the statute which provides for right to bring a particular claim before the tribunal. Whilst time limits cannot be waived (either by the tribunal or the parties), tribunals can, in most cases, extend the time limit if certain criteria are met. Each statute that provides for the right to bring a claim also sets out the circumstances in which a tribunal has the power to extend time; the so called 'escape clauses'. Where a statute is silent on the matter, a tribunal has no power to extend time. From an employer's perspective, it is important to bear in mind that claims can be knocked out at a preliminary hearing, *without consideration* of the substantive merits of the complaint, merely by establishing that proceedings are out of time. For obvious reasons, establishing that a claim is out of time can result in significant savings in terms of costs.

[5.2] As most time limits, such as that for claiming unfair dismissal, go the issue of the tribunals' jurisdiction (*Dedman v British Building and Engineering Appliances Ltd* [1973] IRLR 379) they can be raised at any time either by the parties or by the tribunal of its own volition (regardless of the view the parties) (*Rogers v Bodfari (Transport) Ltd* [1973] IRLR 172).

[5.3] This chapter looks at the process both of ascertaining whether a claim is in time and, if not, the criteria for extending time contained in the escape clauses.

Time limits for presentation of claims: the five-stage test

[5.4] A tribunal, when considering whether it has jurisdiction to hear a claim, will:

- Establish whether a time limit is applicable to a claim and, if so, what that time limit is;
- Identify the event upon which the claim is based and from which time, for the purposes of the relevant limitation period, begins to run ('the trigger event');
- Calculate the time that has elapsed between the event and the presentation of the claim to the tribunal ('the period');
- Accept jurisdiction where the period is less than or equal to the statutory time limit; and
- Where the period exceeds the time limit, go on to consider whether, applying the relevant criteria, the time limit can and should be extended.

A tribunal will consider these issues in strict chronological order and will first determine whether a claim is 'in time' before going on to consider whether, having regard to all the surrounding circumstances, time ought to be extended. Each of these steps will be considered below.

Stage one: what time limit applies?

[5.5] The time limits applicable to the claims that the tribunal has jurisdiction to hear are set out in **appendix I – claims a tribunal can hear**.

For cases where the 2004 dispute resolution procedures apply, it is important to bear in mind that under the Employment Act 2002 certain time limits are automatically extended. Detailed consideration of these procedures is outside the scope of this book, however for a summary of information on the 2004 dispute resolution procedures see **chapter 4: dispute resolution**.

Stage two: identify the trigger event

[5.6] All the statutory provisions which create the right to bring a claim, refer to a particular event, or 'trigger' that starts time running for the purposes of presenting a claim to the tribunal. Unsurprisingly, different 'trigger' events apply to different claims.

Unfair/wrongful dismissal claims

[5.7] In general, a claim for unfair dismissal must be presented to the tribunal 'before the end of the three months beginning with the effective date of termination' (*Employment Rights Act 1996 (ERA 1996), s 111)*). The 'trigger' date, therefore, from which time starts to run, is the effective date of termination ('the EDT').

Section 97(1) of the *ERA 1996* provides that for an employee:

'(a) whose contract of employment is terminated by notice, whether given by his employer or by the employee, the EDT is the date on which the notice expires;

(b) whose contract of employment is terminated without notice, the EDT is the date on which the termination takes effect, and

(c) who is employed under a limited-term contract which terminates by virtue of the limiting event without being renewed under the same contract, the EDT means the date on which the termination takes effect.'

[5.8] Hence, where an employee is dismissed *with* notice, the EDT is the date on which the notice expires, irrespective of whether or not the employee was actually required to work during the notice period. When calculating the precise EDT it is important to bear in mind that where an employee is given notice of termination, the notice period runs from the day after receipt and not from the day on which notice was given (*West v Kneels Ltd* [1986] IRLR 430). So if an employee is given one month's notice, time for the purposes of calculating the month starts to run from the day after receipt of the notice .

On the other hand, where an employee is summarily dismissed, or dismissed *without* notice the EDT is the date on which he is dismissed or ceases to work.

[5.9] In practice, the difference between these two options can often result in an employee having an extra month to bring a claim before the tribunal (ie the four-week notice period). It is important, therefore, to consider with care the basis of dismissal and to ensure that the letter of dismissal clearly sets out the option that is chosen.

[5.10] Where an employer terminates the employment the termination is only effective upon communication to the employee. Hence, where a dismissal was communicated to an employee in a letter which arrived whilst she was away, the contract of employment did not terminate until the employee had actually read the letter or had had a reasonable opportunity to read it (*Gisda CYF v Lauren Barratt* [2010] UKSC 41). The reasonableness of the employee's behaviour could be considered when determining whether they had had such a 'reasonable opportunity'.

[5.11] Where proceedings are issued either before notice of termination has been served, or prior to the date of dismissal, a tribunal has no jurisdiction to hear a claim for unfair dismissal. So, for example, where an employee issued proceedings upon being told that their fixed-term contract would not be renewed, but before the contract expired, their application was held to be premature and hence outside the jurisdiction of the tribunal (*Throsby v Imperial College of Science and Technology* [1978] ICR 357).

[5.12] By way of exception to this general rule, the *ERA 1996, s 111(3)* permits a tribunal to hear claims that are presented during an employee's notice period (ie prior to the EDT but after notice of termination has been given). This exception applies also to claims for constructive dismissal where an employee, having given notice, issues a claim prior to the expiry of the notice period. This encourages claims to be brought as early as possible.

[5.13] In claims for wrongful dismissal, which are essentially claims by employees seeking compensation for dismissal in a manner contrary to their contractual terms of employment, the 'trigger' date is also the EDT. There is no requirement (as there is in relation to a claim for unfair dismissal) for an employee to have worked for 12 months before bringing a wrongful dismissal claim.

Discrimination claims

[5.14] In claims involving discrimination under the Equality Act 2010, proceedings may not be brought after the end of the period of three months starting with the date of the act complained of, or, in certain circumstances, such other period as the tribunal thinks just and equitable (*Equality Act 2010, s 123(1)*).

For discrimination claims arising out of events which occurred prior to the coming into force of the Equality Act 2010, the relevant statutes or regulations state that 'a tribunal shall not consider a complaint… unless it is presented to the tribunal before the end of the period of three months beginning when the act complained of was done' (see, for example, *Sex Discrimination Act 1975, s 76(1), Race Relations Act 1976, s 68(1), Disability Discrimination Act 1995, Sch 3, para 3(1)* and *Employment Equality (Religion or Belief) Regulations 2003, reg 34(1).*

In general, therefore, time starts to run from the date that the act complained of occurred and not from the date on which the disadvantaged party became aware of the discriminatory conduct (*Virdi v Commissioner of Police of the Metropolis* [2007] IRLR 24).

[5.15] For a long time it was thought that the 'act complained of' was required to have taken place whilst an employee was employed. The House of Lords, in *Relaxion Group plc v Rhys-Harper* [2003] UKHL 33, however, emphatically rejected this proposition, holding that tribunals have jurisdiction to consider complaints under the various discrimination legislation, concerning matters which take place after the employment relationship has ended. For this jurisdiction to exist what was required was a substantive connection between the allegedly discriminatory act and the previous employment relationship. This decision was later confirmed by an amendment to the discrimination statutes, enabling an employee to challenge a reference given to him after his employment had ended on the grounds that it was discriminatory. Such a claim would be subject to the ordinary time limits with his being required to present his complaint within three months of the act of discrimination (which is likely to be the date the reference was sent).

In addition, the *Equality Act 2010* expressly prohibits discrimination which 'arises out of and is closely connected to a relationship which used to exist' between the employer and employee (*s 108(1)*), thus making it crystal clear that the tribunal has a broad jurisdiction to hear complaints of discrimination so long as they are sufficiently connected to the employment relationship.

[5.16] In a claim alleging that a dismissal was discriminatory time begins to run not from the date of the employer's decision to dismiss, but from the date on which the employee's notice period ends (ie the EDT; see *British Gas Services Ltd v McCaull* [2001] IRLR 60).

[5.17] Time only starts to run from the date when an employer is in a position to implement a decision. This was confirmed in *Swithland Motors plc v Clarke* [1994] ICR 231, a case concerning a prospective purchaser of a business who decided, prior to purchasing the business, that certain employees would be dismissed in the event that the purchase was successful. The tribunal held that time only began to run from the date that the purchaser was in a position to implement their decision, which in practical terms meant that time began to run from the day after they had purchased the business and told the employee that she was dismissed.

[5.18] For the purposes of calculating when 'an act complained of occurred', conduct extending over a period of time is treated as being done at the end of the period (*Equality Act 2010, s 123(3)*). This reflects the position adopted by the courts in respect of discrimination claims brought under the various discrimination statues prior to the *Equality Act 2010* coming into force. Consequently, the principles underlying the guidance provided by the courts as to what amounted to 'an act extending over time' under the earlier statutes, are likely to remain broadly applicable in considering claims under the *Equality Act 2010*.

So for example, it is likely that, in determining what amounts to 'an act extending over time', tribunals will be expected to continue to follow *Hendricks v Metropolitan Police Comr* [2003] IRLR 96, and to focus *not* on whether there is something which can be characterised as a policy, rule, scheme, regime or practice, but rather on whether there was an ongoing situation or continuing state of affairs in which the claimant was treated less favourably. This approach led the Court of Appeal in *Hendricks* to conclude that the acts of harassment evidenced a general culture of discrimination, which did amount to an on-going state of affairs, which fell within the meaning of the *Sex Discrimination Act 1975, s 76*. The claimant, who was able to establish that the last act of discrimination occurred within the preceding three-month period, was therefore able to include in her claim a significant number of other acts extending back over many years.

[5.19] By way of further example, where an employer operated a policy under which only men were eligible for a mortgage subsidy, the refusal to grant a female employee a subsidy was held to be a discriminatory act that continued throughout the lifetime of the policy. Since the policy was still operating when the applicant resigned, she was entitled to bring a sex discrimination claim within three months of the date of her resignation, despite the fact that the act complained of (ie the refusal of her application for a mortgage subsidy) had taken place five months earlier (*Calder v James Finlay Corpn Ltd* [1989] ICR 157. See also *Barclays Bank plc v Kapur* [1991] ICR 208 where the applicants were allowed to bring claims 17 years after joining the pension schemes).

[5.20] What is equally clear, however, is that when considering whether there has been a continuing act, a claimant cannot rely on an act occurring after presentation of the complaint (*Robertson v Bexley Community Centre t/a Leisure Link* [2003] IRLR 434).

[5.21] Another example of a continuing discriminatory act is where an employer, having given assurances to an employee who has complained of discriminatory abuse, then fails to satisfactorily implement those assurances (*Littlewoods Organisations plc v Traynor* [1993] IRLR 154). In these circumstances, the act will extend until satisfactory remedial action has been taken. A failure to do something is to be treated as occurring when the person in question 'decided on it'. For these purposes and in the absence of evidence to the contrary, a person (P) is to be taken to decide on failure to do something when P does an act inconsistent with doing it or if P does no inconsistent act, on the expiry of the period in which P might reasonably have been expected to do it (*Equality Act 2010, s 123(3)(b)* and *(4)*). It remains to be seen how this provision, which is likely to give rise to difficult questions of fact and interpretation, will be applied in practice.

[5.22] It remains important to distinguish between a continuing discriminatory 'act' and an act that has continuing discriminatory 'consequences'. In this context, it is critical to differentiate between a single act, such as a failure to promote, and a general regime that has a continuing discriminatory effect. The mere fact that a person continues to experience the discriminatory consequences of a decision will not justify extending the time limit. Only where the act itself is continuing will time be extended. A practical example of this distinction can be found in *Sougrin v Haringey Health Authority* [1992] ICR 650, a claim involving a nurse who alleged that her failure to be promoted at an internal appeal was due to racial discrimination. The Court of Appeal rejected her argument that the loss of pay she suffered as a result of not being promoted amounted to a continuing act of discrimination. In their view, the loss of pay was an inevitable consequence of the decision not to promote her, and that the time for bringing her claim started to run from the date that she lost her internal appeal; namely five months before she presented her claim to the tribunal.

Redundancy claims

[5.23] The general rule is that any claim for redundancy must be made within six months of the 'relevant date'. The *ERA 1996, s 164(1)* defines the various ways that an employee can make a claim for redundancy, and confirms that an application will be in time where, within six months of the relevant date if one of the following occurs:

- a redundancy payment is agreed and paid;
- the employee has made a claim, in writing, to the employer for such a payment;
- a question as to the employee's entitlement to, or amount of, the payment has been referred to a tribunal; or
- a claim for unfair dismissal has been presented to the tribunal.

[5.24] Rather uniquely, therefore, employees are permitted to present a claim for a redundancy payment either to the employer or the tribunal. So long as this occurs within six months of the relevant date, the claim will be 'in time'. The relevant date, which is taken into account when calculating the limitation period is defined in the *ERA 1996, s 145* as follows:

- where a contract of employment is terminated without notice, the relevant date is the day that the termination takes effect;
- where a contract of employment is terminated with notice, the relevant date is the day that notice expires;
- where a contract of employment is for a fixed term, the relevant date is the last day of the fixed term.

[5.25] Historically, where an employee presented a claim before the relevant date, a tribunal was thought not to have jurisdiction to hear the complaint (*Pritchard-Rhodes Ltd v Boon and Milton* [1979] IRLR 19). With the subsequent change in the law relating to unfair dismissal so as to allow claims for unfair dismissal to be brought within the notice period (*ERA 1996, s 111*), it is likely that a tribunal would now accept jurisdiction to hear a claim for redundancy presented during the notice period.

Tribunals are given a special discretionary power to extend time for a further six months in circumstances where it considers it just and equitable that an employee should receive a redundancy payment (*ERA 1996, s 164(2)*). This discretion may not be exercised, however, where a redundancy payment was agreed and paid within the first six months (ie the first category of *s 164(1)* above).

[5.26] There are two exceptions to the time limit generally applicable to claims for redundancy. First, where a civil servant or Crown employee refers a question to a tribunal concerning their entitlement to the equivalent of redundancy pay (*ERA 1996, s 177*) the normal six-month limitation period does not apply. Instead, such a reference must be made within the ordinary contractual limitation period of six years (*Greenwich Health Authority v Skinner* [1989] IRL 238).

Second, where the Secretary of State has failed to make a redundancy payment on behalf of an insolvent employer (*ERA 1996, s 166*), an employee may, under *section 170* of the *ERA 1996*, refer this issue to a tribunal. No time limit is prescribed for this type of reference.

Equal pay claims

[5.27] A claim for breach of the equality clause (the equality clause which is implied into every contract of employment with a view to ensuring that the totality of the terms and conditions of employment for a woman are no less favourable than for a man) must be referred to a tribunal either whilst an employment contract is in existence, or within six months of the contract terminating (*Equality Act 2010, s 129*; for cases arising prior to the commencement of the 2010 Act, see *Equal Pay Act 1970* (*EPA 1970*), *s 2(4)*). It is important to note that a tribunal has no discretionary power to extend this time limit. Having said this, there are a number of exceptions to the six-month time limit: for example cases of 'concealment' where the employer has deliberately hidden any fact which is relevant to the breach to which the proceedings relate.

Unauthorised deduction of wages

[5.28] A claim for unauthorised deduction of wages time must be presented to a tribunal within three months, beginning with the date of alleged failure to pay any sum owed to an employee under their terms of employment (*ERA 1996, s 23*). In a similar manner to discrimination claims, where it can be established that there was a *series* of unlawful deductions, time will begin to run from the date of the last failure to pay the employee.

Contract claims

[5.29] Claims for breach of contract must be presented to a tribunal within three months beginning with the EDT (claims for breach of contract are brought under the *Employment Tribunal Extension of*

Jurisdiction (England and Wales) Order 1994). It is important to remember that tribunals can only hear breach of contract claims that are brought *after* the termination of employment. A tribunal has no jurisdiction to hear a claim for breach of contract, where the complaint is made during the currency of a worker's employment (*Capek v Lincolnshire County Council* [2000] IRLR 590).

It is also important to bear in mind that employees retain a parallel entitlement to bring a breach of contract claim in the ordinary civil courts within the six year limitation period applicable to contract claims pursuant to the *Limitation Act 1980*.

Failure to provide written particulars

[5.30] Every employer is required to provide his employees with a written statement of particulars of employment and an itemised pay statement (*ERA 1996, s 1(1)* and *s 8*). An employee who wishes to bring a claim alleging that these statutory requirements have not been complied with may do so at any time during their employment or within three months of the termination of the contract of employment.

Stage three: calculating time

Presenting a claim

[5.31] Having identified the 'trigger event' a tribunal will then go on to determine whether the claim has been presented to the tribunal within the prescribed statutory time limit (there are exceptions to this general rule; for example claims for redundancy – where the complaint can be made to the employer).

For the purposes of the *Employment Tribunals (Constitution and Rules of Procedure) Regulations 2004* a claim is validly presented on the day that it is physically delivered to the appropriate tribunal. In practical terms this means that an originating application can be served by post, fax or hand delivered. It is crucial to bear in mind that 'presentation' of a claim occurs on the day that the originating application is *received* by the tribunal and *not* on the date when it was posted to the tribunal.

[5.32] Confirmation of receipt of the originating application should *always* be obtained so as to safeguard against the risk that the application has been lost or delayed in the post or not received as a result of transmission problems with the fax. A party should not delay in seeking confirmation. A tribunal will have little sympathy for an applicant who, having sent their originating application and not received confirmation of receipt, delays unreasonably in verifying that it has arrived (*Camden and Islington Community Services NHS Trust v Kennedy* [1996] IRLR 381).

Calculating time

[5.33] In carrying out the calculation, any reference in a statute or rule to a month or months is taken to mean 'calendar' month(s) (*Interpretation Act 1978, Sch 1*), and any reference to a specific date is deemed to include the whole 24-hour period. Consequently, so long as a claim is presented before midnight of the last day of the statutory time limit, the claim is deemed to have been presented 'in time'.

Where a statute indicates that time runs *beginning with* a particular event, the statutory period for bringing the claim *includes* the date when this event occurred (see *Pruden v Cunard Ellerman Ltd* [1993] IRLR 317 for a full summary of the rules for calculating time).

[5.34] Note that all calculations of time for acts required to be done under the *2004 Rules* will be made in accordance with *reg 15*. This provides that where an act must or may be done:

(i) within a certain number of days or from an event, the date of the event shall not be included;
(ii) not less than a certain number of days of or from an event, the date of that event shall not be included in the calculations;
(iii) not less than a certain number of days before or after an event, the date of that event shall not be included in the calculations.

Regulation 15(5) further provides that where the tribunal is required to send the parties notice of a hearing (14 days before the date of the hearing) this requirement is satisfied by the tribunal placing the notice in the post 14 days before the date of hearing. Unless the contrary is proved, the tribunal shall be deemed to have sent the parties notice on the date of the accompanying letter.

Examples

Example 1: In a claim for unfair dismissal, the three-month period within which to bring a claim 'begins to run' from the EDT. If the EDT is 22 March, a claim for unfair dismissal will need to be presented to the tribunal before midnight on 21 June.

Where the time limit for bringing a claim begins to run *'of, from or after'* a particular date, the statutory period for bringing the claim *excludes* that date.

Example 2: In a claim for equal pay the six-month limitation period begins to run from the date a person terminates their employment. So, for example, an employee who left his job on 6 January will have until 6 July to present a claim to a tribunal.

Where, having calculated the period of time, there is no corresponding date in the appropriate month, the limitation period is deemed to expire on the last day of that month.

Example 3: Where the EDT is 1 September, the three-month time limit should expire on midnight of 31 November. However, since November only has 30 days, the time limit will, in fact, expire on the last day of the month (ie 30 November).

This rule can give rise to some rather strange results. For example, whether the EDT is 1 December or 30 November, the limitation period will expire on the same day; namely midnight of 28 February (or 29 February in a leap year).

Example 4: A respondent is sent a copy of a claim on 1 October. Under the 2004 Rules he must present a response to the Employment Tribunal Office within 28 days of the date on which he was sent the copy. The last day for presentation of the response is 29 October.

[5.35] When considering whether or not a claim is 'in time' tribunals are strict in their application of the three-month limitation period. The fact, for example, that the last day for presenting a claim falls on a Saturday, Sunday or Bank Holiday does not affect the date when the limitation period expires. This was confirmed in *Swainston v Hetton Victory Club Ltd* [1983] ICR 341, where the Court of Appeal rejected the applicant's submission that, although the time limit expired on Sunday 6 December, the fact that his claim had been presented to the tribunal on the next working day, namely Monday 7 December, meant that it was presented 'in time'.

[5.36] In *Consignia plc v Sealy* [2002] IRLR 624 the Court of Appeal reaffirmed the decision in *Swainston* and gave useful guidance concerning postal applications:

- a party who sent his application by first class post at least two working days before the expiry of the relevant time limit would ordinarily be entitled to an extension of time (this is consistent with the deeming provisions in *Civil Procedure Rules – CPR, rr 6.14* and *6.26*);
- where a time limit expires on a weekend/bank holiday *and* the tribunal has no letterbox or other means of receiving communication during weekends/bank holidays, there is no automatic extension of time to the next working day. In these circumstances, however, a claimant who is prevented from presenting his complaint on the last day can seek to extend time by arguing that it was not reasonably practicable for the complaint to have been presented within the prescribed period.

In *Initial Electronic Systems Ltd v Avdic* [2005] IRLR 671 the EAT confirmed that Consignia did not create an obligation on claimants to prove an unforeseen circumstance; instead it established a test of objective reasonable expectation against which the claimant's act of sending his claim form needed to be considered. The EAT further confirmed that once one of the Consignia criteria are established (ie a Tribunal lacking a post box and thus preventing presentation of the claim at the end of the limitation period) a claimant is ordinarily free from justifying his earlier delay.

When calculating the limitation period a tribunal will not make allowances for any anomalies that arise due to the way that months are calculated. So, for example, in a claim where the EDT was 30 April and the complaint was presented one day of out of time, on 30 July, the EAT rejected the applicant's submission that the claim was in time since, had the EDT been one day later (ie 1 May), the time limit would not have expired until 31 July (*University of Cambridge v Murray* [1993] ICR 460).

Stage four: is the claim in time?

[5.37] If a claimant has presented his claim within the relevant statutory time limit the tribunal should accept jurisdiction.

Under the Employment Act 2002, an employee who failed to comply with the requirements of the statutory grievance procedure (ie who failed to lodge a grievance with their employer) was barred from bringing a claim before an employment tribunal (*section 32(2)* of *Employment Act 2002*). These provisions were repealed by the Employment Act 2008 and, from 6 April 2009, have been replaced by a more flexible regime under which a failure to raise a grievance no longer acts as a bar to bringing a claim before a tribunal. Note, however, that an employee who fails to follow the new regime (namely the ACAS Code of Practice: Disciplinary and Grievance Procedures) may have any award of damages reduced (see **chapter 4: dispute resolution** and **chapter 24 – remedies: calculating likely awards**).

As indicated in **chapter 4** the majority of claims will now fall to be considered under the new regime, which does not provide for automatic extensions of time. There will, however, be a diminishing minority of claims that will still fall to be considered under the old statutory dispute resolution procedures. The transitional provisions which govern the claims in relation to which the old statutory dispute resolution procedures, are identified in **chapter 4**. Given that these transitional provisions make it clear that the old statutory dispute resolution procedures only apply to grievances or acts which took place prior to 5 April 2009 and/or 4 October 2009, there would appear to be little or no scope for the automatic extensions of time previously applicable under the old regime to have any continuing impact on claims issued in 2011.

Stage five: extending the time limit

Jurisdiction

[5.38] A tribunal has no jurisdiction to hear a claim that is brought outside the relevant statutory time limit (see *Grimes v Sutton London Borough Council* [1973] ICR 240, as confirmed in *Radakovits v Abbey National plc* [2009] EWCA Civ 1346; [2010] IRLR 307). This means that parties cannot simply agree to have a case heard where the claim has been presented out of time. Moreover, as with all jurisdictional issues, a tribunal has an obligation to satisfy itself that a claim has been presented in time irrespective of whether the point is taken by either party. This is a continuing obligation and the issue of whether or not a claim has been brought within time can be raised at any point during proceedings (*Rogers v Bodfari (Transport) Ltd* [1973] IRLR 172 – any decision of a tribunal on a claim brought outside a time limit may be challenged on the basis that the tribunal lacked jurisdiction, irrespective of whether this point was argued before the tribunal. In this case, having made a finding that the dismissal was unfair, the claim was adjourned to consider compensation. At the adjourned hearing, time limits were raised for the first time and the tribunal felt compelled to dismiss the complaint).

[5.39] In most cases, however, a tribunal has a statutory discretion to extend time and thereby hear a claim. The relatively few claims where a tribunal has no power to extend time and can therefore never hear an 'out of time' claim include:

- claims to which the now repealed statutory grievance procedures applied and which were brought more than one month after the expiry of the normal statutory time limit in circumstances where no grievance has been raised;
- claims relating to equal pay etc under the *Equality Act 2010* (formerly under the *Equal Pay Act 1970*);
- appeals against an unlawful act notice from the Equality and Human Rights Commission under the *Equality Act 2006, s 21*;
- applications for compensation where a tribunal has made a declaration of unjustifiable disciplining of trade union members under the *Trade Union and Labour Relations (Consolidation) Act 1992 (TULR(C)A 1992), s 66*);
- applications for interim relief under the *ERA 1996, s 128* or pending determination of a complaint of unfair dismissal under the *TULR(C) A 1992, s 161(2)* (the time limit for bringing a claim for interim relief is extremely restrictive – an employee may only bring a claim either prior to the EDT or within seven days of the EDT);
- appeals against a notice of underpayment issued by HMRC under the *National Minimum Wage Act 1998, s 19*.

Extending the time limits

[5.40] Where an applicant has failed to present a claim within the relevant time limit, they may seek to persuade the tribunal to extend time under one of the so-called 'escape clauses'.. The higher courts have repeatedly stressed that the exercise of the discretion to extend time is the exception rather than the rule (see, for example, *Robertson v Bexley Community Centre* [2003] EWCA Civ 576; [2003] IRLR 434 and

Chief Constable of Lincolnshire Police v Caston [2009] EWCA Civ 1298; [2010] IRLR 327).

The criteria that a tribunal is required to consider, when deciding whether or not to extend time, will vary from claim to claim. In practice, however, there are effectively two types of 'escape clause' that apply to the vast majority of claims.

The first, and most common clause, allows a tribunal to consider a claim that has not been presented within the principal time period (for example, in a claim for unfair dismissal, three months from the EDT) but which the Tribunal is satisfied has nevertheless been presented:

> 'within such further period as it considers reasonable in a case where it is satisfied that it was *not reasonably practicable* for the complaint to be presented before the end of that period of three months' (*ERA 1996, s 111(2)(b)*).

The second type of clause that applies to claims for discrimination enables a tribunal to extend the principal time period where it considers it *'just and equitable'* to do so in all the circumstances. This is a far more relaxed test than the 'reasonably practicable test'.

(1) 'Not reasonably practicable'

[5.41] The burden of proving that it was not reasonably practicable to present a claim 'in time' rests squarely with the claimant. If he persuades the tribunal that it was not reasonably practicable he must also go on to show that the time within which the claim was eventually presented was reasonable. In the case of *Walls Meat Co Ltd v Khan* [1979] ICR 52, the Court of Appeal provided useful guidance of what is meant by 'reasonably practicable':

> 'The performance of an act, in this case the presentation of a complaint, is not reasonably practicable if there is some impediment which reasonably prevents, or interferes with, or inhibits such performance. The impediment may be physical, for instance illness of the complainant or a postal strike; or the impediment may be mental, namely the state of mind of the complainant in the form of ignorance of, or mistaken belief with regard to essential matters'.

[5.42] In order to fully understand this test it is necessary to appreciate that it incorporates two distinct considerations; namely one of 'reasonableness' and one of 'practicability'. Both have to be satisfied before a tribunal will consider extending time. An employee will therefore have to provide evidence:

- as to the matters that rendered it impracticable to present the complaint in time; and
- that establishes that these matters were themselves reasonable, having regard to all the surrounding circumstances.

Consequently, even if it is accepted that an employee was, for example, ignorant of their legal rights, and that therefore it was not practicable for them to have brought the claim in time, a tribunal will go on to consider whether ignorance was, in all the circumstances, 'reasonable'. This will involve an assessment of the employee's explanation of their ignorance and, in particular, whether or not they had access to legal advice, what steps were taken to find out about their rights and whether they were misled or deceived.

[5.43] The 'reasonableness' test is objective. A tribunal is therefore entitled to refuse to extend time where it considers that an employee ought to have known or been aware of their rights. For obvious reasons a tribunal is more likely to reach such a conclusion when faced with an intelligent well-educated employee who could have reasonably been expected to have investigated their rights within the time limit.

[5.44] Bearing in mind the increasing public awareness of unfair dismissal, and employment rights generally, it is becoming ever more difficult for an employee to establish that an ignorance of their rights is reasonable. It is certainly arguable that, even where an employee has only a general idea as to the availability of a remedy, it would be reasonable to expect them not to delay in making suitable enquiries.

[5.45] When considering factors that may have physically prevented the employee from presenting their claim, a tribunal will tend to attach greater weight to impediments that arose in the closing stages of the limitation period (*Schultz v Esso Petroleum Ltd* [1999] ICR 1202). So, for example, an employee who was physically incapacitated in the last month of the limitation period is more likely to succeed in having time extended than one who was ill for only the first month. The reason for this is that it will be more difficult for the latter to justify his subsequent failure to present the claim in the two months that remained.

[5.46] Where an claimant has knowledge of his rights, but chooses to delay making a claim for fear of jeopardising his commercial arrangements with his previous employer, this is unlikely to amount to a good reason (in terms of reasonable practicability) to extend time (*Birmingham Optical plc v Johnson* [1995] ICR 459).

Other common reasons justifying delay

[5.47] **Error of advisor**: The extent to which an employee can rely on an error of their advisor, to demonstrate that it was not reasonably practicable for the claim to have been presented in time has been the subject of some debate. If a professional advisor, such as a solicitor, has been instructed by the employee to advise or act for him, then any wrongful or negligent advice or action on his part which results in the time limit being missed will be attributed to the employee with the result that he will ordinarily be unable to rely on the escape clause (*Dedman v British Building and Engineering Appliances Ltd* [1973] IRLR 379). If a claimant engages a skilled advisor to act for him and that advisor mistakenly advises as to the relevant time limits to the claimant's prejudice, the remedy lies against the advisor. Although the rationale underpinning the *Dedman* principle has been questioned, the correctness of the approach was confirmed by the Court of Appeal in *Marks & Spencer plc v Williams-Ryan* [2005] IRLR 562.

[5.48] Where, on the other hand, an employee is misled by the advice of someone that they have not retained or engaged, for example a tribunal employee, they are likely to be entitled to rely on the escape clause, subject of course to establishing that reliance on the advice and subsequent actions were 'reasonable' (*Jean Sorelle Ltd v Rybak* [1991] IRLR 153 and *London International College v Sen* [1993] IRLR 333). The rationale underlying this distinction appears to be that an advisor who is engaged to assist in a case is potentially liable for any incorrect advice, and it is he and not the employer who should compensate the employee for any loss suffered as a result of this advice.

Where an employee has received incorrect advice from more than one source, a tribunal will attempt to identify the advice that was the substantial cause of the late application. So, for example, in the case of *London International College v Sen* [1993] IRLR 333, where an employee received incorrect advice both from a solicitor and the tribunal, the Court of Appeal took the view that since the substantial cause of the late application was the 'reasonable' reliance on the incorrect advice given by the tribunal, the employee should benefit from the escape clause despite the fact that he had had access to skilled advice.

There is some doubt as to whether an employee who seeks the advice of a Citizens Advice Bureau or a similar voluntary body is to be treated in the same way as one who engages a solicitor. In *Marks & Spencer plc v Williams-Ryan* [2005] IRLR 562 the Court of Appeal left open the possibility that a claimant could assert that it was not reasonably practicable to have brought proceedings earlier because they were relying upon the erroneous advice of a CAB. As Lord Phillips MR put it, the answer will depend on who gave the advice and in what circumstances.

[5.49] Lastly, it is worth noting that a solicitor remains under a continuing obligation to confirm with the tribunal receipt of the complaint by the tribunal (*Palmer v Southend-on-Sea Borough Council* [1984] ICR 372). The fact therefore that a claim was sent well within time but was not received by the tribunal is only likely to amount to a valid justification for extending time where appropriate attempts have been made to confirm receipt.

[5.50] Delay caused by internal appeal/other proceedings: Where the sole reason for an employee having delayed presenting their complaint is the fact that they had an ongoing appeal under the employer's internal dispute procedure or statutory procedures, this is unlikely, by itself, to justify extending time under the escape clause. As many of the leading cases in this area were decided before the introduction of the statutory grievance procedures it is unlikely, in the view of the authors, that their abolition will result in a significant reappraisal of these underlying principles.

Similarly, the fact that an employee delays presenting a complaint until after other proceedings (whether civil or criminal) have been determined is unlikely to satisfy the criteria. In *Palmer v Southend-on-Sea Borough Council* [1984] IRLR 119, two employees who had been convicted of stealing petrol and dismissed were told that if their criminal convictions were overturned, the Council might reconsider their dismissal. The convictions were overturned but the Council refused to reinstate the employees. The time limit for challenging the original dismissal had expired and the Court of Appeal refused to extend time on the basis that it had been reasonably practicable to present the complaint in time.

By way of exception to this general rule, a tribunal may be willing to extend time where the employee delays presenting a claim to the tribunal, pending the decision of an internal appeal, at the specific request of the employer (*Owen v Crown House Engineering Ltd* [1973] IRLR 233).

[5.51] Ignorance of material facts: Where, as a result of the late discovery of a fact or facts that enable a claim to be made, an application is presented out of time, tribunals have been willing to apply the 'escape clause'. In determining whether or not the late discovery of a fact justifies extending the time limit, a tribunal will apply a three-stage test, conveniently laid out in the case of *Machine Tool Industry Research Association v Simpson* [1988] IRLR 212. Under this test an employee is required to establish that:

- it was reasonable for them not to be aware of the factual basis upon which they could bring an application to the tribunal during the limitation period;
- the knowledge gained has, in the circumstances, been reasonably gained by them, and is either crucial, fundamental or important to their change of belief and realisation that they have reasonable grounds for bringing a claim (it is important to note that there is no requirement for the employee to establish the truth of the new fact(s), only the reasonableness of a belief in it – *Marley (UK) Ltd v Anderson* [1996] ICR 728; and
- the acquisition of knowledge is, in any event, crucial to their decision to bring the claim.

In practice, this justification is often raised in cases involving redundancy dismissals. In *Machine Tool Industry Research Association v Simpson,* for example, an employee who, after being made redundant, became aware that another employee had been re-engaged to carry out a substantially similar job, decided to bring a claim for unfair dismissal. The Court of Appeal accepted that it was only after she discovered that another employee had been re-engaged did she become suspicious as to the 'real' reason for her dismissal, and that since this occurred after the expiry of the three-month time limit, the escape clause ought to be operated in her favour. See also the guidance provided in *Cambridge and Peterborough Foundation NHS Trust v Crouchman* [2009] ICR 1306.

[5.52] As with all applications for an extension of time it remains incumbent on an employee to act with all due speed once they become aware of their right to make a claim. This is neatly illustrated by the decision in *Cook (James W) & Co (Wivenhoe) Ltd (in liquidation) v Tipper* [1990] IRLR 386, a case where eight shipyard workers were made redundant but at the same time given assurances that they would be re-engaged when work picked up. In relying on this assurance, they did not bring a claim for unfair dismissal. When, after the time limit had expired, the shipyard was closed down, the workers realised that there had never been an intention of keeping it open and sought to bring a claim for unfair dismissal. The Court of Appeal accepted that time should be extended, but held that only the employees who had presented a complaint within two weeks of the closure should benefit from the 'escape clause'.

[5.53] **Postal delay**: Historically, where it could be established that the failure to present a complaint in time arose as a result of an unforeseen delay in the postal services, this was normally considered to be an acceptable reason for extending time (*Dedman v British Building and Engineering Appliances Ltd* [1974] ICR 53). Any extension of time was of course subject to the employee and/or their advisor establishing that they had a reasonable expectation that the claim would arrive in time.

It is important to bear in mind that the burden of proof is on the employee. In the past, this burden was relatively light since tribunals were generally willing to accept that a person who posted their application by first class post had a reasonable expectation that it would arrive the next day. Consequently, the mere fact that an employee waited until the penultimate day of the limitation period to post their application was rarely, of itself, considered 'unreasonable'. In more recent decisions, however, tribunals, recognising the increasing unreliability of the postal service, have indicated that less tolerance should be shown to those who wait until the penultimate day before posting their complaints (*St Basil's Centre v McCrossan* [1991] IRLR 455 – 'mere evidence of expectation of delivery of a first class post may not, in the future, provide an adequate explanation'). In *McCrossan* it was suggested that the 1985 *Practice Direction* referred to in that case, relating to the delivery of documents in the High Court, offered useful guidance as to what amounted to a reasonable expectation. Under the provisions of these directions, first class post is deemed to arrive on the second working day after posting, whereas second class post is deemed to arrive on the fourth working day.

[5.54] When considering whether to extend time a tribunal will pay particular attention to the reason for the delay in presenting the application. So, for example in *McCrossan*, a case where an originating application was dictated on a Friday, but was only typed and posted on the following Tuesday (the penultimate day of the limitation period), the EAT gave a clear indication that, in future, this sort of delay might well be considered 'unreasonable'.

The issue was considered in *Consignia plc v Sealy*[2002] IRLR 624 by the Court of Appeal who confirmed that:

- a party who sent his application by first class post at least two working days before the expiry of the relevant time limit would ordinarily be entitled to an extension of time (this is consistent with deeming provision in Civil Procedure Rules, r 6.14 and *McCrossan*);
- where a time limit expires on a weekend/bank holiday *and* the tribunal has no letterbox or other means of receiving communication during weekends/bank holidays an applicant who is prevented from presenting his complaint on the last day can seek to extend time by arguing that it was not reasonably practicable for the complaint to have been presented with the prescribed period.

[5.55] Where, on the other hand, an application has been lost in the post, a tribunal is only likely to extend time where it is satisfied that the employee and/or their advisor have taken all reasonable steps to check that it has been received in time. This test requires an employee to make appropriate enquiries at or near the time when a reply from the tribunal ought reasonably to have been received (*Camden and Islington Community Services NHS Trust v Kennedy* [1996] IRLR 381). The fact that an employee cannot simply rely on the presumption that 'what is posted will be delivered' is highlighted by the case of *Capital Foods Retail Ltd v Corrigan* [1993] IRLR 430. In this case, although it was accepted that the application had been posted five weeks prior to the expiry of the limitation period, the EAT refused to extend time because, in their view, the solicitors had acted 'unreasonably' by not taking any steps to check that application had been received until three months after the limitation period had expired.

[5.56] Time limits applicable to the escape clause: Where a tribunal accepts that it was not reasonably practicable for an employee to have presented their claim in time, it must then consider whether the claim was in fact presented within a reasonable time thereafter. Only where it is satisfied that the employee has acted with all reasonable speed after the impediment that was preventing the presentation of the claim had been removed will a tribunal extend time to the date that the claim was actually presented.

There is no general rule as to what constitutes a 'reasonable time'. In *Marley (UK) Ltd v Anderson* [1996] IRLR 163 the decision by a tribunal to treat a four-week delay as inherently unreasonable, without looking at the surrounding circumstances, was held to be wrong in law. Whether the delay in presenting the claim was reasonable will depend on the particular circumstances of each case.

(2) 'Just and equitable'

[5.57] Under this second 'escape clause', which applies primarily in cases of discrimination (*Equality Act 2010, s 123*) (*SDA 1975, s 76(1), RRA 1976, s 68(1), DDA 1995, Sch 3, para 3(1) and 34(3) ERRB 2003*) tribunals may grant an extension of time if it thinks it is 'just and equitable' to do so. Although this is a far less restrictive test than the 'not reasonably practicable' formula, and gives tribunals a significantly wider discretion to extend time, there is no presumption that a tribunal should extend time – 'the exercise of the discretion remains the exception rather than the rule' (*Robertson v Bexley Community Centre (t/a Leisure Link)* [2003] EWCA Civ 576).

Practical examples where time has been extended, in circumstances where it is unlikely that it would have been extended under the 'not reasonably practicable' test, include where:

- an employee delayed in presenting a claim in reliance on incorrect legal advice (*Hawkins v Ball and Barclays Bank plc* [1996] IRLR 258);
- an employee delayed presenting a complaint pending an internal appeal (*Apelogun-Gabriels v Lambeth London Borough Council* [2001] EWCA Civ 1853 confirmed that this was a relevant factor in deciding to extend time but expressly rejected the suggestion in *Aniagwu v London Borough of Hackney* [1999] IRLR 303 that there is a general principle that an extension should always be granted where a delay is caused by the applicant invoking an internal appeal);
- an employee who discovered evidence which formed the basis of his race discrimination claim nine years after the expiry of the time limit (*Afolabi v Southwark London Borough* [2003] EWCA Civ 15; [2003] IRLR 220);
- a judicial decision clarifies the law so as to give an employee a new right (*Biggs v Somerset County Council* [1996] IRLR 203).

[5.58] These examples are provided merely by way of illustration and should not be construed as indicative of a general rule. Whether or not it is just and equitable to extend time will depend on the particular facts of each case. So, for example, where contrary to union advice an employee delayed presenting a complaint pending an internal appeal, a tribunal has refused to extend time.

It is also worth emphasising that under the just and equitable test, a tribunal is required to consider the prejudice that both parties will suffer as a result of allowing or refusing to extend time. With this in mind, a tribunal will endeavour to ascertain the extent to which each party has contributed to the delay.

[5.59] In deciding whether an employee should benefit from the 'escape clause' a tribunal will pay particular attention to the following:

- the length and reasons for any delay;
- the extent to which the delay may have affected the reliability or availability of the evidence;
- any steps taken by the employee to ascertain the factual position and/or their legal rights (including obtaining suitable legal advice);
- the speed with which the employee acted once they became aware that they were able to make a claim; and
- the extent to which the employer contributed to the delay.

If the employee is at fault, this is a relevant factor for the tribunal to consider in weighing up whether it is just and equitable to allow the claim to proceed (*Virdi v Commissioner of Police of the Metropolis* [2007] IRLR 24).

In *Hutchison v Westward Television Ltd* [1977] IRLR 69, the EAT confirmed that 'circumstances of the case' referred to the facts relevant to the application to extend time and not the merits of the substantive claim.

Claims under EC Law

[5.60] The treatment of EU law in this book is of necessity summary.

In short, however, claims based on either:

- a directly applicable provision of the *Treaty of Rome* (eg *Art 141 – equal pay*); or
- a directly effective European Council Directive (eg *Equal Pay Directive 75/117/EEC*);

are not subject to any specific time limits, whether under EC or UK domestic legislation. The European Court of Justice (ECJ) has ruled on numerous occasions that time limits for the enforcement of EC rights are a procedural matter to be determined by the national legislation of

Member States. This is subject to the proviso that any such time limits are not less favourable than those applicable to similar domestic actions and do not render virtually impossible the exercise of the EC right/law (*Emmott v Minister for Social Welfare*: C-208/90 [1993] ICR 8; *Fisscher v Voorhuis Hengelo BV: C-128/93,* [1995] ICR 635; *Preston v Wolverhampton Healthcare NHS Trust (No 2)* [2001] ICR 217 – where, after a reference to the ECJ, the House of Lords held that the six-month time limit under the *Equal Pay Act 1970* was neither less favourable than nor rendered impossible the exercise of EC rights/law).

[5.61] Tribunals do not have jurisdiction to hear claims from private sector employees based solely on EC law. As the Court of Appeal held in *Biggs v Somerset County Council* [1996] ICR 364 (see also *Barber v Staffordshire County Council* [1996] ICR 379), EC law may only be relied on before a tribunal, so as to displace a provision of domestic legislation which is considered incompatible with a directly effective article or directive. As a result of this decision, it is clear that a private sector employee may only bring proceedings before a tribunal under existing UK legislation. This in turn means that, even where a private sector employee wishes to rely on EC law (ie directly effective directives or under provisions of the Treaty in the Functioning of the European Union which entered into force on 1 December 2009), any proceedings will still be subject to the time limits applicable to the statutory claim (ie the claim under existing UK legislation) that they choose to bring before the tribunal.

[5.62] The position is somewhat different for state employees (eg civil servants) who may bring a claim based on a directly effective directive, even where the directive has not yet been implemented/fully integrated into national legislation. The time limit for bringing these claims starts to run from the date that the directive is fully implemented into national law (*Emmot v Minister for Social Welfare: 208/90* [1991] IRLR 387 – see also *Biggs* where the Court of Appeal held that this principle only applied to directives that required implementation). This means that proceedings may be issued years after the circumstances or events upon which the claim is based took place.

[5.63] The Court of Appeal's decision in *Biggs* has effectively barred retrospective proceedings based on new interpretations of EC law, for claims where the statutory test for extending the time limit is whether 'it was reasonably practicable to have brought the claim in time'. In that case, the applicant, relying on a subsequent House of Lords decision in

R v Secretary of State for Employment, ex p Equal Opportunities Commission [1994] ICR 317, sought to bring a retrospective claim for unfair dismissal 18 years after she was dismissed. She submitted that, as a result of the decision in ex p EOC, it was now clear that the exclusion of part-time workers from the right to claim unfair dismissal was discriminatory, and that she should be entitled to bring a claim for unfair dismissal within three months of the date of that decision. The Court of Appeal rejected her argument that prior to the decision in *ex p EOC*, it had not 'been reasonably practicable' to bring the claim due to the uncertainty that existed as to the state of the law. In its view, it had been open to the applicant to have lodged a claim in 1976 and raised the arguments at that stage. It therefore refused to treat her application as in time.

[5.64] In relation to statutory claims where an extension of time can be granted on 'just and equitable' grounds, however, there would appear to remain far greater scope for bringing retrospective proceedings based on new interpretative decisions of EC law. In the case of *DPP v Marshall* [1998] ICR 518, for example, the EAT allowed a transsexual to bring a claim under the SDA 1975, within three months of the ECJ decision that gender reassignment fell within the ambit of the *Equal Treatment Directive (76/207/EEC)* (*P v S C-13/94* [1996] ICR 795), although this was some three years after the cause of action arose. This generous approach to just and equitable was further confirmed in *Cannon v Barnsley Metropolitan Council* [1992] All ER (D) 194, in which it was confirmed that it was likely to be just and equitable to extend time to a claimant to when the Directive had been implemented into national law.

Do's and Don'ts for claimants

Do:

- Where applicable comply with the ACAS Code of Practice: Disciplinary and Grievance Procedures before presenting a complaint to a tribunal.
- Take reasonable steps to obtain advice as soon as you think that you might have a claim.
- Identify without delay the act complained of and the relevant time limit for bringing a claim.
- Present the claim promptly and in any event before the expiry of the relevant time limit.
- Send documents by recorded delivery and keep the relevant records.

- Keep contemporaneous notes of conversations identifying the date and the names of parties.
- Be proactive and take reasonable steps to confirm that documents have been received by the tribunal.
- Present a claim form (which complies with the requirements set out in **chapter 6**) which contains the prescribed information and outlines the facts that you feel may give rise to a claim, the identity of the respondent etc well before the statutory time limit expires.
- Act promptly if outside the statutory time limit you become aware of facts which support a claim or a further claim – ie present a claim or amended claim as soon as reasonably practicable after becoming aware of these facts.

Don't:

- Wait until the penultimate day of the limitation period for presenting a claim and, if you do, hand deliver the claim and obtain a receipt.
- Delay in confirming receipt of documents, making applications or enquiries.
- Delay in making a claim merely because there is an internal appeal pending or due to ongoing negotiations to settle.
- Underestimate the difficulty of obtaining an extension of time.

Do's for respondents

Do:

- Seek clarification where there is doubt as to when the act complained of occurred.
- Give all parties (including the tribunal) as much written notice as possible of the reasons why you consider the claim to be out of time or any other reason why you consider the tribunal to lack jurisdiction.
- Seek guidance at an early stage from the tribunal as to whether it is appropriate to determine, as a preliminary issue, the question of whether the claim is in time.
- Prepare for a hearing on time limits with the appropriate legal test in mind – 'reasonably practicable' or 'just and equitable'.
- Remember that time limits can be raised at any stage during proceedings, even at a remedies hearing.

Chapter 6

Making a claim: the Claim Form (ET1)

Introduction

[6.1] Since 1 October 2005 employment tribunal proceedings are commenced by presenting a a claim in the prescribed form to an Employment Tribunal Office. This prescribed form is referred to as an 'ET1'.

The Claim Form is available online from www.employmenttribunals.gov.uk, or from any Employment Tribunal Office (see **chapter 9 – communicating with the tribunal**). Forms are usually also available from the majority of advice centres, Citizens Advice Bureaux, job centres and ACAS. An accompanying booklet, entitled 'Making a claim to an Employment Tribunal' (URN 10/516) gives guidance on filling in the form and on other matters including the appropriate Employment Tribunal office to which to present the claim.

A copy of the ET1 appears in **appendix III: application to an employment tribunal**.

One of the most significant and draconian changes introduced by the Employment Tribunals (Constitution and Rules of Procedure) Regulations 2004 ('the 2004 Regulations') was the mandatory requirement for claim forms to contain certain 'required' information. Failure to provide this information will result in the claim form being rejected by the tribunal – claimants should note that tribunals do not have any discretion as to this issue –if the 'required' information is not included in the claim form then it will be rejected and the claim will not be registered. In those circumstances the only option will be to apply to the tribunal for a review of its decision to reject the claim under rule 34 (see **[6.7]** below) or, if the decision reveals an error of law, appeal to the EAT (see **chapter 28 – steps after the decision II: appeal**).

In broad terms the ET1 sets out:

- the essential 'required information' (this is defined below);
- what the claim is for (eg unfair dismissal, sex discrimination etc);
- the essential facts upon which the claim is based;
- the relevant required information stipulated by the Rules; and
- basic information about the claimant's employment, such as pay and length of service.

An effectively drafted ET1 helps create a positive first impression on both the tribunal and the respondent. It is therefore very important for claimants to set out the basis of their claim as clearly and concisely as possible.

Sample details of a claim for unfair dismissal and of sex discrimination can be found in **appendix v – case study**, which should be read in conjunction with the notes below.

Submitting the ET1

[6.2] *Rule 1* of the *2004 Rules* sets out in full the requirements which need to be complied with in order to start a claim.

A claim is commenced by a claimant 'presenting to an Employment Tribunal Office the details of the claim in writing' (*rule 1(1)*). Those details must include all the 'required information' and must be made using the form prescribed by the Secretary of State, ie the ET1.

The claim form can be presented by hand, post, fax, email or online (rule 61(1) and *Tyne and Wear Autistic Society v Smith* [2005] ICR 663). Except where the claim is completed online the claim form should be sent or delivered to the appropriate Employment Tribunal Office. The appropriate office is determined by reference to the postcode for the place where the claimant normally worked or the postcode for the place where the matter complained of occurred. The booklet, entitled 'Making a claim to an Employment Tribunal' (URN 10/516), provides a list of postcodes from which the appropriate office can be located.

The required information is listed in rule 1(4) as:

(a) each claimant's full name;
(b) each claimant's address;
(c) the name of each person against whom the claim is made ('the respondent');
(d) each respondent's address; and
(e) details of the claim.

Completing the ET1

[6.3] The form itself denotes the information which must be provided by law. The details which are mandatory are indicated by the symbol ' * '. It is important to bear in mind that failure to provide the relevant required information may result in the claim being rejected (see **[6.7]**).

The sections of the form are described below.

- **Section 1 – 'Your details'**
  The claimant must provide his first name (*), surname (*) and address (*). Where the Claim Form is to be used by multiple claimants (which is permitted under rule 1(7) if their claims arise out of the same set of facts) their names and addresses should be provided separately. In addition to these mandatory requirements the claimant should provide their date of birth and contact details. Claimants are asked to indicate their preferred method of communication with the tribunal (email or post).
- **Section 2 – 'Respondent's details'**
  The name and address of respondent (*) are mandatory. It is important to include accurate information about the respondent including the full address of the head office of the company in order to avoid delays as this information will be used by the tribunal to send the claim to the respondent. There is space to include details of an additional address to that provided in section 2.2 if the claimant worked at an address different from that already provided. Hence, if the claimant worked for a supermarket it would be appropriate to provide the supermarket's head office address at section 2.2, and with the address of the particular store at section 2.3.
  Details of additional respondents can be included at section 11 (see below).
- **Section 3 – 'Employment details'**
  When employment started, whether it is continuing and if not when it ended. The claimant should also state what job he does or, as appropriate, did. The guidance for completing the form states that this information should be supplied by workers as well as employees, treating the questions as though 'employment' referred to their working relationship with the respondent.

- **Section 4 – 'Earnings and benefits'**
  In this section the claimant should set out the average number of hours worked each week, pay and other benefits. If the claimant has obtained alternative employment details of their new employment should also be provided.
- **Section 5 – 'Your claim'**
  In this section the claimant provides details of the substance of their claim. The claimant must tick one or more of the boxes provided which describe the event or events that have caused him to bring the claim (*). The claimant is asked to indicate whether his is:
  a. claiming to have been unfairly dismissed (including constructive dismissal)
  b. claiming to have been discriminated against on the grounds of:
     - sex (including equal pay)
     - race
     - disability
     - religion or belief
     - sexual orientation
     - age
  c. claiming a redundancy payment
  d. that he is owed:
     - notice pay
     - holiday pay
     - arrears of pay
     - other payments
  e. other complaints

  Section 5.2 (*) is arguably the most important section of the form: it is in this box that the claimant must set out the background and details of the claim. The details of the claim and the date(s) when the event(s) complained about happened should be included in this section. This section needs to be completed in sufficient detail for the tribunal and the respondent to be able to fully understand the complaint, whilst at the same time not referring to matters which are irrelevant to the claim being brought. For further discussion of this section, see **6.5** below.
- **Section 6 – 'What compensation or remedy are you seeking?'**
  The form states that "Completion of this section is optional, but may help if you state what compensation or remedy you

are seeking from your employer as a result of this complaint". Despite this section not being mandatory, it is nevertheless suggested that it should, where possible, be completed since it provides the respondent with a clear indication as to what practical steps need to be taken to prevent the litigation continuing (and might thereby help the parties reach an amicable settlement).

- **Section 7 – 'Other information'**
  The form expressly states that claimants should not send a covering letter with the form. Section 7 provides an opportunity for claimants to add any additional information which the tribunal needs to know about. It may be used to explain why a claim has been presented out of time or to make an application, for example, seeking specific disclosure of certain documents.
- **Section 8 – 'Your representative'**
  If the claimant is represented full details should be given in this section of the representative's name, organisation, address, telephone number, case reference number and preferred means of communication.
  If this section of the form is completed, the tribunal will send any future correspondence about the case to the representative rather than to the claimant. It is therefore important that a claimant only names a representative where that person is assisting with the case on an ongoing basis, rather than simply advising on how to fill in the form.
- **Section 9 – 'Disability'**
  If the claimant considers that he has a disability this box should be ticked. The claimant is asked to state what the disability is and what assistance, if any, he will need as the claim progresses through the system including for any hearings that may need to be held at Tribunal Service premises. The accompanying guidance gives examples such as converting documents to Braille or larger print, providing information on disc and paying for sign language interpreters.
- **Section 10 – 'Multiple cases'**
  The claimant is asked to indicate whether, to his knowledge, "is your claim one of a number of claims against the same employer arising from the same, or similar, circumstances". Ticking this box assists in processing the claim more efficiently.

- **Section 11 – 'Details of additional respondents'**
  In these boxes the claimant can provide details of additional respondents. A claimant may use this section where, for example, he brings a claim for discrimination against his employer and at the same time a claim for harassment against a fellow employee where the harassment and discrimination arise out of the same set of facts.

What the Tribunal does on receipt of a claim form

[6.4] The Claim Form will first come before a tribunal Secretary who under rule 2(1) will decide whether the claim or part of it should be accepted in accordance with rule 3. The Secretary will decide whether:
a. the claim has been presented using the prescribed form;
b. the form contains the relevant information; and
c. the tribunal has jurisdiction to consider the claim.

The Secretary cannot accept the claim unless it includes all the relevant required information and the tribunal has jurisdiction to hear the claim (see **chapter 1 – tribunals today**) (rule 3(1) and (2)). Where a particular form is prescribed and has not been used the Secretary is unable to accept the claim and is required to 'shall not accept the claim and return it to the claimant with an explanation of why the claim has been rejected and provide a prescribed form' (rule 3(1)).

As a failure to comply with the procedural requirements in starting claim will will often result in the tribunal concluding that it lacksing jurisdiction to accept a claim form, it is imperative that all relevant required information is included. Furthermore, because of the inevitable risk of mistakes, these strict procedural requirements provide an additional incentive for issuing the claim early – so in this way if the claim form is returned the claimant still has time to make the corrections and resubmit it to the tribunal.

If the Secretary decides to accept the claim, a copy will be sent to the respondent (rule 2(2)). If only part of the claim is accepted the Secretary will notify the parties that the rejected aspects of the claim will not be dealt with unless they are accepted at a later date.

The date on which the claim is sent to the respondent will be recorded by the Tribunal in writing. There is a presumption that this date will be the date on the tribunal's letter accompanying the claim form. From the respondent's perspective this date is if of great importance, since the 28 days in which he is required to file a response starts from the day after this date.

If the Secretary decides not to accept the claim he will refer his decision to an Employment Judge who will either confirm or reverse the decision.If the Employment judge decides not to accept it then he must inform the claimant of this decision as soon as reasonably practicable and provide details as to how to appeal or review his decision.The Employment Judge's decision to reject to a claim can be reviewed under rule 34. Insofar as the review is unsuccessful the decision can be appealed to the Employment Appeal Tribunal on a point of law.

It is fair to say that this aspect of the Rules has not been popular. Indeed, the EAT has been at pains to emphasise that the Rules are not to be over rigidly construed so as to deny a claimant access to the employment tribunal system (see *Grimmer v KLM Cityhopper Ltd* [2005] IRLR 596 and, more recently, *Hamling v Coxlease School Ltd* [2007] IRLR 8).

In order to avoid injustice the EAT has stressed the need to have regard to the overriding objective when applying these seemingly mandatory aspect of the Rules. So, for example, in *Richardson v U Mole Ltd* [2005] IRLR 668, despite the claimant having failed to use the new mandatory form and having failed to indicate that he was an employee (in circumstances where it was common ground that he was in fact an employee.), the EAT held that the claim form should have been accepted. In the view of the EAT the claimant's completion of the section entitled 'Please give the dates of your employment' sufficed to make clear that he was an employee and, even if this was incorrect, the claim form should have been accepted on review as the errors were immaterial and/or justice and equity required it.

Details of the claim: Section 5

[6.5] This is where the claimant sets out the basic facts which form the essential elements of their claim. This section is all about achieving a balance between giving sufficient, but not excessive, information about the essential elements of the claim. In the view of the authors there are now obvious advantages in including details of the precise remedy sought given the power of the tribunal to enter judgment in default against the respondent if the latter's ET3 is not accepted (see **chapter 7 – the employer's response (ET3)**)

Advantages of well drafted details complaint

[6.6] There are some obvious benefits in filing a well drafted claim form:

- It will be the first impression that the respondent and the tribunal receive of the claim.
- Some details of the complaint are mandatory therefore a failure to provide sufficient this information will result in the claim being rejected by the tribunal.
- Giving sufficient, but not excessive, information about the claim may prevent an application or order that further information be provided (see **chapter 10 – post-claim request for further information)**.
- Failure to mention something fundamental could have serious consequences if the claimant seeks to raise that fact at the full hearing. For example, if at the hearing it is mentioned for the first time that a particular individual has discriminated against the claimant, the tribunal might either postpone the hearing to give the respondent an opportunity to prepare its response, making a costs award against the claimant or might even prevent the claimant from relying on that fact at all. Even if the tribunal allows this complaint to be raised, if there is no good reason for failing to include it in the claim form, the tribunal is likely to be sympathetic to submissions from the respondent questioning the credibility of such a late complaint.

Drafting the details of complaint

[6.7] Many claimants (or their advisors) agonise about how much detail to include in this section. The purpose of the ET1 is to set out the essential elements of the claim. The claimant should be careful not in include excessive or irrelevant information which makes it difficult to identify what the real issues in the case are. Having said this, however, claimants should not, where appropriate, be afraid to attach additional sheets to the claim in order to adequately set out the details of their complaint.

A good rule of thumb is to ask 'what information should be included to enable the tribunal to understand the issues in the case and the respondent to understand the case it has to meet?' Approaching the issue that way helps prevent an application for further information from the respondent.

The case of *Ali v Office for National Statistic* [2005] IRLR 201 highlights the strict approach that is taken in determining the scope of the complaint. In that case the claimant had made a complaint of direct race discrimination and, in light of material which came out during the hearing of his claim, applied to introduce a claim of indirect discrimination. The Court of Appeal held that this was a new cause of action and that the proper approach was for the matter to be remitted to the tribunal for it to consider whether it was just and equitable to allow this claim to be introduced out of time.

The guidance for making a claim provides the following assistance in relation to what to include:

- **Unfair dismissal or constructive dismissal claims:** Why the claimant considers he was unfairly dismissed; whether the claimant disagrees with the reason the respondent gave for dismissing him and, if so, what he considers the reason to have been; a description of the events leading up to dismissal and how the dismissal took place, including dates, times and people involved; if it is claimed that the respondent's actions led to the claimant resigning, details of the circumstances surrounding this.
- **Discrimination claims:** A description of the incidents which the claimant believes amounted to discrimination, the dates of these incidents and the people who were involved; an explanation of the way in which the claimant believes he was discriminated against. If the complaint relates to discrimination during an application for a job, to state what job was being applied for. If the complaint relates to more than one type of discrimination separate details of the act (or acts) of discrimination should be detailed. If the claimant is unable to give the dates of all the incidents complained about, they must at least give the date of the last incident or tell the tribunal if the discrimination is ongoing. The guidance also suggests that claimants may wish to describe how they have been affected by the events complained about. This will assist the tribunal in assessing the remedy.

Do's and Don'ts when drafting the details of complaint

Do:

- Ensure that the relevant required information is contained in the claim form.
- Use the correct Claim Form.
- State the legal basis of the claim (e.g. unfair dismissal, sex discrimination etc).
- Include sufficient facts which demonstrate why you consider that the conduct of the respondent was unlawful.
- Structure those facts around the legal test that the tribunal will apply in deciding whether the respondent has acted unlawfully.

Don't:

- Include detailed explanations as to how the claimant will prove the above.
- Include detailed legal arguments or exaggerate.

In order to achieve this, the claimant or his representative will need to have a good basic knowledge of the area of employment law in which the claim arises. The following example illustrates the above points. It may also be helpful to look at the example of an ET1 (in a specific factual context) in **appendix III: application to an employment tribunal (ET1)**.

Example

1. *Background*: The claimant's claim is for unfair dismissal. The claimant was employed by the respondent as a sales manager from 2000 – 2010. On 1 December 2010, the claimant was sent a letter by the respondent in which he was informed that the latter was contemplating dismissing him on the basis that his position had become redundant and inviting him to attend a meeting to discuss that matter. On 6 December 2010, the claimant attended a meeting with the respondent in which he was informed that, due to a drastic downturn in business, his position had become redundant and that, in accordance with his notice period, his last day of employment would be 6 January 2011. The claimant exercised his right to appeal against

that decision. Despite requesting a hearing he was denied such a hearing. Instead he was informed that his appeal was rejected and that the decision to dismiss him on grounds of redundancy was maintained. His employment therefore terminated on 6 January 2011.

2. *Grounds of complaint*: The claimant alleges that his dismissal was unfair for the following reasons:

2.1. The expressed reason for dismissal, redundancy, was not the real reason. The claimant will contend that the real reason was capability and that his dismissal for that reason was unfair. The claimant will rely upon the fact that the issue of redundancy was raised at the same meeting on 6 December 2010 at which the claimant was informed that he had failed to meet his performance targets etc.

If, which is denied, redundancy was the reason for the claimant's dismissal, the claimant will contend that the respondent acted unreasonably in all the circumstances in treating this as the reason for dismissal. In so asserting, the claimant will rely, inter alia, upon the following:

(a) The requirement of the company for a person to carry out the type of work undertaken by the claimant had not ceased or diminished. After the claimant was dismissed, a Mr X was employed to perform the tasks the claimant had been carrying out during the last two years of his employment. No other employees were made redundant.

(b) The respondent did not carry out a fair procedure because:

(i) The hearing on 6 December 2010 took place without the claimant being given any prior notice of the basis upon which the respondent alleged he was redundant. It was only 20 minutes into the meeting, after a direct question from the claimant, that he was told the reason was a drastic downturn in business. He was given no further details as to the form which the downturn had taken. Neither were such details given after this meeting.

(ii) It failed to consult properly or at all with the claimant over his redundancy (include basic facts in support);

(iii) It failed to adopt a fair selection criteria (include basic facts in support); and

(iv) It failed to make any, or any sufficient, attempts to find alternative work for the claimant within the respondent's organisation (include basic facts in support).

By reason of the above the claimant has suffered loss and claims relief based on the following schedule of loss (see **chapter 24: remedies**).

The above example structures the factual basis of the claimant's claim around the law of unfair dismissal, namely:

- What was the reason for the dismissal?
- Was it a potentially fair reason (i.e. in this example, redundancy)?
- Did the respondent act reasonably in treating it as a reason to dismiss the claimant (including the adoption of a fair procedure)?

In deciding how much to include, the claimant should consider which facts should be included to give the respondent a proper idea of the claim it has to meet. The advantage of this approach is that it requires the factual basis of the claim to be marshalled around the legal issues, making the grounds of complaint instantly more comprehensible to the tribunal.

The consequences of an incomplete ET1

[6.8] The golden rule remains that so long as the ET1 contains the prescribed information, it should be submitted in time, even if it is otherwise incomplete.

The regime of acceptance and rejection of incomplete ET1s is set out in rules 2 and 3 of the 2004 Rules. The principle features of the regime, however, can be summarised as follows:

- An ET1 which is missing any of the required information set out in rule 1(3) above will be rejected and returned by the tribunal.
- If a claim is rejected it is not treated as lodged for the purposes of the relevant time limit.
- A claim will not be rejected unless the Secretary has certified that required information is missing or that the tribunal does not have

jurisdiction to hear the claim and referred the claim, with his reasons for rejecting it, to an Employment Judge who then confirms or reverses the decision.

- An Employment Judge's decision to reject to a claim can be reviewed under rule 34 (see **chapter 27: steps after the decision i: review**). Insofar as the review is unsuccessful the decision can be appealed to the Employment Appeal Tribunal on a point of law.

Where, due to proximity of an expiring time limit, it has not been possible to include all the relevant information, it is suggested that the sensible course to adopt is as follows:

- Indicate on the claim form in the relevant places that the information missing will be supplied as soon as possible (preferably giving a specific date), explaining why it has not been supplied to date.
- When the missing information is obtained, send the fully completed ET1 to the tribunal immediately under cover of an application to amend the ET1. The sooner this is done the better, since it is likely to influence the decision of the Employment Judge on whether to accede to the application.
- If, by the time of being invited to make oral or written submissions, the relevant information still has not been obtained, be ready to give the tribunal an explanation of why it has not been possible to obtain the information and a timescale as to when it is expected to be received.

However, note: these points relate to *relevant* information as opposed to the information which has to be provided as prescribed by rule 1(4) of the 2004 Rules: if the latter has not been provided the form will simply be rejected by the tribunal.

If, for whatever reason, a claimant is unable to insert the prescribed information, the ET1 should nevertheless be sent to the tribunal within the statutory time limit for bringing the claim. It will be open to the claimant to challenge the tribunal's rejection of the claim form by way of a review under rule 34.At the review the claimant will have an opportunity to explain why he was unable to insert the prescribed information before sending the claim form. If he can establish one of the grounds set out in rule 34 (3) the claim will be allowed to proceed. It has to be said, however, that it is hard to conceive of circumstances in which an employee will be unable to insert the prescribed information.

Challenging rejection of the claim form

[6.9] The only options available to a claimant whose ET1 has not been accepted is to seek a review of the decision under *rule 34* or to appeal on a point of law to the EAT (see **chapter 26 – steps after the decision II: appeal**).

A decision not to accept a claim form may be reviewed on two of the five grounds provided for by *rule 34(3)*, these being:

- The decision was wrongly made as a result of an administrative error (sub-paragraph (*a*)); or
- The interests of justice require such a review (sub-paragraph (*e*)).

The application for a review must be made within 14 days of the date when the decision not to accept the claim was sent to the parties, although this may be extended if the Employment Judge considers it just and equitable to do so (*rule 35(1)*). The application must be in writing and must identify the ground(s) upon which the application is made (*rule 35(2)*).

Administrative error

Under the 2001 Rules the comparable ground of review (*rule 13(1)(a)*) expressly referred to a decision which was wrongly made 'as a result of an error on the part of the tribunal staff'. The 2004 Rules widened the ambit of the rule so that this ground of review encompasses not only both tribunal staff and Employment Judges, but also is also capable of including errors by the parties and their legal representatives (*Sodexho Ltd v Gibbons* [2005] ICR 1647).

Interests of justice

The 'interests of justice' ground has been held to be a broad 'residual category' designed to confer a wide discretion on Employment Judges (*Flint v Eastern Electricity* [1975] ICR 395). It must, however, be exercised with due respect for the principle of finality in tribunal proceedings. The extent to which a tribunal will be able to take in to account the merits of the claimant's substantive case (ie the likelihood of successfully defending the claim) is something of a grey area. In the view of the authors, this may be a relevant factor although it is unlikely to be enough, of itself, to result in a favourable exercise of discretion. The tribunal's principle focus area of concern is likely to be on the reason why the claim form was not accepted and the explanation advanced for this.

An illustration of the initial approach taken by the EAT can be found in *Grimmer v KLM Cityhopper Ltd* [2005] IRLR 596). This case involved a claimant, who wished to complain about a refusal to allow her flexible working to enable her to look after her children, but who submitted a claim form which simply alleged that the company refused her request for flexible working on the grounds that, if they acceded to it, others would make similar requests. The Employment Judge refused to accept a claim on the grounds that she had failed to provide adequate 'details of her claim' as required. In overturning the decision the EAT emphasised that the threshold for access to the tribunal should, in the interests of justice, be kept relatively low. In the EAT's view, in determining whether the absence of the required details should prevent access to the tribunal the question was 'whether it can be discerned from the claim as presented that the claimant is complaining of an alleged breach of an employment right which falls within the jurisdiction of the employment tribunal'.

The subsequent decision in *Hamling v Coxlease School Ltd* [2007] IRLR 8 cast doubt over the relaxed approach adopted in *Grimmer.* In *Hamling* solicitors on behalf of a claimant submitted a claim form which omitted her address, while giving the solicitors' full address. Her claim was rejected. On review an Employment Judge held that there was no room for the exercise of judgment: the requirement of the rules was clear and unambiguous. In allowing the appeal, the EAT held that the task of an Employment Judge was:

- Not confined to the mechanistic exercise of checking-off the list of required information in rule 1(4) against the content of the form;
- To ask whether any omission from the claim form was (1) a 'relevant' omission, and (2) a 'material' or overriding omission; and
- Required to have regard to the overriding objective in asking and answering both questions.

The approach in *Hamling*, whilst clearly not representing a return to a prescriptive approach to the requirements of the Rules, does reflect a retreat from the relaxed merits driven approach in *Grimmer.*

Hamling was identified as the preferred approach by the EAT in *Unison & Anor v National Probation Service South Yorkshire & Anor* UKEAT/0339/09/SM. It is noticeable, however, that despite adopting this slightly more restrictive approach, the claimant's appeal was again alllowed. In Unison, whilst the form ET1a was missing (ie the form which has to be submitted by a second Claimant), the ET1 contained details a claim by Unison (the second Claimant). In practice, therefore, the only missing detail was Unison's address. This did not, in the EAT's view, amount to a material omission having regard to the contents of the ET1 which set out in detail the grounds of the claim.

For more guidance on the grounds of review, see **chapter 25 – steps after the decision I: review**.

A party should always ensure that their review application is fully argued and accompanied by the necessary evidence to make out the ground relied upon. Needless to say the arguments and/or evidence should be focussed on addressing the shortcomings identified in the decision rejecting the claim form.

Note there is no necessity for an Employment Judge to list the case for hearing – he can decide it on the papers. If an application is not accompanied by sufficient evidence in support it risks being dismissed. How that evidence is presented will always depend upon the circumstances. It will frequently be sensible to adduce a witness statement exhibiting relevant documentation.

When the application for a review is received by the tribunal the Employment Judge will consider whether there is a ground for review which has a reasonable prospect of success (*rule 35(3)*). If he decides that question in the affirmative, he will go on to consider whether to confirm, vary or revoke the original decision (*rule 36(3)*).

If the review is successful the claimant will be allowed back in to the proceedings. If the claimant is unsuccessful he may appeal to the Employment Appeal Tribunal (EAT) on a point of law.

Amending the claim form

[6.10] Any alteration or addition (such as submitting more detailed grounds of complaint) to the ET1 must be done through an application to amend. The majority of such applications are dealt with by an Employment Judge alone reviewing the papers. .

The application to amend should include:
(a) the proposed amendment/addition (in precise form); and
(b) briefly, the reason why the information was not included in the original application.

The application should be made in accordance with the provisions of rule 11.

So long as there is a good reason for the initial failure to include the information tribunals are often willing to allow amendments to claim forms where the application is made early on in the proceedings. In considering an application it will apply the overriding objective (see **chapter 8 – fairness: the overriding objective**). This means that in the tribunal will usually balance the likely hardship caused to the claimant by a refusal of the amendment against the likely hardship caused to the respondent by permitting it. The main barrier to success therefore is prejudice to the respondent. This means that the earlier the claimant makes the application the better as the respondent will be less able to argue that they have been prejudiced in the preparation of their case. The extent of and reasons for the original failure to include the amendment in the original claim and delay in seeking to amend is also likely be relevant – especially if the respondent has contributed to the delay.

If the proposed amendment would have the effect of bringing a claim outside the statutory time limits the tribunal will consider whether time should be extended to allow the late introduction of the claim (see **chapter 5: time limits**). For obvious reasons such an application is unlikely to succeed in the absence of a good reason for the delay in making the claim. Whether this arises depends substantially on whether the application is simply 'a change of label' (seeking to rely on the same facts but to rely on them in support of a different legal claim, e.g. sex discrimination as well as unfair dismissal) or is in reality an entirely new claim based on new grounds. As *Ali v Office for National Statistic* [2005] IRLR 201 makes clear, the former is more likely to be allowed than the latter (which requires an assessment of whether it was reasonably practicable and/or just and equitable for time to be extended).

When amending the details of complaint (section 5.2 of the claim form), it is common practice amongst professional representatives to make the amendments on the original written details, which are then headed 'Amended Details of Complaint'. The practice is to underline additional words and strike through words that are being deleted so that they are still legible. The advantage of doing this is that the tribunal need only look at one document to get a complete view of the application, as opposed to looking at the initial grounds and then at the amended grounds, which can be confusing.

Do's and Don'ts

Do:

- Remember that a failure to provide the required information will result in the automatic rejection of the ET1.
- Submit the ET1 in time and then apply to amend later if necessary.
- Try and make applications for amendments as soon as possible to avoid arguments of prejudice by the respondent or alternatively warn the respondent that you will be making an application to amend when further information becomes available.

Don't:

- Confuse the details of complaint with a detailed witness statement – give sufficient information for the respondent to know the case it has to meet and to enable the tribunal to identify the issues in the case.
- Forget that effective grounds of complaint can defeat an application for further information.

Pre-action checklist

[6.11]

For the claimant

Have you:

- Identified the type of complaint you wish to make?
- Taken the required steps under the current Disciplinary and Grievance Procedures set out in the ACAS Code of Practice? Remember the Code should be complied with where possible, but not to the extent that this jeopardises complying with the necessary time limits.
- Engaged in any appropriate pre-action communication, such as serving a question form (in discrimination cases) or a letter before claim aimed at resolving the dispute (see **chapter 3**)?
- Identified the correct name of the respondent (it is useful to clarify this is pre-claim correspondence)?
- Confirmed that the claim is one which the tribunal has jurisdiction to hear?
- Had regard to time limits?
- Considered taking advice (see **chapter 2**)?

For the respondent

Have you:

- Appraised the strength of your case, including a review of any relevant documentation, such as internal memos, correspondence and notes of meetings and hearings?
- Engaged in pre-claim correspondence with a view to forming a valid compromise agreement (see **chapter 16 – settlement of claims**)?
- Complied with the current Disciplinary and Grievance Procedures set out in the ACAS Code of Practice and considered whether the potential claim is in time (see **appendix I**) or whether there is any other possible challenge on grounds of jurisdiction?
- Considered whether it is necessary to seek specialist advice/ secure representation for a hearing? (see **chapter 2**)

Stages leading to full hearing checklist

[6.12]

- What information should be included in the claim form and employer's response? (see **chapter 6 – making a claim** and **chapter 7 – the employer's response**)
- Have the issues been properly defined, or is there a need for a request for further information? (see **chapter 10 – post claim requests for further information**)
- Is there are any basis for requesting a pre-hearing review? (see **chapter 13 – pre-emptive strikes**)
- Is there documentation which should be requested from the other side (see **chapter 11 – disclosure**) or from a third party? (see **chapter 14 – witness orders and orders for the production of documents**)
- If the chairman has not already directed that one take place, should you request a case management discussion in order to make any applications, or is it better to make the applications separately in writing? (see **chapter 13 – pre-emptive strikes** and **chapter 6 – making a claim**)

- What witnesses do you need – is a witness order likely to be necessary? (see **chapter 14 – witness orders & orders for the production of documents**)
- Is your case prepared for full hearing? (see **chapter 17 – preparing for the full hearing**)
- Has settlement of the claim been explored? (see **chapter 16 – fixed conciliation periods & settlements of claims**)

Chapter 7

The Response (ET3)

Introduction

[7.1] When a claim to an employment tribunal is made the tribunal Secretary will send the respondent (in most cases the claimant's employer) a copy of the claimant's completed claim form (or 'ET1') together with a response form (known as an 'ET3') for the respondent or its representative to complete. The respondent must use the ET3 response form as any other method of responding will be rejected; thereby denying the respondent any further right to participate in the subsequent proceedings.

A copy of the ET3 appears in **appendix iv**.

[7.2] As with the ET1, a booklet is published (URN 10/792) entitled 'Responding to a claim to an employment tribunal' which includes guidance on completing the response form. Again, as with the ET1, the ET3 must contain certain specified 'relevant required information'. A failure to include this prescribed information automatically results in the response being rejected.

[7.3] From the employer's perspective, the ET3 is the first opportunity to tell both the tribunal and the claimant its version of events. An effectively drafted ET3, which shows an understanding of the legal principles upon which the tribunal will decide the case, is important for the following reasons:

- to win a case an employer often needs to show that, at the time of the relevant events, it acted with an awareness of essential employment law principles. If a poor understanding of such principles is exhibited in the ET3 the claimant will be given a head start; and

- a carelessly completed ET3 may create the damaging impression that the employer has not taken the dispute seriously.

Whilst this may be unfair, tribunals tend to expect higher standards of drafting from employers than employees.

Time limits

[7.4] If the tribunal accepts the claim form the Secretary will, amongst other things (*rule 2(2)*):

(a) Send a copy of the claim to each respondent and record in writing the date on which it was sent;

(b) Inform the parties in writing of the case number of the claim (which must from then on be referred to in all correspondence relating to the claim) and the address to which notices and other communications to the Employment Tribunal Office must be sent;

(c) Inform the respondent in writing about how to present a response to the claim, the time limit for doing so, what may happen if a response is not entered within the time limit and that the respondent has a right to receive a copy of any judgment disposing of the claim;

(d) When any enactment relevant to the claim provides for conciliation, notify the parties that the services of a conciliation officer may be available to them; and

(e) If only part of the claim has been accepted, inform the claimant and any respondent which parts of the claim have not been accepted and that the tribunal shall not proceed to deal with those parts unless they are accepted at a later date.

[7.5] As with the strict time limits for commencing a claim, the respondent is similarly obliged to respond in a timely fashion. The respondent has 28 days from the date on which the tribunal sends a copy of the claim form in which to respond (*rule 4(1)*). That the time limits are strict is confirmed by the approach in *Moroak (t/a Blake Envelopes) v Cromie* [2005] IRLR 535 in which the tribunal at first instance rejected a response that was 44 minutes late. Although this decision was reversed on appeal, because it was just and equitable to do so (see below), it illustrates the importance of presenting the response within the prescribed time limits.

[7.6] It is important to note that the 28-day time limit is from the date on which a copy of the ET1 is sent to the respondent, not from the date on which it is received by the respondent (*Bone v Fabcon Projects Ltd* [2006] ICR 1421). If the respondent fails to respond within the time limit or at all an Employment Judge may issue a default judgment (*rule 8*) or the Secretary may refuse to accept the response (*rule 6(2)*).

[7.7] The date on which the tribunal sends the claim form will be recorded and the tribunal should notify the respondent of the date on which the response is due. In calculating this time limit the date on which the respondent is sent a copy of the claim form is *not* included in the calculation. If, therefore, the copy of the ET1 is sent on 1 October the last day for presentation of the ET3 is 29 October (see *reg 15* of the *2004 Regulations*). If there is a significant delay (for example because of a postal strike) between the sending of the ET1 by the tribunal and its receipt by the respondent, so that there is insufficient time to respond, this may well amount to good grounds on which to seek an extension of time (see below). In this situation the application should be made as soon as possible explaining the delay and a record should be kept of when the ET1 was in fact received.

Extending the time limit

[7.8] Where the 28 day period has not yet elapsed the respondent may apply for an extension of time in which it is present its response (*rule 4(4)*). The application must explain why the respondent cannot comply with the time limit. If an application to extend time is made and the respondent is legally represented in relation to the application, the respondent or its representative must at the same time as the application is sent to the tribunal provide all other parties with the following information in writing:

(a) Details of the application and the reasons why it is made;
(b) Notification that any objection to the application must be sent to the Employment Tribunal Office within seven days of receiving the application or, if a hearing of any type is due to take place before the expiry of that seven-day period, before the date of that hearing; and
(c) That any objection to the application must be copied to both the Employment Tribunal Office and all other parties.

The respondent or its representative must also confirm in writing to the tribunal that these requirements have been complied with (rule 4(4A)). If the respondent is not legally represented the tribunal will undertake requirements (b) and (c).

[7.9] An Employment Judge shall only extend the time within which a response may be presented if he is satisfied that it is 'just and equitable to do so' (rule 4(4)). In *Kwik Stores Ltd v Swain* [1997] ICR 49 the EAT stated that in exercising this discretion Employment Judges must take account of all relevant factors, including the explanation or lack of explanation for the delay and the merits of the defence, and must reach a conclusion which is objectively justified on the grounds of reason and justice, taking into account the possible prejudice to each party (see also *Pendragon plc (t/a CD Bramall Bradford) v Copus* [2005] ICR 1671). All relevant documents and material must be put before the tribunal to explain both the non-compliance and the basis on which it is sought to defend the case.

[7.10] In making an application under *rule 4(4)* the respondent should ensure that sufficient explanation is given for the reasons for any past delay or anticipated delay. The respondent should explain:

- Whether there was any material delay in the respondent receiving notification of the claim (for example, was there a postal strike which may have delayed receipt of the claim?)
- The speed with which the respondent has acted upon receipt of the claim
- The length and reasons for the proposed delay (ie where there was a delay in receipt of the copy of the claim form)
- Whether the difficulties in complying with the statutory time limit is in any way attributable to the claimant's actions (for example, did the claimant notify the respondent before commencing the claim?)
- The nature of the application made by the claimant which makes responding within 28 days impractical or impossible (for example, are there multiple allegations of discrimination involving numerous alleged discriminators over a long period of time?)
- The respective prejudice to the parties caused by granting or refusing an extension of time

[7.11] The quality and completeness of the application will be important. Broad explanations such as 'difficulties in obtaining legal advice' or 'pressure upon resources' are unlikely to be sufficient to satisfy the tribunal. Full details of the reasons for the delay should be given including, where appropriate, a chronology which demonstrates that the respondent has taken all appropriate steps promptly.

[7.12] An application for an extension of time made within the original time period is, in the view of the authors, likely to be viewed more favourably by the tribunal than one which accompanies an application to review a default judgment or decision not to accept a claim.

Submitting the ET3

[7.13] *Rule 4(1)* provides:

> 'If the respondent wishes to respond to the claim made against him he must present his response to the Employment Tribunal Office within 28 days of the date on which he was sent a copy of the claim. The response must include all the relevant required information. The time limit for the respondent to present his response may be extended in accordance with paragraph (4).'

The 'relevant required information' is listed in *rule 4(3)* as:
(a) the respondent's full name;
(b) the respondent's address;
(c) whether or not the respondent wishes to resist the claim in whole or in part; and
(d) if the respondent wishes to so resist, on what grounds.

[7.14] Since 1 October 2005 it has been mandatory to use the ET3 response form. If a response is required to be presented using an ET3, but the prescribed form has not been used, the Secretary will not accept the response and will return it to the respondent with an explanation of why the response has been rejected and provide a prescribed response form (rule 6(1)).

[7.15] For an ET3 to be presented it must be received by the tribunal – the mere fact of sending it is not enough. It is sensible, therefore, to send it by recorded delivery or keep a fax transmission record or to check, before the end of the 28 days, that the response has been received

Completing the ET3

[7.16] The form itself denotes the information which must be provided by law. The details which are mandatory are indicated by the symbol ' * '. It is important to bear in mind that failure to provide the relevant required information may result in the response being rejected (see **7.18**).

- **Section 1 – 'Claimant's name'**
  This section is to be used to provide the Claimant's name.
- **Section 2 – 'Respondent's details'**
  The name and address of respondent (*) are mandatory. The respondent's full name should be provided and an indication of its legal status, ie whether the respondent is a sole trader, a partnership, a limited liability company, a plc, a limited company etc. There is space to provide a contact name – it is advisable to include such a point of contact, particularly where the respondent has not appointed a representative.
  The respondent's address (*) must be included. It is advisable to include additional contact details.
  The respondent is also asked to provide details as to the type of business in which it is engaged and the size of the organisation.
- **Section 3 – 'Employment details'**
  If the claimant is, or was, a worker providing services to the respondent, the guidance to completing the form states the answers to the questions in this section should be answered as if "employment" referred to the claimant's working relationship with the respondent. The respondent is asked to confirm whether the dates of employment given by the claimant are correct: if not, what were the dates and why is there disagreement; whether the employment is continuing; whether the claimant's description of his job title is correct and if not, what it should be.
- **Section 4 – 'Earnings and benefits'**
  Whether the claimant's details about pay, hours of work and notice are correct and, if not, what they should be and why notice was not worked or paid. The respondent should also comment upon any pension or additional benefits, such as a company car, medical insurance etc, which the claimant has provided details of.
- **Section 5 – 'Response'**
  Whether the respondent resists the claim (*) and, if so, the full grounds on which it is resisted. If only part of the claim is resisted, the 'Yes' box should be ticked and explained in section 5.2. The guidance on completing the response form states:

  > 'If you have ticked 'Yes', please explain the grounds on which you are resisting the claim. If the claim is about more than one issue, you will need to respond to each issue. Clearly explain what points you disagree with and give information to support your argument. If the respondent dismissed the claimant, explain the procedure you followed before the

actual dismissal and give full reasons why you dismissed the claimant. If the claim is about discrimination, please provide a response to each of the statements made by the claimant and describe the action you took when the claimant raised the matter with you. Give full reasons if you disagree that your organisation owes the claimant money or if you disagree with the amount claimed. At this stage you should not send any documents to support your response. However, you may have to produce them if the claim goes to a hearing. If there is not enough space, please continue on a separate sheet and attach it to this form.'

- **Section 6 – 'Other information'**

  As with the ET1, the guidance to completing the form states that no covering letter should be sent with the form, but that this section should be used to give any extra information which needs to be drawn to the tribunal's attention, for example any special needs because of a disability. The box could also be used to raise matters such as unavoidable dates when key witnesses will not be available or requirements for technological facilities at the hearing (such as video equipment). It could also be used to draw attention to preliminary issues which may require determination, such as whether the claimant's claim is out of time or whether there needs to be a preliminary hearing to determine whether the claimant is disabled in a disability discrimination case.
- **Section 7 – 'Your representative'**

  This section should be completed where the respondent has appointed a representative and provides for details of the representative's name, organisation, address, telephone number, reference and preferred means of communication. As with the ET1, this box should only be used if the representative has been appointed to act in an ongoing capacity in the proceedings, and not where they have simply given advice on completing the form.

  Sample grounds of resistance can be found in appendix v – case study.

What the tribunal does on receipt of a response

[7.17] On receiving a response the Secretary will consider whether the response should be accepted in accordance with *rule 6* of the *2004 Rules*. If the response is not accepted it will be returned to the respondent and the claim will be treated as if no had been presented (*rule 5(1)*). If the Secretary accepts the response he will send a copy of it to all other parties and make a written record of the date on which he does it (*rule 5(2)*). The case will then be dealt with by the tribunal under its case management powers (see **chapter 9**).

Circumstances in which a response will be rejected

[7.18] *Rule 6* of the *2004 Rules* provides:

> **When the response will not be accepted by the Secretary**
>
> 6.
>
> (1) Where a response is required to be presented using a prescribed form by rule 4(2), but the prescribed form has not been used, the Secretary will not accept the response and will return it to the respondent with an explanation of why it has been rejected and with a copy of the prescribed response form.
>
> (2) The Secretary will also not accept the response if it is clear to him that any of the following circumstances apply--
>
> (a) the response does not include all the required information (defined in rule 4(3));
>
> (b) the response has not been presented within the relevant time limit.
>
> (3) If the Secretary decides not to accept a response for either of the reasons in paragraph (2), he is required to refer the response together with a statement of his reasons for not accepting the response to an Employment Judge. The Employment Judge is then required to determine, in accordance with the criteria in paragraph (2), whether the response should be accepted.
>
> (4) If the Employment Judge decides that the response should be accepted he will inform the Secretary in writing accordingly and the Secretary will accept the response and then deal with it in accordance with rule 5(2).
>
> (5) If the Employment Judge decides that the response should not be accepted he is required to record his decision together with the reasons for it in writing in a document signed by him. The Secretary is then required to inform

> both the claimant and the respondent of that decision and the reasons for it. The Secretary is also required to inform the respondent of the consequences for the respondent of that decision and how it may be reviewed or appealed.
>
> (6) Any decision by an Employment Judge not to accept a response can be reviewed in accordance with rules 34 to 36. If the result of such a review is that the response is to be accepted, then the Secretary will accept the response and proceed to deal with the response as described in rule 5(2).

[7.19] Note:

- The Secretary must refer the response to the Employment Judge with a view to its rejection if (a) a time limit has not been complied with or (b) the required information has not been provided.
- Upon referral by the Secretary, the Employment Judge, if satisfied that the response does not contain the required information or was received late by the tribunal, *will* reject the response.
- As with decisions to reject a claim form, the Employment Judge's decision to reject a response is subject to review (see **chapter 25: steps after the decision i: review**) or to an appeal on a point of law (see **chapter 26: steps after the decision ii: appeal**)).
- Where the extent of the default is simply a failure to use the prescribed form, this will result in immediate non-acceptance by the Secretary who will provide the employer with a prescribed form. However, if the response has been presented very late in the 28-day period, this may result in the correctly presented response being out of time and therefore being rejected. It is therefore important to ensure that the correct form is used or that, if it is not used for any reason, the response is sent in good time and an application for an extension is made at the same time.

Challenging non-acceptance

[7.20] The only option available to a respondent whose ET3 has been rejected is to seek a review on restricted grounds of the decision not to accept the response under *rule 34* or to appeal on a point of law to the EAT (see *Butlins Skyline Ltd v Beynon* [2007] ICR 121). An application for a review will prevent a default judgment being issued (see **7.7**).

[7.21] The application for a review must be made within 14 days of the date when the decision of non-acceptance was sent to the parties, although this may be extended if the Employment Judge considers it just and equitable to do so (*rule 35(1)*). The grounds of review are limited to:

(a) the decision was wrongly made as a result of an administrative error; or
(b) the interests of justice require such a review (*rule 34(3)*).

The application, which must be in writing, must identify one or both of these grounds as being the basis of the review (*rule 35(2)*). Bearing in mind the mandatory nature of the powers the circumstances in which a point of law will arise so as to justify an appeal rather than a review are likely to be very limited.

[7.22] The administrative error ground is self-explanatory – it refers to an administrative error by the tribunal (whether a member of the tribunal's staff or the Employment Judge) as opposed to the party. In addition to an error it has to be shown that the error caused the wrong decision, ie the decision to reject the response.

[7.23] The 'interests of justice' ground has been held to be a broad 'residual category' designed to confer a wide discretion on Employment Judges (*Flint v Eastern Electricity* [1975] ICR 395). It must, however, be exercised with due respect for the principle of finality in tribunal proceedings. The extent to which a tribunal will be able to take into account the merits of the respondent's substantive case (ie the likelihood of successfully defending the claim) is something of a grey area. In the view of the authors, this may be a relevant factor although it is unlikely to be enough, of itself, to result in a favourable exercise of discretion. The principal focus of the tribunal is likely to be on the reason why the response was not accepted and any accompanying explanation by the respondent.

Whilst the case *Hamling v Coxlease School Ltd* [2007] IRLR 8 concerned a claimant, as opposed to a respondent, the underlying principles identified by the EAT in concluding that the threshold for access to the tribunal should, in the interests of the overriding objective, be kept relatively low, would broadly speaking seem to apply equally to respondents. In *Hamling* the EAT stressed that Employment Judges should approach their task as a mechanistic exercise of checking-off the list of required information, but instead should have regard to the overriding objective and consider whether any 'relevant' omissions were 'material' and sufficient to justify preventing access to the tribunal.

Consequently, whilst it is acknowledged that tribunals tend to expect respondents to be better equipped to comply with procedural requirements, and are thus at times less willing to excuse procedural failures by respondents, case law does nevertheless suggest that the correct approach is one which accords with the overriding objective and which, where errors are purely technical, allows access to the employment tribunal system.

For more guidance on the meaning of 'interests of justice', see **chapter 25**, which deals with review in general, including review of decisions of non-acceptance.

[7.24] A party should always ensure that their review application is fully argued and accompanied by the necessary evidence to make out the ground relied upon. The arguments and/or evidence should be focussed on addressing the shortcomings identified in the decision rejecting the response. There is no necessity for an Employment Judge to list the case for hearing – he can decide it on the papers. Hence, if an application is not accompanied by sufficient evidence in support it risks being refused. How that evidence is presented will always depend upon the circumstances. It will frequently be sensible to adduce a witness statement exhibiting relevant documentation.

[7.25] When the application for a review is received by the tribunal, the Employment Judge will consider whether there is a ground for review which has a reasonable prospect of success (*rule 35(3)*). If he decides that question in the affirmative, he will go on to consider whether to revoke the original decision. He may take this decision without a hearing. The review decision will be taken by the Employment Judge who made the original decision unless it is not practicable (*rule 35(3)*). If the review is successful, the employer will be allowed back in to the proceedings. If it is unsuccessful a respondent may appeal to the Employment Appeal Tribunal (EAT) on a point of law.

Consequences of a response not being presented or accepted

[7.26] There are two principal consequences for an employer if the response is not accepted; both of which are significant. Firstly, the respondent is no longer a party to the proceedings and can take no further part in the proceedings, save for limited procedural steps (*rule 9*). Secondly, judgment in default can be entered in favour of the claimant (*rule 8*). These two consequences will now be considered in turn.

Taking no further part in the proceedings

[7.27] A respondent who has not presented a response or whose response has not been accepted by the tribunal is, pursuant to *rule 9*, not entitled to take part any further part in the proceedings except to:

(a) make a request for written reasons (*rule 30*);
(b) make an application for a review of a default judgment under *rule 33*;
(c) make an application for a preliminary consideration of an application for review under *rule 34*;
(d) be called as a witness by another person; or
(e) be sent a copy of a document or corrected entry in accordance with *rule 8(4), 29(2)* or *37*.

As *Rule 9* therefore makes very clear the respondent is prevented from taking any part in the proceedings except to the very limited extent provided for in paragraphs (a) – (e) above. In practical terms this means that the respondent will be unable to counter the claimant's version of events at any subsequent hearing (unless called as a witness by another party). For obvious reasons this is likely to result in defeat for the respondent unless the claimant's case or evidence, even taken at its highest, is insufficient to make out the claim.

Default judgment

[7.28] *Rule 8* of the *2004 Rules* provides:

Default judgments

8.

(1) Subject to paragraphs (2A) and (6), in any proceedings if the relevant time limit for presenting a response has passed, an Employment Judge shall, in the circumstances listed in

paragraph (2), issue a default judgment to determine the claim without a hearing.

(1A) If the Employment Judge is not satisfied that he has sufficient information to issue a default judgment, he shall make an order (as described in rule 10(2)(b)) requiring such additional information as he considers appropriate to enable him, subject to paragraphs (2A) and (6), to issue a default judgment.

(1B) Where an order is made as described in paragraph (1A), and the additional information requested has not been received within the specified time limit, a default judgment shall be issued in accordance with paragraph (1).

(2) Subject to paragraphs (2A) and (6), those circumstances are when either--

(a) no response in those proceedings has been presented to the Employment Tribunal Office within the relevant time limit;

(b) a response has been so presented, but a decision has been made not to accept the response either by the Secretary under rule 6(1) or by an Employment Judge under rule 6(3), and the Employment Tribunal Office has not received an application under rule 34 to have that decision reviewed; or

(c) a response has been accepted in those proceedings, but the respondent has stated in the response that he does not intend to resist the claim.

(2A) No default judgment need be issued where the Employment Judge--

(a) is not satisfied that the tribunal has jurisdiction to consider the claim, or part of it; or

(b) has sufficient evidence to conclude that the claim form has not been received by the respondent.

(3) A default judgment may determine liability only or it may determine liability and remedy. If a default judgment determines remedy it shall be such remedy as it appears to the Employment Judge that the claimant is entitled to on the basis of the information before him.

(4) Any default judgment issued by an Employment Judge under this rule shall be recorded in writing and shall be signed by him. The Secretary shall send a copy of that judgment to the

> parties, to ACAS, and, if the proceedings were referred to the tribunal by a court, to that court. The Secretary shall also inform the parties of their right to apply to have the default judgment reviewed under rule 33. The Secretary shall put a copy of the default judgment on the Register (subject to rule 49 (sexual offences and the Register)).
>
> (5) The claimant or respondent may apply to have the default judgment reviewed in accordance with rule 33.
>
> (6) A default judgment shall not be issued where the parties have settled the proceedings (either by means of a compromise agreement or through ACAS). If a default judgment is issued in these circum-stances it shall have no effect.
>
> (7) When paragraph (6) applies, either party may apply under rule 33 to have the default judgment revoked.

Prior to an amendment to the rules in 2008, the Employment Judge had a purely discretionary power in relation to whether enter default judgment, ie to do what he considered to be 'appropriate'. Whilst this general discretion remains in relation to certain criteria, for proceedings which commenced on or after 6 April 2009, Employment Judges are now required to enter a default judgment where :

(a) no response has been presented at all;
(b) the Secretary has rejected the response because the respondent did not use the prescribed form and no application to review the decision has been received; or
(c) a response was presented and accepted but the respondent has stated in the response that it does not intend to resist the claim.

[7.29] The judgment in default can relate to either liability only (ie the employee was unfairly dismissed/unlawfully discriminated against) or to both liability and remedies (ie to include the relief the employee is entitled to as a result of the act of unfair dismissal/unlawful discrimination, etc). If it includes remedy, the relief will be for such remedy as the claimant appears entitled to on the basis of the information before the Employment Judge. As a default judgment appears to be a paper-only exercise, the extent to which a remedy judgment is possible would seem to depend entirely on the amount of information included by the claimant in the claim form. It should, however, be borne in mind that if a remedy hearing was arranged in order to give the claimant the opportunity to set out his case on remedy, the respondent would not be permitted to play any part in such a hearing because of *rule 9*, and would therefore not be able to challenge the claimant's evidence.

[7.30] The Employment Judge retains a discretion not to enter default judgment where there is sufficient evidence to conclude that the claim form has not been received by the respondent or is not satisfied that the tribunal has jurisdiction to consider the claim, or part of it. Hence, a claimant should not be able to achieve a result which he would otherwise have been prevented from pursuing merely through the respondent's default.

Challenging a default judgment: the review procedure (rule 33)

[7.31] *Rule 33* of the *2004 Rules* provides:

> **Review of default judgments**
>
> 33.
>
> (1) A party may apply to have a default judgment against or in favour of him reviewed. An application must be made in writing and presented to the Employment Tribunal Office within 14 days of the date on which the default judgment was sent to the parties. The 14 day time limit may be extended by an Employment Judge if he considers that it is just and equitable to do so.
>
> (2) The application must state the reasons why the default judgment should be varied or revoked. When it is the respondent applying to have the default judgment reviewed, the application must include with it the respondent's proposed response to the claim (where that has not been received by the Employment Tribunal Office), an application for an extension of the time limit for presenting the response and an explanation of why rules 4(1) and (4) were not complied with.

(2A) An application under paragraph (1) may be given preliminary consideration (without the need to hold a hearing) by an Employment Judge, who may refuse the application if the requirements of paragraph (2) have not been met.

(3) A review of a default judgment shall be conducted by an Employment Judge in public unless all the parties to the proceedings consent in writing to the review without a hearing. Notice of the hearing and a copy of the application shall be sent by the Secretary to all other parties.

(4) The Employment Judge may--
   (a) refuse the application for a review;
   (b) vary the default judgment;
   (c) revoke all or part of the default judgment;
   (d) confirm the default judgment;

   and all parties to the proceedings shall be informed by the Secretary in writing of the Employment Judge's judgment on the application.

(5) A default judgment must be revoked if the whole of the claim was satisfied before the judgment was issued or if rule 8(6) applies. An Employment Judge may revoke or vary all or part of a default judgment if the respondent has a reasonable prospect of successfully responding to the claim or part of it.

(6) In considering the application for a review of a default judgment the Employment Judge must have regard to whether there was good reason for the response not having been presented within the applicable time limit.

(7) If the Employment Judge decides that the default judgment should be varied or revoked and that the respondent should be allowed to respond to the claim the Secretary shall accept the response and proceed in accordance with rule 5(2).

(8) An Employment Judge may on his own initiative review a default judgment on the grounds listed at rule 34(3)(a), (b) and (e).

In order to apply for a review it is necessary to write to the tribunal within 14 days of the judgment being sent to the parties. There is provision for this period to be extended where it is just and equitable to do so, but any application for this should be made very promptly and with compelling reasons as any delay places yet another obstacle in the way of a respondent seeking to have the judgment revoked. In applying to the tribunal a party should include the following:

- A proposed response to the claim which contains sufficient detail to demonstrate that the respondent has a reasonable prospect of successfully defending the claim.
- An application to extend time. The provision for review of default judgment provides a mechanism for a retrospective application to extend time (see *rule 4(4)* which provides that normally such an application must be made within 28 days of the ET1 being sent to the respondent). It seems likely that a 'just and equitable' test will be applied to consideration of whether to grant such an extension.
- An explanation for why *rules 4(1)* and *4(4)* (presentation of a response containing the required information within 28 days or application for an extension within that time) were not complied with, including showing whether there was good reason for the response not being presented within the time limit.

[7.32] Even where the respondent has a reasonable prospect of successfully defending the claim, this will not necessarily lead to judgment being revoked. The outcome is likely to turn on the respondent's explanation for failure to present the response, or an application to extend time, within the time limits: in other words, are there sufficiently compelling extenuating circumstances to justify the respondent's delay in responding to the claim or applying to extend time. The tribunal has a broad discretion whether or not to set aside a default judgment and is entitled to take into account all matters relevant to that discretion including the prospects of success (*Pendragon plc (t/a CD Bramall Bradford) v Copus* [2005] ICR 1671).

[7.33] Although either party may apply to review the default judgment, in reality it is difficult to foresee circumstances in which the claimant would wish to do so, having the benefit of a judgment against the respondent. However, it is possible that if a settlement included terms more favourable to the claimant (eg a positive reference or an agreement to reinstate) than would be likely to be ordered by the tribunal by way of a judgment, then there might conceivably be an advantage to the claimant in having the default judgment revoked to allow the settlement to take place.

Drafting the grounds of resistance

[7.34] Remember to address the issues which the tribunal will have to decide, not simply to answer the specific allegations in the ET1, which may be minimal in nature. If, for example, the grounds of complaint simply state: 'I was unfairly dismissed because my manager continuously picked on me', the tribunal will ask:

- was there a dismissal?
- what was the reason for the dismissal?
- was it a potentially lawful reason?
- did the respondent act reasonably in all the circumstances in treating it as a reason to dismiss the claimant (including any procedures that were or should have been applied)?

The grounds of resistance need to address all of those issues. Drafting effective grounds involves, therefore, a two-step process.

Step one: Identify the basic legal issues that the tribunal will have to decide. Examples of typical issues in unfair dismissals can be found in the paragraph above. In cases of discrimination, the issues will often be:

(a) was the claimant subjected to less favourable treatment?
(b) if so, was this on account of their sex, race, disability etc?
(c) if there was less favourable treatment on grounds of sex, race, disability etc, did the respondent take all reasonable steps to prevent such treatment taking place?

Step two: Structure the facts which (if found to be proven by the tribunal) demonstrate that the employer acted lawfully around those issues. For example, in relation to issue (a) above: The respondent denies that it subjected the claimant to less favourable treatment (= legal issue). The claimant was treated fairly by the respondent at all times. In May 2010, the claimant was disciplined for persistent late attendance at work in accordance with procedures which apply to all staff regardless of sex/race etc (= facts in support of the case).

Preserving the employer's position

[7.35] Remember, where appropriate, to preserve the employer's position in respect of each of the issues in the case. This can be done through use of phrases such as 'if, which is denied…', 'without prejudice to the contention that…', and even the slightly less legalistic 'in any event'.

Example

It is denied that the claimant was treated less favourably than her chosen comparator (include facts in support). If, which is denied, the claimant was treated less favourably, it is denied that this was on grounds of her sex (include facts in support). Without prejudice to this assertion, it is contended that the respondent took all reasonable steps to prevent its employees carrying out acts of discrimination (include facts in support).

It can be seen from the example that the employer is defending its position in respect of each of the hurdles which the claimant will have to cross with use of such phrases as 'if, which is denied' and 'without prejudice'.

In addition, if the information given by the claimant is insufficient for the respondent to provide a response (ie the claimant has failed to identify the individual(s) who are allegedly bullying him), then this should be made clear by using phrases such as 'if, which is not admitted due to the absence of relevant particulars,...', or 'no admissions are made at present as to the un-particularised allegation the appellant was bullied at work. The respondent will seek further particulars as to the identify of the individual(s) who allegedly bullied the appellant at work and, once this information is obtained, will seek to amend its response accordingly'.

How much should be admitted?

[7.36] Careful thought is required as to what, if anything, should be admitted by the employer in the grounds of resistance. Remember that issues can be conceded much closer to the hearing date. Equally, credit may be lost with the tribunal if the employer seeks to dispute an aspect of the case that ought to have been conceded from the outset. A general rule of thumb is this: ask whether, if the tribunal accepted the employer's position in relation to a particular issue, that would still result in a finding against it (on that issue). If the answer is yes, then it may be appropriate to concede on that issue, unless there is some hope of further evidence emerging.

Example

An employee claims that she has been victimised by a manager on grounds of her sex over a period of three months, including one instance of being sent home from work. An investigation has been carried out by the respondent under its grievance procedure, the outcome of which is a report by a senior manager that, whilst sex discrimination and victimisation did not take place, the employee was erroneously sent home on a particular occasion and told to return the next day. The senior manager has found, however, that the reason for that treatment was not the employee's sex, but rather the mistaken (yet honest) belief of the junior manager that she was due to work the night shift that day.

How should the grounds of resistance be drafted? It should be admitted that the employee was mistakenly sent home. This should be conceded in a way which does minimum damage to the case, for example: 'The respondent denies that the claimant was victimised or treated less favourably on grounds of her sex over a period of three months' (then give facts in support, including investigation). 'The respondent accepts that on [...] the claimant was mistakenly sent home. The respondent's internal investigation found that the reason for this had no connection with the claimant's sex, but was due to the erroneous belief of the manager concerned that the claimant was due to work the night shift that day.'

How much detail should be provided in the grounds of resistance?

[7.37] Just as the employer needs to know from the claimant what case it has to meet, likewise the claimant is entitled to have notice of the major facts and events upon which the employer will rely in support of its case. A failure to do so can have serious consequences at a later stage. It is necessary, therefore, to include, important events and facts in support of the employer's case, but it is often best to steer clear of detailed explanations as to precisely *how* the employer's case will be proved in relation to those events.

Example

The claimant maintains that he was dismissed after a single incident of gross misconduct on 6 January 2005. The employer, while stating that he was dismissed for gross misconduct, also relies upon several past incidents of misconduct. The claimant needs to be given notice of this in order to respond. Include: 'The claimant was dismissed for an act of gross misconduct, namely fighting in the work place on 6 January 2005. In deciding whether dismissal was the appropriate sanction' the respondent took into account the claimant's disciplinary record, in particular the fact that he had on three previous occasions within the previous year been issued with formal disciplinary warnings for misconduct of a similar nature.'

Do's and Don'ts in the drafting of grounds of resistance

Do:

- Include the required information and use the ET3 form.
- Include the essential facts which (if found to be proven by the tribunal) demonstrate that the respondent acted lawfully.
- Structure those facts around the legal test, which the tribunal will apply in deciding whether the respondent has acted lawfully.
- Submit a holding ET3 where you have not yet taken full instructions from your key witnesses and make a subsequent application to amend if necessary. Remember that applications to amend are more likely to succeed the earlier they are submitted.
- Provide as much relevant information as possible when drafting the ET3 so as to minimise the chances of a possible application for further information from the claimant.

Don't:

- Include detailed explanations as to how you will prove the above.
- Include detailed legal arguments.
- Be afraid to make an application to amend, giving full reasons for the delay and referring to the overriding objective.

Responding to the claim – reminder of key points

- The response must be made on Form ET3.
- The form must be presented to the tribunal within 28 days of the ET1 being sent by the tribunal to the employer (the date on which it was sent should appear on the correspondence from the tribunal).
- If the response is late or omits required information it will be rejected and the employer will be prevented from taking any part in the proceedings and/or may have default judgment entered against it.
- If in doubt as to when the claim was sent, send in the response earlier rather than later.
- Keep proof that the ET3 was received by the tribunal in time (ie recorded delivery slip/fax confirmation).
- Any application for an extension of time must be made before the end of the 28 day period and should include an explanation of why it is not possible to submit the response in time. The extension will only be granted if the Employment Judge considers it just and equitable to do so.
- If at all possible, present the response in time even if it needs to be amended later.
- Provide all the information required by the rules in the form. This includes the details of why you are resisting the claim.
- It is possible to seek a review of a decision to reject the response or a review of a default judgment. Even if such a review is supported by proper grounds and is made in accordance with the procedural requirements set out in *rules 34* and *33*, success is far from guaranteed. It is always preferable to present a properly constituted response within time even if an application to amend is subsequently required.

Chapter 8

Fairness: the Overriding Objective

Introduction

[8.1] First introduced in 2001, the overriding objective is the guiding principle in determining how tribunals and Employment Judges should exercise their discretionary powers. When exercising any procedural powers, whether following an application by the parties or of its own volition, tribunals are required to give to effect (so far as practicable) to the 'overriding objective'. The parties are required to assist the tribunal in furthering the overriding objective.

Insofar as any conflict arises the overriding objective takes precedence over any case law relating to the exercise of procedural powers decided prior to the introduction of the overriding objective. Since, as many chairmen (now Employment Judges) observed when it was first introduced, the notion of the overriding objective merely formalised the principle which had in practice always guided the exercise of their discretionary powers (ie in accordance with common sense principles of fairness, with a view to doing justice to the dispute and the parties) it was unlikely that any significant conflict would arise with pre-overriding objective case law (see **8.7** for further discussion on the status of previous case law). This has in fact provided to be the case, with the overriding objective being applied in way that continues to ensure that employment disputes are dealt with in accordance with the key principles of justice, fairness and proportionality.

The overriding objective is often cited by a tribunal when:

- Exercising its powers to manage proceedings under *rule 10, 11* or *12* of the *2004 Rules*. Examples of such decisions include directing that there should be a case management discussion or a pre-hearing review.
- Considering any application made during the course of the proceedings. For example: in deciding applications for a review

of a default judgment or other decisions, applications to amend, to extend time, requests for further information, witness orders, applications for costs, applications to strike out, disclosure and issues of admissibility of evidence during the hearing.

If making or defending any such applications, it is therefore imperative to advance a case with reference to the criteria laid down in the overriding objective.

What is the overriding objective?

[8.2] *Regulation 3(1)* of the *2004 Regulations* states that:

> 'The overriding objective of these Regulations and the rules…is to enable tribunals and Employment Judges to deal with cases justly.'

Regulation 3(2) provides the definition:

> 'Dealing with a case justly includes, so far as practicable: –
> (a) ensuring that the parties are on an equal footing;
> (b) dealing with cases in ways which are proportionate to the complexity or importance of the issues;
> (c) ensuring that it is dealt with expeditiously and fairly; and
> (d) saving expense.'

Each of these concepts is considered separately below. However it should be noted that this definition is a non-exhaustive list of examples of what dealing with a case justly involves, and therefore other considerations may also be appropriate.

Ensuring that the parties are on an equal footing: This is a broad concept which seeks to ensure that each party has:
- a sufficient understanding of the case it has to meet;
- sufficient time to meet it both in terms of preparation and the ability to call witnesses; and
- is not disadvantaged by the fact that it has less resources and legal expertise at its disposal than the other party.

In essence, it is about providing, so far as is practicable, 'a level playing field'.

Dealing with cases in ways which are proportionate to the complexity or importance of the issues: This means that a tribunal must balance the complexity and importance of the issue(s) at stake when making a relevant decision. This will involve striking a balance between the complexity and importance of the issues and the burdens which may be placed on each parties. It is significant that there is no express reference to the amount of damages at stake. In essence, this principle aims to avoid placing an excessive burden, whether in terms of the amount of preparation or costs, on either party which is greater than is necessary to fairly decide that issue (having regard to the relative importance of the issue(s) in the wider context of the employment proceedings).

Ensuring that it is dealt with expeditiously and fairly: Here there is recognition of the old adage that 'slow justice is no justice'. Tribunals should bear in the mind the importance of a swift determination of disputes when considering how best to achieve justice between the competing interests of the parties to a claim.

Saving expense: The expense referred is the expense of the parties as a consequence of a decision being taken (or not taken). Included in this might be administrative and legal costs.

The above are all matters which a tribunal will weigh in the balance in deciding how to 'deal with the case justly'. No single factor is likely to be determinative of itself. The importance and influence of each will depend upon the facts of the individual case and the view taken by individual tribunals of how best to deal with the case 'justly'. In broad terms, however, Employment Judges are likely to be sympathetic to applications relating to issues which are central to the dispute, which are made in a timely manner, which do not request excessive material and which do not cause the other party any or any significant prejudice.

Applying the overriding objective in practice

[8.3] When making or defending applications to the tribunal, it is good practice to relate your arguments or submissions to the criteria contained in the overriding objective, since the tribunal is obliged to give effect to it in exercising its procedural powers.

There are circumstances where, on any approach to the overriding objective, it is almost inevitable that an application will be granted.

Example 1

Shortly after the respondent has served his response (ET3), and before a date for hearing has been set down, the respondent applies to amend his ET3 to include the fact that the claimant was dismissed as a consequence of stealing three brown envelopes full of cash, not one. Doing justice between the parties will almost invariably dictate that such an application is allowed. If not, the respondent could be prevented from relying on that information at the full hearing, hampering the presentation of its case. By contrast, the claimant suffers little or no prejudice – the amendment is unlikely to delay the determination of the dispute particularly because it was made early on in the proceedings. Having said this, however, it would be sensible for the respondent to include an explanation for why the error was made.

Often, however, deciding what is in accordance with the overriding objective is not cut and dried. The competing interests of the respective parties, coupled with the need to allocate a proportionate amount of the tribunal's resources and time to the dispute, requires tribunals to carry out a delicate balancing exercise, the outcome of which is far more difficult to predict. Take for example the following scenario.

Example 2

The claimant complains, in the ET1, of acts of discrimination by specific individuals.

In addition to the specific allegations, the claimant alleges that there is a 'widespread culture of discrimination' throughout the respondent organisation.

The respondent makes an application seeking further information of 'the facts upon which the allegation that there is a widespread culture of discrimination is based, including details of any acts of discrimination which have given rise to the alleged culture, the perpetrators of the acts, the dates upon which the acts took place and the places where the acts took place'.

The claimant refuses a voluntary request from the respondent to provide the details. The matter proceeds to argument by the parties at a pre-hearing review, where the respondent seeks a formal direction from the tribunal.

The respondent's argument

The application is necessary to understand the case it has to meet and deal with the case justly. The phrase 'culture of discrimination' is vague and could mean anything. It is not clear whether the claimant is going to rely upon additional acts of discrimination not referred to in the ET1. The parties will not be on an equal footing if the case proceeds to a full hearing and the claimant raises allegations at the last minute which the respondent has not had an opportunity to respond to (*reg 3(2)(a)*). The respondent will be ambushed (*reg 3(2)(c)*). If the application is not granted there is a risk that the substantive hearing will need to be postponed for the respondent to respond to the fresh allegation which will inevitably cause delay and give rise to additional expense (*reg 3(2)(d)*).

The claimant's response

The respondent has ample information to understand the case it has to meet and the information requested is unnecessary to do justice between the parties. Far from placing the parties on an equal footing, this request would place the claimant at a disadvantage, by compelling disclosure at an early stage of matters which are more appropriately included in witness statements. The claimant does not have the same resources as the respondent. Having made the allegation that there is a culture of discrimination, it is entitled to see what evidence the respondent produces in response, before giving further details (*reg 3(2)(a)*). The phrase 'culture of discrimination' has a clear enough meaning, and to make an order would be disproportionate to the complexity of the issue (*reg 3(2)(b)*).

How the tribunal decides: balancing unfairness

[8.4] It can be seen from the above example that both sides can formulate an arguable case applying the criteria laid down in the overriding objective. For the tribunal, which is deciding the matter, it is frequently a question of asking which side will suffer a greater degree of injustice or unfairness if the order sought is or is not made. For obvious reasons the decision that is made may vary from tribunal to tribunal; there being scope for different decisions to be taken as to how best to achieve justice between the parties, all of which are consistent with the overriding objective and which are correct in law (see also **8.6**). Again, not unsurprisingly, tribunals often reach decisions which strive to strike a middle ground between the competing interests of the parties.

Balancing the unfairness

[8.5]

Example 3

In an application by the claimant for disclosure of documents, the tribunal may ask:

(a) How important is the issue to which the application goes?
(b) What is the potential importance of the information/documents in relation to that issue?
(c) What delay will be caused by requiring the production of the information?
(d) What are the administrative burdens and expense that an order would impose on the respondent?

It will determine whether (c) and (d) are outweighed by the combined effect of (a) and (b). If the application is granted, it will be because it decides the potential importance of the information outweighs the delay and costs that the respondent (bearing in mind its size and resources) will incur as a consequence.

Example 4

A postponement becomes necessary in the middle of a hearing because the claimant, who is unrepresented, suddenly raises a new allegation to which the respondent has not had an opportunity to respond. The respondent seeks an order for costs. The claimant says that he has no resources. He would have raised the allegation earlier but did not know this was necessary. In considering the application in light of the criteria set out in *rule 40(3)* (ie whether the claimant has behaved unreasonably or vexatiously etc) the tribunal is likely, in balancing the respective unfairness to each party, to consider the following:

- How obviously relevant to the dispute is the issue which the claimant seeks to raise at the 11th hour?
- How credible are the reasons given for failing to refer to the issue in light of the nature of the issue and dispute?
- Was there a case management discussion or pre-hearing review where the importance of raising all relevant issues was explained fully to the claimant?
- Was the claimant represented at any stage during the proceedings?
- How, in other respects has the claimant behaved in progressing the claim?
- Could the respondent have pre-empted this situation by making a request for further information?
- What is the size and resources of the respondent?
- What is the claimant's ability to pay a costs order?

Choosing a middle way

[8.6] Often, 'giving effect to the overriding objective' will mean that the tribunal does not do what either party wants, but instead adopts a middle way or compromise. So, in example 2, it *might* make an order simply that the claimant gives a general indication, no more than a paragraph long, of what it means by the phrase 'culture of discrimination'. In example 3, it could direct disclosure in much more limited terms than that sought by the claimant, for example that the respondent provides a written summary of the information which is sought, rather than all the original documentation. In example 4, a far smaller costs award than that which is asked for by the respondent may be awarded. If either party receives a strong indication from the tribunal that it is unwilling to make the order that is sought, it is often sensible to address the tribunal on a possible middle course.

Do's and Don'ts

Do:

- Treat the overriding objective as a tool when making and defending applications.
- Consider the extent to which the final determination of the dispute will be delayed.
- Consider whether your concerns could be addressed by a costs order against the other side.
- Approach the issue by objectively balancing the respective unfairness to the parties.

Don't:

- Forget that the criteria in the overriding objective apply equally to both parties.
- Use case law predating the introduction of the overriding objective without considering the extent to which, if relevant, the principles in the case have been altered by the introduction of the objective.
- Forget that the overriding objective is intended to be flexible and is designed around the changing needs of individual cases.

Chapter 9

Communicating with the Tribunal and Case Management

Introduction

[9.1] The following chapters of this book address specific aspects of case management, that is to say the steps taken by the tribunal and the parties to prepare the case for the final Hearing (through, for example, case management discussions, disclosure of evidence, pre-hearing reviews, strike-out applications etc). This chapter provides an overview of the tribunal's case management powers and of communication between the parties and the tribunal.

The tribunal's response

[9.2] On receiving the ET1 the tribunal will first consider whether the claim should be accepted or rejected (in whole or in part). For further information on this process see *rule 3* of the *2004 Rules* and **chapter 6 – making a claim – the claim form (ET1)**. Assuming that the claim (or part of it) is accepted, the tribunal will proceed to take the following steps (*rule 2*):

- Send a copy to each respondent, recording in writing the day on which it is sent;
- Inform the parties in writing of the case number of the claim and the address to which all notices and other communications to the tribunal must be sent;
- Inform the respondent in writing about how to respond to the claim, including the time limit, the consequences of failing to enter a response within the time limit, and the respondent's right to receive a copy of any judgment disposing of the claim;
- Notify the parties, where appropriate (which it is in most cases), that the services of a conciliation officer (through ACAS) may be available to them; and

- If only part of the claim has been accepted, inform the parties which parts of the claim have not been accepted and that the tribunal shall not proceed to deal with those parts unless they are accepted at a later date.

Note in particular that the claimant can, relatively quickly after the ET1 is sent to the tribunal, expect to receive written notification from the tribunal giving, amongst other things, the address for correspondence with the tribunal and the case number. The case number should be quoted in all future correspondence with the tribunal or the other party. It is normal for the claimant to wait until receipt of the respondent's response form (which will be sent by the tribunal) before contemplating further contact with the tribunal.

Sending the ET1 to the respondent

[9.3] As explained above, once the tribunal has received the claim form and decided to accept all or part of the claim, a copy of the ET1 will be sent to the respondent, together with:

- Written notification of the claim number and address for correspondence with the tribunal;
- Written information about matters such as time limits (and the consequences of not entering a response within the time limit) and the availability of conciliation;
- Written information about which parts of the claim, if any have been rejected and the consequences of that decision; and
- A blank ET3 form for use as the response form, together with a booklet giving guidance on completing the form.

The completed response form must be presented to the tribunal (ie returned and received by the tribunal) within 28 days (see *rule 4(1)* and **chapter 7 – the employer's response – (ET3)**). The respondent may wish to consider making any appropriate applications for case management orders at the same time as returning the response form (see below).

Action by the tribunal upon receipt of the response form

[9.4] As with the ET1, the first step which the tribunal will take on receiving the ET3 is to consider whether it should be accepted or rejected (see *rule 6* and **chapter 7 – the employer's response – the notice of appearance (ET3))**. Assuming that the response is accepted, the tribunal will send a copy of the form to all other parties and record in writing the date on which this is done (rule 5(2)).

Action by the Employment Judge

[9.5] Upon acceptance of the response form, both it and the claim form are usually placed before an Employment Judge in order to review whether the case can proceed directly to a Hearing, or whether there are preliminary matters which need to be addressed. Expect the Employment Judge to have regard, in particular, to the following:

- Whether a case management discussion is necessary;
- Whether there is an issue relating to jurisdiction (eg time limits) suitable for being dealt with by way of a pre-hearing review (under *rule 18*);
- Whether further particulars are needed;
- Whether there are any other steps which need to be taken to ensure that the case can proceed to a final Hearing;
- The estimated length of Hearing (see **9.7**).

In a growing number of cases, tribunals are listing cases for case management discussions of their own motion – often at short notice. Tribunals have been quick to appreciate the advantage of identifying the central issues to a dispute early on in proceedings thus enabling parties to appreciate the relative strength of their cases (and hence promote settlement) and minimise the need for lengthy Hearings (ie by restricting evidence to matters which are relevant to the legal issues which the tribunal will need to determine). Furthermore, active case management discussions reduce the need for Hearings to be adjourned because of allegations being raised for the first time late in the day.

Early communication by the parties

[9.6] If a party wishes for one of the above steps to be taken, it is sensible to make an appropriate application as early as possible, ideally so that when the Employment Judge comes to review the case upon return of the response form, he will have the application before him. So the respondent might, for example, want to accompany the response form with an application, for further particulars of the claim (as to making applications, see below); or to complete section 6 of the response form indicating dates to avoid.

Listing the case for full Hearing

[9.7] Under the rules all references to Hearings with a capital 'H' are to the final hearing where the substantive dispute between the parties is resolved.

A large number of tribunals, though not all, now use a pre-listing enquiry system. The parties are sent a form informing them of the month in which it is proposed the case will be heard and requiring them, within a short timescale, to inform the tribunals of any dates upon which they (or their witnesses) are unable to attend. It is essential that this form is filled in accurately – failure to do so might well jeopardise an application for an adjournment due to non-availability at a later date. In cases where no pre-listing questionnaire is sent out, parties should inform the tribunal as early as possible of dates to avoid in the following six months. Many cases are now heard within a six-month time period, in accordance with the Tribunals Service's target.

Length of Hearing

[9.8] The Employment Judge, upon examination of the file, will attempt to form a view as to the anticipated length of the Hearing according to the issues in the case. Often this will be difficult for him to do because, for example, there is no way of knowing the number of witnesses that will be called. Where there is concern that a Hearing may be listed for less time than is necessary, it is sensible for the parties to inform the tribunal, as soon as possible, of the likely number and relevance of the witnesses who it is intended to call. If the Employment Judge decides to have a case management discussion, it is here that a time estimate and date will often be fixed for the Hearing. Parties should therefore come to case management discussions with their dates to avoid and an estimated length of the Hearing based on the evidence they are likely to rely on.

If it is impossible to estimate the likely length of the Hearing – say for example because the allegations in the claim form are insufficiently particularised so the respondent cannot say which witnesses they will need to call – then this fact will be useful ammunition to support an application for further particulars.

The notice of Hearing

[9.9] In all cases, parties receive a notice of hearing giving the Hearing date. *Rule 14(4)* states that in the case of any hearing other than a case management discussion, this notice must be *sent* by the tribunal to the parties not less than 14 days before the hearing unless the parties agree to a shorter period. In the case of case management discussions, the notice must be 'reasonable' and, as indicated above, tribunals have shown an increasing willingness to list these hearing at fairly short notice.

[9.10] Whilst it is plainly in everyone's interest for the Hearing to be listed, where possible, on a date which all parties can manage, there will be occasions when the date chosen by the tribunal causes either or both parties difficulties. One of the most common problems which arise is that a witness is not or is no longer available due to pre-booked holidays or professional commitments. In such situations, where an application for a postponement is necessary, act promptly. The same applies if the case has been listed for insufficient time.

The tribunal's general power to manage proceedings (*rule 10*)

[9.11] Historically tribunals have always had broad powers to regulate their own procedures. Modern tribunals, faced with a huge growth in cases, have adopted an increasingly active role in the management of cases as they progress towards a final Hearing. This 'hands on' approach to case management is fully reflected in the *2004 Rules* which provide tribunals with many tools to progress a case to swift resolution. These case management powers are considered below.

The tribunal's powers of case management

[9.12] *Rule 10(1)* gives the tribunal a wide power, whether acting on the application of a party or on the Employment Judge's own initiative, to 'make an order in relation to any matter which appears to him to be appropriate' in terms of the management of proceedings. Such orders may be made on the basis of a consideration by the Employment Judge of the papers in the absence of the parties or at a hearing (subject to any express provision in the rules requiring a hearing).

[9.13] *Rule 10(2)* provides a non-exhaustive list of examples of the types of order which may be appropriate. Examples of these are orders:

- Governing the manner in which proceedings are conducted, including time limits to be observed.
- For additional information, witness orders or orders for disclosure, or for written answers to questions put by the tribunal or Employment Judge.
- Extending time limits or staying all or part of proceedings, or postponing or adjourning any Hearing.
- That different parts of the proceedings be dealt with separately or that different claims be considered together.
- That non-parties who may be liable for the remedy be joined as respondents, or dismissing the claim against respondents who are no longer directly interested in proceedings, or that any person considered to have an interest in the proceedings be joined as a party.
- Varying or revoking other orders, or giving notices of hearings or pre-hearing reviews or of possible strike-out orders.
- Giving leave to amend a claim or response.
- For the preparation or exchange of witness statements or as to the use of experts or interpreters in the proceedings.

Many of these types of order are addressed in more detail in the following chapters or are self-explanatory. Any order made under *rule 10* may specify the time and/or place at which compliance is required and may impose conditions. Parties will be warned by the tribunal of the consequences of non-compliance (which may include strike-out or costs: *see rule 13*). Orders will be recorded in writing, signed by the Employment Judge, and parties will be notified by the tribunal as soon as is reasonably possible after the order is made (*rule 10(8)*).

It is open to a party to apply for an order to be varied or revoked (*rule 10(4)*). Where the order has been made without the parties having been given an opportunity to make representations the order itself will contain a statement notifying the parties of their right to apply to have the order varied or revoked (*rule 12(2)*).

The application of the tribunal's case management role

[9.14] The tribunal's case management role starts from the day upon which the claim form is accepted and continues until the conclusion of the case. There are two ways in which the tribunal's case management powers may be exercised:

- *Of the tribunal's own motion*: this will normally arise where the Employment Judge reviews the case file and considers that case management steps are necessary (for example when reviewing the file at the time the response form is accepted). This reflects the modern role of the tribunal in actively managing cases.
- *As a result of an application by one of the parties*: The parties should seek to co-operate as far as possible in progressing the case towards a hearing, including agreeing case management steps between themselves wherever possible. However, where they cannot agree over any issue of case management (for example, disclosure of evidence), either party can apply to the tribunal to ask it to exercise its powers of case management (see below – making applications for orders).

[9.15] It is important for the parties to be aware of the importance of active case management by the tribunal, whether of its own motion or otherwise. This plays a significant part in modern tribunal proceedings, and reflects the importance of the overriding objective (see **chapter 8 – fairness: the overriding objective**). The tribunal, in managing the case, will seek to give effect to this objective. It should be borne in mind, of course, that *reg 3(4)* of the *2004 Regulations*, which sets out the overriding objective, places a positive duty on the parties to "assist the tribunal or the Employment Judge to further the overriding objective".

There are two points to be particularly aware of when considering the tribunal's case management role:

- First, significant case management concerns of the tribunal in any case will be to avoid unnecessary delays and to ensure that the full hearing is ready to proceed on the day upon which it is listed. Parties should therefore manage their own cases, including the preparation of evidence and the making of any applications, with this concern in mind. and
- Secondly, the fact that the parties are in agreement over a particular course, such as an adjournment or the adducing of late evidence in breach of an order, does not necessarily mean that the tribunal will agree (though it will always be a relevant factor).

Case management hearings

Case management discussions

[9.16] *Rules 14(1)(a)* and *17* provide for case management discussions (for a full discussion see **chapter 12 – case management discussions & orders**.) These are interim hearings at which procedural matters and management of the proceedings are dealt with, for example any of the case management orders set out in *rule 10(2)* (see above). They are conducted by a chairman and are heard in private (see **chapter 21: private hearings**). Case management discussions are intended only for procedural case management issues and not for decisions concerning the substantive rights of the parties. So for example, an Employment Judge will be willing to consider ordering a party to provide further information but will not be willing to give a decision as to whether the tribunal has jurisdiction to hear an aspect of the claim – the latter being a decision which relates to the substantive rights of the claimant. Matters which cannot be dealt with in a case management discussion, but must be dealt with at a pre-hearing review (see *rule 18*) or Hearing as appropriate include:

- a determination of a person's civil rights or obligations;
- any judgment or order:
  - as to the entitlement of any party to bring or contest the proceedings,
  - striking out all or part of a claim or response, or
  - making a restricted reporting order.

Case management orders may also be made in the course of a pre-hearing review.

Electronic hearings

[9.17] It is worthy of note that *rule 15* provides that case management discussions and pre-hearing reviews may be conducted 'by use of electronic communications' (which in practice usually means by telephone) provided that the Employment Judge or tribunal conducting the hearing considers it just and equitable to do so. In practice where both parties are represented, the hearing is unlikely to last longer than an hour and the issues are relatively straightforward, case management discussions are routinely conducted by telephone. Such telephone hearings therefore avoids the need (and cost) of parties and/or their representatives attending the tribunal in order to deal with short and straightforward issues. However, several points may be made in respect of telephone hearings:

- If the hearing is required by the rules to be heard in public (not case management discussions – see *rule 17*), then the electronic hearing must be held 'in a place to which the public has access and using equipment so that the public is able to hear all parties to the communication'. In practice, with a telephone hearing this presumably means in a public hearing room with the parties on speakerphone in a conference call.
- Telephone hearings are more likely to be used where the case management issues are standard or straightforward, or where the parties have been given little advanced notice and are legally represented. This is because protracted discussion of complex case management issues where the parties to the call are unfamiliar with tribunal procedure are likely to be difficult and unsatisfactory.
- If a telephone hearing is to be held, it is even more important that the issues have been clearly identified in advance so that all parties are fully prepared and the hearing can be conducted clearly and efficiently. It is useful to try and agree a set of proposed orders which can be faxed and emailed through in advance to the tribunal Employment Judge to consider before the case management discussion.

Case management during the course of a Hearing

[9.18] The Employment Judge will continue to manage cases actively during the Hearing itself. This is part of the general power under *rule 10(1)* to manage proceedings by making 'an order in relation to any matter which appears to him to be appropriate'. So, if the Employment Judge believes that a question is being asked of a witness which is irrelevant or which that witness is not in a position to answer, he may intervene regardless of whether the other party objects. Similarly, if one party seeks to adduce new evidence on the day of hearing which has not been previously disclosed the tribunal may, of its own motion, refuse to allow the evidence to be introduced. In deciding whether to admit the evidence the tribunal are likely to be influenced by matters such as the prejudice to other party, the effect on the timetable of the Hearing and whether an adjournment will be required.

[9.19] Other case management steps prior to or at the outset of the Hearing are common, for example timetables imposing limits on the length of examination or cross-examination of witnesses, or orders for chronologies or skeleton arguments (usually only where parties are legally represented).

Unfavourable case management decisions

[9.20] A case management decision is an 'order' for the purposes of *rule 28(1)(b)*, which states that Employment Judges or tribunals may make an 'order' in relation to interim matters which will require a person to do or not to do something. *Rule 28* provides that the order will either be issued orally at the end of a hearing or reserved to be given in writing at a later date. *Rule 30(1)(b)* provides that a tribunal or Employment Judge is only required to give oral or written reasons for an order if a request for reasons is made before or at the hearing at which the order is made. If such a request is made, the reasons may be given orally at the time of issuing the order or reserved to be given in writing at a later date. In relation to orders, written reasons are only required if requested by the Employment Appeal Tribunal.

Effectively, therefore, tribunals are not obliged to give any reasons for an order unless a request is made at the time of the hearing at which the order is made. Furthermore, there is no requirement for the reasons to be given *in writing*, unless requested by the Employment Appeal Tribunal. In practice, however, where the matter has been the subject of a dispute between the parties, Employment Judges are likely to give brief reasons for making or refusing to make any case management order. Certainly, the absence of any reasons in circumstances where the order causes significant hardship to one party is likely to support an application under rule 11 (see below) to have the order revoked or varied.

[9.21] The question, then, is what can a party do if dissatisfied with a case management order? The short answer is 'very little'. The legislative draftsmen plainly intended to give tribunals not only extensive powers to manage cases but a certain degree of immunity from challenge in relation to their case management orders. This is, in part, achieved by excluding orders from the definition of decision in respect of which parties may apply for a review under *rule 34*. Consequently, no application under *rule 34* can be made to review an order in relation to which a party is dissatisfied.

[9.22] However, there are a number of steps which a party can take both before and after a case management order to minimise the chance of an unfavourable order being imposed:

- First, it is important to remember that the best means of securing a favourable case management decision are:
  - to agree matters, as far as possible, with the other party (this will be persuasive although not conclusive when the tribunal considers the matter);
  - to set out clearly and persuasively the reasons for seeking or objecting to the order in the first place (see below);
- Secondly, the application may be renewed, or an application may be made to vary or revoke a case management order, at any time under *rule 11*, subject to the time limits for doing so (see below). However, although the original decision will not be binding on an Employment Judge considering the matter at a later stage, an application to vary or revoke is more likely to be successful if:
  - it is made on grounds which, for some good reason, were not raised or fully appreciated when the order was first made;
  - there has been a change of circumstances since the order was first made;
- Thirdly, where the order has been made by an Employment Judge of his own motion, without the parties having been given an opportunity to make representations, they have an automatic right, under *rule 12(2)(b)*, to apply to vary or revoke the order.
- Fourthly, in some circumstances it may be possible to appeal against the order, although this can only be on a point of law (see **chapter 26: appeal**). However, it should be borne in mind that:
  - the circumstances in which an appeal is likely to be possible are extremely limited, primarily because of the wide discretion afforded to tribunals in their case management powers. On rare occasions, it may be possible to argue that the exercise of discretion was so clearly wrong (ie perverse) so as to amount to an error of law: so, for example, a refusal of a timely application, supported by medical evidence, to postpone a Hearing, on the grounds that the claimant's inability to attend due to the fact that he has been involved in a serious car accident, is likely to be susceptible to challenge on the grounds of perversity of failure to give effect to the overriding objective;
  - an appeal against a case management decision will not normally have the effect of delaying the substantive proceedings in the tribunal: these will normally continue in the interim and the

appeal on the procedural issue will only be considered after the conclusion of the case.

Practice directions

[9.23] By *reg 13* of the *2004 Regulations*, the President of Employment Tribunals has the power to make, vary or revoke practice directions about the procedure of employment tribunals in the area for which he is responsible. Practice directions constitute a further set of rules running alongside the existing procedural rules, either for all cases or for specific types of proceedings or hearings.

An up-to-date list of relevant practice directions can be found on the HM Courts and Tribunals Service website (www.justice.gov.uk). Practice directions set out more precisely how the tribunal should aim to manage certain types of cases where there is a one employer being sued by a number of former employees or where certain proceedings should be dealt with in a certain way because, for example, they raise a common but at that stage disputed issue in law.

Making applications for orders – rule 11

[9.24] Under *rule 11* parties are, at any stage in the proceedings, entitled to apply for any case management order to be made, varied or revoked by the tribunal. The most common examples of orders which a party may wish to apply for are:

- an extension of a time limit;
- for the provision of further particulars;
- for disclosure;
- for the postponement of a hearing / Hearing;
- for the attendance of certain specific witnesses;
- for the case to be listed for a case management discussion or pre-hearing review; or
- an application that the other side show cause why their case should not be struck out.

How should the application be made?

[9.25] Rule 11 provides for a specific procedure for the making of applications. It is important that this procedure is respected; indeed, the requirements set out in Rule 11 provide a useful checklist of things that need to be included in order for the application to be successful.

Rule 11

11

(1) At any stage of the proceedings a party may apply for an order to be issued, varied or revoked or for a case management discussion or pre-hearing review to be held.

(2) An application for an order must be made not less than 10 days before the date of the hearing at which it is to be considered (if any) unless it is not reasonably practicable to do so, or the Employment Judge or tribunal considers it in the interests of justice that shorter notice be allowed. The application must (unless an Employment Judge orders otherwise) be in writing to the Employment Tribunal Office and include the case number for the proceedings and the reasons for the request. If the application is for a case management discussion or a pre-hearing review to be held, it must identify any orders sought.

(3) An application for an order must include an explanation of how the order would assist the tribunal or Employment Judge in dealing with the proceedings efficiently and fairly.

(4) When a party is legally represented in relation to the application (except where the application is for a witness order described in rule 10(2)(c) only), that party or his representative must, at the same time as the application is sent to the Employment Tribunal Office, provide all other parties with the following information in writing—

  (a) details of the application and the reasons why it is made;

  (b) notification that any objection to the application must be sent to the Employment Tribunal Office within 7 days of receiving the application or, if a hearing of any type is due to take place before the expiry of that 7 day period, before the date of that hearing;

  (c) that any objection to the application must be copied to both the Employment Tribunal Office and all other parties;

and the party or his representative must confirm in writing to the Employment Tribunal Office that this rule has been complied with.

(4A) The time limit described in sub-paragraph (4)(b) may be amended where the Employment Judge or tribunal considers it in the interests of justice to do so.

(5) Where a party is not legally represented in relation to the application, the Secretary shall (except where the application is for a witness order described in rule 10(2)(c) only) send a copy of the application to all other parties and inform them of the matters listed in sub-paragraphs (4)(b) and (c).

(6) An Employment Judge may refuse a party's application and if he does so the Secretary shall inform the parties in writing of such refusal unless the application is refused at a hearing.

Key points of note when making an application

[9.26] The main points to remember are:

When bringing the application

- The application *must* be made in writing to the tribunal and must include the case number.
- The tribunal may deal with it orally or at a hearing: if it is dealt with at a hearing, this will take the form of a case management discussion (see **chapter 12 – case management discussions**) or pre-hearing review (see **chapter 13 – pre-emptive strikes: pre-hearing reviews**).
- It must be made as soon as possible: at least ten days before the date of the hearing on which it falls to be considered. Although it is possible for the tribunal to agree to abridge that time, the need for this should be avoided by an application at the earliest possible stage: if a late application results in an adjournment of a hearing, there may be costs implications. If it is unavoidable to bring the application at the last minute, the application should include an explanation of why it could not be made earlier and a specific request that time be abridged.
- It is not enough simply to ask for the order. The party seeking it must provide the reasons for the request, identify any orders

sought (ie in draft terms), and explain how the order would assist the tribunal or Employment Judge in dealing with the proceedings efficiently and fairly. Parties should bear in mind the requirements of the overriding objective. Where relevant, documents should be attached: for example, in the case of a request for further particulars, the document setting out the precise particulars sought should be attached to the application.

- When the person making the application is legally represented in relation to the application, they *must*, at the same time as the application is sent to the tribunal, send a copy of the information set out in *rule 11(4)* to all other parties: essentially, details of the application and the reasons for seeking it, notification of the requirement, procedure and time frame for the other party to notify any objection to the order. Further, they must confirm in writing to the tribunal that this has been done.
- Even where the party making the application is not legally represented, it is good practice to copy the application to all other parties. The greater the notice that is given to other parties, the less scope there is for the hearing to be adjourned because other parties are not in a position to deal with the application.

When responding to the application

- Any objection to the application should also be made in writing. It should include the case number.
- The objection must be sent to the tribunal within seven days of receiving the application or at least seven days before the date of the hearing on which it falls to be considered, whichever is the sooner. In reality it should be sent as soon as possible so that both the tribunal and the party making the application have the opportunity to consider it in good time before the hearing. A last-minute objection which results in an adjournment of the hearing may have costs consequences.
- The objection must be copied to both the tribunal and all other parties (not just the party making the application).
- Although the rules do not specifically say so, as a matter of good practice the objection should set out the reasons for objecting to the application. If an alternative order is put forward as an alternative, this too should be set out.

[9.27] Where the case has been listed for a case management discussion parties should, where possible, use this opportunity to make any application for a specific issue to be considered at the hearing.

Parties should avoid leaving it until the day of the case management discussion to make an application; this is particularly so where the matter could have been raised in writing and within the time limits as required by *rule 11*. However, if something urgent arises late in the day or something happens on the day of a hearing that demands an oral application, for example an application for an adjournment to deal with an unexpected and unforeseeable development, then this should be made orally and the tribunal should be asked to dispense with the notice requirements in the interests of justice. In the case of urgent applications, it is often sensible to fax or email rather than post the application. If at all possible a record should be kept showing the date on which the application was sent and received by the tribunal and the other parties.

[9.28] Unlike in the county court, there is no prescribed form that the parties should use to make an application. It is important, however, that the written request complies with the requirements of *rule 11* set out above. Employment Judges are inundated with letters from parties requesting various orders. If the order sought is clearly set out, with persuasive and compelling reasons, the application is more likely to be granted by the tribunal, possibly even without the need for a hearing. A well-drafted application will enable the tribunal (and other parties) to understand precisely what the tribunal is being asked to order and why.

Examples of structure of application and response

Re: Case No 56940/2010 *Jones v Smith and Co*: Application for an order under *rule 11*.

Order sought from the tribunal: The claimant/respondent seeks an order under [identify relevant tribunal rule] that the respondent/claimant [specify order sought]. For example:

> 'The claimant seeks an order, under *rule 11(b)*, that the respondent provide the further particulars set out in the attached document dated [...] and headed 'Request for Further Particulars'.

Grounds for seeking the order: The grounds should be set out concisely, but persuasively. Any attempts that have been made to obtain the other side's consent to what is requested should also be set out, enclosing any relevant correspondence. The party making the application should have regard to the to the legal criteria which the Employment Judge will apply in deciding whether to make the order (see relevant chapter relating to the power in question eg **chapter 11 – disclosure, chapter 14 –witness orders and orders for the production of documents** etc) and to the requirements of *rule 11*. The overriding objective is likely to be central in most applications. For example:

> 'The 'Request for Further Particulars' attached to this application was sent to the respondent on [date] and [date]. No particulars were received; neither was any formal response received indicating why the respondent was unable to reply to the request. This application is made because the claimant considers that the respondent will not provide this information unless ordered to do so by the tribunal. If this information is not provided, the claimant is unable to understand fully the case he has to meet because [give brief details]. An order would also assist the tribunal in dealing with the proceedings efficiently and fairly because it will assist in defining the issues between the parties and identifying precisely which witnesses and other evidence the claimant needs to call to address the respondent's allegations. The claimant submits that this order can be made without the need for a hearing, but if the tribunal considers that a hearing is required, the claimant asks that a case management discussion be arranged'.

Where the party applying for the order is legally represented: In these circumstances the requirements of *rule 11(4)* must also be met. For example:

> 'The claimant's representatives sent a copy of this application, including the reasons why it is sought, to the respondent on […] and informed the respondent that any objection to the application must be sent to the tribunal within seven days of receiving it, [or before the hearing on [date], whichever date is earlier, if appropriate] and copied to all other parties. The claimant therefore confirms that *rule 11(4)* has been complied with'.

Where the other party wishes to object to the application: In these circumstances the reasons for the objection should be set out concisely, again having regard to the legal criteria which the Employment Judge will apply, to the requirements of rule 11 and to the overriding objective. For example:

> 'The respondent objects to providing the [eg redundancy scoring sheets for the other employees in the claimant's team] requested because of its duty of confidentiality to its other employees and because the request amounts to a request for evidence rather than a request for information. The appropriate evidence will be exchanged in the normal course of disclosure and an order is therefore unnecessary. The respondent informed the claimant by telephone on [date] of its reasons for objecting to the request. The respondent therefore requests that the application be refused or that the matter be considered at a case management discussion'.

The response from the tribunal

[9.29] When the Employment Judge has considered the application, he will write to the parties with his decision, usually giving brief reasons, unless the matter needs to be determined at a case management discussion or other hearing, in which case notice of the hearing will be sent out to all parties.

Do's and Don'ts

Do:

- Address the legal criteria which the tribunal will apply in deciding whether to make a particular order.
- Address the overriding objective, including the prejudice to the respective sides if the order is / is not made.
- Present your applications concisely and clearly, providing cogent reasons.
- Give the information required by *rule 11*: in particular the reasons for requesting (or objecting to) the order and an explanation of how the order would assist the Employment Judge or tribunal in dealing with the proceedings efficiently and fairly.

- Explain precisely what the tribunal is being asked to order and why.
- Make the application at the earliest reasonable opportunity and at the very latest within the timescale set out in *rule 11*.
- Seek the agreement of the other party, if timescales allow it, to avoid the need for an order.

Don't:

- Phrase the application in a manner which assumes it will be granted.
- Ask for an order in general terms (eg 'the respondent to disclose all personnel documents as they may be important'): it is important to be clear about precisely *what* the tribunal is being asked to order and *why* the order is sought with reference to the legal issues arising in the dispute.

Remember: the golden rule is 'what' and 'why': what the tribunal is being asked to order the other party to do; and why the order is necessary.

The consequences of failure to comply with orders

[9.30] By virtue of *rule 13*, if a party does not comply with a case management order, an Employment Judge or tribunal may take one of the following steps:

- Making an order in respect of costs or preparation time (see *rules 38* to *46*);
- At a pre-hearing review or a Hearing, make an order striking out the whole or part of the claim or response and, where appropriate, debarring a respondent from responding to the claim altogether;

Where the order with which a party has failed to comply stated that failure to comply with the conditions of the order would result in the claim/response being struck out without further notice, the proceedings will be automatically terminated on the day after the last date for compliance. In these circumstances there is no need for a further hearing (*rule 13(2)*). It is therefore of paramount importance that if an order is made, parties comply with that order and, if unable to do so for good reason, apply to the tribunal under *rule 11* (see above) for the order to be varied or revoked. Further, if an application is made by the other party for an order to be made and it is known that compliance will be problematic, then it is all the more important to respond in a timely manner objecting to the application under *rule 11* (see above) and explaining any difficulty, rather than simply failing to respond and risking an order being made.

Communicating with the tribunal

[9.31]

> *Checklist*
>
> - Send important documents, such as the ET1 and ET3, by recorded delivery or where these documents are submitted online be sure to retain a print-out confirming that they have been transmitted to the tribunal.
> - Make a note of the case number and quote it on all correspondence and applications and in the subject field of any email.
> - Think from the outset about the number of witnesses needed, dates to avoid and any applications that need to be made.
> - Make applications that clearly set out the order you seek and the grounds for seeking it and comply with the requirements of *rule 11*.
> - Keep in mind the administrative burden on tribunals and their desire to avoid unnecessary delays.

Contacting employment tribunals

General tips about correspondence with the tribunal

[9.32] Tribunals now permit correspondence from parties by email as well as by letter or fax. The case number must be used not only in any correspondence by letter or fax, but also in the subject field of any e-mail communication with the tribunal. Tribunal guidance on communicating with the tribunal by e-mail states that:

- Any documentary attachments to an e-mail must be sent in a 'Word' compatible format or they will not be accepted. Any documents sent by the tribunal will be sent by enclosure or attachment using 'Word XP' software.

- The tribunal will send an electronic acknowledgment of any e-mail correspondence: if no such response is received within two working days of the e-mail being sent, it may be advisable to check with the tribunal that the e-mail has been received.
- If a party wishes the tribunal to communicate with them by e-mail, they should indicate this on the claim form or response form, giving a valid e-mail address. By doing so, that party is agreeing that they check for incoming e-mail at least once a day and that the e-mail address may be passed to other people involved in the claim (eg other parties, ACAS).
- Copies of non-electronic documents, or those requiring an Employment Judge's signature (eg a judgment or other decision), will be sent to the parties by post even if they have requested that communication with the tribunal be by e-mail.

[9.33] The tribunals can also accommodate disabilities or special needs when communicating with parties if this is requested by contacting the tribunal offices. Examples of this include converting documents to large print or Braille, providing information on audio-tape, or providing signing or foreign language interpreters.

It is important to remember that it is the duty of the parties to ensure that any correspondence (including e-mail) is received by the tribunal within any applicable time limit.

How to contact the tribunals

[9.34] A large amount of information (including downloadable ET1 and ET3 forms and guidance on making a claim) can be found at the HM Courts and Tribunals Service website (www.justice.gov.uk).

Hearing Centres: England and Wales

- Ashford Employment Tribunal
  Ashford House
  County Square Shopping Centre
  Ashford
  Kent
  TN23 1YB

Tel: 01233 621346
Fax: 01233 624423
Email: ashfordet@hmcts.gsi.gov.uk

- Bedford Employment Tribunal
  8–10 Howard Street
  Bedford
  MK40 3HS

Tel: 01234 351306
Fax: 01234 352315
Email: bedfordet@hmcts.gsi.gov.uk

- Birmingham Employment Tribunal
  Phoenix House
  1–3 Newhall Street
  Birmingham
  B3 3NH

Tel: 0121 236 6051
Fax: 0121 236 6029
Email: birminghamet@hmcts.gsi.gov.uk

- Brighton Employment Tribunal
  [Correspondence should go to the Southampton Employment Tribunal]

- Bristol Employment Tribunal
  Ground Floor
  The Crescent Centre
  Temple Back
  Bristol
  BS1 6EZ

Tel: 0117 929 8261
Fax: 0117 925 3452
Email: bristolet@hmcts.gsi.gov.uk

- Bury St Edmunds Employment Tribunal
  100 Southgate Street
  Bury St Edmunds
  IP33 2AQ

Tel: 01284 762 171
Fax: 01284 706 064
Email: buryet@hmcts.gsi.gov.uk

- Cardiff Employment Tribunal
  Caradog House
  1–6 St Andrews Place
  Cardiff
  CF10 3BE

Tel: 029 2067 8100
Fax: 029 2022 5906
Email: cardiffet@hmcts.gsi.gov.uk

- Exeter Employment Tribunal
  Keble House
  Southernhay Gardens
  Exeter
  EX1 1NT

Tel: 01392 279665
Fax: 01392 430063
Email: exeteret@hmcts.gsi.gov.uk

- Leeds Employment Tribunal
  4th Floor
  City Exchange
  11 Albion Street
  Leeds
  LS1 5ES

Tel: 0113 245 9741
Fax: 0113 242 8843
Email: leedset@hmcts.gsi.gov.uk

- Leicester Employment Tribunal
  5a New Walk
  Leicester
  LE1 6TE

Tel: 0116 255 0099
Fax: 0116 255 6099
Email: leicesteret@tribunals.gsi.gov.uk

- Liverpool Employment Tribunal
  1st Floor
  Cunard Building

Pier Head
Liverpool
L3 1TS

Tel: 0151 236 9397
Fax: 0151 231 1484
Email: liverpoolet@hmcts.gsi.gov.uk

- London Central Employment Tribunal
  Ground Floor
  Victory House
  30–34 Kingsway
  London
  WC2B 6EX

Tel: 020 7273 8603
Fax: 020 7273 8686
Email: londoncentralet@hmcts.gsi.gov.uk

- London East Employment Tribunal
  2nd Floor
  Anchorage House
  2 Clove Crescent
  London
  E14 2BE

Tel: 0207 538 6161
Fax: 0207 538 6210
Email: eastlondon@hmcts.gsi.gov.uk

- London South Employment Tribunal
  Montague Court
  101 London Road
  West Croydon
  CR0 2RF

Tel: 020 8667 9131
Fax: 020 8649 9470
Email: londonsouthet@hmcts.gsi.gov.uk

- Manchester Employment Tribunal
  Alexandra House
  14–22 The Parsonage

Manchester
M3 2JA

Tel: 0161 833 6100
Fax: 0161 832 0249
Email: manchesteret@hmcts.gsi.gov.uk

- Newcastle Employment Tribunal
  Quayside House
  110 Quayside
  Newcastle Upon Tyne
  NE1 3DX

Tel: 0191 260 6900
Fax: 0191 222 1680
Email: newcastleet@tribunals.gsi.gov.uk

- Nottingham Employment Tribunal
  3rd Floor
  Byron House
  2a Maid Marian Way
  Nottingham
  NG1 6HS

Tel: 0115 947 5701
Fax: 0115 950 7612
Email: nottinghamet@hmcts.gsi.gov.uk

- Reading Employment Tribunal
  5th Floor
  30–31 Friar Street
  Reading
  RG1 1DX

Tel: 0118 959 4917
Fax: 0118 956 8066
Email: readinget@hmcts.gsi.gov.uk

- Sheffield Employment Tribunal
  14 East Parade
  Sheffield
  S1 2ET

Tel: 0114 276 0348
Fax: 0114 276 2551
Email: sheffieldet@hmcts.gsi.gov.uk

- Shrewsbury Employment Tribunal
  Prospect House
  Belle Vue Road
  Shrewsbury
  SY3 7NR

Tel: 01743 358341
Fax: 01743 244186
Email: shrewsburyet@hmcts.gsi.gov.uk

- Southampton Employment Tribunal
  3rd Floor Duke's Keep
  Marsh Lane
  Southampton
  SO14 3EX

Tel: 023 8071 6400
Fax: 023 8063 5506
Email: southamptonet@hmcts.gsi.gov.uk

- Watford Employment Tribunal
  3rd Floor
  Radius House
  51 Clarendon Road
  Watford
  WD17 1HP

Tel: 01923 281 750
Fax: 01923 281 781
Email: watfordet@hmcts.gsi.gov.uk

Hearing Centres: Scotland

- Aberdeen Employment Tribunal
  Mezzanine Floor
  Atholl House
  84–88 Guild Street
  Aberdeen
  AB11 6LT

Tel: 01224 593137
Fax: 01224 593138
Email: aberdeenet@hmcts.gsi.gov.uk

- Dundee Employment Tribunal
  Ground Floor
  Block C
  Caledonian House
  Greenmarket
  Dundee
  DD1 4QX

Tel: 0138 222 1578
Fax: 0138 222 7136
Email: dundeeet@hmcts.gsi.gov.uk

- Edinburgh Employment Tribunal
  54–56 Melville Street
  Edinburgh
  EH3 7HF

Tel: 0131 226 5584
Fax: 0131 220 6847
Email: edinburghet@hmcts.gsi.gov.uk

- Glasgow Employment Tribunal
  Eagle Building
  215 Bothwell Street
  Glasgow
  G2 7TS

Tel: 0141 204 0730
Fax: 0141 204 0732
Email: glasgowet@hmcts.gsi.gov.uk

Chapter 10

Post-claim requests for additional information

For pre-claim requests for further information, including the use of question forms in discrimination claims under the Equality Act 2010, see ***chapter 3 – pre-claim requests for information****.*

Introduction

[10.1] As discussed in previous chapters (see **chapter 6 – making a claim** and **chapter 7 – the employer's response**), claimants and respondents are required by the *2004 Rules* to provide certain prescribed information relating to their claim or response. Where this information has not been provided and is material the Secretary ought not to accept the claim or response as the case may be.

In addition to this prescribed information parties are expected to explain in sufficient detail the basis of the complaint or defence. Where this is not done the tribunal can order a party to provide additional information or, as it sometimes referred to, for further particular. Such an order can be made on by the tribunal of its own motion, or in response to an application by the other party. . This chapter describes the circumstances when such a request is appropriate and the procedure which should be followed by a party wishing to make such an application.

The request for additional information

[10.2] An order that a party provide further particulars of its case can be made either pursuant to an application by the other party to the claim or by the tribunal of its own motion. The power to order a party to provide additional information arises under *rules 10(1) and (3), and*

11 of the 2004 Rules. An application for additional information may be made orally (for example at a case management discussion hearing) or in writing (see **chapter 9 – communicating with the tribunal** at **9.17**).

[10.3] A request for additional information commonly takes the form of the requesting party formulating a series of written questions, usually relating to the grounds set out in the ET1 or ET3, with a view to clarifying the way that the other party is putting their case. The purpose is to provide the party making the application with information about the case it has to meet and/or the tribunal with information about the issues it is likely to have to decide.

[10.4] The possible advantage of such a request can be summarised as follows:

- It enables a party to properly prepare its case and not be 'ambushed' at a full hearing.
- It provides protection (in terms of costs) to the requesting party in relation to fresh allegations being raised for the first time at the substantive hearing of the dispute.
- It may have the effect of exposing vulnerable areas in the other side's case which causes them to lose confidence at an early stage and settle or concede.
- Non-compliance with an order may enable a strike out application to be made (on notice) or alternatively an application for costs – both under *rule 13*.
- Non-compliance will also enable the innocent party to invite the tribunal at the full hearing to draw adverse conclusions from the failure to provide the additional information.
- A request and any reply received might serve as a useful forerunner to an application for a pre-hearing review or for a deposit under *rule 20* (see **chapter 13 – pre-emptive strikes: pre-hearing reviews**).

[10.5] As with all tactical decisions, the advantages have to be weighed against possible disadvantages. If there is a weakness in a particular aspect of the other side's case, which is for the other side to remedy, there may be advantages in not alerting them to it. Be careful, however, not to prejudice the preparation of your own case. The more obvious the flaw in the case the more a tribunal will expect a legally represented party to have sought further particulars of the claim. It is important to remember that tribunals are required, under the overriding objective, to act in a way that places both parties on an equal footing. Where the other side is unrepresented, the tribunal may be unsympathetic to a party who claims to be taken by surprise at a full hearing when the matter could (or should) have been clarified by an earlier request for further information. If, however, further particulars have been sought, the tribunal may refuse the other party permission to make a new allegation which has not been raised in their response to the request for full particulars, or at the very least will be sympathetic to an application both for an adjournment to deal with the new issue and for the resulting costs (see **chapter 15 – postponements and adjournments** and **chapter 22 – costs**).

Making the application

[10.6] An application for an order for further information must be made in accordance with *rule 11* of the *2004 Rules*. Hence the application must be made not less than ten days before the date of any hearing at which it is to be considered) unless it is not reasonably practicable to do so, or the Employment Judge or tribunal considers it in the interests of justice that shorter notice be allowed. The application must (unless an Employment Judge orders otherwise) be in writing and include the case number for the proceedings and the reasons for the request (*rule 11(1)*) (see **10.7**).

[10.7] As the Employment Judge or tribunal considering the application will need to have regard to the overriding objective (see **chapter 8 – fairness: the overriding objective**), the application must include an explanation as to how the order would assist the tribunal or Employment Judge 'in dealing with the proceedings efficiently and fairly' (for the criteria to be considered when making such an order, see below at **10.12**). Where a party is legally represented in relation to the application, that party or his representative must, at the same time as the application is sent to the tribunal, provide all other parties with the following information in writing:

(a) details of the application and the reasons why it is sought;
(b) notification that any objection to the application must be sent to the tribunal within seven days of receiving the application or, if a hearing of any type is due to take place before the expiry of that seven day period, before the date of that hearing; and
(c) that any objection to the application must be copied to both the tribunal and all other parties.

The party or his representative must also confirm in writing to the tribunal that these requirements have been complied with (*rule 11(4)*).

[10.8] Examples of where a request for additional information might be appropriate are given below. An example of how to lay out the request can be found in **appendix v – case study**, although there is no proscribed form for doing so. It is important, however, that full reasons are provided for any application that is made.

[10.9] When considering a written application, a tribunal will usually expect the party seeking the order to have first sought the particulars from the other side voluntarily. It may be possible to avoid this if making the request at a directions hearing. However, even in this situation, it remains good practice to notify, where possible, the other party of the request that will be made so that they are not taken by surprise at the hearing. For obvious reasons the longer and more difficult the request the more important it is to give the other party prior notice. If making the application in writing it is sensible to enclose the formal request for particulars with the application itself (the reasons in the application may be brief if the request speaks for itself), together with a copy of inter-party correspondence setting out prior attempts that have been made to obtain clarification of the case. It is also important (indeed imperative for parties who are legally represented) to copy in the other side to any written application made to the tribunal.

[10.10] If the application is made orally, a copy of the request for particulars requested is sufficient. Generally, applications are more likely to succeed the earlier they are made, although in theory an application can be made at any time prior to the conclusion of proceedings.

[10.11] Sometimes, the information contained in the ET1 is so sparse or clearly insufficient that the respondent can lodge a 'holding ET3' (which merely formally denies or does not admit the matters set out in the claim and indicates that further particulars are being sought), whilst making a simultaneous application for further particulars, which, once provided, will enable it to serve a detailed ET3 setting out its position in response to the allegations made by the claimant (see **chapter 7 – the employer's response**).

The criteria for making an order

[10.12] The tribunal will determine an application for additional information in accordance with the principles set out in the overriding objective (see **chapter 8 – fairness: the overriding objective**). It will balance the relevance of the request against such matters as the prejudice to the other side by having to answer it. The case law in this area predates the overriding objective. Having said this, however, the principles enunciated in those cases are likely to remain relevant when considering the application of the overriding objective. They include *White v University of Manchester* [1976] ICR 419; *International Computers Ltd v Whitley* [1978] IRLR 318; *Byrne v Financial Times Ltd* [1991] IRLR 417.

[10.13] In broad terms a tribunal will usually make an order if it considers that further clarification of the case is proportionate and necessary for the requesting party to understand the case it has to meet and to be able to prepare accordingly. If, on the other hand, the tribunal forms the view that a request goes further than is necessary to achieve this objective, it will either not make the order at all or make it in modified form – namely restricting the order to the information which it considers reasonable and sufficient for the requesting party to understand the case it has to meet.

[10.14] Tribunals are unlikely to entertain requests for 'oppressive' requests. Oppressive requests usually ask not so much for clarification of the other side's case but rather detailed questions about how they are going to prove it, for example which witnesses they intend to call and which documents they intend to adduce to prove a particular aspect of their case (see *P & O European Ferries (Dover) Ltd v Byrne* [1989] ICR 779). Remember that these matters, crucial as they are, are best dealt with through processes such as disclosure and directions for exchange of witness statements. Requests for additional information should be used to clarify the other party's case not to 'fish' for evidence. Other examples of oppressive requests include requests for matters which are irrelevant to the issues between the parties or wholly disproportionate requests for minute details of the other side's case. In determining whether a request is oppressive the tribunal is likely to have regard to the resources of the respective parties to the dispute.

[10.15] In making and defending such applications, parties should make full reference to the overriding objective, including issues such as placing the parties on an equal footing, the saving of expense and doing justice to the complexity of the issues. These criteria can be used as tools both in making and defending applications. Tribunals will be particularly anxious to ensure that the issues are properly defined before the full hearing takes place in order to avoid delays, overly long hearings and injustice.

Examples of requests

The claimant has alleged that managers within the respondent organisation 'continuously discriminated against her over a period of ten months', but has not provided further details. The respondent might request all or some of the following information if it has not been provided in the grounds of complaint:

- who, in the respondent organisation, the claimant alleges discriminated against her;
- the specific act/s of discrimination relied upon with the relevant dates; and
- the basis upon which the claimant asserts that she was subjected to less favourable treatment on grounds of sex/race, including details of any comparator upon whom the claimant wishes to rely.

It can be seen from this example that each request relates to the issues which the tribunal will have to decide in the case.

In an unfair dismissal case, the respondent has relied upon capability as the reason for dismissal and alleged that the claimant's performance was inadequate over a period of six months, without providing further details. The claimant might wish to request:

- details of the precise duties that the respondent alleges were carried out incompetently;
- what aspect of the claimant's performance was considered to be inadequate;
- whether the claimant was ever notified of this dissatisfaction and, if so, when, by whom and in what format; and
- details of dates.

The tactical advantages of such a request are obvious, particularly if the claimant considers that the respondent will not be able to provide such information. Where a claimant alleges that they were treated differently from other employees, and alleges that this amounted to unfairness, the respondent will often be entitled to details of which employees the claimant alleges were treated more favourably.

Consequences of failing to comply with a request for further particulars

[10.16] Where a tribunal makes an order, it will give a deadline for the provision of further particulars. If that deadline is not complied with (or the particulars provided are inadequate), the party in whose favour the order was made can make an application under *rule 13(1)* that the other party show cause why the tribunal should not strike out the ET1 or ET3 or part thereof. In practice, a tribunal *may* be reluctant to impose such a draconian penalty applying, as it must, the overriding objective. Instead, it may chose to make an award for costs or preparation time, to compensate the innocent party who has incurred additional costs arising from the enforcement (*rule 13(1)(a)*). However, what is clear is that the more protracted or flagrant the failure to comply with orders, the more likely that the tribunal will lose patience and strike out the whole or part of the party's case – for, as has already been stated, the overriding objective applies equally to both parties, and there will come a time when a tribunal concludes that that the party in default has been given more than sufficient opportunity to put his case, and that it would be simply unfair on the other party, for the former to be shown any further indulgence (especially in circumstances where the failure to respond prevents the other party and/or the tribunal understanding the basis of the claim and/or response).

[10.17] Alternatively, the tribunal may order the party in default to pay a deposit in respect of the aspect of the case which it has failed to particularise (see **chapter 14 – witness orders**).

[10.18] Where the case proceeds to a full hearing, any failure to comply with the requests should be highlighted by the disadvantaged party. The tribunal's attention should be drawn to the fact that the other side has been given every opportunity to particularise its case but has failed to do so. If particulars emerge at the full hearing which should have been given in answer to an earlier request, the tribunal should be invited either not to consider the this information, attach little weight to it, or to grant an adjournment in order for the new matters to be answered, with costs payable by the party in default.

The power to order written answers

[10.19] An alternative to the requesting of additional information is a request for written answers. The power to order written answers to questions put by the tribunal or Employment is contained in *rule 10(2)(f)*. In practice, there is considerable overlap between the power to order the provision of additional information and the power to order written answers. There is no hard and fast rule as to when a request for written answers, as opposed to a request for additional information, should be made. In the majority of cases there will be little practical difference between the two, and in those circumstances a request for additional information is the most common course. There is usually little that can be achieved through a request for written answers that cannot be equally well achieved by a well-drafted request for further particulars. One example of the use of written answers might be to obtain information in a discrimination case that has not been previously sought in a questionnaire, and where the time limit for filing a questionnaire has expired. Whether a tribunal accedes to such an application will, however, depend upon the individual circumstances of a case. The tribunal may, of its own motion, decide to ask a party a series of questions about its case. Such questions will be for the purpose of clarifying the issues that the tribunal has to decide.

Do's and Don'ts in the drafting of requests

Do:

- Decide what additional information to seek by reference to what is reasonably necessary to understand the case. Remember that the purpose of a request is to clarify the issues that are in dispute and not to try and force the other party to disclose how it is going to prove a certain aspect of its case.
- Make reference to the overriding objective in making the application.
- Ensure that any request is proportionate and relates to issues that are central to the dispute.
- Keep in mind the nature of the issues the tribunal will have to decide and phrase the requests with these in mind.
- Make the request as early as possible and explain any delay in making the application.
- Ask for the particulars to be provided voluntarily first and copy the other side into any application made to the tribunal, giving as much notice as possible (at least ten days where a party wishes to raise something at a hearing set down by the tribunal).

Don't:

- Ask questions about what legal arguments the other side will adduce.
- Phrase the request unnecessarily officiously or aggressively.
- Make oppressive requests – in particular requests which relate to evidence as opposed to clarification of the case.

Tactics

- An effective request for additional information can expose weaknesses in the other side's case and encourage them to settle.
- An effective request helps a party prepare their evidence, restricts the issues which are to be determined at the final Hearing and thus can save considerable expense.
- Remember, it is only one of a number of tools at your disposal.
- If an order is made, include the request for particulars and any answers in the bundle for the full Hearing, and do not be afraid to refer the tribunal to it where appropriate. The wing members are unlikely to have copies of their own and the Employment Judge may have lost sight of it amongst the mass of papers in the file.

Chapter 11

Disclosure and Inspection

Introduction

[11.1] Disclosure is the process by which parties notify each other of evidence or documents which exist or have existed that are relevant to the claim. Inspection (which is often included within the term 'disclosure') refers the parties allowing each other to view and/or be given copies of those documents. In practical terms, therefore, the process of disclosure and inspection enables each party to have sight of relevant documentation in the other's possession.

Parties should give thought to disclosure as early as possible in proceedings. Given that it will often be the employer who has the majority of relevant documentation, it is particularly important that the respondent properly assembles and organises that documentation at an early stage. Very often, it is not until disclosure takes place that a party is able to properly prepare its case and gain a realistic view as to the prospects of success.

Parties should first attempt to agree matters of disclosure voluntarily and, only if they are unable to reach an agreement, seek an order from the tribunal. In seeking to agree disclosure parties should bear in mind that, whilst there is no automatic duty of disclosure, a Tribunal is unlikely to be impressed by an unreasonable failure to disclose material which is obviously relevant to issues which are central to the claim.

[11.2] Usually, disclosure relates to the claimant's personnel file and contemporaneous documents, such as notes of disciplinary hearings, memorandums between relevant managers and correspondence. Such documents often have greater evidential value than witness statements and oral evidence produced at the hearing. This is because they:
- are created nearer the time of the relevant events; and
- are not written directly for the purpose of a tribunal hearing.

Traditionally disclosure is thought of as a process that benefits the recipient of the information rather than the party disclosing it. The benefits can, however, run both ways. Disclosure of documentation forces the parties, at an early stage, to focus on the merits of their case, and to take a pragmatic view as to the likely outcome and/or cost of proceeding with the dispute. In addition, it ensures that preparation for the final hearing is done in good time, facilitating compliance with directions. Although the respondent may hold most of the documents, it should never shrink from seeking disclosure of relevant papers in the claimant's possession.

The extent of the duty of disclosure

[11.3] There is no automatic duty of disclosure (save insofar as is implied by the overriding objective) by the parties in tribunal proceedings. In the majority of cases disclosure takes place either by agreement between the parties or as a consequence of an order by the tribunal. Cases where there is no disclosure, whether formal or informal, are few and far between. Disclosure usually takes one of three forms:

(a) Disclosure by agreement between the parties.
(b) Disclosure pursuant to an order from the tribunal.
(c) Disclosure as a consequence of an order requiring the parties to prepare an agreed bundle.

Even in (a), the parties often agree the extent of disclosure with reference to the powers of the tribunal (see **11.9**).

[11.4] Disclosure is one of the matters that the tribunal usually has regard to at the case management discussion (see **chapter 12**), where an order for disclosure is frequently included amongst other directions, with a view to ensuring that the case is ready for full hearing. A fair hearing usually cannot take place in circumstances where important and relevant documents are either not before the tribunal or are only produced at the last moment, thereby depriving the other side of producing evidence in rebuttal. Tribunals strive to avoid this scenario, where the full hearing has to be postponed in order for full disclosure to take place, by giving a clear order early on in proceedings. Where orders for disclosure have been made and not complied with, or a party has failed to serve on the other side copies of documents which are clearly likely to be in dispute the party in default faces a real risk of having to pay the wasted costs arising from his unreasonable behaviour (see **chapter 22 – costs**).

[11.5] The duty of disclosure is one which continues throughout the course of the proceedings. Hence, even after a party has complied with an order for disclosure, if it subsequently discovers further relevant documents, it would expect to disclose them to the other party. In *Scott v IRC* [2004] EWCA Civ 400, [2004] ICR 1410, the respondent employer was criticised for not disclosing an amended retirement policy which was made after the employee was dismissed but before the tribunal Hearing took place because it had a material impact on the level of compensation which should have been awarded.

Which documents need to be disclosed

[11.6] For the purposes of disclosure, 'document' means anything in which information is recorded and a copy of a document is anything onto which information contained or recorded in the document has been copied by whatever means, whether directly or indirectly (*Civil Procedure Rules* (*CPR*), *rule 31.4*). This therefore includes electronic communications (such as email).

It also includes copies of documents that contain modifications, obliterations or other markings or features on which a party intends to rely or which adversely affects his own case or another party's case or supports another party's case. So, for example annotated minutes of meetings would, if the annotations were relevant, be disclosable as would previous versions of a recruitment policy document if those previous versions when read alongside the current document be relevant.

[11.7] Documents which are held or stored electronically are specifically included, hence parties should be aware that they may have to disclose emails and other electronic communications, word processed documents and databases (*CPR, Practice Direction 31A, paragraph 2A*).

[11.8] In a typical unfair dismissal or discrimination case it is common to see disclosure (by one or of the means outlined above) of the following documents:

- The claimant's letter of appointment.
- The claimant's contract of employment, including any amendments.

- The respondent's internal procedures and guides relevant to the issues in dispute: for example, disciplinary codes, sickness absence procedures, redundancy procedures (including selection criteria), and equal opportunities policy.
- An employee's handbook (if one exists).
- Relevant correspondence, internal memorandums and emails between:
  (a) the respondent and the claimant; and
  (b) management within the respondent organisation.
- Attendance notes of all relevant meetings involving the claimant.
- Minutes of all relevant meetings, including disciplinary and appeal hearings.

This list is not intended to be exhaustive. What is relevant will depend upon the circumstances of each case.

[11.9] Where the parties voluntarily chose to make disclosure they must not be unfairly selective in choosing which documents it provides to the other side. In *Bird's Eye Walls Ltd v Harrison* [1985] ICR 278 it was said that once a party had disclosed certain documents to the other side it becomes his duty not to withhold any further documents in his possession or control "if the effect of withholding them might be to convey to his opponent or to the tribunal a false or misleading impression as to the true nature, purport or effect of any disclosed document".

The tribunal's power to order disclosure

[11.10] As part of his general case management powers an Employment Judge may at any time, either on the application of a party, or on his own initiative, make an order 'requiring any person in Great Britain to disclose documents or information to a party or to allow a party to inspect such material as might be ordered by a county court' (*rule 10(2)(d)*). The tribunal's powers in relation to disclosure and inspection are identical to those of the county courts under the *CPR*. The relevant rules are contained within *Part 31* of the *CPR* and *Practice Directions 31A* and *31B*. It is useful therefore to consider the tribunal's likely approach in the context of the county court's powers to order disclosure and the guidance which can be found in post CPR case law.

[11.11] The county courts, in applying *Part 31* of the *CPR*, distinguish between two types of disclosure: 'standard disclosure' and 'specific disclosure'.

Standard disclosure

[11.12] In proceedings before both an employment tribunal and a county court, disclosure is limited to 'standard disclosure' unless otherwise ordered. Standard disclosure refers to general disclosure of documentation relevant to the issues in dispute. The tribunal may give a direction for standard disclosure (whether of its own motion or in response to an application) at a case management discussion or at any other stage of the proceedings. Alternatively, the tribunal may simply order 'standard disclosure by list' (see **11.15**). An application for standard disclosure, provided it is made in reasonable time, is likely to be successful since it entitles a party to documentation which, upon an application of the overriding objective, is necessary to do justice between the parties (see **11.8**).

The meaning of standard disclosure

[11.13] Standard disclosure requires a party to disclose documents :

- on which a party relies;
- which adversely affect his own or another party's case or which support another party's case; and
- which he is required to disclose by a relevant practice direction (*CPR, rule 31.6*).

[11.14] Parties are required to carry out a reasonable search for such documents (*CPR, rule 31.7(1)*). The duty to carry out a 'reasonable search' for documents is considered in the context of:

- the number of documents involved;
- the nature and complexity of the proceedings;
- the ease and expense of retrieval of any particular document; and
- the significance of any document which is likely to be located during the search.

Parties should not adopt a biased or partisan view in deciding whether a document supports the other side's case, but consider the issue from the perspective of an objective bystander. Non-disclosure of documents which arguably assist the other side can have serious consequences, ranging from an order for costs against the offending party to more serious consequences if there is evidence of a deliberate attempt to conceal documents of this nature.

[11.15] In practice, the documents 'upon which a party intends to rely' includes not simply documents that assist that party, but also relevant background documents which are necessary in order to give the tribunal a complete factual picture of the case. It is best to avoid the situation where a case proceeds to a final Hearing and a party is unable to provide the tribunal with any document which the latter considers to be relevant: this causes delay and further expense if the tribunal decide to adjourn the case. Even if the tribunal decides to proceed with the hearing they are unlikely to be impressed with the failure to produce a document which they regard as material.

Specific disclosure

[11.16] Specific disclosure, as the name suggests, relates to a particular document or category of documents. Once again, such orders are usually made prior to the full Hearing (at a case management discussion or otherwise), but there is nothing to prevent a tribunal making them at a full Hearing. Sometimes an application for specific disclosure follows a failure to disclose a document through standard disclosure.

Disputes about disclosure

[11.17] Where the parties cannot agree, it is possible to make an application to the tribunal either for standard or specific disclosure of a specific document or a class of documents. A party can take advantage of a case management discussion (see **chapter 13**) to make this application, or make it in writing to the tribunal (see **chapter 9 – communicating with the tribunal** at **9.17**).

[11.18] In determining such an application, , the tribunal will apply the same test as would a county court, namely the overriding objective as set out in *Part 1* of the *CPR*. Fortunately this is worded in a very similar fashion to the overriding objective applicable to tribunals, but with some notable differences. First, in the area of proportionality, a court, and hence a tribunal, should exercise its power in a manner which is not merely proportionate to the complexity of the issues (as under the tribunal rules), but also to the amount of money involved, the importance of the case and the financial position of the parties. Secondly, both courts and tribunals are required to ensure that cases are dealt with 'expeditiously and fairly'.

Applying the overriding objective in deciding disputes over disclosure

[11.19] In deciding in accordance with the overriding objective whether an order for disclosure is necessary in order to deal with the case justly, a tribunal is likely to ask all or some of the following questions:

- What degree of relevance (or potential relevance) and probative value do the documents sought have in relation to the issues raised in the case?
- Is the extent and volume of the disclosure sought out of proportion to its importance (or potential importance) to the issue/s in question?
- Is the extent and volume of the disclosure sought out of proportion to the importance of the case taken as a whole?
- Is the cost of complying with the requested of disclosure disproportionate to the potential value of the claim?
- To what extent would making an order for disclosure delay the determination of the proceedings or render them longer than justice demands?
- Is the application for disclosure premature?
- Has the other side been notified of the application and, if so, what, if any, are its reasons for refusing to disclose the documents requested (NB a party who is legally represented is, under *rule 11(4)*, obliged to send a copy of such an application to the other parties within prescribed time limits).

[11.20] If a tribunal decides that the document in question falls into one of the three categories covered by standard disclosure, then an application will be difficult to resist. As such a party who unsuccessfully and unreasonably refuses to disclose a document runs the risk of having to pay the costs of the application. However, the tribunal will not necessarily order a party to disclose documents where, at the date of the application, it is unclear whether they will be relevant and their disclosure necessary. The correct approach, as advocated by the EAT in *South Tyneside Metropolitan Borough Council v Anderson* [2005] All ER (D) 91 (Jun), is for the tribunal to order the disclosure of such documents as appear relevant at that stage and, in relation to other material, to consider if necessary an application for specific disclosure later on (when their potential relevance has been clarified).

Examples of disputes about disclosure

[11.21] Many disputes concerning disclosure relate to allegations of unfair treatment in comparison to other employees. For example in discrimination and equal pay cases, a comparison with other employees is commonly the means of proving less favourable treatment. These cases can therefore give rise to applications for disclosure of relevant documents which shed light as to the respective treatment of the claimant and the comparator. Because of the critical importance of the relative treatment of the claimant and comparator in these cases, tribunals are likely to be more sympathetic to reasonable applications for disclosure (for the special considerations which apply to discrimination cases see *Leverton v Clwyd County Council* [1989] AC 706; *and West Midland Passenger Transport Executive v Singh* [1988] ICR 614).

There is no hard and fast rule as to when tribunals will order disclosure. Applications are inherently fact sensitive – hence the scarcity of case law which provides anything but the most general guidance. Individual tribunals will take different views as to the necessity of disclosure. The overriding objective should be used as an instrument both in making and defending applications. A useful tip is to ask whether the application relates to a specific allegation that the other party has already made, or whether it is simply what is known as a 'fishing expedition' – an attempt to trawl through the other side's documents in the hope of finding material which would justify making fresh allegations. Tribunals rarely accede to applications for disclosure where it is felt that the application amounts to a fishing expedition.

Example

An employee in a company with 40 employees is dismissed for gross misconduct, namely hitting another employee.

Scenario (a): She seeks disclosure of documents relating to all gross misconduct dismissals in the past ten years. This is likely to be refused as the dismissal of another person for a different reason in different circumstances is unlikely to be relevant to any issue the tribunal has to decide. In addition, the extent of the disclosure requested (ie all gross misconduct dismissals in the past ten years) may be considered excessive.

> *Scenario (b)*: She seeks disclosure of all documents relating to fights between employees. This, again, is likely to be refused, particularly if it does not relate to a specific allegation of disparate treatment.
>
> *Scenario (c)*: She alleges in the ET1 that, six months before her dismissal, a particular employee was not dismissed following a more serious incident of violence. Disclosure of relevant documents in relation to the other incident is likely to be ordered because she has made a clear allegation of disparate treatment, and is probably entitled to sight of the documents relevant to this allegation.

Failure to comply with an order for disclosure

[11.22] A party who fails without reasonable excuse to comply with an order for the discovery, recovery or inspection of documents is guilty of an offence and liable on conviction to a fine (*Employment Tribunals Act 1996, section 7(4)*). In practice this is unlikely to occur, therefore a more useful option for the party seeking disclosure is to make an application to the tribunal to have the defaulting party's claim or response stuck out. The correct course in these circumstances, is for the party in whose favour the order was made, to make an application under rule 13(1) for the other party to show cause why the ET1 or ET3 should not be struck out or alternatively to pay the costs arising from the failure to comply.

Representations as to why the party should be struck out should be made with the application. The tribunal will apply the overriding objective (see **chapter 8 – fairness: the overriding objective**) in deciding whether the whole or some of a claim/defence should be struck out.

An alternative option open to the tribunal is to draw an adverse inference from the non-disclosure of the document. In any event, whatever the outcome of any interim applications, any unreasonable failure to disclose should be drawn to the attention of the tribunal conducting the full Hearing wherever appropriate.

Disclosure against third parties

[11.23] The power of the tribunal, under rule 10(2)(d), to order a third party to disclose documents or information (and the attendance of that party), is dealt with in **chapter 14 – witness orders and orders for the production of documents**.

Method of disclosure

[11.24] Disclosure can take place 'by list'. This means that a party is given a list of documents upon which the other intends to rely and it can then request copies of specific documents (known as 'inspection'). Alternatively, all the documents can be physically supplied. The question of which method is more suitable is one for the parties to agree or the tribunal to direct. Often, the claimant will not have seen much of the documentation and it is frequently in their interests to request copies of everything not in their possession. For an employer, its list for disclosure frequently takes similar form to the index for the bundle at the full Hearing; another reason why compiling an organised list at this stage can be both productive and time saving.

Documents protected from disclosure

[11.25] There are certain categories of document that the parties are not obliged to disclose and which they are entitled to keep confidential. Included in this are documents in the following categories.

Legal professional privilege

[11.26] The law recognises that, as a matter of public policy, parties should be free to seek and receive legal advice without having the content of that advice revealed to the other side. This is sometimes referred to as 'legal advice privilege'. The protection extends to any communication made by or to a solicitor, barrister or similarly qualified legal executive in their professional capacity where the dominant purpose was the giving or obtaining of legal advice or assistance (*O'Shea v Wood* [1891] P 286, CA and *Kennedy v Lyell* (1883) 23 Ch D 387 at 404, CA). In *Three Rivers District Council v Bank of England* [2004] UKHL 48; [2005] 1 AC 610 the House of Lords confirmed this protection covered communications between a lawyer and his client in respect of matters not simply confined to informing the client of the law but also offering advice as to what should prudently and sensibly be done in the relevant legal context.

[11.27] Note, however, that the mere fact that, in the course of extensive communications between solicitors and clients, there were some letters which were written for the dominant purpose of seeking legal advice (and hence privileged), this did not itself confer privilege on the entire correspondence. Communications from unqualified lawyers are not privileged. Human resource managers should, therefore, be cautious when giving written advice to a manager within the same organisation as this document would be unlikely to be covered by legal advice privilege, nor would written advice given by employment advisors who are not qualified lawyers (*New Victoria Hospital v Ryan* [1993] ICR 201). By contrast, legal advice from a qualified in-house lawyer would be covered (*Alfred Crompton Amusement Machines Ltd v Customs and Excise Commissioners* [1974] 2 AC 405). However, where proceedings are contemplated or pending, communications with unqualified advisors whose dominant purpose is seeking advice in relation to the litigation are likely to be privileged. This is often referred to as 'litigation privilege' as opposed to 'legal advice privilege'.

The difference, therefore, between 'litigation privilege' and 'legal advice privilege' is that the former is capable of extending beyond advice given by qualified lawyers, and will embrace communications with third parties and documents prepared by third parties, when they are made for the purposes of legal proceedings.

Communications (not limited to communications with lawyers) for the purpose of obtaining advice or evidence in contemplated or pending legal proceedings

[11.28] In order to be covered by litigation privilege the dominant purpose for which the document was created must have been for the purpose of obtaining advice or evidence in contemplated or pending legal proceedings. In addition, the litigation must be reasonably in prospect at the time the document was created – in other words a party cannot rely on a fanciful risk of future litigation. It is important to emphasise that for litigation privilege to arise both these criteria need to be met: that is to say that not only does litigation need to be in contemplation, but the dominant purpose of correspondence needs to relate to the litigation (and not for example to an internal grievance etc).

An example of 'litigation privilege' is provided by *Grazebrook v Wallens* [1973] IRLR 139 in which the National Industrial Relations Court held it would extend to agents other than lawyers who were giving advice with an actual view to the litigation in hand. The correctness of this decision was confirmed by Mr Justice Elias in *Mrs Howes v Hinckley & Bosworth Borough Council* UKEAT/0213/08

Further examples of where such privilege might apply are:

- The claimant writes to a former colleague in the respondent company asking them to be a witness in the case.
- The respondent asks its own doctor to report on an assertion made by the claimant in the ET1 that they had a severe mental illness which rendered them disabled within the meaning of the *Disability Discrimination Act 1995*. Note, however, that if there was a report by the doctor on this issue before tribunal proceedings were contemplated, it would not be protected by privilege.

Parties should not forget that communications with experts, whether doctors or others, *will* be privileged if made primarily for the purpose of obtaining advice or evidence in *contemplated or pending* legal proceedings.

Medical reports and other confidential documents

[11.29] The fact that a document is 'confidential' (whether medical or otherwise) is *not*, in itself, a bar to its disclosure in tribunal proceedings (*Science Research Council v Nasse* [1980] AC 1028). There is no presumption against the disclosure of confidential documents. Where an objection is taken by a party to disclosure of a confidential document, the court will apply the overriding objective in deciding whether to order disclosure. For this reason, parties both making and defending applications for disclosure should have regard to whether such disclosure is necessary to do justice between parties in the case. The fact that the information is sensitive or embarrassing is unlikely, of itself, to prevent disclosure although where sensitive material is involved the tribunal ought to be concerned to ensure, before making any order, that the information sought cannot be obtained elsewhere and the disclosure only goes as far as is necessary to determine the issues arising in the claim.

So, for example, where there is an issue in relation to whether a claimant is disabled, a tribunal is unlikely to order disclosure of their entire medical records, merely records relevant to the issue of their disability. Similarly, the tribunal may order that the names of certain individuals be deleted to protect confidentiality (see *Oxford v Department of Health and Social Security* [1977] ICR 884). A good example of a case where the order of disclosure was limited to anonymised statements to protect the confidentiality of witnesses is the decision in *Asda Stores Ltd v Thompson* [2002] IRLR 245 (and [2004] IRLR 598). In that case the employer was allowed to protect the identity of its employees who had been assured that the information they provided during an investigation into the use of illegal drugs would remain confidential.

ACAS officers

[11.30] Communications with ACAS officers are privileged, unless expressly waived by the party involved (*Employment Tribunals Act 1996, section 18(7)*).

Without prejudice communications

[11.31] The phrase 'without prejudice' is often used to describe negotiations by the parties made with a view to settling or compromising a dispute. The courts have held that it is in the public interest that such communications, whether oral or written, are not disclosed save with the consent of both parties (*Independent Research Services Ltd v Catterall* [1993] ICR 1 and *Cutts v Head* [1984] Ch 290). The issue in respect of privilege is whether the communication contains genuine negotiations which constitute an attempt to settle a dispute. The fact that a document is, or is not, headed 'without prejudice' is not determinate of this issue – the tribunal will look beyond any 'label' the parties have attached to the document and consider the substance of the communication itself (*South Shropshire District Council v Amos* [1986] 1 WLR 1271). That said, it is sensible for a party, when conducting such negotiations, to clearly mark any written document 'without prejudice'.

[11.32] The EAT's judgment in *BNP Paribas v Mezzotero* [2004] IRLR 508 demonstrates a fairly permissive approach to employees who wish to rely on discussions which purportedly took place on a without prejudice basis. In that case, which involved allegations of sex discrimination, the employee wished to rely on a 'without prejudice' meeting which occurred after her return to work, where the employer offered her a redundancy package. At the meeting the employer made it clear that this offer was separate to the grievance that she had raised concerning discrimination. The EAT, allowing her to rely on this evidence, held that:

(i) given their unequal relationship it was unrealistic to hold that there had been an express agreement that the meeting would be 'without prejudice';
(ii) her internal grievance did not raise a complaint concerning termination of her employment; and
(iii) the meeting was not a genuine attempt to settle the dispute, since it related to the termination of her employment and not the matters raised in her grievance.

Public interest immunity

[11.33] This usually relates to documents in the possession of public bodies where disclosure may be withheld on the basis that it is harmful to the public interest. If satisfied that the document would under ordinary principles be disclosable the tribunal is required to balance the public interest in concealment against the public interest which lies in the effective administration of justice. 'Public interest', in the former sense, includes the extent to which non-disclosure is necessary for the proper functioning of the public service in question (see *Evans v Chief Constable of Surrey Constabulary* [1989] 2 All ER 594; *Barrett v Ministry of Defence* (1989) The Independent, 23 January; *R v Bromell* [1993] QB 278). Public interest, in the latter sense, includes issues such as the importance of the disclosure in the case and the extent to which it is necessary for the fair disposal of the case.

[11.34] Immunity may be sought in respect of an entire class of document ('class claim') or merely in respect of the contents of a particular document ('contents claim'). With a class claim, it is irrelevant whether the contents of particular documents would be harmful to the public interest – "the point being that it is the maintenance of the immunity of the class from disclosure in litigation that is important" (per Lord Wilberforce in *Burmah Oil Co Ltd v Bank of England* [1980] AC 1090). In practice the types of situation in which a class claim can now be maintained is limited following successive judicial decisions favouring greater scrutiny of assertions of immunity. The fact that a class of documents is held to be for disclosure does not prevent a contents claim being made in respect of a particular document within it.

[11.35] In both class and contents claims, tribunals have been instructed by the Employment Appeal Tribunal to exercise extreme care in the making of any order (*Halford v Sharples* [1992] 1 WLR 736). In respect of the class claims, the power to order disclosure should not be exercised without giving the party against whom it is made the opportunity to appeal (*Halford*).

National security

[11.36] With a limited number of tribunal claims (*Employment Rights Act 1996, s 202(2)*), disclosure cannot take place if a minister of the Crown is of the opinion that it would be contrary to national security. The tribunal has no power, in those circumstances, to enquire further into the reasons for the minister's opinion.

[11.37] Note also, that in cases where national security considerations arise, *rule 54* provides that the procedures in *Schedule 1* to the *2004 Regulations* (referred to in this book as the *2004 Rules*) may be modified by *Schedule 2*.

Waiver

[11.38] A party can waive the privilege attaching to a document and disclose it. Sometimes this will be the right course to adopt. For example, where a doctor has, in contemplation of tribunal proceedings, given clear and unequivocal advice that a person is or is not disabled, it might be best to disclose that advice if it is beneficial to the party involved. Note, however, that parties cannot 'cherry pick' what they disclose – so, if for example, a party discloses a medical report he is then obliged to disclose all medical reports (however unfavourable) written by that same medical expert.

The mere reference to a document in a witness statement does not waive privilege in that document: there must at least be reference to the contents and reliance (see *Bourns Inc v Raychem Corporation* [1999] FSR 641)

Once privilege on a document has been waived, however, it cannot be retracted. If a document is included in a list of disclosable documents by accident, immediate steps should be taken by the party involved to correct the error by informing the other side of the mistake. Where a document is physically disclosed, even if in error, any attempt to retract it will generally be unsuccessful. Note, however, that without prejudice correspondence (see **11.21**) cannot be disclosed without the consent of both parties.

Disclosure: step by step

[11.39]

- Remember, the earlier you address issues of disclosure the better. You should certainly address your mind to it soon after service of the ET1 or ET3.
- Make a list of all relevant documents in your possession. Whilst not compulsory, it is probably best to apply the criteria for standard disclosure contained in the *CPR* since, if a dispute occurs, the tribunal will be bound by these rules in deciding whether to make an order.
- Decide which, if any, of those documents are privileged and should not be disclosed. Do not include them in the list of disclosed documents.
- Structure the list as you would for a tribunal bundle – there is no need, unless so ordered by the tribunal, for parties to file a formal disclosure statement, as would be required by *rule 31.10* of the *CPR*.
- Make a list of all the documents you require from the other side (many of which can be identified from the ET1 or ET3 or pre-action correspondence).
- Write to the other side to agree when disclosure will take place and the method of disclosure – a normal agreement would be for standard disclosure (whether by list or supply of all documents) within, say, 14 days.
- Upon receiving disclosure, review whether you think it is complete. If it is missing documents (or if a review of the disclosed documents reveals a need for further material), write to the other side requesting them within a reasonable period.
- If the request is not complied with, consider applying for an order under *rule 10(2)(c)* or *(d)*. Set out clearly which issue/s the documents are relevant to and the attempts which have been made to secure voluntary disclosure. This can be done in writing, or alternatively you can request an oral hearing.

Tactics

- Requesting relevant and proportionate disclosure from the other side can exert pressure on them and expose weaknesses in its case.
- If documents which ordinarily one would expect an employer to have completed or retained copies of are not disclosed, don't hesitate to request an explanation for the employer's inability and/or refusal to produce them.
- If an application for disclosure is unsuccessful, make a full note of it, and bring it to the tribunal's attention at a later stage if appropriate: eg where the requested documents are subsequently produced for the first time at the hearing.
- If you accidentally fail to disclose a document, immediately bring it to the other side's attention, with an explanation for the error.
- If a party who has denied the existence of documents subsequently produces copies of the same, do refer the tribunal to previous attempts made to obtain copies of these documents.
- If you accidentally disclose a privileged document (whether by list or otherwise), immediately inform the other side that the disclosure was accidental, the reason why the document is privileged and request its return.

Chapter 12

Case management discussions and orders

Introduction

[12.1] Chapter 9 – communicating with the tribunal described the wide ranging case management powers of the tribunal. One of the central powers is that contained in rule 10(1) of the *Employment Tribunals (Constitution and Rules of Procedure) Regulations 2004* which states that:

> 'Subject to the following rules, the Employment Judge may at any time either on the application of a party or on his own initiative make an order in relation to any matter which appears to him to be appropriate ... Subject to the following rules, orders may be issued as a result of an Employment Judge considering the papers before him in the absence of the parties, or at a hearing ...'

As can be seen *rule 10(1)* provides Employment Judges with a general power to give orders to the parties with a view to ensuring the smooth, fair and efficient conduct of the case. This power, which is intentionally broad, must be exercised in accordance with the overriding objective (see **chapter 8 – fairness: the overriding objective**).

[12.2] Orders can be made by an Employment Judge orally, at a hearing, or on the papers, and either of his own volition or in response to an application from one of other of the parties. 'At any time' means exactly what it says: namely from the lodging of the application to the conclusion of proceedings. In practice tribunals will often arrange an interim hearing in order to deal with matters of procedure and case management: these hearings are referred to as case management discussions or sometimes abbreviated to 'CMDs'.

What are orders?

[12.3] *Rule 10(2)* provides a non-exhaustive list of examples of orders which can be made (see also **9.10**). These include orders:

- as to the manner in which proceedings are to be conducted (including time limits for compliance);
- requiring a party to provide additional information or written answers put by the tribunal;
- requiring a party or non-party to disclose documents or information or attend a hearing;
- subject to specific rules, extending any time limits.

Case management discussions (CMD)

[12.4] Case management discussions are interim hearings, conducted by an Employment Judges sitting alone, and are held in private (*rule 17(1)*). At a case management discussion the Employment Judge may deal with matters of procedure and the management of the proceedings and for that purpose may make the kinds of orders listed in *rule 10(2)* (see **12.3**). The hearings ordinarily take place fairly soon after a claim and response have been filed, and deal with matters of procedure and case management (see **12.6**). The Employment Judge will aim to set a realistic timetable for the future conduct of the case. An Employment Judge will *not*, however, rule on the merits of any aspect of a complaint at these hearings. Employment Judges are specifically prohibited from determining 'a person's civil rights or obligations' at a case management discussion and therefore *cannot* make orders or judgments as to, for example, a party's entitlement to bring or contest the particular proceedings or striking out any part of the claim or response. Such orders and judgments can only be made at a Pre-Hearing Review (see **chapter 13 – pre-emptive strikes: pre-hearing reviews**) or at the final Hearing.

[12.5] The orders discussed in this chapter and throughout the book can, and frequently are, made upon the written application by the parties without the need for a hearing. Indeed it is important to remember that orders can be made by the tribunal at any time and without prior notice to the parties (although the parties are then given an opportunity to make representations on the orders made).

Case management discussions at the instigation of the Employment Judge

[12.6] After submission of the ET1 and ET3, an Employment Judge will invariably review the case; not least to ensure that they are on the appropriate forms and contain the requisite information. In lengthy or potentially complex cases, or in cases where the issues are not entirely clear he will usually decide that a case management discussion is necessary in order to ensure that the case is prepared for full hearing. The importance of holding case management discussions has been emphasised by the higher courts, particularly in cases where the disputed facts and/or the law is not straightforward (see, for example, *Goodwin v Patent Office* [1999] IRLR 4).

[12.7] Whilst there is no fixed period of notice that needs to be given, the parties must be given reasonable notice of any case management discussion hearing. The parties will be informed of the date of the case management discussion by letter, which will often include similar terms to the following:

> 'Employment Judge Smith considers that a Case Management Discussion is desirable in this case. The hearing will take place at [...] on [...] before a chairman sitting alone to:
> (a) clarify the issues in the case and give any necessary orders for additional information (see **chapter 10 – post claim requests for additional information**);
> (b) consider what, if any, orders are required in relation to disclosure of documents (see **chapter 11 – disclosure**) and the attendance of witnesses (see **chapter 14 – witness orders and orders for the production of documents**);
> (c) arrange, if possible, for agreement as to documents;
> (d) consider how long the case is likely to last and give directions as to the date and length of the hearing; and
> (e) give any other orders which may be necessary for the fair and expeditious disposal of the case.'

The letter usually states that the parties should attend in person or through a representative and that, if there is no attendance, directions may be given in their absence. Instead of listing the hearing for the parties to attend in person, the tribunal may direct that the hearing will be conducted on the telephone. Where the hearing is to be held via telephone the parties will be notified as to the arrangements.

In addition to the matters stated in the letter, parties should expect an Employment Judge to give orders directing the preparation of a joint bundle and possibly also a chronology (see **chapter 19 – preparing for the full hearing**). This task is commonly entrusted to the Respondent due to the perception that ordinarily the employer has greater resources at his disposal.

Case management discussions at the instigation of one or both of the parties

[12.8] There is nothing to prevent either party requesting a case management discussion themselves under *rule 11*. It is particularly sensible to do so where you consider that the other party is likely to present their case at full hearing in an unpredictable manner, whether by raising new issues or calling unexpected evidence.

Generally, case management discussions are listed at the request of the parties (or party) in four instances:

- Where an application has been made on paper by one or both of the parties which (in the view of the Employment Judge) merits a hearing (note that an Employment Judge might decide to deal with the application on the papers, see **9.18**).
- Where one or both of the parties expressly requests a case management discussion. This request might be made in the ET1 or ET3 itself or may be made in correspondence with the tribunal at a later date.
- Where a hearing is necessary for the purpose of modifying earlier orders which have not been complied with. Where a sanction is being sought against the party in default the proper course is to make an application for a pre-hearing review, where the Employment Judge can strike out all or part of the claim, and/or award costs. As indicated above, at a case management discussion an Employment Judge cannot make any decisions concerning the entitlement of a party to bring a case – he is therefore unable, for example, to strike out a case at a case management discussion.
- Where a hearing is necessary for the purpose of making an order as to costs or preparation time which has been occasioned by non-compliance with previous orders.

You should make use of a case management discussion to ensure that all outstanding pre-full Hearing issues are dealt with, having regard to the checklist of issues described above.

Preparing for a case management discussion

[12.9] In preparing for a case management discussion hearing each party should:

- define the issues as they see them which arise in the case – this can be usefully set out in a case summary which parties should try and agree and forward to the Employment Judge prior to the hearing;
- decide what additional information (as opposed to evidence) is needed from the other side (see **chapter 10**);
- consider what orders, if any, should be obtained in relation to disclosure (see **chapter 11**);
- consider if there are any other orders needed – for example, consolidation with another claim/s which involve similar issues of fact or law, or issues relating to reporting restrictions etc;
- decide how many witnesses they intend to call;
- have in mind a time estimate for the full Hearing;
- make a note of dates to avoid for a full Hearing (it is crucial to obtain accurate information prior to the hearing as to the dates upon which witnesses/representatives cannot attend. An application for a postponement at a later date may well be refused if the party was given a full opportunity to provide dates to avoid).

[12.10] A case management discussion should not be confrontational. Employment Judges will expect the parties to adopt a reasonable attitude and to have had at least a brief discussion as to what can properly be agreed. Such agreement may be:

- prior to the day of the hearing, by mail, fax, email or telephone; and/or
- immediately prior to the hearing, at the tribunal itself.

Where the dispute is complex, consider whether the tribunal would be assisted by the preparation of a case summary, chronology and/or short skeleton argument. Where possible the case summary and/or chronology should be agreed between the parties. This can assist in marshalling the arguments prior to the making of an application. Make sure that the skeleton argument is just that – ie skeletal (see **chapter 17**). Ensure that both documents are provided to the other party prior to the hearing.

Using the case management discussions to make applications

[12.11] One advantage of a case management discussion, particularly one instigated by the tribunal, is that it can (and should) be used by the parties to make applications for orders in areas where they cannot agree, without necessarily giving advance written notice to the tribunal of the fact that an application will be made. Having said this, however, wherever possible it is undoubtedly good practice to notify the tribunal and the other side (if possible ten days before the hearing) of any specific application that may be made – this is particularly appropriate where a party is going to seek an unusual order or an order they know is likely to be contested. Employment Judges are unlikely to look kindly at behaviour which amounts to an unreasonable attempt to 'ambush' the opposing party at the case management discussion. In relation to orders which are commonly given at case management discussions Employment Judges will usually allow an application to be made on the day (under *rule 11(1)*) for an order for:

- additional information (see **chapter 10**);
- disclosure (see **chapter 11**);
- witness orders (see **chapter 14**).

The structure of the hearing and the order

[12.12] *Rule 14(2)* specifically requires tribunals to avoid, as far as possible, formality in its proceedings. Whilst each Employment Judge will conduct the hearing in his own way, it .is common however for an Employment Judge to start by asking which, if any, matters are agreed. He will then form a view on whether the directions which have been agreed are appropriate from the tribunal's perspective, in accordance with the tribunal's overriding responsibility for case management.

With areas of dispute, the Employment Judge will usually hear first from the party who is seeking a particular order or direction before hearing the response. It is therefore important for parties to have prepared their reasons for requesting or denying the appropriateness of an order.

When seeking and defending such applications, parties will have to persuade the tribunal according to the criteria in **chapter 8 – fairness: the overriding objective,** and any relevant case law. Remember that the powers in question are intended to be operated flexibly by tribunals according to the specific factual circumstances before them.

The order

[12.13] The Employment Judge will usually make his order orally on the day of the hearing, although there may be a short break after completion of the submissions before it is delivered. The order will also be written down and sent to the parties as soon as reasonably practicable. Whilst it is possible to appeal an interim decision, in practice this is likely to be very difficult (see **chapter 26 – steps after the decision II: appeals**).

Varying or revoking orders

[12.14] If a party is unhappy that an order has been made (or made in particular terms) they may apply to the tribunal under *rule 11* to have it varied or revoked. The application should be made in writing (see **chapter 9**). Generally speaking, such applications will only be successful where the party has not had a full opportunity to present their case (ie because the order was made following a written application) or if there has been a change of circumstances since the direction was made (ie due to unforeseen circumstances witness availability has changed). It is possible to appeal to the Employment Appeal Tribunal against an order made by an Employment Judge, but this will only be successful if it can be demonstrated that the Employment Judge acted irrationally (ie reached a decision that no reasonable chairman could have reached), in a manner that was plainly contrary to the overriding objective, failed to take into account a relevant factor or took into account an irrelevant factor. In practice, this is very difficult to show, since the reasons accompanying any order are only required to be brief.

Enforcing orders

[12.15] What happens if a party does not comply with directions or orders given by the tribunal? *Rule 13 (1)* and *(2)* state that:

(1) If a party does not comply with an order made under these rules … or a practice direction, an Employment Judge or tribunal—
    (a) may make an order in respect of costs or preparation time under rules 38 to 46; or

(b) may (subject to paragraph (2) and rule 19) at a pre-hearing review or a Hearing make an order to strike out the whole or part of the claim or, as the case may be, the response and, where appropriate, order that a respondent be debarred from responding to the claim altogether.

(2) An order may also provide that unless the order is complied with, the claim or, as the case may be, the response shall be struck out on the date of non-compliance without further consideration of the proceedings or the need to give notice under rule 19 or hold a pre-hearing review or Hearing.

Pursuant to *rule 19*, unless the order not complied with provides otherwise, the power to strike out a claim or part of a claim will not be exercised unless the party against whom the order is to be made has been sent notice of the intended order and given an opportunity to make representations.

[12.16] Where a party has failed to comply with a material part of an order, the correct course is to write to the tribunal requesting that the other side show cause why the whole or the relevant part of the claim or response should not be struck out. The effect of a claim or response being struck out is that the application cannot either be brought or defended. Sometimes the default will only relate to part of the claim, for example the allegation of sex discrimination, in which case the application should be limited to striking out that part of the claim.

Parties should bear in mind that failure to comply with orders is common and should, where appropriate, adopt a reasonable and proportionate approach. Where the strict terms of an order have not been complied with (ie a particular step was taken the day after is should have been taken pursuant to the terms of the order), but little or no prejudice has been suffered, any application to the tribunal for a sanction is unlikely to be successful. In other cases, where the default continues, it is certainly good practice, except in urgent cases, to request an explanation from the party in default, putting them on notice that absent a response providing good reasons for the failure to comply with the order in question and confirmation that the order will be complied within a reasonable period, an application to strike out the relevant part of their claim or response, under *rule 13*, will be made.

[12.17] Whether to strike out the whole or part of the claim or response is a matter for the discretion of the tribunal. Barring a party from pursuing a good claim or legitimately defending a claim for a failure to comply with procedure is undoubtedly draconian. The tribunal will have regard to the overriding objective and the alternative penalties available to it, in determining the appropriate sanction for non-compliance. Often, where an application under *rule 13* is made, it has the effect of prompting the other party to comply with the original order. In those circumstances, the tribunal may exercise its discretion not to strike out, in accordance with the overriding objective, on the basis that the other side has not suffered any long-term unfairness as a consequence of the default which cannot be compensated by an appropriate order for costs. Another common step taken by tribunals is to make an 'unless order', namely that the claim will not be struck out if the party in default complies with the order within a further period of, say, 14 days.

Partial compliance

[12.18] There will be instances where a party has partially complied with an order. For example, the answer to a request for further information is incomplete, or disclosure is only partial. In those circumstances, it is still possible to take enforcement action under *rule 13*. The tribunal will, generally, be less willing to strike out if there has been at least some compliance; the extent of the tribunal's reluctance reflecting the extent of compliance and the reasons for any non-compliance.

In all cases where there has been non-compliance, it is sensible, at the very least, for the party who has obtained the direction to flag this up at the time, whether in correspondence or at a hearing. This can become extremely useful at a later stage, particularly where the other party has failed to comply with an order on more than one occasion.

Flagging up non-compliance

[12.19]

Example

The respondent writes to the claimant requesting details of the additional employees within the organisation whom the claimant claims were discriminated against by a particular manager. She refuses. A case management discussion has already been listed at the instigation of the Employment Judge in order to ensure the case is ready for full Hearing. At that hearing, the respondent applies for a direction that further particulars of the individuals in question be provided, in order to understand the case it has to meet. The tribunal makes that direction, whilst stressing that the claimant has the alternative, if she chooses, of simply withdrawing the allegation. The particulars are not provided, and the respondent seeks to enforce the order by making an application under rule 13 for a pre-hearing review where the tribunal can consider the application to strike out the part of her claim relating to discrimination against the other unnamed individuals.

The Employment Judge, exercising his discretion and applying the overriding objective, declines the application. He comments, however, that, if the claimant does not provide the necessary details, then less weight is likely to be attached to her evidence on that issue. The respondent expressly asks the tribunal to note that, if details are given on the day of the hearing, necessitating a postponement, it will make an application for costs. When the full Hearing takes place, the allegation is repeated, and details are provided. No reasonable explanation is provided for why these details were not provided earlier. The respondent reminds the tribunal of the attempts which were made to seek particulars of the individuals concerned. It asks that, in the circumstances, the tribunal attach no weight to the claimant's evidence that others in the organisation were discriminated against by the manager in question or alternatively the claimant to pay the cost of an adjournment to allow it an opportunity to obtain evidence in rebuttal. Many tribunals are likely to offer the claimant the option of pursuing this aspect of the claim whilst paying for the costs arising from the adjournment or proceeding with the hearing with little weight being attached to the details produced for the first time at the hearing.

Note: Employment Judges have a wide discretion as to whether strike out. The approach to non-compliance will vary considerably according to the facts concerned, the extent of the non-compliance and the individual Employment Judge hearing the case. Having said this, given the draconian nature of this sanction, it is safe to say that it is normally only applied in response to fairly significant and protracted material non-compliance.

Do's and Don'ts

Do:

- Remember that orders can be given orally or in writing by the tribunal.
- Make full use of a case management discussion to avoid the need for further interim hearings.
- Give consideration as to whether the time estimate for the case management discussion is sufficient.
- Make contact with the other party beforehand to establish areas of agreement so as to avoid, where possible, the need for further case management discussions. Keep copies of correspondence which can be produced at the case management discussion as evidence of your reasonableness or the other side's behaviour.
- Inform the tribunal of any proposed agreed timetable.
- Request a case management discussion where you consider it would be useful and necessary, giving reasons why.
- Consider what orders are appropriate immediately after submission of the claim and on receipt of response.
- Prepare thoroughly for case management discussions and behave reasonably to assist the tribunal where possible in managing the case.
- Give thought, before requesting a case management discussion, as to whether you need an oral hearing (whether in person or via telephone) or whether an application can be dealt with on the papers.
- Make a careful note of orders which are and are not made, and refer to them if they become relevant at final hearing, eg disclosure or further particulars.
- Make reasonable applications to enforce orders which have not been complied with and which cause you or could cause you real prejudice.

Don't:

- Adopt a confrontational approach unless necessary.
- Forget the basic purpose of orders – namely to promote a fair hearing.
- Apply for orders which are oppressive and go further than is necessary.
- Forget to ask, where appropriate, for costs arising from a party's failure to comply with orders.

Chapter 13

Pre-emptive strikes: pre-hearing reviews

Pre-hearing reviews (PHR)

[13.1] Obtaining an appropriate order (ie an order striking out the whole or part of a claim/response, or requiring payment of a deposit) at a pre-hearing review (PHR) is a useful method of deterring the progress, at an early stage, of factually very weak cases, cases which can be determined on a point of law, cases where there has been significant non-compliance with orders or cases where issues as to the tribunals' jurisdiction arise. The powers of a tribunal at a PHR are contained in *rule 18* of the *Employment Tribunals (Constitution and Rules of Procedure) Regulations 2004 (SI 2004/1861).*

Under the previous rules tribunals had separate powers to order a PHR or, alternatively, a preliminary hearing. The powers that a tribunal could exercise at these hearings differed. Under the new rules preliminary hearings are abolished and tribunals are given a global power to determine all relevant preliminary issues (both procedural and substantive) at a PHR.

Under the new rules a PHR can be sought (or ordered by the tribunal of its own volition) in relation to any issue of jurisdiction, or allegation contained in either the ET1 or the ET3, although in practice it is usually the former which is scrutinised in these circumstances. A party can also apply where there has been a sufficiently serious failure by the other party to comply with orders of the tribunal or practice direction (contrary to *rule 13*) for a PHR.

It is important for parties to recognise that a PHR is quite distinct from a case management discussion. An application for a PHR should only be made when a party wishes the tribunal to determine a substantive issue in the claim. A case management discussion, on the other hand, is appropriate where parties wish to set out the procedural agenda for determining the complaint.

Issues suitable for a PHR

[13.2]

Rule 18(2) provides that, at a PHR an Employment Judge (or tribunal) may:

'(a) determine any interim or preliminary matter relating to the proceedings;
(b) issue any order in accordance with *rule 10* or do anything else which may be done at a case management discussion;
(c) order that a deposit be paid in accordance with *rule 20* without hearing evidence;
(d) consider any oral or written representations or evidence;
(e) deal with any application for interim relief made under *section 161* of *TULR(C) A* or *section 128* of the *Employment Rights Act*.'

Rule 18(7) expressly states that an Employment Judge may make an order striking out a claim or response, or any order dealing with the entitlement of a party to bring or contest the claim.

In broad terms a PHR is appropriate where there is a self-contained legal or factual issue which is capable of deciding the entire case or, as the Employment Appeal Tribunal (EAT) has put it, 'a knockout point which is capable of being decided after only a relatively short hearing' (*CJ O'Shea Construction Ltd v Bassi* [1998] ICR 1130, EAT and *Wellcome Foundation v Darby* [1996] IRLR 538, EAT). Parties should be aware that tribunals are generally unwilling to embark on anything other than very limited fact finding processes at PHR's.

The tribunal will give effect to the overriding objective in deciding whether there should be a PHR (see **chapter 8 – fairness: the overriding objective**).

PHRs are intended to be a *time saving* process, relieving the tribunal and the parties of the need and cost of preparing for and considering the substantive complaint(s), when there is aself contained issue which can be fairly determined and will (or is likely to be) determinative of the entire or a particular aspect of the case. They are also intended to act as a *warning device*, whereby parties with weak cases can objectively (ie by the tribunal) be given notice of the consequences of failing with their claim. PHR's are not appropriate where the preliminary point cannot be separated from other factual issues in the case or can only be fairly determined by hearing substantial amounts of evidence.

Examples of legal issues suitable for determination at a PHR are whether:

- the claim has been presented within the relevant time limit (see **chapter 5 – time limits**).
- the claimant is employed or self-employed.
- the claimant has the necessary qualifying period of continuous employment for an unfair dismissal claim.
- the claimant was dismissed or resigned (in a claim for constructive dismissal).
- an essential statutory element for bringing the claim has been fulfilled.
- the claim is of a type the tribunal has jurisdiction to hear.
- the claim or an aspect of the claim should be struck out for non-compliance with orders.
- due to the overall weakness of the claim it is appropriate to strike it out or order the payment of a deposit.

Parties should note, however, that sometimes there will be an issue which falls into one of the above categories, but which is not suitable for determination at a preliminary hearing because it cannot be properly separated from other factual issues in the case.

Issues suitable for a PHR

Time limits

[13.3] Commonly, the issue of whether the tribunal has jurisdiction to hear a claim (ie whether the complaint has been presented in time and, if not, whether time should be extended) is suitable for determination at a PHR. This is particularly so in cases, both of unfair dismissal or discrimination, where it is common ground that the claim was presented outside the three-month time limit. In such cases the only issue is whether it was reasonably practicable (in unfair dismissal cases) to present the claim in time, or whether it is just and equitable (in discrimination cases) to extend the time limit until the date the claimant issued the claim.

In discrimination cases, however, the position is often more complex involving, for example, allegations of a continuous course of discriminatory conduct, with only the last act having taken place with the three-month time limit preceding the issuing of the claim. In these cases the tribunal has to try and decide whether the last act of discrimination, which is 'in time', can in fact properly be said to be linked with the previous acts, and hence form part of a course of conduct. In this instance (particularly where it is alleged that the respondent had in place a discriminatory policy), it is submitted that the tribunal may wish to hear all the facts before forming a view, and may therefore decline to proceed with a PHR (see **chapter 5** and **appendix I – claims a tribunal can hear**).

Employed or self employed

[13.4] In this instance, the preliminary issue, if decided against the claimant, will be determinative of the case.

Qualifying period of employment

[13.5] The tribunal will make a finding at the PHR in relation to issues such as when the effective date of termination was and whether the employment was continuous (see **chapter 5** and **appendix I**). If, for example, in a straightforward complaint of unfair dismissal, the claimant is unable to establish that his employment has lasted a year the tribunal will have no jurisdiction to consider the complaint.

Dismissal or resignation

[13.6] In principle, this is an issue suitable for a PHR provided it is determinative of the case. Caution should be exercised, however, to ensure that it can properly be separated from other issues in the case. Tribunals are generally unwilling to permit substantial amounts of evidence to be called at PHR since this rather defeats the purpose of PHRs: namely to save costs and time. Parties should also note that the issue of whether a person was constructively dismissed is *not* suitable for dealing with at a preliminary hearing.

Essential statutory element not fulfilled

[13.7] Examples of where a statutory element is fulfilled include whether an employee is suffering from a disability for the purposes of the Disability Discrimination Act or, in an unfair dismissal case, whether the employee does not have the necessary qualifying period of employment. A further example is whether the named respondent is the relevant employer for the purposes of proceedings. The parties should look at the particular provision of substantive law under which the claim is brought and decide whether there is an isolated issue, capable of being determinative of the claim, or aspect of the claim and which is suitable for dealing with by way of a PHR.

The type of claimant which the tribunal has no jurisdiction to hear

[13.8] Occasionally, the claim is of a type which the tribunal simply has no power to hear (see **appendix I**). An example is where an claimant brings a claim for personal injury, or fails to define in the ET1, a claim which the tribunal is entitled to hear. In these circumstances, a PHR is appropriate and may well be directed to take place by the tribunal of its own motion.

Whether the claim should be struck out or whether a party should be required to pay a deposit as a condition of continuing with the claim

[13.9] The power to consider whether a weak claim should be struck out is considered in detail in **13.15**. Where a party considers that, objectively, an allegation or, indeed, the entire claim or response has *little* reasonable prospect of success, it can apply for an order, under *rule 20(1)*, requiting the other party to pay a deposit of up to £500 as a condition of continuing with the proceedings. The test with such an application is slightly less onerous than with a strike out, in that the tribunal need only be satisfied that the claim or response has *little* (as opposed to *no*) reasonable prospect of success. Accordingly, it is quite common for a party seeking to strike out a claim to make an application for a deposit "in the alternative" and as a back up in case the strike out application fails.

Cases which are not suitable for dealing with by way of a PHR

[13.10] Where a case turns on a significant conflict of evidence which requires the assessment of substantial amounts of witness evidence or an event or course of events in relation to which: (a) the parties are in dispute about what occurred; and (b) each party intends to call direct and potentially credible evidence, a PHR is unlikely to be appropriate.

> **Example**
>
> At a meeting with four senior managers, the claimant (in an unfair dismissal and sex discrimination case) claims that she was told: 'I am afraid the bottom line is we can't afford to employ pregnant women in your sort of job'. All four managers deny saying this.
>
> It is unlikely that a tribunal would order the claimant to pay a deposit because there is no objective reasons why it should prefer the evidence of the managers. The mere fact that the employer is able to rely on 4 witnesses (all of whom have a vested interest in denying the allegation) is unlikely to make a material difference. The tribunal will only be in a position to determine whether the allegation is true by hearing the managers and the claimant give oral evidence, and assessing any documentary evidence. This should be done at a substantive hearing and a tribunal would be unlikely to accede to an application for a PHR.

Applying for a PHR

[13.11] It is sensible, if possible, to first agree with the other side as to whether it is appropriate for there to be a PHR before making the application under *rule 11*. The application should be made in writing specifying:

- the issue (ie non-compliance) or allegation(s) in the ET1 or ET3 in relation to which the PHR is sought (making reference to the specific criteria *rule 18(2)*).
- why this relates to the entitlement of a party to bring or contest proceedings.
- how a PHR will assist in progressing the dispute, defining the issues, saving costs and/or the time of the tribunal etc.

In addition, it is usually appropriate to refer to the criteria in the overriding objective, which the tribunal is obliged to give effect to in deciding whether such a hearing should take place, in particular, *regulation 3(2)(b)*, *(c)* and *(d)* of the *Employment Tribunals (Constitution and Rules of procedure) Regulations 2004* (see **chapter 8 – fairness:the overriding objective**).

A party who wishes to strike out an allegation (whether contained in the claim or response) should make an application under *Rule 11* for 'the claimant/respondent to show cause why the claim or response should not be struck out' (this wording is taken from *rule 19(1)*).

Whichever course is adopted, however, notice of the application must be served on all parties in accordance with *rule 19(1)*. The reason why the order is sought or the order which the party has failed to comply with should be clearly set out (and if possible attached in its original form) as should the basis upon which the breach is alleged (eg failure to provide the particulars sought). The other party must be given the opportunity, either in writing or orally, to show cause why the claim should not be struck out.

Upon receipt of the application, the Employment Judge will, if he decides it appropriate, list the case for a PHR. If it is decided that it would not be appropriate for a PHR to take place, written notice of the decision with summary reasons will be sent to the party seeking the review. If sufficiently aggrieved, a party can either seek a review of this refusal (if it appears that the chairman has clearly misunderstood the basis for the application or if additional information has come to light) or appeal against the decision. Parties should be aware, however, that appeals against interim case management decisions are rarely successful. In practice, only where an Employment Judge's decision is clearly materially wrong in law or one that no reasonable Employment Judge could have reached *and* causes a party substantial prejudice is the EAT likely to interfere with a case management decision.

The hearing

[13.12] The hearing will normally conducted by an Employment Judge alone. Parties may make a written request for the PHR to be heard by a full tribunal. Such a request must be served at least 10 days prior to the hearing (*rule 18(3)*).

It is advisable in cases involving a number of factual issues to prepare and serve well in advance of the hearing witness statements and a bundle of relevant evidence. Similarly, if the case involves complex issues of law, it is useful to prepare a skeleton argument which cites the relevant authorities, all of which should be disclosed to the other side in advance, with copies prepared for the tribunal (four copies of all relevant authorities should be prepared for the tribunal and the other side).

.The usual course will be for the Tribunal to hear any evidence first and then submissions. The party who has applied for the review should be prepared to address the tribunal first, although the chairman may start the hearing by asking the other party to address certain concerns which the tribunal has identified. In time limit cases, where it is accepted that the application to the tribunal has been made late, the tribunal will usually hear from the claimant first, since he bears the burden of establishing why time should, exceptionally, be extended.

The power of the tribunal at a PHR

[13.13] *Rule 18(7)* sets out the power of the tribunal to make orders as to the entitlement of a party to bring or contest proceedings (*rule 18(7)(a)*). The tribunal is expressly provided with the power to strike out a case or response where it considers that there are *no* reasonable prospects of success (rule 18(7)(b)), or to decide any substantive issues arising from the complaint (ie to finally determine an allegation contained in the claim or response).

Alternatively, where the tribunal decides that a matter has *little* reasonable prospects of success (as opposed to *no* reasonable prospect), it may, under *rule 20(1)*, order a party to pay a deposit of up to £500 as a condition of continuing with the proceedings.

The tribunal conducting the PHR is precluded from conducting the full merits Hearing (*rule 18(9)*).

The Tribunal's approach at a PHR

[13.14] In deciding what is the appropriate order to make at a PHR, the tribunal must seek to give effect, so far as is practicable, to the overriding objective (see **chapter 8 – fairness: the overriding objective**). Whilst, as with all these decisions, a great deal depends on the specific facts of the case and the individual approach of tribunal members, it is safe to say that generally only in the clearest cut cases do tribunals deny parties the chance of a hearing.

Striking out

[13.15] *Rule 18(7)(b) – (f)* set out the circumstances where the tribunal has the power to strike out the claim or response, and may make an order:

> '...
> (b) striking out or amending all or part of any claim or response on the grounds that it is scandalous, or vexatious or has no reasonable prospect of success;
> (c) striking out any claim or response (or part of one) on the grounds that the manner in which the proceedings have been conducted by or on behalf of the claimant or respondent (as the case may be) has been scandalous, unreasonable or vexatious;
> (d) striking out a claim which has not been actively pursued;
> (e) striking out a claim or response (or part of one) for non-compliance with an order or practice orders;
> (f) striking out a claim where the chairman or tribunal consider that it is no longer possible to have a fair hearing in those proceedings.'

Note that a strike out, with the exception of (d) and (f) above, can apply to both the claimant and the respondent.

In respect of each of the categories set out above, the tribunal will apply a two-stage test:

- have the criteria for striking out under that category been met (see below);
- is a strike out consistent with the overriding objective (see **chapter 8**).

A strike out is, as the name suggests, a draconian measure that knocks out the other party's case permanently without giving them the opportunity of having a full Hearing. It is only really suitable for exceptionally weak cases, where it is readily apparent that there is no reasonable prospect of success.

Category (b) meaning of 'no reasonable prospects of success'

[13.16] Broadly speaking, a claim or contention which has no reasonable prospects of success will fall into one or both of two categories:

(a) the claim, on the evidence taken at its highest (i e even if accepted as true by the tribunal) does not even have a remote or fanciful prospect of success; or

(b) there are no realistic prospect of the party in question proving their claim or contention. It is generally harder to strike out a claim on this basis because the Court of Appeal has made clear that disputes of fact which relate to the central issues in the case are not suitable for determination at a PHR (see below). Note that in this context it is frequently sensible to have first sought (and failed to obtain a satisfactory reply) further particulars concerning the claim before applying for a PHR.

Example of (a): An employee resigns in response to his manager's comment 'sorry to see your team got hammered last night', relying upon this single incident as a repudiatory breach of contract giving rise to a claim for constructive dismissal A tribunal is likely to conclude at a PHR that, even if the employee's account is true, the incident in question is not even arguably serious enough to constitute a fundamental breach of the contract of employment and that therefore the claim has no reasonable prospect of success.

Example of (b): In a race discrimination case, the claimant claims that he was not selected for promotion solely because the manager was a member of the National Front. He has provided further particulars of this allegation, in which he simply states that he was told of it by 'reliable sources'. He is not prepared to disclose either the name of the source of the circumstances in which he received the information, nor does he intend to adduce any other evidence in support of the allegation he is making The respondent has objective documentary evidence that the manager in question has been a member of the labour party for years. The tribunal may conclude, in these circumstances, that the claimant has no reasonable prospect of proving that the manager in question discriminated against him. NB some tribunals may think that in such a scenario the claimant had *little* reasonable prospect of success and, instead of striking his claim out, order the payment of a deposit in respect of that contention.

The high threshold which must be crossed in order for a party to demonstrate that a claim has no reasonable prospect of success was emphasised by the Tribunal in *Balls v Downham Market High School & College* [2011] IRLR 217, where it was stated as follows:

> '[T]he tribunal must first consider whether, on a careful consideration of all the available material, it can properly conclude that the claim has *no* reasonable prospects of success. I stress the word "no" because it shows that the test is not whether the claimant's claim is likely to fail nor is it a matter of asking whether it is possible that his claim will fail. Nor is it a test which can be satisfied by considering what is put forward by the respondent either in the ET3 or in submissions and deciding whether their written or oral assertions regarding disputed matters are likely to be established as facts. It is, in short, a high test. There must be *no* reasonable prospects.'

In *North Glamorgan NHS Trust v Ezsias* [2007] EWCA Civ 330, [2007] IRLR 603, [2007] ICR 1126, the Court of Appeal held that a strike out is generally not appropriate where there was a dispute of fact as to a central issue in the case:

> 'It would only be in an exceptional case that an application to an employment tribunal will be struck out as having no reasonable prospect of success when the central facts are in dispute. An example might be where the facts sought to be established by the applicant were totally and inexplicably inconsistent with the undisputed contemporaneous documentation.'

Categories (b) and (c): 'scandalous, vexatious and unreasonable'

Scandalous

[13.17] There is very little case law defining scandalous conduct. Scandalous, therefore, should be given its every day meaning. By way of general guidance it is likely to include reprehensible conduct that is significantly outside the range of reasonable professional behaviour. So, for example, a party who knowingly makes irrelevant or fabricated allegations, unsupported by evidence, with the intention of smearing the other side might be found to have guilty of scandalous conduct. In practice, there is considerable overlap between this and the 'vexatious' category. What is clear, however, is that the behaviour has to be fairly extreme before a tribunal will even begin to consider striking out a claim or response.

Vexatious

[13.18] In *Marler Ltd v Robertson* [1974] ICR 72, it was established that vexatious included situations where the parties actions were influenced by some improper motive. This includes situations where the party has no real expectation of success, but is simply bringing proceedings with the intention of harassing or embarrassing the other side.

The 'vexatious' category includes claims where an claimant attempts to re-litigate a matter which has already been finally determined in earlier proceedings or in another forum. The strike out occurs on the basis that, applying the doctrine of estoppel (see below), the claim constitutes an 'abuse of process'.

Circumstances where estoppel arises: estoppel can arise:

- where the claimant brings the same factual complaint on a different legal basis (known as 'cause of action estoppel') (*Blaik v Post Office* [1994] IRLR 280, EAT).
- where

  > 'a particular issue forming a necessary ingredient in a cause of action has been litigated and decided and in subsequent proceedings between the same parties involving a different cause of action to which the same issue is relevant, one of the parties seeks to reopen that issue'.

  (*Arnold v National Westminster Bank plc* [1991] 2 AC 93, HL, see also *Munir v Jang Publications* [1989] ICR 1, CA). This is known as 'issue estoppel'.

- where the claimant had the opportunity to bring the claim in earlier proceedings but failed, without reasonable excuse, to do so. This is known as 'Henderson v Henderson' rule (see *Divine-Bortey v Brent London Borough Council* [1998] ICR 886, CA, also useful general case on estoppel).

An example of the latter might be a claim that a dismissal (which has already been the subject of a tribunal decision concerning fairness) was also discriminatory. Note that estoppel operates as a defence to a claim and should be specifically raised in the response.

When alleging that a party is 'estopped' due to previous tribunal proceedings, it is necessary to show that there has been a relevant 'judgement' in previous proceedings. Judgement is defined in *rule 28* as a final determination of the proceedings or of a particular issue in the proceedings (ie a strike out or decision at the final Hearing).

Under the previous rules a claim was considered to be automatically dismissed upon withdrawal. Whether the withdrawal would estop a future application would depend on the circumstances of the withdrawal (see *Barber v Staffordshire County Council* [1996] IRLR 209, CA (claim estopped), *Sajid v Sussex Muslim Society* [2002] IRLR 113, CA (claim not estopped) and *Ako v Rothschild Asset Management Ltd* [2002] IRLR 348, CA (High Court claim not estopped after withdrawal of tribunal claim).

Rule 25, however, introduces an important procedural change which requires respondents to make an application for claims that are withdrawn to be formally dismissed. Respondent are required to make this application within 28 days of notice that the claim has been withdrawn having been sent to them by the tribunal. This 28-day time limit can be extended where a tribunal considers it to be just and equitable. After a tribunal has, in response to an application by the respondent, formally dismissed the claim, the claim can never be re-activated (subject to claimant's right to challenge the dismissal by way of review or appeal). The dismissal of a claim therefore acts as an absolute bar from further proceedings relating to the same dispute.

The clear implication of *rule 25* is that unless the respondent formally applies to have the claim dismissed, the claimant will be able to 're-activate' the claim that has been withdrawn. How a claimant goes about re-activating the claim is not entirely clear. However, it would reasonable to expect tribunals to require a written application to re-activate the claim accompanied by an explanation for the withdrawal and subsequent change of heart. A claimant would also be well served by referring to the appropriate parts of the overriding objective (bearing in mind that it applies equally to both sides).

Whilst the rules do not expressly provide for a time limit restricting the claimant's right to re-activate a claim, it is likely that the longer the delay the better the chances of a respondent successfully applying to strike out the re-activated claim (on the grounds for example that it is no longer possible to have a fair Hearing – *rule 18(7)(f)*).

For cases on the exercise of discretion to strike out for abuse of process (including estoppel), see *Barber v Staffordshire County Council* (above), *Department of Education and Science v Taylor* [1992] IRLR 308; *Ashmore v British Coal Corpn* [1990] ICR 485, CA; *Mulvaney v London Transport Executive* [1981] ICR 351 EAT; *Acrow (Engineers) Ltd v Hathaway* [1981] ICR 510; *Telephone Information Services Ltd v Wilkinson* [1991] IRLR 148, *EAT*).

Unreasonable

[13.19] The 'unreasonable' category only applies to the conduct of proceedings as opposed to the contents of the originating application and notice of appearance. It is difficult to see precisely what it adds to the 'scandalous and vexatious' categories for strike out.

Category (d): not been actively pursued

[13.20] This category arises where a claimant has caused 'inordinate and inexcusable delay'. In *Evans' Executors v Metropolitan Police Authority* [1992] ICR 151 the Court of Appeal considered that Tribunals should follow the approach of the House of Lords in *Birkett v James* [1978] AC 297 (relating to the test applicable at that time to the striking out of civil claims for want of prosecution). This requires that there should either be intentional or contumelious default, or inordinate and inexcusable delay such that there is a substantial risk that it would not possible to have a fair trial of the issues, or there would be substantial prejudice to the respondents. In the modern climate of pro-active case management of cases by the tribunal (including targets for bringing cases to full hearing), it is unlikely that a claim would be allowed to 'go to sleep' for sufficient time so as to give rise to a strike out application under this rule. One example of where, under the old rules (which applied a similar test of 'want of prosecution') it was applied was where a postponement was granted upon the claimant's request in order to attempt settlement, but the claimant failed (despite frequent reminders) to keep the tribunal informed as to the current position (*O'Shea v Immediate Sound Services Ltd* [1986] ICR 598, EAT).

Category (e): striking out for failing to comply with orders or Practice Orders

[13.21] Where the tribunal makes an order under *Rule 10*, for example for the provision of further particulars or disclosure, with which a party fails to comply, the other party may make an application to strike out either the claim or response (whilst the application is made under *Rule 11* reference should also be made to *Rule 13* which deals with non-compliance with orders). Parties should bear in mind, however, that striking out a case tends to be regarded as very much the sanction of last resort, and hence is used sparingly. A decision on whether to do so will involve consideration of the overriding objective, including such matters as the degree of fault and the prejudice caused to the innocent party by the non-compliance.

The tribunal may decline to strike out if they consider that this would be a disproportionately harsh penalty, but instead warn the offending party that their non-compliance may prejudice their case at full hearing. Alternatively it may give the offending party one last chance to comply by setting a date for compliance of the order with a warning that failure to comply with this order will result in the claim or response (or relevant part thereof) being struck out. This is often referred to colloquially as an 'unless order'. Even in circumstances where a strike out application is unsuccessful, the party making it should consider asking for its costs arising from the non-compliance.

Regardless of whether a strike out application is made or is successful, the party in whose favour the original order was made should not hesitate to flag up non-compliance at a later stage should it be relevant to do so. For example, if, during the course of a full hearing, a party seeks to adduce matters which should have been disclosed through the provision of particulars or disclosure, the other party should object to the late introduction of the evidence, emphasising any prejudice that they suffer and invite the tribunal to attach no or little weight to the evidence.

Category (f): no longer possible to have a fair Hearing

[13.22] This category introduces a new concept in employment law. There is therefore at present relatively little case law as to how this category is likely to be interpreted. It is submitted that it is likely to be used relatively sparingly and in circumstances where, for example, due to the unavailability of key witnesses (perhaps due to sickness or repatriation) it is no longer possible to fairly determine the issues in dispute between the parties. A further example of where this category may be relevant is in applying to strike out a claim which, having been withdrawn (see *rule 25* above), is re-activated after a significant delay –

see *Abegaze v Shrewsbury College of Arts & Technology* [2009] EWCA Civ 96, [2010] IRLR 236

Order for a deposit and costs warning

[13.23] If the tribunal decides that an allegation or, indeed, the entire claim or response has little reasonable prospect of success (as opposed to *no* reasonable prospect – where the appropriate order would be to strike out the matter), it may, under *rule 20(1)*, order a party to pay a deposit of up to £500 as a condition of continuing with the proceedings. This deposit must be paid within 21 days of notice of the order being sent to the parties. The tribunal will record its reasons in summary form for making an order for a deposit.

When deciding whether to make a deposit order under *SI 2004/1861 Sch 1 r 20(1)*, a tribunal is permitted to have regard to the prospects of a party establishing the essential factual elements of its case. In carrying out that exercise, it is permitted to reach a provisional view as to the credibility of the contentions advanced by the parties *(Van Rensburg v Royal Borough of Kingston-upon-Thames* (EAT/95/07, 16 October 2007). Elias J emphasised in that case, however, that the tribunal must have a "proper basis for doubting the likelihood of the party being able to establish the facts essential to the claim or response' (para 27). In practice, where a case turns on credibility an order for a deposit is very much the exception rather than the norm. It remains the case that factual issues should generally be determined at the full hearing. Strong and cogent evidence is required in order to persuade a Tribunal that a factual contention has little prospect of success.

In deciding whether to order payment of a deposit the tribunal must make reasonable enquiries into the party's financial ability to pay the deposit and have regard to the overriding objective (see **chapter 8**).

The tribunal must send a written notice setting out the grounds upon which the order was made and warning that, if the party against whom the order is made, persists with the claim, or aspect of the claim, he risks losing the deposit *and* having a costs order made against him at the conclusion of the full Hearing (*rule 20(3)*).

The written order requiring a party to pay a deposit (which is accompanied by a costs warning) enables the party to make an informed decision (since the notice contains the reasons why the tribunal is of the view that the claim is weak) as to whether or not to proceed, with an indication of the possible consequences should the claim or response be unsuccessful.

Failure to pay the deposit

[13.24] The party against whom the order is made must pay the deposit within 21 days of the date (recorded upon the order) when the notice is sent to them, or alternatively within an additional 14 day period where such an extension has been granted by a tribunal in response to an application made by the party within the original 21-day time limit. There is no requirement for a cheque to clear within the relevant period – it is sufficient that the cheque is in the hands of the Tribunal before that period expires (*Kuttapan v London Borough of Croydon* [1999] IRLR 349, EAT). If payment is not made within the relevant period, the claim or contention in respect of which the order was made, will be automatically struck out and the party prevented from pursuing it at the full Hearing. A claimant against whom a deposit order has been made can apply for an extension of time for payment of the deposit under r *10(2(e)*, even if the time for payment has expired (*Sodexho Ltd v Gibbons* [2005] IRLR 836).

Whilst an order to pay a deposit is not a decision or order that can be reviewed by the Tribunal, a party can make an application under rule 11for the Tribunal to use its general case management powers under rule 10(2)(n) to revoke or vary the decision to make deposit order. The first decision should not be interfered with, however, unless the facts or the law has changed or there are exceptional circumstances which justify that course (*Hart v English Heritage (Historic Buildings and Monuments Commission for England)* [2006] ICR 655, EAT and *Maurice v Betterware UK Ltd* [2001] ICR 14, EAT).

Where the claim has already been struck out, a striking out order under *r 20(4)* is capable of being reviewed under *r 34* (*Sodexho Ltd v Gibbons* [2005] IRLR 836, [2005] ICR 1647, EAT).

Costs if the matter proceeds to full Hearing

[13.25] If the party pays the deposit and the case proceeds to full Hearing, the deposit will be refunded unless the party is unsuccessful for similar reasons as were given by the tribunal which ordered the deposit to be paid.

If the party succeeds at full Hearing, the deposit will be refunded. If, on the other, the claim or response proves to be unsuccessful at the full Hearing and no award of costs or preparation time is made against the party for any other reason, a tribunal will go on to consider whether the party should forfeit all or part of the deposit on the grounds that it acted unreasonably in persisting in having the claim or issue determined (*rule 47*).

The basis upon which the tribunal decides whether to make a costs award at full Hearing will differ from the usual criteria for deciding costs. As indicated above, the tribunal will have first considered and declined to make such an order under the normal criteria contained in *rules 39/42*. It will then go on to consider whether:

- the party acted unreasonably in pursuing the matter which was the subject of the deposit; and
- the reasons which led the tribunal to find against that party on the matter in question were substantially the same as the reasons given by the tribunal at the PHR. As already noted no member of the tribunal who heard the PHR may sit at the full hearing (*rule 18(9)*).

In deciding this issue the tribunal will pay particular attention to whether or not the reasons the party was unsuccessful were substantially the same as those identified by the tribunal who made the order for a deposit. Clearly, a party who has received written notice of the reasons why the claim has little reasonable prospect of success, and who subsequently loses the case for the reasons identified in the notice, can expect to forfeit some or all of the deposit (See also **chapter 22 – costs** and, in particular **22.11** for further discussion on applicable costs where a party has been required to pay a deposit) .

Do's and Don'ts

Do:

- Remember that an order at a PHR can be limited to a particular aspect of a party's case and need not extend to the whole claim/ response.
- Remember that only limited evidence can be called at a PHR relating to discrete issues: tribunals are loathe to embark on mini-hearings.

- Make any application in writing setting out why the matter in respect of which the PHR is sought has no reasonable prospects of success. Ensure that the other party is given adequate notice of your application.
- Prepare and serve on the tribunal and other parties a skeleton argument/written submissions for use at a PHR together with copies of authorities and bundle of evidence which you intend to rely on.
- Remember that if the deposit is not paid within 21 days (and no extension of time sought within that period), the matter will be struck out.
- When applying to strike out for non-compliance with an order, set out the full history of default, including any letters sent.
- Consider whether it would be most appropriate to strike out or apply for a deposit.
- Address the overriding objective – minor default is unlikely to lead to a strike out.
- Consider making a simultaneous application for costs arising from the other side's non-compliance.
- Remember that, with claims which have no reasonable prospects of success, but are not completely hopeless, the tribunal may be more willing (applying the overriding objective) to order payment of a deposit at a PHR.

Don't:

- Apply for a PHR in cases where there is a substantial and credible dispute as to facts.
- Make an application unless it has some prospect of success – this may be counterproductive and result in an award of costs against the party applying.
- Be casual when faced with a strike out application but demonstrate to the tribunal that you have taken it seriously.
- Seek to deny mistakes or administrative errors when they occur.

Chapter 14

Witness orders and orders for the production of documents

Introduction

[14.1] The tribunal has the power, in appropriate circumstances, to compel witnesses who are able but unwilling to give relevant evidence to attend tribunal proceedings where they. Similarly, the tribunal can require individuals to disclose, or allow the inspection of, documents or information to a party. These powers arise under *rule 10(2)(c)* and *(d)* of the *2004 Rules* which state that a tribunal may make an order:

(*c*) requiring the attendance of any person in Great Britain either to give evidence or to produce documents or information; or

(*d*) requiring any person in Great Britain to disclose documents or information to a party or to allow a party to inspect such material as might be ordered by a County Court (or in Scotland, by a sheriff).

Parties should note that these two powers are not mutually exclusive – it is therefore possible to obtain an order for the attendance of the witness and the production of documents.

[14.2] As with all of the Tribunal's general case management powers, these powers can be exercised either on the tribunal's own motion or in response to an application by one or either party. Where a legally represented party wishes to make an application for either order, the application should be made in writing in the usual way as set out in *rule 11*. It should therefore:

- Be made at least ten days before the date of any hearing at which it is to be considered.
- Include the reasons for the request and an explanation of how the order would assist the tribunal in dealing with the proceedings efficiently and fairly.

- Be copied to all other parties together with notification that any objection to the application must be sent to the tribunal and all parties within seven days of receipt. However, note that this requirement is waived where the application is limited to a witness order under *rule 11(4)*).

In deciding whether to accede to the application the tribunal will have regard to the overriding objective (see **chapter 8, fairness: the overriding objective**). It is therefore sensible to formulate any application with reference to the criteria of the overriding objective as well as the criteria set out below.

[14.3] Failure without reasonable excuse to comply with an order under *rule 10(2)(c)* or *(d)* is a criminal offence punishable by a fine not exceeding level 3 on the standard scale (currently £1,000) (*Employment Tribunals Act 1996, s 7(4)*). The amount of the maximum fine must be set out in the body of the order (*rule 10(6)*).

Witness orders

[14.4] There are three requirements which need to be fulfilled before a tribunal will exercise its discretion to make a witness order (see *Dada v Metal Box Co Ltd* [1974] ICR 559; [1974] IRLR 251):

- An order is necessary because the witness will not, or may not, attend voluntarily;
- The witness is able to give *prima facie* and *admissible* relevant evidence (see *National Centre for Young People with Epilepsy v S Boateng* LTL22/12/2010; and
- There is a specific date for the tribunal hearing which can be inserted into the order.

[14.5] *An order is necessary*: a witness should, at first instance, be invited in writing to attend voluntarily. If they decline, equivocate, fail to respond or state that it would be easier for them to attend if there was a formal order, then a party will be in a position to argue to the tribunal that an order is necessary. In practice, a witness order is often of assistance where an employer is unwilling to allow one of his employees to attend a hearing (or where the employee wishes to be compelled to attend so as to avoid jeopardising his relationship with his employer). An application for a witness order is unlikely to succeed where there is no evidence of any previous unsuccessful attempt to secure the witness's attendance voluntarily.

The witness is able to give relevant evidence: the party seeking the order will need to demonstrate that the witness is in a position to give relevant evidence in relation to an issue which the tribunal will have to decide in the case. It is clearly important for parties to adopt a common sense approach to this limb of the test, since in practice tribunals are only likely to make an order where there are reasonable grounds for thinking the witness' evidence will be important in helping determine a central (as opposed to peripheral) issue in the dispute. Hence, it is unlikely that a tribunal would make a witness order requiring the attendance of a witness to prove the claimant's good character (unless this were specifically in dispute) or to establish a matter about which there was agreement between the parties.

Specific date: the tribunal will not make an order unless there is a specific date for the hearing the witness is required to attend. Parties should note that if the hearing date changes following a postponement, an application will need to be made for a revised order with the new date added.

[14.6] Whilst tribunals enjoy a wide discretion as to whether to make a witness order (*Noorani v Merseyside TEC Ltd* [1999] IRLR 184), it is important to emphasise that the key issue in such applications is likely to be on the relevance of evidence which the witness can provide (considered in the context of other evidence available).

Lastly under this heading, it is worth noting that, unlike any other application under the rules, an application for a witness order can be made without informing the other party of that fact (*rule 11(4)*). The same does *not* apply to an application for the production of documents (see below).

Example of application to the tribunal

[14.7] The claimant seeks an order, under *rule 10(2)(c)*, that Bill Smith attend the tribunal on 9 June 2010 to give evidence.

The order sought The claimant seeks an order, under *rule 10(2)(c)*, that William Smith attend the tribunal on 9 June 2010 to give evidence in the case of *Jones v White PLC* at the hearing on 28 September 2010.

The grounds for making the application The order is necessary because the claimant wrote to William Smith on [...] asking him to confirm, as a matter of urgency, that he was willing to give evidence on the claimant's behalf (copy of letter and proof of recorded delivery attached), and there has been no response. The claimant believes that an order is necessary to secure his attendance.

Mr Smith (a colleague of the claimant at the relevant time) is able to give relevant evidence in relation to the issue of whether the claimant was fairly dismissed for theft. The claimant's case is that during the course of its investigation into the theft the respondent was told by Mr Smith that the claimant was present with him outside the premises at the time when the theft was committed. The claimant alleges that the respondent failed to take this into consideration in reaching its decision. The respondent denies that Mr Smith ever gave this information during the investigation. His evidence is therefore central to determining the issues before the tribunal.

Potential risks of obtaining an order

[14.8] *The hazard of hostile evidence.* The power of the tribunal to compel the attendance of witnesses provides an important tool to the parties, but one which should be exercised with caution. Parties should consider carefully whether a witness who is compelled to attend will provide *helpful* evidence. In carrying out this analysis it is important to identify the reason why the witness is unwilling to attend to give evidence. Clearly a witness who has just been fired and who is likely to harbour a grudge against his ex-employer is a very different proposition than a witness who does not want to be seen to side with his employer and therefore wants to be compelled to attend the Hearing.

Whether to seek an order presents a tactical dilemma in which the potential value of the expected evidence needs to be balanced against the risk that different and prejudicial evidence will be given to the tribunal. Such a judgement can only be made on the facts of each individual case.

Parties should note that a witness who attends pursuant to an order they have secured is still 'their witness', and their evidence forms (however detrimental) part of the party's case. In other words, where a witness gives evidence which undermines the case of the party who calls him, that party cannot seek to go behind that evidence by challenging the evidence given or by cross-examining that witness.

Only in very limited circumstances will a tribunal give a party permission to treat their own witness as 'hostile' and cross-examine of otherwise challenge them as if they were giving evidence for the other side. Parties should note that, if the tribunal perceives that the order seeks to compel the attendance of a hostile witness, it may exercise its discretion and refuse to make the order (*Pasha v DHSS* EAT 556/80).

Orders for the production of documents

[14.9] An order for the production of documents can be made either against a party to the proceedings or a third party. Before such an order can be made three conditions need to be complied with:

- The party has declined to provide the documents voluntarily.
- The documents are admissible and relevant to a material issue the tribunal has to determine.
- The tribunal is satisfied that the disclosure sought is necessary in order to dispose fairly of the claim *or* save expense (*rule 10(5)*). – NB this latter requirement is mandatory in relation to third parties and therefore any application for an order of third party disclosure must make reference to these criteria explaining how the order sought is necessary to dispose of the dispute fairly or more cheaply).

Example of application to the tribunal

[14.10] The claimant (Peter Murray) has resigned and claimed constructive dismissal. The Respondent believes that the claimant, prior to the resignation, had already applied for a post in another company (Jones and Co) which he now occupies.

The order sought The respondent seeks an order that Anne Jones, personnel director of Jones and Co, provide within 14 days all documents in the possession of Jones and Co (or any associated or subsidiary company) relating to the application of Peter Murray

for a position within Jones and Co (or any subsidiary or associated company), including (but not limited to):
(a) the application form submitted and/or letter of application;
(b) the CV and covering letter;
(c) any letters sent by Jones and Co pursuant to the application, including letter of appointment; and
(d) the contract of employment and/or statement of particulars of employment.

The grounds for seeking the order A formal order is sought because Ms Jones has failed to respond to a number of letters (attached) requesting the above information.

The documents sought are relevant to the following issues:
(a) whether Mr Murray (the claimant) left the respondent organisation in consequence of the alleged breach of contract or due to the fact he had already secured a position elsewhere, and
(b) the extent of the claimant's loss.

The respondent has reason to believe that the claimant was intending to leave the respondent's organisation and that his departure was not motivated by the alleged breach of contract. Ms Jones is the personnel director of Jones and Co and has access to all of the documents requested.

[14.11] Save where a legally represented party is applying for a witness order under *rule 10(2)(c)* he is always obliged to notify other parties of his application in accordance with rule 11(4) (see **9.17**). Where a party is not legally represented the tribunal secretary is obliged to inform the other parties of the nature of the application, the reasons for the application and their right to make objections to the application within seven days of the notification (ie the information listed in *rule 11(4)*). Where, however, the application relates solely to a request for a witness order there is no obligation to serve a copy of the application on the other side.

[14.12] If the tribunal makes the order sought, the other party/parties will be served with it. If they have not had an opportunity to make representations prior to the order being made, it is open to them to make an application for the order to be varied or revoked under *rule 11(1)*. They will, however, need to show reasons why, on the merits of the application, the order should not have been made.

Even where, prior to the order being made, a party has notified the tribunal of its objections and the tribunal has nevertheless made the order, an application to revoke or vary the order can be made in light of fresh information which comes to light. If, however, the dissatisfied party has no additional evidence to put forward, and is simply of the view that the tribunal erred in law in rejecting its arguments, then the correct approach is to appeal the order.

Do's and Don'ts

[14.13]

Do:

- Name an individual in the application: organisation names alone are not sufficient.
- Provide full details of the steps already taken to secure the attendance of the witness or obtain the documents.
- Provide a full explanation of the reasons why the witness/document is needed for a fair and proportionate disposal of the dispute etc.
- Where appropriate, notify the other parties of the application that is being made and their right to object to the order that is being sought.
- Be precise in the wording of the proposed order. The witness is only obliged to comply with the strict wording of the order – so make sure it is tightly worded and covers, where appropriate, such matters as subsidiary or associated companies.
- Obtain a revised witness attendance order where the case is postponed or adjourned.
- Consider whether it is necessary to obtain both a witness attendance order and an order for the production of documents.

Don't:

- Forget to include in the application:
  (a) evidence of attempts which have been made to obtain what is sought voluntarily;
  (b) an explanation of the relevance of what is sought to the issue(s) the tribunal has to decide;

(c) the name of the individual against whom the order is made;
(d) (in the case of a witness attendance order) the date of the tribunal hearing they are required to attend; and
(e) (in the case of production of documents) the time span in which you want the documents provided (for example 14 or 21 days).

Chapter 15

Postponements and Adjournments

Introduction

[15.1] There will be occasions when one or both parties cannot or do not wish to proceed with a hearing, whether an interim hearing or the final Hearing of the dispute, on the date upon which the hearing has been listed. In these circumstances the tribunal may postpone the hearing to another date convenient to the parties. An increasingly common situation is where the hearing cannot be accommodated because of a lack of time or tribunal members. This reflects the number of claims currently before tribunals and the constraints on their budgets.

[15.2] The tribunal's power to postpone or adjourn a hearing arises from the general power to regulate their proceedings but finds specific recognition in *rule 10(2)(m)* of the *2004 Rules*. Little guidance is contained within the rules as to how this power is to be exercised: *rule 10(2)(m)* simply states that a tribunal may make an order 'postponing or adjourning any hearing.

[15.3] In tribunal proceedings, a postponement is a decision to move to a different date a hearing which has not yet begun. An adjournment applies to a partially completed hearing which the tribunal decides should be completed on another day, for whatever reason.

The criteria for deciding whether to grant an application

[15.4] The decision whether to postpone or adjourn a hearing is a matter for the discretion of the tribunal (*Jacobs v Norsalta* [1977] ICR 189). In deciding whether to grant a postponement or adjournment the tribunal will apply the overriding objective (see **chapter 8 – fairness: the overriding objective**), including the requirement to deal with cases fairly and expeditiously. Parties seeking adjournments should be aware of the tribunal's reluctance to delay proceedings. As under previous versions of the Rules, in considering an application to postpone or adjourn, tribunals will seek to do what is in the best interests of justice (*Carter v Credit Change Ltd* [1979] ICR 908; [1979] IRLR 361). Tribunals are conscious that employment proceedings are intended to provide parties, who often have very different resources at their disposal, with a swift and cost effective resolution of a dispute.

[15.5] In deciding whether, under the overriding objective, a postponement is necessary to deal with the case justly, Employment Judges can be expected to ask some or all of the following the questions:

- To what extent will a refusal to postpone prevent the just disposal of the case or deny a party a fair hearing?
- Has the party acted promptly in seeking the postponement after the reason became known to them?
- To what extent has the need for the postponement arisen due to unforeseen circumstances beyond the control of either party?
- Is the application being made close to the hearing date?
- Are the parties in agreement that there should be a postponement?
- Might the other side be adversely affected if the application is granted?
- Could the application have been avoided if the party seeking it had acted diligently at an earlier stage?
- Is this the first application for an adjournment in the case?
- What is the likely delay which will be caused by granting the postponement?

None of the above matters are conclusive, but will be balanced by the Employment Judge in making the decision. Parties need to be aware, however, that there is a general reluctance to postpone cases (especially ones with lengthy hearings) and parties should ensure that their applications provide a full and frank explanation of why the need for the postponement has arisen and the consequences of not granting the postponement. It is important not to lose sight of the fact that the need to deal with cases expeditiously is only one aspect of the overriding objective; the primary goal remains the just and fair disposal of complaints. Consequently, where a genuine need for a postponement has arisen through no fault of either party (for example due to the unavailability of an important witness due to sickness), in proceedings which have not long been issued, parties should not be afraid of insisting on the postponement, whether by way of renewed applications or appeal against the refusal of their application.

[15.6] The case of *Teinaz v Wandsworth London Borough Council* [2002] ICR 1471, which was decided under the previous rules, provides useful guidance as to how tribunals ought to exercise their discretion in determining applications to postpone or adjourn. In *Teinaz* the refusal to grant the applicant a postponement (the applicant was allegedly too ill to attend the hearing but had failed to supply satisfactory medical evidence) had resulted in his claim being dismissed. In allowing the applicant's appeal, the Court of Appeal made it clear that tribunals should be slow to refuse a postponement where the effect of such a refusal is to deny a party the chance to put its case. In such circumstances Employment Judges should consider using alternative sanctions (such as cost orders) whilst giving the party applying for the postponement a reasonable opportunity to provide evidence substantiating their need for a postponement.

[15.7] Where a postponement is in the interests of justice, but there has been default on the part of one of the parties, the tribunal can make an order that the party in question pay any costs incurred by the other side which arise as a consequence of the postponement, under *rule 40(1)* (see **chapter 22 – costs**). If the party seeking a postponement or adjournment is able to meet such a costs order and any prejudice to the other side is mitigated by such an order, for example by meeting the additional legal expenses incurred by the delay, this would be a good reason why an application may be allowed.

[15.8] There are a number of different reasons why a tribunal might grant a postponement or adjournment. This chapter looks at some of the most common.

Non-availability of the parties, witnesses or representatives

[15.9] It sometime arises that a party, witness or representative is unable to attend a hearing. It is important for parties to avoid applications to postpone or adjourn for this purpose by:

- Accurately completing listing questionnaires sent out by the tribunal;

- If no listing questionnaire is sent, informing the tribunal prior to listing of periods of witnesses' non-availability; and
- If the case is to be set down for full Hearing at a CMD or PHR, come to that hearing with a list of dates to avoid.

[15.10] Where a party, witness or their representative cannot attend at a hearing that has already been fixed, the party seeking the postponement should address in its application for a postponement the general criteria set out above to see if it applies in their case. In particular, the party making the application should explain why (a) the evidence of the witness is relevant to the issues in the case and (b) the reason for their non-availability.

Unavailability of representatives poses more of a difficulty. If a representative is taken ill shortly before the hearing in circumstances where it is difficult or impossible to replace them then a postponement will usually be granted. If, however, there is sufficient time for an alternative representative to be instructed, then Tribunals will frequently expect this course to be adopted, particularly in relatively straight forward cases.

[15.11] There are a number of possible reasons for non-availability:

- **Ill health:** As a matter of best practice, requests for late postponements should be avoided. However, in the case of ill health the situation is often unforeseen and therefore requests for late postponements may be unavoidable. In *Teinaz* guidance was given to the effect that if a party is genuinely unable to attend the hearing due to ill health then a postponement ought to be allowed. However, a party requesting such a postponement should be prepared to submit evidence supporting the application. If no medical evidence is available at the time of making the application, the tribunal may direct that such evidence (usually a doctor's certificate) is provided in due course. In *Andreou v Lord Chancellor's Department* [2002] IRLR 728, the Court of Appeal gave guidance on what matters the medical evidence should address. A party seeking a postponement of a hearing should ensure that medical evidence addresses the following matters:
  - The nature and prognosis of the illness;
  - Whether the individual was/is fit to attend the specific hearing;
  - If the individual was/is unfit to attend, the reasons for this; and

  - The prognosis and specifically, whether the individual will be fit to attend in the future. If so, an estimate should be sought as to the likely timeframe for recovery.

  A doctor's certificate should address the individual's ability to attend a hearing as opposed to merely confirming the ill-health of the witness.
- **Holiday absence**: Important factors include: the promptness in making the application, the date when the holiday was arranged (ie before or after the listing of the hearing) and the possibility of moving the holiday.
- **Economic/organisational reasons**: A postponement for these reasons is likely to prove more difficult. Tribunal proceedings are inconvenient and costly for the majority of employers. In practice, a tribunal will need to be persuaded that there are compelling economic or organisational reasons why the witness cannot attend on that day. Promptness in making the application upon receiving notification of listing and the closeness of the hearing are likely to be relevant factors in any decision.

Alternatives where a postponement is refused

[15.12] Where a written application to postpone is refused the Secretary of the tribunal will notify the parties in writing of the refusal (*rule 11(6)*). Whilst there is no specific requirement under the rules for the tribunal to provide reasons for the refusal of the application, natural justice requires the written notification to contain, in summary form, the reasons why the application was refused. The appeal courts have made it clear that whilst the explanation for the refusal does not need to be exhaustive, it should enable the parties to understand why their application was refused.

If a party is either unable to understand the reason why the application to postpone has been refused, or feels that the refusal fails to properly address the factual basis which has given rise to the need for the postponement, a further application to reconsider making the order should be made under *rule 11*. If, on the other hand, there is very little time before the hearing, the disappointed party should consider appealing against the refusal to postpone. Parties should be aware, however, that the Employment Appeal Tribunal is reluctant to interfere with interim procedural decisions taken by Employment Judges, save where there has been clear injustice (*Bastick v James Lane (Turf Accountants) Ltd* [1979] ICR 778).

[15.13] A party who is compelled to proceed with the original hearing should consider the following options:

- Make use of documentary evidence as a substitute. For example, by preparing a witness statement and asking the tribunal at the outset of (or prior to) the hearing for permission to adduce this as evidence (see **chapter 17 – preparing for the full hearing**). However, the tribunal may, depending on the contents of the statement, attach less weight to this evidence due to the fact that the witness cannot be cross-examined. In addition, make full use of contemporaneous notes and records, such as notes of disciplinary appeals hearing, which you have included in the bundle (see **chapter 17**).
- Consider renewing your application during the hearing if it becomes obvious that a fair hearing cannot be achieved in the absence of the witness. Be prepared for a possible argument on costs in these circumstances (see **chapter 22 – costs**).

There is a pending appeal to the EAT

[15.14] On occasions, there is an appeal against a ruling by the tribunal on a preliminary or interim matter, or an appeal against the tribunal's finding on liability in circumstances where the remedies hearing has yet to take place. Whilst there is no automatic right to a postponement in such circumstances, there are often good grounds (in terms of saving of costs etc) which can be used to support an application. Ultimately, whether one is granted will be a matter for the discretion of the Employment Judge, in relation to which the Employment Appeal Tribunal (EAT) will be reluctant to interfere. The tribunal should be addressed on the overriding objective when making and defending such applications (see **chapter 8**). Two examples of where the EAT has refused to interfere with the exercise of the chairman's discretion are:

- where an adjournment of the full Hearing was refused in circumstances where there was a pending appeal against the tribunal's preliminary ruling as to the identity of the employer (see *Sperty Corporation (incorporated in USA) v Morris* EAT 528/80); and
- where the chairman refused to postpone a remedies hearing in order to await the outcome of the appeal on liability (see *Nevin Lonsdale Ltd v Saunders* EAT 388/79).

The parties are engaged in related proceedings in the High Court or County Court

[15.15] Such situations are now less common as tribunals have jurisdiction to hear claims for wrongful dismissal and contractual disputes (arising from the termination of employment) which used to be heard in the civil courts. They are more likely to occur in cases where the amount claimed is in excess of the total amount the tribunal is allowed to award for unfair or wrongful dismissal. So, in a case concerning a company director who is paid £150,000 a year and is entitled to one year's notice of termination, it may make sense for tribunal proceedings for unfair dismissal to be stayed pending determination of a High Court claim for wrongful dismissal. If that claim is successful, it is likely that the claim for unfair dismissal will be discontinued. There will be other instances where the two proceedings 'overlap' in the issues they have to decide. Where identical issue/s are concerned, the Court or tribunal hearing the case second is likely to be bound by the findings of the first (see *Divine-Bortey v Brent London Borough Council* [1998] ICR 886). The tribunal will need to consider carefully the degree of overlap between the proceedings (*Muscolino v BUPA Care homes (CFC Homes) Ltd* [2006] ICR 1329).

The case concerns a point of law that is awaiting resolution elsewhere

[15.16] Whether the tribunal postpones for this reason will be a matter for its discretion, which will be exercised in accordance with the overriding objective. The extent to which the case turns wholly on the point of law in question (*Pearson v British Airports Authority* EAT 324/82) and the closeness of 'decision day' in the other case are both likely to be important factors. Parties should note that tribunals may, save in exceptional circumstances, be reluctant to grant postponement for this reason, if only because it is unlikely to be able to control what goes on in other proceedings, which may be settled or withdrawn. The tribunal will not grant a postponement in order to await the coming into force of new legislation (*Willow Wren Canal Carrying Co Ltd v British Transport Commission* [1956] 1 All ER 567).

Examples

Example one: A company receives a notice of hearing. The hearing has been listed in the middle of the holiday of the manager who made the decision to dismiss and is the respondent's primary witness. The day after receiving notification of the hearing, and well before the proposed hearing date, the respondent makes an application to the tribunal for a postponement, listing any further dates on which its witnesses cannot attend. A postponement will probably be granted. Applying the overriding objective, the case cannot be dealt with justly without the presence of the manager in question. The application has been made promptly, and will not cause more than minimal delay to the determination of the dispute and/or prejudice the other side.

Example two: As above, except that the holiday in question is booked two weeks after the company receives notification of the hearing date and the company delays three weeks after receiving such notification in making the application to postpone. The application *may* be refused, on the basis that the company had the opportunity to avoid the postponement and has delayed too long in making the application. The closer to the hearing that the application is made the less likely that it is to be granted.

Example three: A case is listed for a three-day hearing, starting on a Monday morning. On the Friday, one of the claimant's most important witnesses contracts a severe bout of flu. The claimant does not send in a medical certificate but applies for a postponement to which the respondent objects. The tribunal may refuse the application, but indicate that the individual's evidence can, if necessary, be taken 'out of turn' at the end of the hearing, or an adjournment can be ordered at a later stage if it becomes clear that the individual cannot attend and their evidence is material. Note: even if these indications are not made, a party should consider making such applications themselves once the full hearing has started.

Procedure for applying for a postponement prior to the hearing

[15.17] A party who wishes to apply for a postponement must make an application in accordance with *rule 11*. Save where the application is made at a hearing it should be made in writing. The application must state the reasons for the application and explain how the postponement will assist the tribunal in determining the matter fairly. The application should set out in full the grounds for the postponement (see **chapter 9 – communicating with the tribunal** (**9.18**)) and should be phrased with reference to the overriding objective.

[15.18] Where the application is being made shortly before the hearing or just before the 14 days preceding the hearing date, it can be faxed or emailed to the tribunal. In moments of total desperation, the tribunal can be telephoned, the clerk will record in writing the reasons for the application and place them before the tribunal. For obvious reasons, this is a measure of last resort. Indeed, the requirement under *rule 11* is for all applications to be in writing unless the Employment Judge orders otherwise. For that reason, anyone telephoning the tribunal should include an explanation as to why they are unable to make a written application.

[15.19] If the party is legally represented it must comply with *rule 11(4)* which requires the party to serve written notice on the other side of the application, the reasons for the application and of the right to object to the application within seven days of the date of receipt of notification. In relation to parties who are not legally represented the tribunal secretary will notify other parties of the application and the right to object.

[15.20] Upon receiving the application, the tribunal will invariably seek the response of the other side (if these have not already been received). The application will be placed before an Employment Judge who will then make a decision accompanied by brief reasons.

Adjournments during a hearing

[15.21] Sometimes it becomes necessary, during the course of a hearing, to request that the case be adjourned to another day. Commonly, this occurs where a party needs time to obtain evidence in response to some fresh allegation or evidential issue which has arisen unexpectedly during the course of evidence. A not unusual scenario is where the other side suddenly produces a document which has not been disclosed before and which requires the gathering of evidence in response. Again, the tribunal will apply the overriding objective (see **chapter 8**) in deciding whether to grant the adjournment. If it concludes that a fair hearing demands the granting of an adjournment, it is likely to make that order. Expect the tribunal, however, to make a costs order if the adjournment is due to the default of one of the parties (especially if legally represented), such as failure to prepare their case properly at the outset, give details of their case to the other side, or make proper disclosure of relevant documents.

Alternatives to adjournments during a hearing

[15.22] Tribunals are reluctant to adjourn cases part heard. Quite apart from the additional delay and the unsatisfactory effect of the hearing being broken up, it causes severe administrative problems for the tribunal since it requires finding a new date when all those involved – the Employment Judge, lay members and the parties – can attend. For that reason, the tribunal will expect parties to strive to find an alternative, including the following:

- If you need to obtain additional documentary evidence, see if there is any viable way of obtaining that document whilst the hearing proceeds.
- Where it is necessary to call an additional witness, explore whether there is scope for that witness appearing at any time during the hearing, even if the evidence is taken out of turn.
- Do not be afraid of saying to the tribunal that a new matter has arisen which requires a short adjournment of say, 30 minutes, for you to consider with your colleagues/client.

Do's and Don'ts

Do:

- Try and avoid the need for postponements by giving the tribunal up to date availability of witnesses prior to a case being listed and notifying your witnesses promptly as to when they need to attend.
- Make written applications for postponements promptly.
- If time is short, fax or email the application to the tribunal.
- Address why the refusal to grant a postponement would adversely affect the fairness of the proceedings, as compared to the minimum delay or prejudice caused by the postponement.
- Ensure you give complete information, including the reasons why the application could not have been avoided.

- Explain how long a postponement is required providing up to date witness availability so as to enable the hearing to be re-listed immediately, and thus minimise the delay.
- Where possible obtain the agreement of the other side before making the application, enclosing copies to the tribunal of relevant correspondence.
- Consider renewing your application during the full Hearing if it becomes clear that fairness cannot be achieved unless an adjournment is granted.
- If refusal is maintained, make a clear note of the reasons why. Politely draw the tribunal's attention to refusal to grant an adjournment/postponement in final submissions if appropriate, for example stating that you would have wanted the opportunity to adduce evidence in response to a particular issue.
- Consider the alternatives where a postponement is refused, such as relying on documentary evidence and witness statements.

Don't:

- Assume that a postponement will be granted – this is always at the discretion of the tribunal.
- Attempt to gloss over lack of diligence or errors on your part that will be obvious to the tribunal – admit them frankly before focusing on why a postponement is necessary in order to deal with the case justly and is unlikely to cause significant prejudice to the other parties.
- Forget to apply the overriding objective – including balancing the respective unfairness to the parties if the postponement is/is not made.

Chapter 16

Settlement of claims

Advantages of settlement prior to hearing

[16.1] A large number of cases settle prior to the full Hearing. Settling a case has the advantage of:

- dispensing with the risk, cost, disruption and anxiety of proceeding to a determination of the claim by the tribunal;
- enabling the claimant to avoid having state benefits deducted from a tribunal award, a factor which can be used as a bargaining tool by the respondent employer;
- enabling the parties to agree matters which the tribunal has no jurisdiction to order, such as a reference and/or confidentiality clause.

[16.2] A claim or potential claim can be settled at any stage of a dispute, from before an application is made to the conclusion of a remedies hearing. Further, tribunals usually decide the issue of remedy after reaching a decision on the substantive dispute. In these circumstances, they often give the parties an opportunity to reach a settlement in order to avoid a remedies hearing.

Parties should be aware that negotiations aimed at settlement of proceedings are privileged and therefore should not be disclosed to the tribunal whose task it is subsequently to determine the proceedings. If one party does disclose the content of negotiations to the tribunal hearing the case, it is open to the other party to apply for the case to be listed in front of a new tribunal on the basis that their case has been prejudiced, with all of the attendant costs implications.

[16.3] A decision as to whether to settle usually involves assessing the risks of proceeding to a full Hearing and deciding upon a figure for settlement which reflects those risks. In addition, it may involve a consideration of one or more of the following factors:

- *The cost of proceeding to full Hearing.* Since, ordinarily, costs arising from employment proceedings are not recoverable, this is often an important consideration for both sides. Employer and employees alike should consider the cost and expense of preparing for and attending the hearing, bearing in mind the legal costs, time spent in preparation, and the anxiety and disruption of normal duties in proceeding to a full Hearing. It is often in both parties' interest to adopt a pragmatic attitude in settlement negotiations with both sides giving credit for the savings in costs achieved by an early settlement.
- *Issues of principle.* Occasionally, an employer believes a case is so unmeritorious that little or no money should be spent on settlement, or a claimant is determined to obtain a positive finding from a tribunal in their favour, regardless of an offer in settlement from the other side. Whilst legitimate, such stances should be adopted with caution and any decision taken rationally as opposed to emotionally.
- *The possibility of negative publicity.* A very small minority of cases attract publicity. Save in rare circumstances, Hearings are in heard in public, which therefore provides the press with unfettered access to the tribunals. The press are often on the look out for cases which will be of interest and therefore the possibility of publicity is a factor which can affect settlement.

[16.4] A settlement usually includes one or more of the following features:

- a sum of money (common in most cases) (see **16.5**);
- an offer to reinstate (unusual) (see **16.6**);
- a further benefit, such as an apology or an agreed reference, which can be important for claimants yet to find new employment (see **16.7**);
- a confidentiality clause, in cases where the employer and/or employee are concerned to keep the settlement and/or dispute confidential (see **16.9**).

Features of a settlement 1: sum of money

[16.5] Deciding upon the right sum for settlement usually involves a three-stage process for both parties:

(i) assessing what compensation the claimant is likely to receive if successful, including any reductions for contributory fault or a Polkey deduction (*Polkey v AE Dayton Services Ltd* [1988]

AC 344; [1987] IRLR 503; see **24.27**). It may be sensible to draw up a provisional schedule of loss (see **chapter 24 – remedies: calculating likely awards**);

(ii) assessing what percentage chance the claimant has of being successful in relation to all or particular aspects of the claim; and

(iii) assessing the likely cost, length of hearing and disruption to the business which will be caused by preparing and attending a contested Hearing.

The starting point when considering an appropriate settlement figure is to consider (ii) as a percentage of (i). The party should then consider, with reference to the factors outlined above, and in particular the costs of proceeding to a contested Hearing, whether there are any additional reasons why the figure should be reduced or enhanced.

Example

The claimant brings a claim for unfair dismissal. The respondent considers that, due to a procedural defect, there is a 40% chance that the dismissal will be considered unfair. The respondent calculates the award which the claimant is likely to receive, if successful, as £5,000 (see **chapter 24**). It concludes that a reasonable settlement would be 40% of this figure, namely £2,000. The respondent is concerned about the disruption to its operations of two senior managers having to attend a one-day tribunal hearing at a busy time in their year. It decides, however, that the decision to dismiss was justified on the facts, and that it will not therefore increase its 'bottom line' figure of £2,000 (a decision which will vary according to the circumstances). In reaching this view, it is also concerned not to give the impression to other employees that the organisation is an 'easy touch'.

On similar facts, but where the full Hearing is listed for five days (because of the number of witnesses which the claimant intends to call) in a tribunal located some distance away from head office, the respondent might, bearing in mind the legal costs of preparation and disruption to its operations resulting from the managers being unavailable for a lengthier period, adopt a more pragmatic position and offer £2,500 – £3,000.

Note, however, that although this represents a logical approach to negotiating, the process is not mechanistic – is always fact specific and dependent upon the priorities of the parties involved.

Features of a settlement 2: reinstatement

[16.6] Agreements to reinstate or re-engage are relatively rare since a decision by a party to terminate the employment relationship is usually one they are not willing to retract. Furthermore, tribunals recognise that, in practice, little purpose is served by forcefully reuniting an employer and former employee in circumstances where they are unlikely to be able to rebuild the necessary relationship of trust and confidence.

A tribunal is limited to ordering either reinstatement in the original position (with continuity of employment preserved) or re-engagement (a more flexible option). The parties, through a settlement, are not so bound. It is, however, essential (for the sake of avoiding future disputes) to spell out in the terms of any agreement:

- the nature of the employment;
- the remuneration;
- whether continuity of employment is preserved;
- the effect of the settlement on previous rights and privileges accrued by the employee (including pension and seniority rights); and
- any payment which is to be made to compensate the employee in respect of the period when they were out of work.

Features of a settlement 3: reference

[16.7] Where the employee has not obtained new employment, an agreed reference can be extremely important. It can also be a useful bargaining tool for the employer. The usual practice is for the parties to agree upon the terms of a written reference through a process of negotiation. It is increasingly common for references to be taken up on the telephone and claimants should attempt to protect themselves in this respect. Parties might consider using the following wording in an agreement:

> 'X shall, upon request from any prospective employer of Y for a written reference, provide a reference in identical terms to that contained in Appendix A to this agreement and in no other terms. The employer shall respond to all oral (whether by telephone or otherwise) and email enquiries from prospective employers concerning the claimant's aptitude, performance and reasons for leaving the employment of X in accordance with the terms and spirit of the reference in Appendix A.'

The wording of the particular clause will always depend upon the circumstances of the case. For example, parties might agree that telephone enquiries should be answered with a specific form of words – if so this can be incorporated in to the agreement.

[16.8] From the claimant's perspective, the agreed reference should refer to as many of the following as possible:

- duration of employment;
- description of job and duties carried out;
- quality of performance in job;
- character and personality, particularly honesty; and
- reasons for leaving.

Features of a settlement 4: confidentiality clause

[16.9] It is frequently the employer who wishes to keep the terms of a settlement confidential often because they are concerned about the claimant revealing the fact of the settlement and its terms to those still employed by it. For this reason employers sometimes require the inclusion of some form of confidentiality clause. However, it is not always just the employer whose interests are served by such a clause because, for example, the employee may not wish the settlement to be revealed to prospective employers.

[16.10] One difficulty with a confidentiality clause is identifying the consequence of the breach. If no consequence is specified, then the party in breach will be liable for any economic loss flowing from the breach of confidence, in accordance with normal contractual principles. Such losses may however be difficult to prove or quantify. For example, where the respondent, in breach of the confidentiality clause, notifies the claimant's prospective employer of the terms of settlement, it may be difficult for the claimant to establish that, but for the disclosure, he would have been offered the job.

[16.11] A possible option, which is likely to be particularly attractive to the employer, is to require repayment of an agreed sum if the confidentiality clause is broken. The drafting of such clauses is, however, extremely problematic because they have the potential to be interpreted as unenforceable penalty clauses by a court.

Negotiating a settlement

[16.12] There are a number of methods by which the parties and / or their advisors can achieve a settlement. These include:

- negotiating directly amongst themselves;
- conciliation or arbitration through ACAS; and
- mediation through an independent third party.

Because there are restrictions on when an employee can compromise a claim (see **16.13**) the parties should consider which of the above offers the best solution to their dispute. As a basis for negotiations, it is often sensible for the claimant to set out their loss in a schedule, which is sent to the respondent. The respondent can then accept or challenge aspects of that schedule. This may also have the advantage of enabling the parties to prepare for a future remedies hearing. How to conduct negotiations is, of course, a question of tactics which will vary according the circumstances of each case. Commonly, each party will decide upon a 'bottom line', beneath which it will not go.

The form of the settlement

[16.13] The right to take a claim to a tribunal is a statutory right, which can only be contracted out of if strict criteria are met (see *Employment Rights Act 1996 (ERA 1996), s 203* – note that similar provisions apply for other statutory claims). This means that a settlement which purports to prevent an employee from making or pursuing a claim will only have that effect if it is incorporated into:

(a) a valid compromise agreement to that effect;
(b) an agreement made through ACAS; or
(c) an order or decision of the tribunal made with the consent of the parties.

An agreement which purports to prevent an employee from making or pursuing a claim, but which does not fall into any of these categories will not have the effect of preventing a claim being pursued before a tribunal. The employer will almost certainly be given credit, however, for any sums which have been paid when the size of the award is calculated.

Compromise agreements

[16.14] An example of a compromise agreement can be found in **appendix vi – sample compromise agreement**, but should not be used without reading the guidance below.

A compromise agreement can be entered into before or after an application to a tribunal is made. The requirements of a valid compromise agreement are set out in *ERA 1996, s 203(3)* and, broadly speaking, are as follows:

(a) it must be in writing;
(b) it must relate to particular proceedings;
(c) the employee must have received advice from a relevant independent advisor as to the terms of the proposed agreement and, in particular, its effect on their ability to pursue their rights before an employment tribunal;
(d) there must be in force, when the advisor gives the advice, a contract of insurance or an indemnity provided for members of a profession or professional body covering the risk of a claim by the employee or worker in respect of loss arising in consequence of the advice;
(e) the agreement must identify the advisor; and
(f) the agreement must state that the conditions regulating compromise agreements under the relevant Act are satisfied.

[16.15] A compromise agreement can relate to more than one possible complaint (eg unfair dismissal and sex discrimination) to a tribunal, but these should be expressly specified (*Lunt v Merseyside TEC Ltd* [1999] ICR 17). It is not sufficient to state that the employee is prevented from taking 'any claim before a tribunal'. Such wide wording is very unlikely to be enforceable. Whilst *section 203* refers to 'proceedings' being compromised, it is not necessary for a claim to have been commenced for a compromise agreement to be valid. However it is unlikely that such an agreement would be valid where there is only a possibility of a potential complaint arising (see *Lunt* and *Hinton v University of East London* [2005] EWCA Civ 532; [2005] ICR 1260). The agreement should specify the particular claim or claims with reference to the section of the statute under which the claim is made (see **appendix i – claims a tribunal can hear**).

[16.16] A 'relevant independent advisor' is defined by *section 203(3A)* and includes:

(a) a qualified lawyer, ie a solicitor with a practising certificate or a barrister (who is either in independent practice or employed to give legal advice);
(b) a worker at an advice centre who has been certified in writing by the centre as competent to give advice and is authorised to do so on behalf of the centre;
(c) an officer, official, employee or member of an independent trade union who has been certified in writing by the trade union as competent to give advice and is authorised to do so on behalf of the trade union; and
(d) a person specified in an order made by the Secretary of State.

An advisor is not 'independent' if:
(a) he is employed by or is acting in the matter for the employer or an associated employer;
(b) the employer who is a party to the compromise agreement is the advice centre or trade union; and
(c) in the case of an advice centre, the employee or worker makes a payment to the advice centre for the advice received.

One of the principal advantages of settling a case through ACAS (see below) is that there is no requirement for the parties to seek advice from an independent advisor.

ACAS – conciliation

[16.17] Where a claim is made to an employment tribunal under one of the relevant jurisdictions (see *section 18(1)* of the *Employment Tribunals Act 1996* (*ETA 1996*)), the tribunal Secretary must send a copy of all documents, orders, judgments, written reasons and notices to a nominated ACAS conciliation officer (unless the Secretary of State and ACAS have agreed otherwise) (*rule 21* of the *2004 Rules*). Where such an application has been presented to the tribunal and the relevant documents have been sent to ACAS the conciliation officer, it is the duty of the conciliation officer if he is requested to do so by the person by whom and the person against whom the proceedings are brought, or if, in the absence of any such request, the conciliation officer considers that he could act with a reasonable prospect of success, to endeavour to promote a settlement of the proceedings without their being determined by a tribunal (*ETA 1996, s 18(2)*).

[16.18] Parties ACAS' conciliation services should be aware of the following:

(a) it is independent;
(b) it will not advise either party on the merits of their case or advise them that a particular offer should be rejected or accepted (*Moore v Duport Furniture Products Ltd* [1982] ICR 84);
(c) communications made to it by either party will be communicated to the other party in an attempt to facilitate settlement;
(d) communications with ACAS are normally privileged and not for disclosure to the tribunal (*ETA 1996, s 18(7)*);
(e) once an agreement has been made through ACAS, it will be extremely difficult to set it aside, unless it can be shown that the ACAS officer acted in bad faith or adopted unfair methods (*Clarke v Redcar and Cleveland Borough Council* [2006] ICR 897);
(f) ACAS may suggest standard wordings for such matters as provision of agreed references and confidentiality clauses, but these can be adapted by agreement;
(g) an agreement concluded through ACAS can operate to bar more than one claim or prospective claim but, as with compromise agreements, all such claims should be precisely specified.

[16.19] Where an agreement has been negotiated ACAS will draw up a binding agreement which complies with statutory requirements. The form used is referred to as a COT 3. Importantly, the involvement of ACAS obviates the requirement for the employee to have received independent legal advice and can therefore be an attractive option for parties (both employees and employers) who wish to avoid the additional cost and delay which is incurred when such advice is sought.

The ACAS officers will draw up a formal agreement which complies with the statutory requirements referred to above, for the parties to sign. The officer will then contact the tribunal to inform them that the case has settled. ACAS can be asked to become involved even at a late stage in negotiations, when the parties have substantially agreed upon the terms of a settlement, but require the assistance of an ACAS officer to finalise the details and incorporate them in a binding agreement. Parties should be aware, however, that ACAS may be reluctant to allow itself to be used simply as a 'rubber stamp'. It will usually require there to be some areas which still require negotiation, even if these relate to the details of the settlement or agreement. This is particularly likely to be so where a fixed conciliation period has expired – ACAS may look unsympathetically upon a party which has not made use of this period and seeks to use its services for reasons of simple convenience at a late stage.

ACAS – arbitration

[16.20] In addition to providing assistance by way of conciliation, ACAS has responsibility for an arbitration scheme in claims for unfair dismissal and pursuant to the flexible working legislation (*Trade Union and Labour Relations (Consolidation) Act 1992, section 212A*). The scheme is intended to offer a quicker, more informal, private and generally less legalistic alternative to a tribunal hearing. The hearings are conducted by an independent ACAS arbitrator who hears from both sides and thereafter makes a binding decision. The arbitrator's award is final and therefore the parties lose their right to take the claim to a tribunal. The scheme is voluntary therefore all parties will need to agree to it.

Orders or decisions of the tribunal made by consent

[16.21] This form of settlement is popular when a case settles on the day of a hearing but can be utilised at any stage after an claim has been made. Usually, the most effective type of decision is an order by the tribunal to stay or dismiss proceedings upon the terms set out in a schedule attached to the order. An example of an order in these terms can be found at the end of this chapter.

An order in this form has four principal advantages:

(a) it enables the claimant to avoid the recoupment provisions (see **16.22**);
(b) it enables the parties to include in the schedule matters, such as an agreed reference or a confidentiality clause, which the tribunal has no jurisdiction to order;
(c) if the agreement is not complied with by either party, it can be enforced in the county court which can also resolve any dispute as to the terms of the agreement (valid compromise agreements or ACAS agreements are also enforceable in the county court (see **16.12**)).
(d) if the employer fails to comply with the agreement, the employee has the alternative option of applying for the stay to be lifted and the claim reinstated. Note this option can only be pursued where the order of the Tribunal is for a stay. It is also sensible to add a clause to the agreement giving the parties liberty to apply in the event of non-compliance with the agreement.

The alternative is for the settlement to be incorporated into the main body of a tribunal order. In these circumstances, the tribunal is limited to ordering the remedies that are within its jurisdiction, and the recoupment provisions (see **16.22** below) will apply to any sum which the tribunal orders to be paid.

The recoupment provisions

[16.22] Where the employee has received either jobseeker's allowance or income support in the period between termination of employment and the date of the award for compensation for unfair dismissal, such amounts are liable to be deducted by the benefits agency from any award which the tribunal makes (see *Employment Protection (Recoupment of Jobseeker's Allowance and Income Support) Regulations 1996*). No other social security benefits will be deducted. If, on the other hand, the parties are able to agree a voluntary settlement no deduction will be made.

Recoupment is a factor which both claimants and respondents should bear in mind when negotiating a settlement. It is in the claimant's interests to avoid recoupment. The respondent may legitimately, however, seek to use this fact to reduce a payment made in settlement. So, if the parties estimate that £2,000 will be deducted from the award, they might agree to 'split the difference' and reduce the amount of the settlement payment by £1,000. The parties should note that, to avoid the recoupment provisions, they must either conclude a compromise agreement, a settlement through ACAS, or agree to a Tomlin order being made by the tribunal. If the amount of the settlement is incorporated into the main body of a tribunal consent order, the recoupment provisions will bite on any sum which is awarded.

Enforcement of the settlement

[16.23] A valid compromise agreement or an agreement concluded through ACAS is a binding agreement enforceable in the county court. Similarly, breach of an agreement scheduled to a court order is directly enforceable in the county court, as is any order for payment of a sum made by the tribunal. The tribunal does not itself deal with enforcement. Where, however, the employer has failed to comply with the terms attached to an order, the claimant is fully at liberty to apply to the tribunal for the stay on proceedings to be lifted, and the claim be reinstated. To enable this to happen, the claimant should ensure that there is a clause stating that the parties have liberty to apply in the event of non-compliance with the terms of the agreement scheduled to the order.

Do's and Don'ts

Do:

- Ensure that any settlement is incorporated into a valid agreement or order.
- Bear in mind the recoupment provisions when deciding whether to settle.
- Calculate as precisely as possible what the claimant is likely to receive if successful at tribunal, and then decide what percentage of that figure to settle for based upon a realistic and objective assessment of the prospects of success.
- Give thought to an agreed reference and confidentiality clause.
- Give thought to the stress, anxiety, cost and disruption to business operations of preparing and attending the final hearing – these issues should not be underestimated.
- Expressly reserve the right to draw any settlement offers to the tribunal's attention should the issue of costs arise (ie after liability and remedies have been determined), in the event of the dispute proceeding to a full Hearing.
- Consider using ACAS to conciliate and draw up the final agreement.
- Remember that negotiations aimed at settlement are privileged and cannot be revealed to the tribunal until after the dispute has been determined.

Don't:

- Shorten the fixed periods of conciliation unreasonably.
- Conclude a settlement without incorporating it into a valid form.
- Open negotiations with your 'bottom line' figure (unless the circumstances demand otherwise).
- Tell the other side that something is your final offer unless that is genuinely the case – this may weaken your credibility.

Specimen consent order

page 1

Note that the terms of any agreement will always vary according to the circumstances of the case.

IN THE LONDON CENTRAL EMPLOYMENT TRIBUNAL CASE NO:

BETWEEN

Joe Bloggs

Claimant

And

Smith and Co

Respondent

ORDER

1. The claim be dismissed upon the terms set out in the attached schedule.
2. The parties to have liberty to apply in the event of a failure to comply with the terms to set out in the attached schedule – *note this only applies where the Tribunal orders a stay. Where there is a dismissal or a stay the parties can enforce the terms of the agreement in schedule 1 in the County Court because it is a binding contractual agreement.*

Signed: either the parties or their representatives should sign the order

Dated:

page 2:

IN THE LONDON CENTRAL EMPLOYMENT TRIBUNAL CASE NO:

BETWEEN

Joe Bloggs

Claimant

And

Smith and Co

Respondent

SCHEDULE

---

1. The Claimant shall not disclose, whether directly or indirectly, to any third party the terms of this settlement..
2. The Respondent shall, upon request from any prospective employer of Y for a written reference, provide a reference in identical terms to those contained in Appendix A (annexed to this agreement) and in no other terms. The employer shall respond to all oral (whether by telephone or otherwise) and email enquiries from prospective employers concerning the claimant's aptitude, performance and reasons for leaving the Respondent's employment in accordance with the terms and spirit of the reference in Appendix A – *note this formulation requires the addition of a further page, marked appendix A and signed by both parties, which contains the reference. A permissible alternative is to substitute the words 'that contained in appendix A' in this paragraph with 'those set out below' and then to write out the reference immediately below the paragraph. This may be the preferred option when the reference is short.*
3. The Respondent shall pay to the Claimant [£] within 28 days of the date of this agreement

Signed:

Dated:

Chapter 17

Preparing for the full Hearing

Introduction

[17.1] Preparation is the key to the effective presentation of your case in a tribunal. Preparation involves:

- Knowing the facts of the case and the issues.
- Ensuring that your case is ready to proceed to full Hearing.
- Presenting your case in a well-prepared and professional manner with an organised bundle and, where appropriate, a chronology and skeleton argument.

[17.2] This chapter looks at some of the key steps in preparing a case for hearing namely:

- Ensuring you have complied with the tribunal's directions.
- Preparing an effective bundle.
- Drafting a chronology.
- Drafting witness statements.

In addition, matters such as the drawing up of a cast list (or *dramatis personae*) and a skeleton argument are examined. All these steps are recognised as good practice and, irrespective of any orders given by the tribunal (which parties are compelled to comply with or risk facing the sanctions and/or seriously weakening their case before the tribunal), should wherever possible be taken in preparing for a dispute.

[17.3] Many (if not all) of the matters mentioned in this chapter are likely to be the subject of standard or specific direction orders made by the tribunal. Where the direction involves a measure of cooperation between the parties, ensure that you have done what is required and you will be able to demonstrate objectively (i.e. through correspondence) that any failure to comply is due to default on the part of the other side.

The bundle

What is the bundle?

[17.4] The bundle comprises the documentary evidence (except witness statements) upon which you rely in the case. There is frequently an order that the parties compile an agreed bundle of evidence so that the tribunal does not have to refer to two different ones. Even where there is no such order, parties should wherever possible attempt to agree a bundle. Parties should be aware that tribunals strongly disapprove of separate bundles being relied on and are likely to be unimpressed by a party who has adopted an unreasonable position with respect to agreeing a bundle. If, however, it proves impossible to agree a bundle, each party should prepare their own. Either way, six bundles are required – three for the tribunal, one each for the parties and one for the witness table. The unfortunate practice of Tribunals is to require parties to bring all copies of the bundles to the Tribunal on the day of the hearing – they generally will not be accepted in advance.

The contents of the bundle

[17.5] A bundle should be:

- Indexed (in the form of a contents page at the start of the bundle with case name/number).
- Paginated, with every page numbered, as opposed to every document.
- Typically it will contain:
  - (a) The pleadings: namely the ET1, ET3 any reply to the ET3 etc.
  - (b) The contract of employment.
  - (c) Relevant company procedures (such as disciplinary procedures and equal opportunities policies).
  - (d) Correspondence – ie letters, emails, memos and file notes.
  - (e) Minutes of meetings.
  - (f) Pay slips and relevant proof of earnings.
  - (g) Any relevant company announcements, for example a notice announcing a redundancy situation, transfer of ownership, change of location etc.

[17.6] An example of a contents page can be found in **appendix v – case study**. You will see that it divides the above into different sections (which may be conveniently separated by coloured dividers), with the exception of correspondence and minutes of meetings, which are combined into one section. Note that it is usual to place the documents in each section in *chronological order*, particularly the correspondence section – tribunals find it irritating and confusing if letters, memos and minutes are not presented in a logical order. Indeed, as is readily apparent, the fact that documents are not in any logical sequence is also likely to hamper a coherent presentation of a party's case.

[17.7] A word of caution, however; the above constitutes broad guidance only. Plainly the type of case and the issues engaged will influence the kind and amount of documents that should be included within a bundle. Each bundle will vary. In discrimination cases, for example, there may be the need to add to the first section of the bundle the questionnaires. In all cases whether there have been requests for further particulars, these (together with any answers) should be added to the first section. Further, it may be, in a discrimination case that an analysis has been undertaken of the ethnic group or sex of certain sections of staff – where these are included is a matter for the compilers of the bundle, but an obvious place would be in third section. Whilst there can never be any hard and fast rules as to what should be included in a bundle, parties should ensure that all relevant material is included whilst avoiding overloading the tribunal with unnecessary paper.

Preparing an agreed bundle

[17.8] Parties should contact each other as soon as possible with a view to agreeing (if there has been no order to that effect) whether there should be an agreed bundle. They should also seek to agree who will prepare it. In most cases, due to the likely disparity in resources and the fact that most documents tend to be in the respondent's possession, it is often the respondent who will be ordered to prepare the agreed bundle. It is not therefore unreasonable for a claimant to request the respondent to prepare the bundle. The parties should also decide on the procedure for agreeing the contents/layout of the bundle.

Example

Since, in practice, most of the relevant documentation in a case tends to be in the hands of the employer (i.e. the employee's employment file, notes of meetings etc), a common route is for the employer to compile a provisional bundle and to send to the claimant the contents page, listing all the documents which it intends to include. The claimant should then reply stating which additional documents (whether in its/the respondent's possession) it wishes to have included and where in the bundle it wishes the documents to be placed. Provided there is no objection from the respondent, those documents should then be incorporated, either in a separate section in the bundle, or chronologically within the body of the existing bundle.

[17.9] Note: agreeing to the inclusion of the other side's documents in an agreed bundle does not mean that the document becomes part of 'your' evidence, or that you will be taken by the tribunal to be relying upon it. A bundle is simply a collection of the relevant evidence for the tribunal to consider. Objections to inclusion should only be based on irrelevance or evidential unfairness. Usually there is little to be gained from arguing over the order in which the bundle is compiled although frequently issues arise as to what documents should be included. The answer is those relevant documents which either or both parties seek to rely upon.

The consequences of coming to a tribunal without a bundle

[17.10] Where it is not possible, or there is insufficient time, to agree a bundle, you should still prepare one for use at the tribunal. This should include all relevant documentation, both helpful and unhelpful to your case whilst excluding privileged documentation (see **chapter 11 – disclosure**). Tribunals increasingly assume that a proper bundle will be prepared. A party, particularly one that is legally represented or a respondent, who has not prepared one is likely to antagonise the tribunal and will create an impression of disorganisation and sloppiness. Where no bundle is available at a hearing parties also run the risk of having the hearing adjourned (with the attendant cost consequences) or dismissed (especially where there has been non-compliance with the standard directions, which are issued in almost all cases, and require a bundle to be produced).

[17.11] Parties should not underestimate the benefits of compiling the bundle well in advance of the Hearing since it was one of the most effective steps in effectively marshalling the facts of the case, identifying evidential weakness and isolating relevant documentation. The practice of most Tribunal is to refuse to accept bundles in advance of the hearing, necessitating one of the parties bringing copies on the day. This does not, of course, dispense with the need for the parties to have copies of the bundle well in advance of the hearing.

The chronology

[17.12] A chronology lists all relevant events in a case in chronological order, with the date on the left and the event in question on the right. An example of a chronology can be found in **appendix v**. Sometimes, there will be a direction from the tribunal that the parties agree a chronology in a particular case although these tend to be in more complicated cases. Even where there is not such a direction, it is useful to prepare a chronology (preferably an agreed one).

The purpose of a chronology

[17.13] A chronology not only assists the tribunal in gaining an understanding of the sequence of events in a case, but is also an invaluable tool in the proper preparation of a case – whilst time consuming and frequently laborious, it enables the advocate to organise the facts and, in the process, identify key weaknesses and inconsistencies in the case, whether in their case of the other side's. It also helps clarifying what evidential issues will be covered, and thus is useful in determining who will need to be called as witnesses, what their statements will need to address and what documentary evidence needs to be obtained.

[17.14] Precisely how you draft the chronology is a matter of individual style, but bear in mind the following:

- It should include all relevant events, not just events helpful to your case.
- It should not be phrased in a biased or self-serving way.

- Where possible, it should include cross-references to the relevant document within the bundle (for example, where a meeting was held on a certain date and notes were taken during the course of that meeting).

Dealing with disputed events

[17.15] Frequently, each side will have different versions of what occurred on the same date. A chronology should not set out only one version of event: the event should either be referred to neutrally (i.e. the fact of a meeting) or give a summary of both versions of events.

Example

18.5.02: Meeting at office between Mr Harris and the claimant. The parties are in dispute as to what occurred on this date. The claimant claims he was told to resign. This is denied by the respondent.

Alternatively, if you consider this is going to make the chronology too difficult, long and cumbersome, simply describe the event itself.

18.5.02: Meeting at office between claimant and the respondent. [You might consider adding]: The contents of this meeting are heavily in dispute between the parties.

Clearly the first style has the advantage of offering the tribunal more information, but may prove impractical on occasions. Whatever style you adopt, try to draft the chronology in a consistent manner.

Chronologies as a tool in preparation

[17.16] You are likely to find, as you prepare a chronology, that good ideas for cross-examination and final submissions spring to mind.

Think about, for your own purposes *only*, putting an additional third column on the page, so that, as you draft the chronology, you can write down ideas that come to mind.

A 'who's who' in the case

[17.17] Where a case involves numerous witnesses it can be useful if a separate 'cast' list is drafted for the tribunal detailing the names and positions of all relevant people (on both sides) in the case. Again, this is not a purely altruistic gesture. It will assist in the organisation and preparation of your own case and create an impression of competence to the tribunal. Where, however, there are only relatively few witnesses, it may be sufficient for their names and job descriptions to be set out at the top or bottom of the chronology, or simply explained during opening submissions.

Witness statements

What are witness statements?

[17.18] Most tribunals will direct and/or expect the evidence of the witness to be contained in a written format which is either read out by the witness to the tribunal or is 'taken as read' (for recent guidance on when statements should be read aloud at tribunal, see *Mehta v Child Support Agency* UKEAT/0127/10/CEA). The major advantage of producing evidence in the form of statements is that they can be written and planned in advance, ensuring that the evidence which the witness gives is both complete and presented in as attractive a manner as possible. Ordinarily parties should strive to agree to mutual exchange of their respective statements prior to the Hearing. Parties should be cautious about disclosing their witness statements to the other side in advance as to do so gives the other side the advantage of preparing their evidence knowing what you are going to say. Sometimes the tribunal will order advanced mutual exchange witness statements.

[17.19] It is imperative that witness statements deal with all the issues relevant to the party's case. Inadequate statements, which result in factual allegations being made for the first time on the day of the hearing, can seriously undermine a party's case. In such circumstances the offending party runs the risk of not being allowed to raise the fresh factual allegations, or being required to compensate the other side for the cost of a postponement (if required to obtain evidence to counter the fresh allegations), or having less weight attached to the new factual issues.

[17.20] Advantages of a well-drafted witness statement include:

- it is written in advance, can be carefully planned and cover all issues relevant to a proper determination of the dispute;
- it can be phrased in a persuasive and structured manner;
- it reduces the level of uncertainty in relation to your own evidence;
- it acts as a 'prop' for the witness who has some idea of what will be expected of him at the hearing; and
- it can be drafted by representatives or advisors (but see warning below).

Drafting witness statements

[17.21] An example of a witness statement in an unfair dismissal case can be found in **appendix v.**

An effective witness statement should:

- include *all* of the relevant events on which that witness is able to give evidence;
- Refer to relevant documents in the bundle which relate to that witnesses' evidence (eg a dismissal hearing or decision letter). It is important that the statement makes reference to the page in the bundle where the document is to be found.
- not refer to evidence about events and incidents which are outside the direct knowledge of the maker of the statement, for example it does not refer to events of which the witness has no direct knowledge;
- be structured around and restricted to the issues the tribunal has to decide;
- read persuasively; and
- written in numbered paragraphs dealing with the evidence chronologically.

Achieving the above involves a three-stage process on the part of the representative:

- define the issues in the case;
- take instructions from the witness in relation to those issues; and
- attractively setting out those instructions in a well structured, chronological and persuasive statement.

Structuring the witness statement

[17.22]

Example

In a sex discrimination case, the manager is accused of denying the claimant promotion due to her sex. The manager's case is that the decision not to promote the claimant had nothing to do with her sex, but was taken on the grounds that she did not satisfy the criteria for the job and there were more able alternative employees. The statement could be structured in the following way:

- First section – sets out the position and duties of the manager (including the number of employees he has charge of), how long he has held that post, any relevant prior experience, and any training in equal opportunities.
- Second section – sets out when the manager first met the claimant, how long they have worked together, the frequency and nature of the contact, with the aim of demonstrating that the manager had ample opportunity to gauge the claimant's performance.
- Third section – describes the claimant's current post/role and sets out a brief description of the claimant's performance in the job. Reference should be made to appraisals or other supporting contemporaneous documentary evidence.
- Fourth section – describes the higher post, ie how the vacancy arose, the duties of the job.
- Fifth section – describes the criteria adopted for deciding who would occupy the position, the interviewing process, who chaired the interview, whether there was a right to challenge the decision.
- Sixth section – describes how the claimant met the relevant criteria and the extent to which she did not.
- Seventh section – describes the other candidates, including how many applied and who was interviewed.
- Eighth section – describes the qualities (and sex if appropriate) of the candidate who was chosen.
- Ninth section – sets out a comparison between the selected candidate and the claimant, explaining why there were reasons unrelated to the claimant's sex for the decision that was made.

- Tenth section – final paragraph detailing witness's personal reaction to being accused of sex discrimination, including whether she exercised any internal right to challenge the non-promotion and if so on what grounds.

The above statement is structured around the legal issue in the case, namely whether there has been less favourable treatment on grounds of sex.

The role of the representative in the drafting of a statement

[17.23] It is common in cases where a party is represented for the representative to draft the statement after taking instructions from the witness concerned. Note, however, that the evidence in the statement is that of the maker alone. Whilst this does not mean that a representative is restricted to reciting word for word the instructions of their witness, it does mean that only the witness's recollection of events should be transcribed. Similarly, since a representative is likely to have a better understanding of the issues which need to be covered in the statement, it is perfectly reasonable for him to indicate to the witness the factual matters which he would like the witness to address.

[17.24] If the witness is 'fed' a version of events by the representative, this is likely to come across in the tribunal, with potentially devastating consequences for the credibility of the witness and the integrity of the representative. At the more extreme end of the scale, inviting a witness to fabricate evidence constitutes attempting to pervert the course of justice, a criminal offence. The role of the representative should be limited to matters of style and structure, that is to say obtaining the witness's version of events in the context of the legal and factual issues which the tribunal has to decide and phrasing it in as strong and persuasive a manner as possible. An essential step in the drafting of a comprehensive statement is the taking of effective instructions from the client: namely asking the witnesses to explain what took place in relation to all relevant issues and, where appropriate, the reasons any actions were taken.

Does a witness statement dispense with the need for the witness to attend?

[17.25] Witness statements do not dispense with the need for the witness to attend at the hearing to be questioned, whether by the other side or the tribunal. Unless you are sure that the contents of the statement are not going to be contentious, failing to call the maker of the statement to give oral evidence is not a wise course, unless completely unavoidable. The tribunal will be bound to consider any unfairness to the other side as a result of not being able to question the witness. There is, however, nothing to prevent you making an application for the statement to be adduced as evidence in the absence of the witness concerned, explaining why the witness cannot attend. Where possible a party who knows that a witness will be unable to attend should try and agree his evidence with the other side. If the statement is allowed in, the tribunal may well attach less weight to it due to the fact that the witness cannot be questioned.

[17.26] The tribunal's approach is likely to depend on the nature of the evidence – the more contentious the allegations of a witness the less weight that the tribunal is likely to attach to the evidence so as to reflect the injustice to the party being denied the opportunity to challenge (by cross examination) the evidence. Other factors which are likely to be relevant is the extent to which the unavailable witness's evidence is supported by other evidence (whether objective or not), the reason for the non-attendance and the prejudice that the other party has in fact suffered by not being able to cross examine the witness.

Be particularly careful where there is a direct conflict between the witness statement and the evidence of a witness who attends to give oral evidence – the tribunal will usually be inclined to prefer the latter evidence.

Skeleton arguments

[17.27] Skeleton arguments, something used for some time by barristers and solicitor advocates, are becoming more common in tribunal proceedings. A skeleton argument outlines your case in relation to some or all of the issues in outline form. It sets out the factual issues of the dispute within the context of the legal issues which the tribunal will have to apply in determining the case.

[17.28] A well prepared skeleton argument enables the tribunal, prior to hearing the evidence or submissions, to gain an understanding of your argument. It can be very useful in influencing the tribunal's approach to the evidence. Advantages of a skeleton argument:

- It forces you to plan and structure your submissions carefully.
- It is a good opportunity to influence the tribunal from the outset.
- It provides the tribunal with a readily accessible account of your case.
- It can be used as a prop when making submissions.

However, a warning: ensure that the skeleton argument does not become a hostage to fortune by tying you to a position or argument which by the end of the hearing you no longer wish to rely upon. For this reason, skeleton arguments are more safely deployed either when the evidence has been heard (ie for final submissions), or in a hearing which involves submissions rather than evidence (for example a legal dispute about whether the tribunal has jurisdiction to hear the evidence in question).

An example of a skeleton argument can be found in **appendix v.**

List of issues

[17.29] At the start of the full Hearing (or before), it is extremely useful if you can agree a list of issues with the other side and place it before the tribunal. Many Employment Judges do this of their own motion and will be grateful if this is done in advance. If there has been a Case Management Discussion or Pre-Hearing Review (see **chapters 12 and 13**) before the full Hearing it is possible that the issues may have been clarified on these occasions. If this is the case reference should be made to these issues and, if no longer accurate, brought to the tribunal's attention at the earliest opportunity.

Do's and Don'ts

Do:

- Prepare and seek to agree a paginated bundle as early as possible.
- Ensure that you have complied with all orders.
- Prepare a chronology and where appropriate a cast list (see **appendix v)** – invaluable tools in personal preparation.

- Consider using, where appropriate, a skeleton argument and list of issues.
- Ensure that a witness reads the statement and is completely happy with the contents of their statement before signing it.
- Ensure that the witness statement addresses all the factual issues that you wish him to give evidence on.
- Ensure your witnesses have copies of their witness statements well in advance of the hearing.
- Where referring to a document in a witness statement, include the page number in the bundle where it can be found.
- Generally, do not agree to advance disclosure of witness statements unless there is mutual disclosure.
- Consider if there is any default on the part of the other side that has prevented you preparing properly for the hearing, and if necessary refer the tribunal to it, with evidence.
- Ensure that a total of six bundles are brought to a hearing before a full Tribunal – one for each of the parties, one for the witness table and one for each of the Tribunal members.

Don't:

- Panic if you come to the tribunal without a witness statement (unless there is an order to this effect) – witness statements are important but not mandatory – *rule 27(2)* provides parties with the right (subject to the Employment Judge's discretion) to call witnesses/evidence.
- Feel obliged to volunteer a skeleton argument unless confident about doing so.
- Forget that thorough preparation is the key to knowing and understanding both your case and that of your opponent.
- Assume that because a matter is not the subject of an order, it is unnecessary.

Chapter 18

The Hearing I: the order of proceedings

Introduction

[18.1] This chapter looks at the order in which proceedings are conducted and also encompasses the steps parties should take upon arrival at the tribunal. It should be read in conjunction with the next two chapters, which address the manner in which tribunals approach issues of procedure and evidence, and describe some of the essential qualities of tribunal advocacy from how to open a case through to final submissions.

Arrival at the tribunal

[18.2]

- You should aim to ensure that all your witnesses arrive at least half an hour before the hearing is due to commence – this allows for both a safety margin for unforeseen delays and the opportunity for the advocate to clarify any residual issues/further developments with the witnesses. Upon arrival at the tribunal you should check in at reception, indicating which party you appear for. You will then be directed to either the respondent's or the claimant's waiting room. Some tribunals have private conference facilities, of which you may wish to take advantage. Tribunals strive to cater for those with disabilities, including hearing difficulties. It is sensible to contact the tribunal well in advance of the Hearing to confirm what arrangements are in place.
- Make contact with the clerk, who will usually introduce themselves to you in the waiting room, giving them copies of all documentation that you wish to place before the tribunal. Commonly, this will

be the bundle (whether agreed or otherwise) and any skeleton arguments, legal authorities, statement of issues or chronologies (see **chapter 17 – preparing for the full hearing**). The last two should, if possible, be agreed with the other side.

- Where appropriate, make contact with your opponent, both as a courtesy and with a view to identifying areas of agreement and disagreement between the parties. Tribunals are extremely grateful where, at the start of the hearing, parties are able to state clearly which areas remain contentious and which facts are agreed. When speaking to your opponent, bear in mind the following:
  (a) Avoid heated arguments, do not re-argue the dispute, do not allow yourself to be unduly pressurised, do not unreasonably reject attempts to settle a dispute, and never inform the tribunal that the parties are in agreement over a matter unless you are sure that this is the case.
  (b) Disclose statements of issues, chronologies and skeleton arguments (see **chapter 17**) to your opponent (if these have not been disclosed already), agreeing the first two where possible.
  (c) Ensure that each side has had sight of and is aware of (in broad terms) the evidence which will be adduced before the tribunal.
  (d) Try to agree a proposed timetable for the hearing, checking whether there is any objection to a particular course which you intend to adopt, such as calling a witness out of turn, or not calling a witness but instead relying on written evidence.
  (e) Disclose any legal authorities upon which you wish to rely, so as to give your opponent an opportunity to read them prior to the occasion when you refer the tribunal to them (sometimes this necessitates disclosure of such authorities prior to the day of the hearing).

  Note that if you do not wish to have any direct contact with the other side, you can ask the clerk to pass documentation to them.
- Speak to your witnesses before the start of the hearing to describe the order of proceedings and practical matters such as the Oath, where to sit and who is on the tribunal. You should also clarify aspects of the case which you do not understand or upon which, if acting as a representative, you need further instructions.

Formalities

[18.3] The Employment Judge is addressed as 'sir' or 'madam'. The parties will be directed where to sit as they enter the room, but it is usual for the respondent to sit on the left (as you face the tribunal) and the claimant on the right. Witnesses occupy the table in between the parties (or, in some tribunal rooms, to one side). Proceedings are conducted, in their entirety, sitting down (apart from witnesses being required to stand when taking the oath/affirming). Parties and witnesses are required to give their evidence on oath or to affirm (*rule 27(3)*). To avoid antagonising the tribunal it is imperative that all parties present at a hearing are silent when the oath or affirmation is taken.

Order and structure of proceedings: who presents their evidence first?

[18.4] It is usual for the party upon whom the burden of proof lies to call their evidence first. The normal order of play in different disputes (ie unfair dismissal or discrimination) is explained below. Parties should be aware, however, that there are cases where the burden shifts according to the issue the tribunal has to decide (ie unfair dismissal – the claimant bears the burden of establishing that the employment was terminated, then the respondent bears the burden of establishing that the correct procedure was applied and the decision was lawful). In these circumstances, it is usually the party upon whom the initial burden lies who will go first.

It is worth noting, however, that tribunals can and do depart from the standard approaches outlined below (especially in claims involving multiple complaints).

[18.5] *Unfair dismissal*: Provided the parties agree that there was a dismissal the respondent will normally present their evidence first, since the burden is on them to prove what the reason for dismissal was. In many cases, the reason for dismissal, eg misconduct, will not be in dispute, and the only issue will be whether the respondent acted reasonably in dismissing for that reason (in relation to which the burden of proof is neutral). Even in these circumstances, it is usual for the respondent to present their evidence first.

Where the fact of dismissal is in dispute: The employee presents their evidence first. Included in this category are claims for constructive dismissal.

[18.6] *Discrimination*: The claimant will go first (since the initial burden lies on them to prove an arguable case of discrimination, which then shifts to the respondent who needs to provide an explanation unrelated to sex, race etc for any unfavourable treatment) unless, for example, the respondent concedes that there has been indirect discrimination, but wishes to assert a defence of objective justification, whereupon the respondent may give its evidence first.

[18.7] *Mixed unfair dismissal and discrimination claims*: Who goes first in these circumstances will be for the tribunal to decide. It will listen, however, to the views of the parties. The claimant may be better placed, particularly in claims of direct discrimination, to argue that they should go first, since the burden of establishing a *prima facie* case of discrimination falls squarely on them, in contrast to unfair dismissal, where the burden of proof in deciding reasonableness is neutral.

[18.8] *Equal pay cases*: The claimant will usually present their evidence first, since the burden is on them to prove the principal components of their claim (shifting to the employer, where applicable, to prove a material factor defence).

Going first: advantage or disadvantage?

[18.9] On balance, going first is probably preferable, but the issue is by no means clear cut and often the reverse can be true. It is important, whether you are going first or second, to maximise the advantages available to you, which are different in kind.

Advantages of going first:

- You have the first and (usually) the last word. The party who goes first will deliver their final submissions last. It may be, however, that the other party will ask for a right to reply in relation to matters raised in those submissions, in relation to which they have not had an opportunity to make submissions.
- You can create a positive first impression of your case in the minds of the tribunal.

Advantages of going second:

- Your witnesses can respond directly to matters raised in evidence by the other side before they are raised in cross-examination.
- You know the case you have to meet and can, if necessary (and provided there is a natural pause in proceedings), review your original plan of attack, although the scope for doing so may be restricted by your existing witness statements.

The order of proceedings: step by step

Step one: introduction by the Employment Judge

[18.10] There is usually a brief introduction by the Employment Judge, who introduces himself and addresses matters such as establishing whether there is agreement over the effective date of and alleged reason for termination, clarifying the issues, establishing the batting order, organising the documentation (eg bundles etc) and confirming whether the parties are ready to proceed or if there are preliminary issues which need to be resolved. Often the Employment Judge will provide an indication of how he proposes to utilise the time allotted for the hearing. If the claimant is unrepresented, the Employment Judge will normally explain the legal basis upon which the tribunal will decide the case.

Step two: (optional) opening speech from the party who is calling their evidence first (party A)

[18.11] The desirability of making an opening speech is discussed in **chapter 20 – the hearing III – the essentials of effective tribunal advocacy**.

Step three: party A calls its evidence

[18.12] Witnesses should be called, if possible, in a logical order. The witness will first read his witness statement, before being asked any supplementary questions in chief by their own side. The witness will then cross-examined by the other side. For guidance upon examination in chief (including the use of witness statements) and cross-examination, see **chapter 20.** After cross examination the tribunal may ask questions to clarify any matters that they feel have not been adequately addressed. The party calling the witness will then have an opportunity to re-examine; that is to ask questions arising from answers given in cross examination and in reply to questions from the tribunal.

Step four: party B calls its evidence

[18.13] Exactly the same process as is described above in relation to party A is then carried out by party B.

Step five: closing submissions

[18.14] Each party, or their representative, addresses the tribunal, at the conclusion of the evidence, as to why the tribunal should find in their favour. The party who has adduced their evidence last (ie party B) speaks first. Guidance on making final submissions is contained in **chapter 22**.

Step six: the decision

[18.15] The tribunal will ask the parties to return to their waiting room whilst they make their decision. Upon being asked to return, the parties will usually be informed that the decision they are about to hear is an oral decision, but that they will be sent a written decision in due course (see **chapter 23 – the decision, chapter 26 – steps after the decision II: appeal**). It is sensible for the losing party to request a written decision at the conclusion of the hearing or within 14 days thereafter. In more complex cases the tribunal will often reserve its decision which means that the parties will be released for the tribunal to consider their decision, a written copy of which will be sent to the parties on some future date.

Step seven: remedies hearing/costs

[18.16] If the claimant is successful in relation to all or part of their claim it is currently the practice of the tribunals, provided there is time, to proceed straight into a remedies hearing (see **chapter 24 – remedies: calculating likely awards**), and cases are usually listed with this in mind. Therefore, always come prepared and ready to prove and argue the case on remedies. There are now, in certain instances, costs sanctions for failing to do so (see **chapter 22 –costs**). If you consider that it is possible to agree an award with the other side the tribunal may agree to a short adjournment for negotiations to take place.

Chapter 19

The Hearing II: the conduct of proceedings by the tribunal

Introduction

[19.1] Tribunals have, subject to two important restrictions, the power to regulate their own procedure. *Rule 60(1)* of the *2004 Rules* states:

> 'Subject to the provisions of these rules and any practice directions, a tribunal or Employment Judge may regulate its or his own procedure.'

In a similar vein, *rule 14(3)* provides:

> 'The Employment Judge or tribunal (as the case may be) shall make such enquiries of persons appearing before him or it and of witnesses as he or it considers appropriate and shall otherwise conduct the hearing in such manner as he or it considers most appropriate for the clarification of the issues and generally for the just handling of the proceedings.'

The effect of these provisions is that tribunals enjoy a broad discretion to conduct their proceedings in the manner in which they see fit, including deciding what evidence they hear, the order in which it is heard and the manner in which it is adduced.

[19.2] There are, however, two important limitations upon this wide ranging discretion. First, tribunals must conduct proceedings in accordance with the rules of natural justice, in relation to which the Employment Appeal Tribunal (EAT) and higher courts have, over the years, laid down guidelines. Secondly, they must do so in accordance with their own procedural rules and Practice Directions which, it must be remembered, place particular emphasis on giving effect to the overriding objective (see **chapter 8 – fairness: the overriding objective**).

[19.3] Failure to be aware of some of the key features of a fair procedure could lead to a party being seriously disadvantaged in the presentation of its case. In particular, parties should bear in mind the following:

- Parties have the right (subject to the Employment Judge's power to control the conduct of hearings) to give evidence, call witnesses, question witnesses and address the tribunal (*rule 27(2)*).
- It is for the parties, not the tribunal, to ensure that all relevant evidence is placed before the tribunal (see *Craig v British Railways (Scottish Region)* [1973] 8 ITR 636 and *Derby City Council v Marshall* [1979] ICR 731, [1979] IRLR 261). Even if a matter is raised in the ET1 or ET3, it is incumbent upon the party concerned to adduce evidence in relation to it, although the tribunals may assist parties by reminding them (particularly those who are unrepresented) of this. If no evidence is adduced, the tribunal will have no factual material upon which it can make a finding for, or against, a particular party.
- The party who calls their evidence first should call *all* of their evidence and not, subsequently, put in cross-examination to the other side's witnesses matters which have not been first adduced in chief from their own (see **chapter 20 – the hearing III: the essentials of effective tribunal advocacy** – *Aberdeen Steak Houses Group plc v Ibrahim* [1988] ICR 550, [1988] IRLR 420).

  Example: The claimant has given evidence about a meeting that took place between her and the manager in the respondent organisation. She alleges that the manager told her she would shortly be made redundant. When the manager gives evidence, the claimant's representative suggests to him that, in addition to saying this, he also told the claimant that she was hopeless at her job. This had never been said by the claimant in evidence and the representative is therefore putting in cross-examination something which has not formed part of her case in chief.
- The party who calls their evidence second must, in cross-examination of the first party's witnesses, put to them all factual matters which are in dispute in relation to which it proposes to call evidence of its own (see *Aberdeen Steak Houses* above). The reason for this is the principle that each party must be given a fair opportunity to deal with the other's case (see **chapter 20**).

  Example: The claimant gives evidence saying that he was unfairly dismissed for an allegation of fighting. It is the respondent's case that the claimant had previously been involved in another fight – a matter which is disputed by the claimant. The respondent, in cross-examination, does not ask the claimant about the previous fight.

When the respondent's manager gives evidence, he mentions it as a factor he took into account in reaching his decision. The allegation in relation to the prior incident of fighting ought to have been put to the claimant in cross-examination to give him an opportunity to deal with it. The tribunal may allow the claimant to be recalled so as to hear the claimant's version of events, or may decide to attach less weight to the manager's allegation. In an extreme situation the tribunal may ignore the allegation.

- Parties should not be taken by surprise by serious allegations which are made at the last minute and which they have not had time to prepare for (*Hotson v Wisbech Conservative Club* [1984] ICR 859, [1984] IRLR 422). Where this occurs, the party against whom the allegation is made is entitled, if necessary, to seek an adjournment (with the attendant cost consequences for the party in default). Again, this is based upon the principle that each party should be given a fair opportunity to deal with the other's case.
- It is for the tribunal to decide who presents their case first – however they are required to exercise this discretion within the confines of fairly strict guidelines laid down by the EAT and higher courts (*Gill v Harold Andrews Sheepbridge Ltd* [1974] IRLR 109, [1974] ICR 294 and *Oxford v Department of Health and Social Security* [1977] IRLR 22, [1977] ICR 884). For further guidance on the order in which evidence is called, see **chapter 18 – the hearing I: the order of proceedings**.
- It is generally for the parties to decide the order in which they call their own witnesses (*Barnes v BPC (Business Forms) Ltd* [1975] IRLR 313, [1975] ICR 390).
- Where evidence is relevant to the issue/s the tribunal has to decide, then it is obliged to hear it, even if it is in hearsay form (*Rosedale Mouldings Ltd v Sibley* [1980] IRLR 387, [1980] ICR 816). The form in which the evidence is presented is relevant only to the weight, or importance, which the tribunal attach to it (see **19.2–19.4**).
- The Employment Judge is under a duty to take a note of the evidence in the case, which may be ordered to be produced on appeal by the EAT (see **chapter 26 – steps after the decision II: appeal**) (*Houston v Lightwater Farm Ltd* [1990] IRLR 469, [1990] ICR 502).

Calling evidence

[19.4] Evidence is the factual material upon which the tribunal reaches its decision. The rules of fairness dictate that there are limitations upon the types and amount of evidence which can be adduced in tribunal proceedings. It is clear from the wording of *rule 14(3)* that the Employment Judge or tribunal has a very wide discretion to restrict or prevent a party from adducing certain evidence or, if it has already been adduced, to exclude it from their minds in coming to a decision. Such evidence is described as 'inadmissible'. By contrast, evidence which can be legitimately considered by the tribunal is described as 'admissible'. 'Admissible' merely means that the tribunal is entitled to consider the evidence and take it into account in reaching its decision. It may ultimately however decide to accept, reject, or attach no weight (ie importance) to it.

Admissible and inadmissible evidence

Irrelevant evidence

[19.5] For evidence to be admissible, it must be relevant to one or more of the issues which the tribunal has to decide. Tribunals have a very wide discretion concerning the evidence which they may consider – indeed *rule 14(2)* specifically provides that tribunals are not bound by any rule of law relating to the admissibility of evidence. Proceedings in employment tribunals are therefore to be distinguished from, for example, criminal cases where very strict rules of evidence govern what evidence may be admitted. Hence, whereas very strict rules apply to the admissibility of hearsay evidence in criminal cases, no such rules apply in claims brought before an employment tribunal.

[19.6] The reliability or accuracy of a piece of evidence is *not*, save in exceptional circumstances, a factor in assessing its relevance, nor does a party need to show that it is important evidence. All such considerations go to the weight and the amount of time which will be allocated to the evidence at the hearing.

[19.7] In assessing relevance, parties should ask whether it is 'probative' of one or more of the issues that the tribunal has to decide. That is to say is it capable, in any respect, of assisting the tribunal in deciding that issue. If it is so capable, even in a very limited way, it will normally be admissible. If the relevance is limited, this is a factor which goes to weight, but not admissibility.

[19.8] It is important for parties to bear in mind the distinction between relevance and weight. On many occasions, evidence will be of dubious, or very limited, relevance. In these circumstances, it will usually be admissible. The opposing party will, however, be well placed to argue that, given its marginal relevance, the tribunal should attach little or no weight to it.

[19.9] Parties should be aware that the mere fact that evidence is arguably relevant will not always mean that it is admitted by the tribunal. As indicated above, tribunals have a wide discretion in determining what evidence to consider and they may decide that allegations made for the first time at a hearing which are not referred to in the pleadings or witness statements, and which cause serious prejudice to the other party are not properly admissible.

Examples: relevance and weight compared

[19.10] *Example one*: An employee is dismissed for theft from his employer which he denies. After the dismissal the respondent discovers that the employee has a criminal conviction for theft ten years ago and seeks to adduce this in evidence. The claimant attempts to get the evidence of the previous conviction excluded on the basis that it is irrelevant. The claimant stands a good chance of succeeding in having the evidence excluded on grounds of irrelevance. In the circumstances of this case, the past conviction is not relevant to the issue which the tribunal has to decide, which is whether having regard to information that was before the employer at the time and upon which the employer based its decision, was the decision lawful and reasonable. Note that depending on the facts surrounding the conviction (and whether it is *spent*) the issue may be relevant in determining the award – ie if the tribunal accepts that the employer would have had reasonable grounds for dismissing the employee on grounds of the previous undisclosed conviction, this may well affect the award he receives.

[19.11] *Example two*: Assuming the same facts as in Example one, except that the previous conviction was a factor which the employer took into account in reaching its decision to dismiss.

The evidence is, in these circumstances, clearly admissible as the tribunal is assessing the reasonableness of the employer's decision at the time and the theft is one of the factors which the employer took into account. The claimant is likely to want the evidence admitted in any event, in order to argue that it was unreasonable for the employer to take into account such an (arguably) irrelevant factor.

[19.12] *Example three*: In a discrimination case, the claimant argues that he was denied promotion on account of race and that a less well qualified person accepted the job. The claimant seeks to adduce evidence that, at a Christmas party which took place after the selection process, the manager responsible was heard making a racist joke. The evidence of the joke is likely to be admitted because it is relevant to the issue of whether there was a racial motive for the non-selection. This does not prevent the respondent arguing, in final submissions, that the tribunal should attach no weight to the evidence, for example on the basis that the evidence is untrue (if applicable) or that that, in any event, no tribunal could safely infer from the making of such a joke that the manager would adopt a racist selection procedure:

Without prejudice communications

[19.13] Offers and negotiations relating to the settling of proceedings are not admissible evidence in tribunal proceedings (save in relation to the issue of costs after liability and the remedy have been determined). For this reason, it is important that documents relating to such negotiations or offers are not included in the evidence presented to the tribunal and that no reference is made to them during the course of proceedings. On occasions, a claimant who is not represented will be unaware of this rule, and will draw the tribunal's attention to an offer which has been made. The Employment Judge will, in these circumstances, indicate to both parties that such evidence is not admissible and will direct the tribunal's lay members to exclude such evidence from their minds in reaching any decision. The respondent may still consider, however, that the tribunal has been prejudiced by the disclosure of the information in question. If the respondent forms this view it should make an application for the hearing to be abandoned and the case listed in front of a newly constituted tribunal. Whether this course is adopted will depend upon a number of factors, including how much of the negotiations were referred to, how prejudicial the terms of the offer were and the size of any offer that has been made.

[19.14] Tribunals are aware that parties do attempt to settle cases and that fact, in itself, is unlikely to prejudice them. Where, however, the offer is sufficiently large to suggest that the respondent recognises there are serious weaknesses in their case, then serious thought should be given to making such an application, which should be made as soon as possible (and preferably immediately) after the wrongful disclosure has taken place. If successful, the respondent should consider making an application for costs arising from the adjournment.

Challenging inadmissible evidence

[19.15] In the criminal jurisdiction, a challenge to the admissibility of the evidence is made in the absence of the jury. This prevents the unsatisfactory and artificial situation arising where the jury is asked to exclude from their minds evidence which they have already heard. This option is not available in civil or tribunal proceedings. The fact remains, however, that the best course is to prevent inadmissible evidence from coming to the attention of the tribunal which makes the decision by agreeing with the other side in advance of the Hearing the evidence which the tribunal will hear. In the majority of cases this will be possible. Where this is not possible or practicable, if possible, resolve any disputes about the relevance of evidence at a pre-hearing review, obtaining a ruling from the Employment Judge as to what evidence can be adduced at the full Hearing. Such disputes are likely to be particularly prevalent in discrimination and equal pay cases.

[19.16] Where the issue as to the admissibility of evidence arises during the course of the Hearing there are a number of options. Sometimes the other side's representative will ask a question of a witness which will put you on notice that inadmissible evidence is about to be adduced. The best course is to object to the question there and then, before the answer is given. State that a question is being asked about an irrelevant matter and explain why. The Employment Judge will then give a ruling on whether the question is permissible. Sometimes, it is best to let such questions 'go by' if they are innocuous in nature and you are confident that the answer will not harm your case. Parties should be aware that, by and large, tribunals do not appreciate the flow of evidence being interrupted by continuous objections (especially concerning relevance) – and therefore parties should, where possible, allow the tribunal (who are well aware of the rules of procedure and evidence) to manage proceedings as they see fit.

[19.17] If inadmissible evidence is adduced, you have a choice whether to refer to it there and then, or to wait until your final submissions. If you believe that an answer has been given which will lead to the adducing of further inadmissible evidence, it is best to object immediately in order to prevent this occurring.

[19.18] When addressing the tribunal during final submissions, draw its attention to any evidence which in your opinion should be excluded from its mind as being irrelevant or incapable of assisting in determining the issues in the case.

Do's and Don'ts

Do:

- Remember the fundamental principle in tribunal proceedings that each party should have a fair opportunity to present their own case and respond to that of the other side.
- Apply for an adjournment (with costs where appropriate) if a new matter is raised by the other side which you have not had an opportunity to respond to and in relation to which you need time to prepare evidence in response. Alternatively, if appropriate, ask for a short break to take instructions.
- If you are going first, ask for a witness to be recalled if the other side give evidence about a matter which ought to have been put to them first in cross-examination.
- Attempt to resolve issues of inadmissible evidence prior to the hearing.
- Use the overriding objective as a tool when challenging the fairness of proceedings.

Don't:

- Object unnecessarily – the tribunal will be unimpressed by a party who objects continuously merely on the grounds that a particular question is not relevant. Unnecessary objections can also give the impression that a party has something to hide.

- Forget that it is the duty of the parties to place all relevant evidence (whether helpful or prejudicial) before the tribunal.
- Be afraid to ask for a witness to be recalled if you have failed to put a matter to them – although the tribunal has a discretion to refuse.
- Be afraid, where appropriate, to apply for a case to be re-listed in front of a newly constituted tribunal where reference has been made to without prejudice negotiations

Chapter 20

The Hearing III: the essentials of effective tribunal advocacy

Introduction

[20.1] Advocacy is, in essence, the art of persuasion. Whilst experience is an invaluable asset for any advocate, there are certain key features of good advocacy which this chapter seeks to address.

Pre-hearing preparation

[20.2] The importance of thorough preparation cannot be overestimated. However impressive someone's ability to 'think on their feet', the reality is that without a clear understanding of the legal issues and facts of a dispute, a party is unlikely to do justice to their case. For most of us the capacity to respond to a witness effectively in cross-examination, answer questions from the tribunal and deal with unexpected developments comes, in large part, from having a thorough knowledge of the facts of the case, an appreciation of the chronology in which relevant events occurred and a clear understanding of the issues arising in a particular case. It also comes from having given careful thought in advance to how the case should be presented. The following are some of the key features of effective preparation.

Prepare a chronology

[20.3] It is a myth that preparing an effective chronology lengthens your preparation time,– usually the reverse is true. In most circumstances, you will do this anyway for the tribunal, so there will be no duplication of effort. A chronology is an invaluable way of ensuring that you have a thorough knowledge of the documentation in the case. It will enable you to organise and marshal the evidence in your own mind. The chronology should contain all significant relevant events in the sequence they occurred. Where the event is recorded in a document, e.g. notes of a disciplinary hearing, the document should be referred to (including the page number where it can be found in the bundle) in the chronology.

[20.4] Chronologies are usually drawn up using the following:

- the bundle of documentary evidence (such as letters, disciplinary notes etc);
- witness statements;
- any additional instructions you may have.

Many advocates prepare chronologies in draft form as they are reading the documents. As you prepare the chronology and marshal the facts, useful thoughts on the presentation of your case will frequently come to mind. For example, you might notice an inconsistency or weakness in the other side's case which provides a useful avenue for cross-examination, or a point may occur to you which could be used in final submissions. Note these down as they occur. How this is done is a matter of choice. You might, for example, wish to have separate sheets of paper headed 'points for cross-examination', 'points for final submissions' and 'matters to be asked of own witnesses'.

After completing your chronology you should be able to turn to any relevant document in the case and be satisfied that, if it is relevant, the event to which it refers is recorded in the chronology.

Identify the issues in the case

[20.5] It is essential to identify the issues which the tribunal will have to decide. Only then can you plan how to persuade the tribunal how to find in your favour in relation to those issues and identify the evidence that you will need to call. In order to identify the issues, you will need to have a knowledge of the relevant area of law. So, in an unfair dismissal case, you will need to be aware that the tribunal must decide:

(a) what the reason was for the dismissal;
(b) whether this was a potentially lawful reason; and

(c) whether the employer acted reasonably (both procedurally and substantively) in dismissing for that reason.

In many such cases, (a) and (b) are not in dispute and the only live issue is (c).

[20.6] If there has been a Case Management Discussion or a Pre-Hearing Review before the final Hearing it is likely that the tribunal will have sought to clarify the issues and will very often have listed the issues that remain in dispute. It is therefore advisable to examine very carefully any directions or orders that the tribunal may have made, either on its own initiative or at the request of the parties, as these may help to refine the issues to be determined at the Hearing.

Plan your objectives

[20.7] Once you have identified the chronology of events and legal issues, plan your objectives in relation to those issues based on your factual knowledge of the case. A claimant in an unfair dismissal case might, therefore, wish to demonstrate that the employer failed to adopt a fair procedure by:

- not interviewing relevant witnesses;
- not giving the claimant a proper opportunity to respond to the allegations;
- failing to take into account relevant considerations, for example the claimant's lengthy service and good record.

[20.8] In a case of alleged discrimination by non-promotion, the respondent may wish to demonstrate that they carried out a fair selection procedure through open advertisement and fair interviewing process where candidates were assessed against objective criteria, and that the non-selection of the claimant was due to his failure to perform adequately at interview when assessed against these criteria. Under each area you might want to make notes of the areas of evidence which are likely to support each proposition, highlighting matters to put in cross-examination and which need to be adduced from your own witnesses in support of your case.

Plan your examinations in chief and cross-examinations and, using your objectives, have a broad framework in mind as to what your final submissions are likely to be.

Advocacy at the hearing

[20.9] *The importance of note taking*: It is essential to take a thorough note of the evidence as it is heard. Proceedings are not tape recorded and your note will (unless you ask the Employment Judge to recite his) be the only record you have of what has taken place. It is surprising how seemingly mundane and non-contentious evidence can become relevant at a later stage, for example if a witness gives an answer in cross-examination which is different from what was said in his statement. It is also important, when making final submissions, to be able to accurately recite to the tribunal important pieces of evidence upon which you rely.

Unqualified people, representing themselves or their companies, are well advised to bring a friend or colleague to help take notes – it is sometimes hard to write, listen, think and ask questions at the same time.

The opening speech

[20.10] There is no obligation upon a party to make an opening statement and this is frequently unnecessary in straightforward cases where the issues are adequately defined at the outset. Tribunals tend to dislike opening speeches unless they are genuinely necessary. It is sensible to ask the Employment Judge whether the tribunal would be assisted by an opening. The objective of your opening speech should be limited to:

- defining the issues in the case, identifying areas of factual/legal conflict; and
- giving the tribunal a very broad outline of your case in relation to those issues.

The latter can be useful, particularly in complex cases, if you wish the tribunal to approach the evidence with a clear idea of what your case is. It is crucial, however, that you do not stray into giving evidence in your opening or make submissions about the strength of the evidence or as to the merits your case.

Do's and Don'ts

Do:

- Ask the Employment Judge if an opening would assist.
- Keep your opening concise.
- Make an opening statement only if you feel that it is necessary to clarify the issues from the outset.
- Confine your remarks to giving a broad view of what your case is in relation to the issues, or the 'theme' of your case.

Don't:

- Describe in detail the evidence which the tribunal is going to hear.
- Make submissions about the strength of your case and the weakness of the other side's – save this for final submissions.
- Allow your opening to become a hostage to fortune by making predictions about the evidence – cases are inherently unpredictable.

Examination in chief

[20.11] Examination in chief is when you ask your own witness to give their version of events to the tribunal. As an advocate you should ensure that your witnesses:

- deal with all relevant issues in relation to which they are able to give evidence;
- presented in as persuasive a manner as possible.

In almost all cases parties will either be expected or otherwise expressly directed by the tribunal to have obtained and exchanged witness statements before the Hearing. It can be of considerable advantage if a thorough statement has been prepared. This can then be read out by the witness, accompanied by supplementary questions (if necessary) to clarify or expand upon the matters in the statement. Where a statement is not prepared, you will have to elicit the necessary evidence from the witness through a series of questions. Where questions are asked of a witness in chief (whether supplementary to a witness statement or otherwise) these questions should be 'non-leading' – the answer must not be suggested in the question (see **20.16**).

Preparing an examination in chief

[20.12] Before your witness gives evidence, you should be clear about all of the matters which you require that witness to cover. This involves identifying which issues in the case the witness is able to give direct evidence about.

Typically, evidence in chief (whether through a witness statement or otherwise) should cover:

- all relevant events and conversations which that person witnessed;
- the basis upon which that person reached any relevant decision, including the matters they took into account (note, in an unfair dismissal case, it is common for these to be recorded by the manager in a contemporaneous memo. Where the memo is complete, the witness statement need simply refer to that document as being an accurate reflection of the basis for the decision); and
- any other relevant matters upon which that witness is able to give relevant evidence.

Examination in chief: step by step

[20.13]

- Inform the tribunal who you are calling.
- The witness, while standing by the witness table, will be asked to take the oath or to affirm, as administered by either the Employment Judge, one of the lay members or the clerk, at the Employment Judge's discretion. The witness then sits for the rest of the proceedings.
- The witness will then usually be asked to confirm their name and address by the Employment Judge. If he does not ask, make this your first question.
- If the witness has a statement, ask that witness to confirm:
  (a) that they have made a statement in the case;
  (b) that they have a copy of that statement in front of them;
  (c) that the signature at the bottom of the statement is theirs; and
  (d) that (subject to any corrections made on the day) the contents are true to the best of their knowledge.
- The witness (if this is not covered in the statement) should be asked to explain his employment/professional duties.
- Where there are parts of the statement which are incorrect – for example a date is wrong – take the witness to that part immediately, and ask them whether it is correct, and, if not, that correct evidence should be, and ask the tribunal to make a note of the correction.

- Practice various between Employment Judges as to whether witnesses should read their statements aloud or if the tribunal is content to treat the statements 'as read'. In *Mehta v Child Support Agency* UKEAT/0127/10/CEA, the EAT (the President presiding) gave guidance as to when statements should be read. Whilst this decision remains within the tribunal's discretion they are now directed to consider whether as a matter of routine statements need to be read aloud. Where there are good reasons for a witness reading their statement aloud (eg affording a nervous witness the opportunity to 'settle themselves' before cross-examination thereby assisting them in giving their evidence).
- If it is decided that the witness will read their statement, as theystop them at any point where an additional point of clarification is warranted or a document needs to be referred to, or alternatively wait until they have read the statement and ask additional questions at that point, referring them back, where necessary, to the relevant numbered paragraph.

The purpose of supplementary questions where a witness statement is used

[20.14] The purpose of supplementary questions is to:

- correct anything which is inaccurate;
- update the statement in relation to recent events;
- add to or clarify particular parts of the statement;
- respond to new points which have been or are likely to be given in evidence by other witnesses;
- refer the tribunal to a document in the bundle which is mentioned in the statement.

Generally speaking, supplementary questions should be directed to clarifying or amplifying that which is contained in the witness' statement or addressing matters which arise from the other party's statements although Tribunals tend to differ as to the level of strictness with which they apply that principle.

[20.15] The questions can be asked either after the statement is read out or as it is being read out, with the witness being stopped at the relevant stage. The latter is usually the best course when you are stopping to refer the tribunal to a particular document in the bundle mentioned in the statement. In these circumstances, you should ask the witness to refer to the page in the bundle and confirm that the document is the one he is referring to in the statement. With important documents, give the tribunal an opportunity to read it there and then, before asking the witness to continue reading the statement.

- Where there is no witness statement, elicit the relevant evidence from your witness through a series of questions, which in contentious matters (ie matters in dispute) should be non-leading.
- The best means of preparing the questions is to write down all the matters upon which you need a witness to give evidence, and then formulate the questions.

Leading questions

[20.16] Any question asked of your own witness, including (where there is a witness statement) supplementary questions, should not be leading in respect of any contentious matter. A leading question is one where the answer is suggested in the question. As a good rule of thumb, a question which can be answered with a simple 'yes' or 'no' may indicate that a leading question has been asked. Similarly, questions starting with 'is it right to say…' or 'would you agree…' are strongly indicative of a leading question. By contrast, questions starting with the words 'why' 'what happened…' or 'to what extent…' are unlikely to be leading. Leading questions can do a disservice to your own witness. A tribunal is likely to attach less weight to an answer which is given in response to a leading question.

Example

You are acting for the respondent. You want to bring out in evidence both that the seriousness of the misconduct and that the claimant's previous formal warning for misconduct were important factors in the decision to dismiss.

Example of a leading question: Is it right to say that the most important factors in coming to the decision to dismiss were the seriousness of the misconduct and the fact that the claimant received a formal warning three months previously? Answer: Yes.

Example of a non-leading question: What were the principal factors in deciding that dismissal was warranted? Answer: The seriousness of the misconduct and the fact that he had been warned three months earlier.

Effectively directing your witness

[20.17] Adducing the evidence you want from a witness without asking leading questions can be extremely difficult. The following should prove useful:

- Use your materials – often you can direct the witness to the area you want by referring them to a particular document. This can act as a signpost. You can ask, for example, what their reaction is to a particular document, whether it is accurate or inaccurate, whether they wish to add something etc.
- Direct your witness to a particular aspect of the other side's case which you want them to deal with. For example, 'what is your reaction to the assertion by x that you lost your temper at the meeting on 12 November…?'.
- Plan your questions in advance: this is important, but remember that evidence rarely goes precisely according to plan so you need to retain an element of flexibility.

[20.18] *Challenging leading questions asked by your opponent*: Do not be afraid to object to a leading question (preferably before the answer is given) if one is asked by your opponent of their own witness. Sometimes, you can nip the question in the bud, for example if you hear the words 'is it true to say that the main reason…'. Politely object to the question on the grounds that the question is being phrased in a leading manner. Tribunals differ in their approach to the asking of leading questions. They are likely, for obvious reasons, to be far more lenient to a claimant who is representing themselves and is unfamiliar with proceedings, than a legally qualified representative. A tribunal will also be keen to prevent proceedings becoming oppressive, or evidence to become disjointed, and will therefore usually only restrict leading questions in relation to matters that go to the heart of the dispute between the parties. Parties should remember, however, that too many leading questions, irrespective of whether they relate to non-contentious issues, can create a bad impression and undermine the weight of evidence.

Cross-examination and putting your case

[20.19] The aim of cross-examination is:

- to elicit the evidence helpful to your case from the other side's witness, usually (in contrast to examination in chief) through a series of leading questions;

- to give that witness an opportunity to deal with your case where it is inconsistent with or at odds with their own. This is an aspect of procedural fairness – namely giving both sides the opportunity to comment on the other side's evidence. This is particularly important with allegations of dishonesty (note, if your side is going first, your own witness should already have given their version of events/what was said when giving evidence in chief – it is usually not permissible, in these circumstances, for the allegation to be put for the first time in cross-examination where your witness has not given evidence of the allegation).

[20.20] A successful cross-examination involves the examiner eliciting the answers they want from the witness through very precise questioning. This involves:

- careful planning;
- an appreciation of the issues in relation to which that witness evidence is relevant;
- the identification of weaknesses in that evidence which you can bring out;
- the setting of realistic objectives for your cross-examination; and
- the formulation of precise questions – usually leading in nature.

In contrast to examination in chief, leading questions are not only permitted, but are generally preferable. They allow you to control the witness and elicit the answers you want from them.

Example

You appear for the claimant in an unfair dismissal case where an employee of eight years standing was dismissed for being three hours late for an important meeting. Whilst preparing the case, you have noticed that the contemporaneous memorandum recording the reasons for dismissal makes no mention of the employee's previous good attendance record. One of your objectives is to demonstrate that this was an important factor which the manager failed to take into account in reaching his decision.

> Q: Do you agree that the claimant's previous good record was a relevant factor for you to consider when taking the decision to dismiss?
>
> A: Yes.

> Q: Please turn to page 40 in the bundle. This is a contemporaneous memorandum which you prepared recording the factors you took into consideration in deciding to dismiss the claimant?
>
> A: Yes.
>
> Q: Did you take care in writing that memorandum?
>
> A: Yes.
>
> Q: Yet you make no mention of that previous good record?
>
> A: No.
>
> Q: I suggest the reason that it is not mentioned in the memorandum is because you didn't in fact consider it to be relevant?
>
> A: ….

Explanation of example

[20.21] There is an old saying: 'never ask a question in cross-examination unless you know the answer'. This would probably be better phrased as 'never ask a question in cross-examination unless you are fully prepared for any possible answer'. Using the above example, some of the questions do admit of more than one answer, but the planning of your questions should ensure that, where possible, the witness is 'cornered' into giving evidence that assists you. If, for example, the witness answers that the previous good record is not a relevant factor, this does not matter. You have still obtained a potentially damaging admission from the manager in that he failed to take into account a relevant consideration. You can simply note this down for final submissions and proceed to the next theme in your cross-examination. As it is, the manager accepts the premise of the question hence the need to take him (and the tribunal) to the document, establish its accuracy and with the final question put the conclusion that you wish the tribunal to make.

Putting your case

[20.22] The obligation to put your case to a witness is an important one. It stems from the principle that each party should have the opportunity to respond to the other side's evidence. This is particularly so when you are first to cross-examine and your own side's evidence is being called second. If you have failed to put an aspect of your case in cross-examination, the tribunal may refuse to admit evidence from your own side in relation to that matter. Alternatively, the other side's witness may have to be recalled in order to give them the opportunity to deal with it. The obligation to put your case extends especially to circumstances where:

- you are alleging that the witness said or did something which has not been mentioned in their evidence in chief; or
- has failed to give a truthful account of an event.

Parties, especially those who may be appearing before a tribunal for the first time, should not, however, be too daunted by the obligation to put their case – important though it is. No one can predict with certainty the course which evidence may take, and even the most conscientious and experienced advocate cannot count on being able to eliminate the risk of surprise altogether. Provided that you do your best to avoid any possibility of unfair surprise to your opponent in the way your evidence is presented, you need not expect the tribunal to be too harsh and censorious if, for any reason, your case has not been fully put. Given a spirit of goodwill all round, consequent risks of injustice can normally be removed through the tribunal authorising the recall of a witness or some other direction, though it is under no obligation to do so.

Example

You represent the respondent in an unfair dismissal case where the respondent maintains that the claimant was not dismissed but resigned. One of the crucial events is a meeting on the final day of the claimant's employment. The claimant gives evidence that, at this meeting, he was told to pack his bags and leave. Your case is that this was never said and further that the claimant said: 'I have had enough of this place, I'm leaving – send me my P45'. You must give the claimant the opportunity to deal with this allegation and you should further challenge his evidence that he was told to pack his bags and leave. Try and do this, however, in a way that is advantageous to your case.

Q: You were told that the purpose of the meeting was to find a way of resolving your problems at the company (refer to document in bundle)?

A: Yes.

Q: At the meeting, you were present, together with two members of management?

A: Yes, John Jones and Bill Smith.

Q: During the meeting, Bill Smith offered you a number of practical solutions for working out your problems at work?

A: No.

Q: You were angry and upset during the meeting?

A: Yes, because of the way they had been treating me.

Q: Both managers remained calm throughout the meeting?

A: I suppose so.

Q: You had been in the room for 30 minutes before you left?

A: Yes.

Q: When you left you were angry and upset?

A: Yes I was.

Q: You were so angry and upset that you told them you were leaving and they should send you your P45?

A: I never said that.

Q: You've since come to regret saying that and you've invented the story that they told you to pack your bags and leave?

A: No, I'm telling the truth.

Explanation of example

[20.23] Note that, with this example, you have built up to the moment of asking the relevant questions by establishing two facts favourable to your version. First, that the Claimant was angry and upset and therefore liable to say something in the heat of the moment. Second, that he had been in the room for 30 minutes, something arguably inconsistent with a dismissal. Both these points can be noted down for final submissions.

Finally, it is important to be realistic when planning your cross-examination of a witness. There will be occasions when cross-examination is unnecessary altogether, for example because the witness' evidence is uncontentious. If you consider that asking questions will not assist your case, do not ask them, unless you have to in order to give the witness an opportunity to deal with your case.

Do's and Don'ts

Do:

- Plan a clear set of objectives for your cross-examination.
- Ensure that your objectives are realistic.
- Ask precise (preferably leading) questions which restricts the responses available.
- Plan for every conceivable answer.
- Be purposeful in your style of questioning.

Don't:

- Be aggressive.
- Engage in an argument with or respond to questions by the witness – move on when the time is right.
- Think that a cross-examination *should* be hostile in tone: if you can get the witness to freely agree with you, this is often an advantage.
- Make comments on the witness's evidence there and then; instead note these down and save them for final submissions.

Re-examination

[20.24] Every party calling a witness has the right to re-examine the witness after cross-examination from the other side. Re-examination must be limited, however, to matters which have been raised in cross-examination. It cannot, without the permission of the tribunal, be used to introduce evidence which should have been given in chief and which does not arise from the cross-examination. Re-examination is a right to be exercised sparingly and should *not* be used to persuade the witness to repeat, or to change evidence they have already given. It is frequently unnecessary, and often inadvisable, to re-examine a witness at all.

[20.25] Examples of where re-examination might be appropriate include the following:

- To give an opportunity to the witness to say something which you know forms part of their evidence but which they either inadvertently failed to mention in cross-examination or were not given an opportunity to do so.
  Example: You act for the claimant in an unfair dismissal case. In cross-examination, the claimant admits that she was warned for misconduct in 2001. Your instructions are that she was told by a senior manager prior to the dismissal hearing that the warning would not count against her. To remind her of this, you might ask: 'Did a manager discuss with you the 2001 warning prior to your disciplinary hearing?'
- To correct a straightforward factual error which the claimant has made in cross-examination.
  Example: 'In cross examination you stated that you wrote to the claimant at the beginning of March complaining of her attendance. Could you turn to page 41 in the bundle. Is that the letter you were speaking of? What is that date of the letter – could you confirm to the tribunal when you sent the letter'.

Closing submissions

[20.26] Closing submissions take place after the evidence has been heard. Their purpose is to persuade the tribunal to find in your favour. The party who adduced their evidence second usually speaks first, with the other party responding. The tribunal has a discretion whether to allow a further response from the first party. Parties should not be afraid of asking for a short adjournment to allow them to formulate or refine their submissions.

Effective submissions should contain a clear and obvious structure. It is usual to structure your submissions around the issues the tribunal has to decide, explaining why, in relation to each one, the tribunal should find in your favour. This involves referring to the evidence which has been heard and:

- drawing the tribunal's attention to evidence, both oral and documentary, which supports your case; and

- where there is a conflict on the evidence, suggesting why the tribunal should accept your side's version of what took place.

[20.27] Do not forget the value of referring the tribunal to undisputed evidence which supports your case. This will not simply be evidence from your own witnesses which has not been challenged, but also advantageous answers which you have been able to obtain from the other side's witnesses in cross-examination.

Where there is a dispute about the evidence, reference to the undisputed facts can again be useful. So, to adopt the example used in cross-examination, in asking the tribunal to find that the claimant was not sacked but stormed out of the room and resigned, you can refer them to the undisputed evidence that he was angry at the time of the meeting, that he had been present in the meeting for 30 minutes before he left (a fact which, depending on the circumstances, could be inconsistent with dismissal). You will, in addition to that undisputed evidence, refer them to the account of what took place given by your managers.

[20.28] Provided that submissions are structured, relevant and persuasive, it is a matter of personal choice as to how they are presented to the tribunal. The following is a short illustration of how you might set about approaching such submissions in a particular case. In practice, your submissions are likely to be longer and to refer to considerably more evidence. Copies of any legal authorities (leading cases etc) on which you intend to rely should be provided to the tribunal and the other party (that is, four copies) no later than the beginning of your submissions.

Example

You act for the claimant in an unfair dismissal case. Your client has been dismissed for misconduct after an incident in which he was caught fighting at work. You concede, on behalf of the claimant, that the reason for dismissal was misconduct, and that this is one of the potentially lawful reasons under the *Employment Rights Act 1996*. You remind the tribunal that the only live issue before them is whether the respondent acted reasonably, in all the circumstances, in dismissing him for that reason.

You state, for the following reasons, that it was not.

First, the dismissal was procedurally unfair because the respondent did not carry out a fair investigation.

- There is undisputed evidence that the respondent made no effort to interview bystanders of the fight whom the claimant had told them would support his version that the other employee had struck the first blow. Without doing so, the respondent could not have gained a proper understanding of a relevant factor, namely the degree of provocation which the claimant faced.
- The respondent failed to take into account a relevant consideration in reaching its decision – namely that the claimant had an immaculate record of employment over many years. Whilst the respondent maintained in evidence that this was taken into account, the weight of the evidence before the tribunal suggests otherwise – there is no mention of it in the memo recording the factors taken into consideration in making the decision to dismiss and it was not until he was referred to it in cross-examination that the dismissing manager mentioned it.

Second, without prejudice to the contention that the dismissal was procedurally unfair, the decision to dismiss was outside the range of reasonable responses open to the employer.

- The claimant had an immaculate record and long service.
- On the claimant's evidence, he faced severe provocation, an assertion which is likely to be correct given his previous good record.
- The undisputed evidence is that he immediately acknowledged that his actions, in fighting, were wrong and showed remorse for them.
- Two months prior to the claimant's dismissal, three employees were giving written warnings for being involved in fighting, but were not dismissed. No reasonable employer would have been so inconsistent as to give those employees a mere warning and subject the claimant to the extreme penalty of dismissal.

This example, in skeleton form, is intended to illustrate how you might set about dealing with the two main issues for the tribunal to decide, namely whether the employer carried out a fair investigation and whether dismissal was within the range of reasonable responses open to the employer.

Do's and Don'ts

Do:

- Make notes of points for final submissions as the case proceeds on a separate piece of paper.
- Structure your submissions logically around the issues the tribunal has to decide.
- Use a skeleton argument in complex cases if you have time to prepare one.
- Plan your submissions carefully – with the aim of persuading the tribunal to find in your favour.

Don't:

- Repeat your best points *ad nauseam* – this will undermine their effectiveness.

Chapter 21

Private hearings and restricted reporting orders

Introduction

[21.1] As with most judicial proceedings in other tribunals and courts, the general rule (other than case management discussions (see *rule 17(1)* of the *2004 Rules*) is that proceedings before an employment tribunal should be held in public. The rationale behind the requirement that hearings take place in public is that it is thought to be in the public interest that hearings be open to public scrutiny rather than take place behind closed doors. However there are two exceptions to this principle of open justice: firstly, the tribunal has discretion in very limited circumstances to order that a hearing (or part of a hearing) be heard in private (pursuant to *rule 16(1)*), and secondly, by imposing restricted reporting orders in cases concerning allegations of sexual misconduct and in cases concerning evidence of a personal nature in disability discrimination cases (pursuant to *rule 50(1)*). As the latter name suggests, such an order does not prevent access to the tribunal by the public and media, but prevents the publication, until promulgation of the decision, of identifying details of individuals.

Hearings in private

[21.2] A tribunal may sit in private (*rule 16(1)*) for the purpose of hearing evidence or representations which, in the opinion of the tribunal or Employment Judge, is likely to consist of information:

(a) which cannot be disclosed without constituting a breach of a specific statutory prohibition;
(b) which has been communicated to a witness in confidence or which has otherwise been obtained in consequence of the confidence placed in them by another person; or

(c) the disclosure of which would cause substantial injury to any undertaking of the witness or any undertaking in which they work.

[21.3] In addition, a tribunal must sit in private where directed to by the Secretary of State in the interests of national security (*rule 54*).

[21.4] In relation to (b), this not only potentially includes medical practitioners or solicitors operating under a professional duty of confidentiality, but may also include those in business and other organisations which, when they receive such information, are under a duty to keep it confidential. An example of the latter might be where the witness is obliged to disclose details of confidential business transactions or trade secrets which they have received subject to a duty of confidentiality. The wording of the rules further suggests that the relevant moment in time for ascertaining whether a duty of confidentiality exists is the moment when the witness received the information. The disclosure of business transactions, trade secrets and confidential negotiations might also engage (c) – namely causing substantial injury to the undertaking.

[21.5] Whenever a tribunal decides to hold a hearing or part of a hearing in private it is required to provide reasons for its decision (*rule 16(2)*).

Sensitive or embarrassing allegations

[21.6] The *2004 Rules* deliberately refer not to the making of allegations but to the disclosure of 'information' by a witness. The mere fact that a damaging allegation is made will not, of itself, enable the hearing to take place in private (although it could form the basis for making a restricted reporting order – see below). Serious allegations are frequently made in tribunals, sometimes without proper evidence, which are embarrassing and/or damaging for those involved. That is unless, in defending that application, the respondent is obliged to disclose information which is likely to cause substantial damage to the undertaking or involve the disclosure of confidential information. The situation could conceivably be different, however, in a (non dismissal) case where the claimant is still employed by the undertaking and wishes to give evidence which could be damaging (this is because the protection extends to any undertaking of the witness or one in which they work).

Making applications for a case to be heard in private

[21.7] The application should be made immediately before the commencement of the hearing. It has been held that it is not appropriate for the application to be decided by the Employment Judge alone, but by the full tribunal (*Milne and Lyall v Waldren* [1980] ICR 138). It is sensible to highlight both to the tribunal and the other side, in advance of the day of the hearing, that the application will be made unless it is thought that this might 'put ideas into their head' about generating publicity. If the parties are in agreement that the hearing be in private, this will not necessarily be conclusive. Restricting the right of the public to observe proceedings is considered to be a serious matter and the tribunal will not make such an order unless satisfied that the criteria in *rule 16(1)* are met. Further, the tribunal has a discretion, even if the criteria in *rule 16(1)* are met, to decline to sit in private. In deciding how to exercise this discretion, it will take into account the overriding objective (see **chapter 8 – fairness: the overriding objective**), the prejudice to the party or parties and will balance the need for privacy against the public interest which lies in proceedings being open.

Restricted reporting orders

[21.8] Restricted reporting orders have the effect of preventing publication of any information which might lead to members of the public identifying a particular person or people in a case. The jurisdiction of the tribunal to make such orders arises both under *rule 50* and the *Employment Tribunals Act 1996* (*ETA 1996*), *ss 11* and *12*. Such orders can be made only in cases involving:

- allegations of sexual misconduct; or
- evidence that is likely to be of a personal nature in disability discrimination cases.

[21.9] 'Evidence of a personal nature' is defined to mean 'any evidence of a medical, or other intimate, nature which might reasonably be assumed to be likely to cause significant embarrassment to the complainant if reported' (*ETA 1996, s 12*). In either case, the order from the tribunal will specify the persons who must not be identified, and a notice to that effect will be displayed on the tribunal door and the notice board displaying the list of proceedings.

[21.10] The order can be made either of the tribunal's own motion or upon the application of the parties. The tribunal has a discretion whether to make the order and must consider whether it is in the public interest that the press be able to communicate the information to the public. There has been considerable debate about whether a restricted reporting order can be made in respect of a corporate body as well as an individual. Whilst there is some conflict in the case law on this point, on balance it is unlikely that corporate bodies can so benefit (see *Leicester University v A* [1999] ICR 701 (no protection for corporate bodies) and *M v Vincent* [1998] ICR 73 (order protecting corporate body permissible)). Such bodies should be aware, however, that if publication of their name is likely to lead to a particular individual being identified, then this would constitute a breach of any order in respect of that person – something which offers them some protection.

[21.11] In contrast to an application for a private hearing, which should be made immediately prior to the commencement of that hearing, an application for a restricted reporting order can be made at any stage in the proceedings. The application can be made in writing to the Employment Tribunal Office, or orally at a hearing and can be determined by the tribunal or an Employment Judge alone exercising his powers under *rule 50(2)*.

[21.12] It is worth noting that the tribunal also has a power to make a temporary restricted reporting order of its own motion (*rule 50(2)* and *(3)*). The parties must be notified, however, that in the absence of an application to have the reporting order revoked or converted into a full order within 14 days of the temporary order having been made, the temporary order shall cease have to effect (*rule 50(5)*).

Do's and Don'ts

Do:

- Consider at an early stage whether the hearing needs to be in private or whether a restricted reporting order is required.
- Consider making contact with the other side to see if they would agree to an order.
- Make an application for a restricted reporting order as early as possible in proceedings.

- Make an application for a private hearing on the day of the full Hearing, but, if at all possible, give the tribunal and the parties notice of the fact that the application will be made.
- In difficult or complex cases, consider seeking specialised legal advice on whether evidence (documentary or otherwise) is likely to be considered confidential.

Don't:

- Assume that because the criteria in *rule 16* or *rule 50* are met the tribunal will make the order.
- Forget that the general principle is that proceedings should where possible be held in public.

Chapter 22

Costs

Introduction

[22.1] The tribunal's powers in respect of costs are set out in *rules 38* to *48* of *Schedule 1* to the *Employment Tribunals (Constitution and Rules of Procedure) Regulations 2004 (SI 2004/1861)*.

Unlike civil court proceedings, there is no general rule in employment proceedings that the successful party has the right to recover their legal costs. Tribunals, in fact, have no inherent power to award costs and may only consider making an award in the restricted circumstances set out in the procedural rules.

The historic reasons for not awarding costs were to preserve tribunals as an accessible forum where parties could bring and defend proceedings without the threat of prohibitive costs awards. As public awareness of employment rights and employment proceedings grew, tribunals found themselves increasingly swamped with unmeritorious cases, whilst lacking the tools to discourage such applications. In an effort to redress the balance the Government has, over time, amended the rules, granting tribunals ever wider powers to award costs. The 2001 Regulations, in particular, significantly increased the maximum level of costs to £10,000, widened the criteria for assessing whether an award should be made, and made it mandatory for a tribunal to consider the making of an award of costs in certain circumstances. Whilst the 2004 rules have continued this trend, the general principle remains that, unlike civil court proceedings, costs do not 'follow the event' in a tribunal case. In other words the successful party is not entitled to its costs merely by virtue of the fact that it has won – something more has to be shown. Costs remain the exception rather than the norm.

The particular types of order available under the 2004 rules

[22.2] The 2004 rules provide for three principle types of order: a costs order, a preparation time order and a wasted costs order.
(a) A 'costs order' applies to parties who are legally represented at the relevant stage in proceedings (see **22.3–22.15** below).
(b) A 'preparation time order' allows those who are without legal representation to receive compensation for the time spent preparing their case (see **22.16–22.23** below). This is an entirely new power, allowing tribunals, for the first time to compensate litigants in person.
(c) A 'wasted costs order' is an order that a party's representative pay personally the cost of all or some of the proceedings. Whilst there has been a long standing provision for this is civil proceedings, the 2004 rules introduce it for the first time in tribunal cases (see **22.24–22.29**).

Costs orders (recovering the cost of legal representation)

[22.3] All costs orders are compensatory in nature – ie they are intended to compensate the receiving party for the costs incurred as a result of the conduct complained of. In order to receive a costs order in their favour a party will have to persuade the tribunal that:
(a) they are eligible for that order because they instructed a legal representative at the material time;
(b) one or more of the criteria for the making of that order is met; and
(c) the tribunal should exercise its discretion to make a costs order.

This chapter examines those three stages in turn. It then goes on to explain: (i) how a tribunal calculates the amount of a costs order; and (ii) how and when a costs application should be made.

Stage one: Eligibility for a costs order

[22.4] *Rule 38(2)*

> A costs order may be made under rules *39*, *40* and *47* only where the receiving party has been legally represented at the Hearing or, in proceedings which are determined without a Hearing, if

> the receiving party is legally represented when the proceedings are determined. If the receiving party has not been so legally represented a tribunal may make a preparation time order (subject to rules 42 to 45). [See rule 46 on the restriction on making a costs order and a preparation time order in the same proceedings.]

Stage two: The criteria for the making of a costs order

[22.5] There are four circumstances where the tribunal *may* make a costs order. These are:

(a) costs resulting from a decision to postpone the case (*rule 40(1)*);
(b) costs resulting from a party's non-compliance with an order (*rule 40(4)*);
(c) costs where a party has behaved vexatiously, abusively, disruptively or otherwise unreasonably *or* brought misconceived proceedings (*rule 40(2) and (3)*).

Further, the tribunal must (absent a special reason) make a costs order where a postponement has been occasioned by the failure of a respondent to be ready, at a remedies hearing, to deal with the issue of reinstatement/reengagement.

Addressing each of these circumstances in turn:

(a) Costs resulting from a decision to postpone the case

[22.6]

Rule 40(1) states that a tribunal may make a costs order

> when on the application of a party it has postponed the day or time fixed for or adjourned a Hearing or pre-hearing review. The ... order may be against or, as the case may require, in favour of that party as respects any [costs incurred, allowances paid or preparation time spent] as a result of the postponement or adjournment.

This rule applies to situations where a postponement or adjournment has become necessary due to the conduct of one of the parties and the result of that postponement/adjournment is that the other party incurs additional costs. Examples include situations where

- a party fails to inform the Tribunal of a date to avoid in relation to a key witness, leading to the postponement of the fixed hearing

- a party requires an adjournment to adduce evidence on a matter which it should have foreseen would be relevant to the proceedings.

It should be noted that there is no requirement for a party to have behaved 'unreasonably' in order for the tribunal to make an order under this rule. That said, the tribunal will, in the exercise of its discretion, usually require the postponement/adjournment to have been caused by some kind of blameworthy conduct on the part of the other party. The Tribunal's powers, in this particular respect, mirror those of a court in civil proceedings. In deciding whether to award costs against a party for causing an adjournment or for not complying with an order, a tribunal is likely to take in to account such matters as:

- the degree of culpability or blameworthiness of the offending party;
- their knowledge of proceedings, particularly if they are acting in person;
- whether an award would have the effect of deterring them from continuing with proceedings.

(b) Costs resulting from a party's non-compliance with an order

[22.7] *Rule 40(4)*

> A tribunal or [Employment Judge] may make a costs order against a party who has not complied with an order or practice direction.

It can be seen that there is no express requirement to show unreasonable conduct in order to qualify for the making of an order under this head. This rule covers situations where there has been a failure by a party to comply with an order for the provision of particulars, disclosure or any other order made by the tribunal. The rule enables the tribunal to compensate parties for the costs incurred in securing compliance with the order or practice direction. Consequently the tribunal will only consider making an award where the innocent party has taken action to enforce compliance. Such action might include asking the tribunal to make an 'unless order' under *rule 13(2)* or making an application to the tribunal that the other party show cause why their case should not be struck out under *rules 18(7)(c) or (e) or 13(1)(b),* or other strike out provisions. Alternatively, it might include a less drastic course, such as writing to the other party to remind them of their default. Note, however, that the tribunal still has a discretion whether to award costs in these circumstances (and if so, how much to award)which will be exercised in accordance with the overriding objective.

Example

The respondent, who is legally represented, secures an order requiring the claimant to provide further particulars of the grounds of complaint within 21 days. The claimant fails to comply. The respondent's solicitor spends 30 minutes (at an hourly rate of £100) making an application to the tribunal that the claimant be asked to show cause why the claim should not be struck out under *rule 18(7)(c)* for unreasonable conduct or *rules 13(1)(b) or 18(7)(e)* for non-compliance with an order. The Employment Judge lists the case for a pre-hearing review to consider these issues. Two days prior to the hearing and one month after the original deadline for providing the particulars, the claimant provides the further particulars. The respondent nevertheless elects to proceed with the strike out application. At the hearing, the Employment Judge decides that, in view of the fact that the particulars have now been provided, and applying the overriding objective, the claim should not be struck out. The respondent applies for their costs arising from the enforcement action. The Employment Judge decides that he will not award the respondent their costs of attending the pre-hearing review, since it ought to have known that, once the particulars were provided, the application was unlikely to succeed. He does, however, award costs of £50 in relation to costs of making the application to strike out. Note, however, that because of *rule 46(2)*, it seems likely that the actual order which the Employment Judge would be likely to make would be along the lines that 'on determination of the proceedings, either costs or preparation time in respect of this strike-out application be awarded to the respondent [assessed by the tribunal in the sum of £50 or on the basis of a time of 30 minutes being spent by the respondent's solicitor]'.

(c) Costs resulting from the bringing or conducting of proceedings

[22.8] *Rule 40(2)*

A tribunal or [Employment Judge] shall consider making a costs order against a paying party where, in the opinion of the tribunal or [Employment Judge] (as the case may be), any of the circumstances in paragraph (3) apply. Having so considered, the tribunal or [Employment Judge] may make a costs order against the paying party if it or he considers it appropriate to do so.

Rule 40(3)

> The circumstances referred to in paragraph (2) are where the paying party has in bringing the proceedings, or he or his representative has in conducting the proceedings, acted *vexatiously, abusively, disruptively or otherwise unreasonably, or the bringing or conducting of the proceedings by the paying party has been misconceived.*

When examining rule 40(3), it is convenient to break it down in to categories where: (a) a party has behaved vexatiously, abusively, disruptively or otherwise unreasonably; and (b) a party has brought or conducted proceedings which are misconceived. Parties, and in particular Respondents, should note that it is sensible, in without prejudice correspondence, to warn the other party in advance of an intention to seek costs, setting out the basis upon which the application will be made and urging that party, if they are unrepresented, to seek legal advice (it is sometimes useful to inform them of the existence of advice centres and CABs from which such advice could be received). Tribunal frequently ask to see evidence of such a warning when considering the issue of costs.

Meaning of vexatious, abusive or otherwise unreasonable

[22.9] In order to succeed in demonstrating that the paying party has behaved *vexatiously, abusively, disruptively or otherwise unreasonably* the receiving party will have to establish a degree of fault on the part of the paying party. In most cases, this will require some relevant evidence, for example as to:

- the paying party's actual motivation for bringing the proceedings, or their knowledge of the weaknesses of their case (and potentially the extent to which they sought to make appropriate enquiries); and
- their subsequent conduct in the light of that motivation or knowledge.

In general, a tribunal will only make an award on the basis that a claim is 'vexatious' or 'abusive' where it is satisfied that there was some improper motive underlying the bringing or subsequent conduct of the claim. This is a stringent test and awards for costs under these headings are uncommon. In practice, Tribunals tend to consider conduct which is vexatious in the context of asking whether a party has acted unreasonably or brought a claim which is misconceived, both of which involve a less restrictive test. The meaning of vexatious was described in the following terms by Lord Bingham in *A-G v Barker [2000] 1 FLR 759*:

> '"Vexatious" is a familiar term in legal parlance. The hallmark of a vexatious proceeding is in my judgment that it has little or no basis in law (or at least no discernible basis); that whatever the intention of the proceedings may be, its effect is to subject the defendant to inconvenience, harassment and expense out of all proportion to any gain likely to accrue to the claimant; and that it involves an abuse of the process of the court, meaning by that a use of the court process for a purpose or in a way which is significantly different from the ordinary and proper use of the court process.'

Bringing or conducting a claim 'unreasonably' is a slightly wider test that covers situations where, taking into account a party's knowledge, their subsequent decision to proceed with a claim is difficult, on any view, to justify. Again, the concentration of the Tribunal will be on the motivation and knowledge of the party against whom the costs order is sought. If it can be inferred that a claimant or respondent pursued their case in the knowledge that it would not succeed then this is likely to be compelling evidence of unreasonable conduct. Similarly, if a party is shown to have lied in relation to a central plank of their case, this will be powerful evidence in support of a costs order on grounds of unreasonable conduct (*Daleside Nursing Home Ltd v Mathew* (EAT/519/08, 18 February 2009). The requirement to demonstrate that the party has lied in relation to a central aspect of the claim is likely to be important in showing that, but for such conduct, the proceedings would not have been brought or (in the case of a respondent) defended and that the receiving party should therefore recover all of its costs. A lie in relation to a peripheral aspect of the claim is unlikely to bring with it the same costs consequences.

It should be noted that conduct prior to the bringing of the claim cannot itself give rise to costs, although it may be relevant to a consideration of whether the subsequent conduct in bringing the claim was unreasonable.

Real and hypothetical examples of conduct falling within the scope of vexatious, abusive, disruptive or otherwise unreasonable conduct include the following:

- A party fails to appear at the hearing without a reasonable explanation. This is an obvious example of unreasonable conduct and one which frequently results in the making of a costs order.

- A person brings or continues a claim which they knew was without merit (although it should be noted that this requires some sort of investigation into the state of knowledge of the paying party and cases of this sort may more appropriately be addressed under the heading of 'misconceived').
- In *Daleside Nursing Home Ltd v Mathew* (EAT/519/08, 18 February 2009), a race discrimination case, the claimant alleged that her manager had made an overtly racist remark and sought to rely on this to assert that other acts were committed on grounds of race. The tribunal found that the remark had never been made. It dismissed the claim but refused the application for costs. The EAT overturned the Tribunal's decision and awarded costs against the claimant, concluding that the claimant had lied in relation to a 'central plank' of her case.
- A person brings a claim, or he or his representative conduct that claim, purely or principally out of spite or for some other improper motive – ie vexatiously (see *Beynon v Scadden* [1999] IRLR 700 EAT where the Employment Appeal Tribunal (EAT) held that the union was improperly using the proceedings to bring pressure on the employers to agree to union recognition; also *Keskar v Governors of All Saints Church of England School* [1991] ICR 493, EAT where costs were awarded on the basis that the claimant was 'motivated by resentment and spite in bringing the proceedings' and there was virtually nothing to support his allegations). Note the new wasted costs provisions may be apt to cover this type of conduct, although it is far from clear whether trade unions are covered by those provisions (see **22.24**).
- A person refuses an offer to settle made by the other side in circumstances where it was unreasonable to do so (*Kopel v Safeway Stores plc* [2003] IRLR 753, EAT). It should be noted, however, that the circumstances where such a situation will be considered unreasonable are likely to be rare: in *Kopel*, the offer was 'generous' and not only did the claimant fail in her claims, but she persisted in making 'frankly ludicrous' and 'seriously misconceived' allegations. It should be borne in mind that a claimant is generally entitled to pursue a claim which has reasonable prospects of success in the tribunals to have a decision in his favour even if an offer is made which represents the most he would be likely to recover even if successful. In *Telephone Information Services Ltd v Wilkinson* [1991] IRLR 148, at para 293 the EAT recognised the importance to be attached to a finding by the Tribunal, regardless of any entitlement to compensation, that an individual's rights at law have been

infringed. The decision in *Kopel*, therefore, does not in any way amount to a departure from the normal principle that there will be no order for costs against a losing party even where an offer to settle has been made. The crucial question is the reasonableness of the rejection of the offer.

Meaning of misconceived

[22.10] This second limb undoubtedly provides a wider basis for awarding costs. The term 'misconceived' is defined as including 'having no reasonable prospect of success' (*Regulation 2* of the *Employment Tribunals (Constitution and Rules of Procedure) Regulations 2004)*. Thus there is no express requirement under the rules for there to be fault or unreasonableness in order for a claim to be misconceived. Whether a claim is misconceived is an objective test based on an assessment of legal/factual criteria. Put simply, where a tribunal is of the view that, despite a party's genuinely held belief as to the validity of their claim/ defence, the application never had any real prospects of success, it *must* then consider whether to award costs.

The bar for concluding, after a full Hearing determining liability or remedy, that a claim had no reasonable prospect of success is likely to be set high, particularly given that the tribunal will generally have had the benefit of having heard all the evidence, including the cross-examination of the witnesses, by the time a decision is taken – an advantage which, of course, the paying party will not have had at the time of bringing or conducting the claim.

Assuming the tribunal find that the bringing or conducting of proceedings was misconceived, it *must* then proceed to decide whether to make a costs order. It is at this point that the conduct of the offending party, and in particular their knowledge or the reasonableness of their refusal to acknowledge the weakness in their case, is likely to become relevant. Other factors which the tribunal might take in to account are whether the party applying for the order was (or ought to have been) aware of the weakness in the other side's case at an earlier stage and taken advantage of available procedures – for example a pre-hearing review or strike out application (see **chapter 13 – pre-emptive strikes:pre-hearing reviews**). Notwithstanding a conclusion that the bringing of proceedings was misconceived, a Tribunal does not have to make a costs order; this is a matter of discretion which turns on the facts of each particular case (see below). If a Tribunal finds that a misconceived claim was brought in the belief that it was well founded, case law suggests it should proceed to consider whether it was properly *pursued* thereafter (*NPower Yorkshire Ltd v Daly* (EAT/0842/04, 23 March 2005, unreported)).

Where a party has been required to pay a deposit at a pre-hearing review

[22.11] If a party thinks that some or all of the arguments put forward by the other side have no reasonable prospect of success, it can make an application at a pre-hearing review for an order under *rule 20* requiring the other party to pay a deposit of up to £500 as a condition of being permitted to continue (see **13.23**) for a more detailed analysis of when it is appropriate to make an application for a deposit).

A tribunal is required to record the grounds for requiring a party to pay a deposit and in reaching its decision a tribunal must take reasonable steps to ascertain, and to have regard to any information it becomes aware of regarding the means of the party who will have to pay the deposit. The Court of Appeal has cautioned tribunals to bear in mind the line to be drawn between effective case management and exerting inappropriate and unfair pressure on impecunious parties. Whether a costs warning will be appropriate will depend on factors such as the nature of and extent of the warning itself and the circumstances and manner in which it is given, and the relative strengths of the parties' cases (*Gee v Shell (UK) Ltd* [2002] EWCA Civ 1479, [2003] IRLR 82).

If the party who has been required to pay the deposit subsequently loses the substantive claim on substantially the same grounds as were set out at the time the deposit order was made, the tribunal (which will not be the same tribunal who made the order for the deposit) will consider whether to make a costs or preparation time order against him on the ground that he conducted the proceedings unreasonably in persisting in having the matter determined (rule 47(1)). Whilst the tribunal will consider this exercise under rule 47, this is in effect a special type of 'unreasonable conduct in bringing or conducting proceedings' award. The fact that the deposit order was made, however, is usually a good indication that the bringing or conducting of the proceedings on substantially similar grounds will be considered to be unreasonable, reducing the need for an investigation of the paying party's state of knowledge. As to the sum payable if a costs order under this rule is made, rule 47(2) states that the deposit shall be used in part or full settlement of that sum. If there is any amount outstanding, it should be refunded to the party which has paid the deposit.

(d) Costs arising from the failure of an employer to be ready to deal with an issue of reinstatement/reengagement:

[22.12] There is one situation in which the 2004 rules make it mandatory for the tribunal to make an award of costs. By virtue of *rule 39* (Costs and Expenses) a tribunal *must* make an order for costs against an employer, where a Hearing in an unfair dismissal claim (whether for merits and remedy or for remedy only) has been adjourned and:

- the claimant has expressed a wish to be reinstated or re-engaged which has been communicated to the respondent not less than seven days before the Hearing; and
- the postponement or adjournment of the hearing has been caused by the respondent's failure, without a special reason, to adduce reasonable evidence as to the availability of the job from which the claimant was dismissed, or of comparable or suitable employment.

The net effect of this rule is that, unless an employer can establish 'a special reason', it will be liable for the costs that the employee incurs as a result of any adjournment needed to allow the necessary evidence to be obtained. The power to make an order under these provisions relates to any costs incurred *as a result of* the postponement or adjournment (*rules 39(2)*..

Stage three – The exercise of discretion by the tribunal

[22.13] As stated above, the fact that the previous two stages have been successfully crossed by the party applying for costs (the receiving party) does not necessarily mean that an order will be made. The only exception to this is *rule* 39(employer not ready to deal with issue of reinstatement/reengagement such that an adjournment/postponement is necessary) where the tribunal must make a costs order unless it is satisfied that there is a special reason for the failure of the employer to secure evidence on the reinstatement/reengagement issue. In all other circumstances, the tribunal has a discretion whether to make the order. This discretion will be exercised in accordance with the overriding objective (see **chapter 8**

Rule 41(2) states that 'the tribunal or [Employment Judge] may have regard to the paying party's ability to pay when considering whether it or he shall make a costs order or how much that order should be'. This reverses the previous position set out by the Court of Appeal in *Kovacs v Queen Mary and Westfield College* [2002] EWCA Civ 352; [2002] IRLR

414 which stated that ability to pay was not a relevant factor in deciding whether to make an order.

Stage four: Calculating the amount of a costs order

[22.14] 'Costs' means 'fees, charges, disbursements or expenses incurred by or on behalf of a party in relation to proceedings' (*rule 38(3)*). The phrase 'on behalf of' makes clear that,by way of example, a Trade Union or other body which has engaged a legal representative can recover the costs of doing so.

A party is limited to recovering the costs which flow from the conduct complained of. If, therefore, the tribunal decides to make an order under *rule 40(1)*, the party can only recover the additional costs it incurred as a result of the postponement or adjournment. By contrast, if a tribunal decides under *rule 40(2) and (3)* that the decision to bring proceedings was unreasonable then the party could, potentially, recover the entire costs of the proceedings.

There is a 'cap' of £10,000 on the amount which a tribunal can itself order a party to pay (*rule 41(a)*). If the costs are greater then the tribunal can make an order that the sum be subject to a detailed assessment by the county court in accordance with the *Civil Procedure Rules* (*rule 41(c))*). Alternatively, the tribunal can make an order in excess of £10,000 with the consent of both parties(41(b)).

It has been held that Tribunals need to be specific about their reasons for settling on a particular sum in a costs order. Failure to do so may result in the conclusion that their discretion was not exercised properly if, for example, they make a substantial award of costs on the basis that the paying party's conduct 'considerably extended' proceedings whilst making no effort to quantify the extent to which the hearing was so extended (*Lodwick v London Borough of Southwark* [2004] EWCA 306; [2004] IRLR 554).

The formalities – when and how to make a costs application

[22.15] Rule 38

> (7) A party may apply for a costs order to be made at any time during the proceedings. An application may be made at the end

of a hearing, or in writing to the Employment Tribunal Office. An application for costs which is received by the Employment Tribunal Office later than 28 days from the issuing of the judgment determining the claim shall not be accepted or considered by a tribunal or [Employment Judge] unless it or he considers that it is in the interests of justice to do so.

(8) In paragraph (7), the date of issuing of the judgment determining the claim shall be either –
(a) the date of the Hearing if the judgment was issued orally; or
(b) if the judgment was reserved, the date on which the written judgment was sent to the parties.

(9) No costs order shall be made unless the Secretary has sent notice to the party against whom the order may be made giving him the opportunity to give reasons why the order should not be made. This paragraph shall not be taken to require the Secretary to send notice to that party if the party has been given an opportunity to give reasons orally to the [Employment Judge] or tribunal as to why the order should not be made.

It is apparent from the above that the rules state that 'a party may apply for a costs order to be made at any time during the proceedings'.

There is no time limit on the making of an application for a costs order *except* where proceedings have been determined. The rules state that, in those circumstances, an application for costs must be received by the tribunal no later than 28 days from the date the judgment is issued. When a judgment is given orally at a hearing the date of 'issue' is the date of the hearing. Where a judgment is reserved the date of issue is the date upon which the judgment was sent to the parties. If the 28-day time limit is not observed, the Employment Judge will not consider the application unless he considers that it is in the interests of justice to do so.

In practice it is strongly advisable, even where proceedings have not been determined, for costs applications to be made promptly (see *Walker v Heathrow Refuelling Services Co Ltd* UKEAT/0366/04/TM referred to above). If, therefore, there are grounds for making a costs application at a case management discussion (for example due to non-compliance with an order) then an application should be made there and then – although this would have to be in the form of an application that the Employment Judge exercise his power under rule 46(2). The EAT have given guidance that, in general, a costs application should be made immediately upon the tribunal giving an unreserved decision. Where the decision is reserved, the party seeking costs should indicate to the tribunal that, if successful, it wishes the tribunal to make a costs order (*Johnson v Baxter* [1984] ICR 675), although arguably the need for this is less great now that the rules expressly provide for written applications, and of course sometimes the possibility of an application only becomes apparent from the judgment itself (for example if the tribunal makes findings of fact that a party has deliberately and maliciously fabricated facts relied upon in a claim or defence). In many cases tribunals will give guidance as to when they wish to be addressed on the issue of costs. So, for example, where a party applies for an adjournment, a tribunal may indicate that it wishes first to decide whether an adjournment is necessary, before going on to consider who, if anyone, should bear the costs arising from the delay.

The general rule therefore remains that an application for costs should be made as soon as it becomes appropriate (see *Andrew Ladies Hairstylists v Baxter* [1985] IRLR 96 where the EAT held that applications for costs should be made as soon as reasonably possible). Tribunals are keen to avoid the extra (and often unrecoverable) expense of additional hearings on costs alone. Moreover, any significant delay may weaken an application since it is likely to be viewed as prejudicial to the party against whom the order is sought.

An application for costs can be made in writing or orally. If the former method is used, the Secretary is required under *rule 38(9)* to give the other party an opportunity to provide reasons why the order should not be made. This does not apply where the application is oral at a hearing when all parties are present, since the party will have been given an opportunity to orally explain to the tribunal as to why the order should not be made. In making a written application, a party must comply with the provisions in rule 11 (see **chapter 9 – communicating with the tribunal: 9.17**). The party should therefore set out (a) the nature of the order sought (including the applicable rule) and (b) the grounds upon which it is sought (ie explaining why, on the facts of this case, the criteria for the making of the order is met and why the Tribunal should exercise its discretion to make the award). The party should also set out the amount of costs which is sought. Note that this should be limited to the costs caused by the act complained of. The party should give a sufficiently detailed breakdown of their costs so as to justify the amount sought.

Preparation time orders (recovering the cost of preparing for Tribunal by those who are without legal representation)

[22.16]–[22.19] The preparation time provisions are intended to benefit those who either represent themselves or who engage a representative who is not a qualified solicitor or barrister to act for them. *Rule 42(2)* states that:

> A preparation time order may be made under rules 43, 44 or 47 only where the receiving party has not been legally represented at a Hearing or, in proceedings which are determined without a Hearing, if the receiving party has not been legally represented when the proceedings are determined

The same four stage test as used in relation to costs orders above will be adopted. As regards both eligibility for benefiting from an order and the criteria for the making of that order, the preparation time provisions mirror those relating to costs orders – the only difference being that the phrase 'preparation time order' replaces the phrase 'costs order'. The principle differences relates to the calculation of the award. A party is not, as the title 'preparation time' suggests, entitled to payment in respect of time spent at the Hearing itself. Furthermore, preparation time is assessed at a standard rate of £25 an hour.

Calculating the amount of a preparation time order

Definition of preparation time

[22.20] *Rule 42(3)*

> For the purposes of these rules preparation time shall mean time spent by –
> (a) the receiving party or his employees carrying out preparatory work directly relating to the proceedings; and
> (b) the receiving party's legal or other advisers relating to the conduct of proceedings;
>
> up to but not including time spent at any Hearing.

Thus, in contrast to a costs order, time spent at the Hearing cannot be recovered under the auspices of a preparation time order. Time which is covered by a preparation time order is likely to include that spent in:

- preparing pleadings or other formal documents relating to the proceedings (ie responses to requests for further particulars)
- preparing a witness statement
- assembling documentation
- reading documentation, correspondence and pleadings from the other side
- researching the law
- having a conference to discuss the case
- taking advice.

Furthermore, *rule 42(3)* makes it clear that, where a party has instructed a representative, the time which that representative spends in conducting the case is recoverable, though limited to a rate of £25 an hour (see below).

Parties should note that, as with a costs order, it is limited to recovering the sum flowing from the conduct complained of. So if the order is made under *rule 44(1)*, it is limited to recovering the additional preparation time it has incurred as a result of the postponement or adjournment. If the order is made under *rule 44(4)*, the party is limited to recovering the additional preparation time caused by the other party's non-compliance with an order etc.

Calculating the amount of a preparation time order engages the tribunal in a two-stage process: Firstly the tribunal or Employment Judge will make a calculation as to the amount of hours of preparation time that should be awarded to the receiving party. The Employment Judge will then multiply that figure by 25 to reach a total figure.

As to stage one, the relevant rule reads as follows:

Rule 45

> (1) In order to calculate the amount of preparation time the tribunal or [Employment Judge] shall make an assessment of the number of hours spent on preparation time on the basis of –
> (a) information on time spent provided by the receiving party; and
> (b) the tribunal or [Employment Judge's] own assessment of what it or he considers to be a reasonable and proportionate amount of time to spend on such preparatory work and with reference to, for example, matters such as the complexity of the proceedings, the number of witnesses and documentation required.

In order to maximise the chance of a favourable exercise of discretion under (b) above, when making an application for an order a party provide a sufficiently detailed by concise breakdown explaining the time which it has spent in preparing the case.

As to stage 2, *rule 45(2)* states that the tribunal will next apply the standard hourly rate of £25 to what has been held to be the reasonable amount of hours expended on preparation. *Rule 45(4)* states that the figure of £25 will be increased at a rate of £1.00 a year commencing with 6 April 2006. It will therefore be £26 on that date, and £27 on 6 April 2007 and so forth.

So, where the Employment Judge has concluded that it was reasonable for a party to have spent 35 hours preparing a case, he will award 35 × £25, making a total of £875. Note that the maximum sum which can be awarded in respect of preparation time is, as with a costs order, £10,000. Unlike a costs order (which can be sent off for a detailed assessment) there is no route whereby a party can obtain more than £10,000.

Ability to pay: As with a costs order, rule 45(3) states that a tribunal 'may have regard to the paying party's ability to pay when considering whether it or he shall make a preparation time order or how much that order should be'.

Cases where a party represents himself at the Hearing (or instructs a non-legal representative) but has had the benefit of a legal representative at an earlier stage: This situation is analogous, in many respects, to that set out in **22.14** above. The party is not entitled to a costs order and can only receive a preparation time order. In the view of the authors, the party may be able to recover, under a preparation time order, the costs of instructing the legal representative, but the tribunal would have no jurisdiction to make an award of more than £25 an hour in respect of that representative's work. The author's construction of the rules turns upon the fact that preparation is defined as including time spent by the receiving party's 'legal or other advisers relating to the conduct of proceedings'. Further reliance is placed upon the terms of *rule 46(2)* – see **22.14** – which appears to envisage that a costs or preparation time costs are recoverable under the auspices of a costs order and vice versa. The issue is, however, finely balanced, and guidance is awaited from the courts.

The formalities – when and how to make an application for a preparation time order

[21.21] The procedure for applying for a preparation time order under *rule 42(5)* is identical to that which applies to a costs order under *rule 38(7)* with the only difference being that the phrase 'Preparation Time Order' replaces 'Costs Order'. Readers are accordingly referred to **22.15** above for an explanation of the correct procedure.

Costs and preparation time orders against employers

[22.22] Although tribunals may award costs/preparation time against either party, as a general rule, awards are more likely to be made against an employee bringing the claim as opposed to the employer defending the application. This is because tribunals have long recognised that an employer 'must be entitled to defend proceedings brought against it' (*Cartiers Superfoods Ltd v Laws* [1978] 315, EAT).

Clearly, however, an employer remains accountable for additional costs that arise due to its unreasonable/misconceived conduct in relation to the proceedings.

Even under the new regime it remains the case that tribunals do not have the power to award costs with respect to conduct preceding the issuing of proceedings (*Davidson v John Calder (Publishers) Ltd and Calder Educational Trust Ltd* [1985] IRLR 97 – where Bristow J held that 'it was the conduct in the course of the proceedings which alone is to be considered' and that the test was whether it was unreasonable for an employer 'to have defended this case as to liability once the application was launched and they had to consider the material available to the [employer]'). Having said this, obviously, the more flagrant the employer's behaviour in dismissing the claimant, the harder it will be for the former to justify a decision to defend proceedings as being 'reasonable'. Events prior to the issuing of proceedings may well be relevant in determining whether conduct after such proceedings was unreasonable.

Expenses orders

[22.23] By virtue of *rule 38(1)(b)* the tribunal has the power to order a party to pay to reimburse the Secretary of State for Trade and

Industry in relation to allowances he has paid to witnesses and other such persons in connection with their attendance at the tribunal. An expenses order is governed by identical provisions to those which apply to costs orders.

Wasted costs orders against representatives

General

[22.24] In the 2004 rules there is, for the first time, provision for the tribunal to make an award of costs against a party's representative in respect of their conduct – commonly referred to as a 'wasted costs order'. The representative may be ordered to pay costs either to the other side or to their own client. Significantly, 'representative' is not limited to those who are legal representatives (although note the 'profit requirement' set out below). If the order is made, that representative is liable to pay the costs personally. This is an important innovation introduced by the 2004 rules. The relevant power is contained in *rule 48(1)* of the 2004 rules, which provides that 'a tribunal or Employment Judge may make a wasted costs order against a party's representative'.

Practical examples of where the power *may* be exercised include the following:

- The representative has failed, without reasonable explanation, to diarise a hearing and/or inform his client (or a witness) of the correct date such that the hearing postponed.
- The representative has, without reasonable explanation, failed to advise his client of the necessity to deal with an issue which is central in proceedings, resulting in a postponement/adjournment.
- The representative has failed to inform his client of the necessity to appear and give evidence to the tribunal at a pre-hearing review in relation to the issue of whether it is just and equitable for a time limit to be extended (discrimination claims) or whether it was reasonably practicable for the claim to be presented in time (unfair dismissal claims).
- Late evidence is disclosed, without reasonable explanation, to the other party which should have been disclosed by the representative at an earlier stage, causing the other party to incur additional costs.
- A representative has failed, without reasonable excuse, to comply with the terms of an order, leading to the incurring of additional costs by the party who subsequently enforces that order.

In the following situations, a wasted costs order may be made, but it is likely to be harder to satisfy the tribunal that the grounds are made out for doing so:

- A hopeless case has been pursued due to the erroneous advice of the representative.
- The representative has prolonged proceedings through unnecessary/irrelevant questioning and submissions.

In short, wasted costs orders are likely to be easier to secure where a clear error, legal or otherwise, can be identified (see below). The first five examples given above fall into the category of error which no reasonable representative, acting at the minimum level of competence, should make. The final two examples engage the tribunal in assessing the representative's judgment, something which is not susceptible to measurement in precise terms and which the tribunal may not be in the best position to evaluate.

The criteria for the making of a 'wasted costs' order

[22.25] Wasted costs are defined (*rule 48(3)*) as costs incurred by a party:

- as a result of any improper, unreasonable or negligent act or omission on the part of any representative; or
- which, in the light of any such act or omission occurring after they were incurred, the tribunal considers it unreasonable to expect that party to pay.

The rules are silent as to the definition of 'improper, unreasonable or negligent'. This is, however, phrased in identical terms to the wasted costs provisions applicable to civil proceedings set out in Part 48.7 of the Civil Procedure Rules 1998. The Tribunal is likely, therefore, to follow the guidance set out by the civil courts.

The leading case on wasted costs in the civil courts is *Ridelagh v Horsfield* [1994] Ch 205, where the Court of Appeal gave comprehensive guidance on the criteria for the making of a wasted costs order. The Court stated that the following three stage test should be applied when considering whether to make such an order:

- Did the legal representative act improperly, unreasonably or negligently? If so
- Did such conduct cause the relevant party to incur unnecessary costs? If so

- Is it in all the circumstances just to order the legal representative to compensate the relevant party for the whole or part of the relevant costs?

Addressing each limb in turn:

Did the representative act improperly, unreasonably or negligently?

[22.25A] 'Improper' covers, but is not confined to, conduct which would ordinarily be held to justify disbarment, striking off, suspension from practice or other serious professional penalty. It is clear that the threshold under this category is very high.

'Unreasonable' describes conduct which is 'vexatious, or designed to harass the other side rather than advance the resolution of the case'. It is not apparent from the Court of Appeal's judgment whether unreasonable is limited to those circumstances. In the view of the authors it is not since the court went on to state that the 'acid test' is 'whether the conduct permitted of a reasonable explanation. If so, 'the course adopted might be regarded as optimistic and reflecting on a practitioner's judgment, but it was not unreasonable'. It appears, therefore, that unreasonable conduct is any conduct which does not permit of a reasonable explanation.

'Negligence' means a failure to act with the competence reasonably expected of ordinary members of the profession. In the authors' view, the practical examples given above fall most conveniently in to the negligence category, although there is an argument that they can also be deemed to be 'unreasonable'.

An extremely useful 'rule of thumb' when asking whether conduct is sufficient to justify a wasted costs order under any of the above heads is the guidance of the Court of Appeal in the cases of *Tolstoy v Miloslavsky v Aldington* [1996] 1 WLR 736 and *Wall v Lefever* (1997) Times, 1 August. In *Tolstoy* the court stated that 'the wasted costs jurisdiction must be exercised in care and only in clear cases.' In *Wall* the court stated that 'it is a summary procedure which is to be used in circumstances where there is a clear picture which indicates that a professional adviser has been negligent.'

Pursuing a hopeless case: For a tribunal to consider making an award under this head, it will be necessary for there to be clear evidence that a hopeless case was brought by the client on the erroneous advice of his representative. Merely acting in a hopeless case is not enough to justify the making of a wasted costs order (In *Horsfield* the court stated that 'a legal representative was not to be held to have acted improperly simply because he acted for a party who pursued a claim or defence which was plainly doomed to fail'.). What is required therefore is either an admission from the representative that the client brought the claim acting on legal advice or a waiver of privilege by the client so that the advice in question can be examined by the tribunal. The court in *Horsfield* made clear that 'it was rare if ever safe for a court to *assume* that a hopeless case was being litigated on the advice of the lawyers involved. They were there to present the case, it was for the judge and not the lawyers to judge it' [emphasis added]. By contrast, a legal representative should not act in an abuse of the court's (or the tribunal's) processes. The court defined abuse of process as using proceedings for purposes for which they were not intended. This is a very broad concept. Examples given by the court included pursuing proceedings for reasons unconnected with success, advancing a case which the representative knew to be dishonest and knowingly conniving in the incomplete disclosure of documents.

Did such conduct cause the relevant party to incur additional costs?

[22.25B] This is a test of causation which will be strictly applied. If the conduct in question did not cause a party to incur costs no order can be made, however reprehensible the conduct. So, if a legal representative fails to disclose important documentation until the day of hearing, necessitating a postponement, a costs order is unlikely to be made if the hearing would have been postponed in any event for some other reason – for example that, due to an overcrowded list, the tribunal was unable to hear the case.

Is it in all the circumstances just to order the legal representative to compensate the relevant party for the whole or part of the relevant costs?

[22.25C] In *Ridelagh v Horsfield* (cited above) the Court of Appeal held that

> Even if the court were satisfied that legal representatives had acted improperly, unreasonably or negligently so as to waste

> costs, it was not bound to make an order, but would have to give sustainable reasons for the exercise of its discretion in that way.

The same applies in tribunal proceedings, although in extreme circumstances, for example dishonesty, the making of the order is likely to follow axiomatically upon a finding that the representative has acted improperly. An example of a situation where a Tribunal may be inclined not to make an award is where there are compassionate circumstances which might make an award unjust, for example a bereavement at the time when the negligent act took place.

Against whom a wasted costs order may be made

[22.26] The order may be made against a party's representative. This is defined in rule 48(4) as

> 'a party's legal or other representative or any employee of such representative or any employee of such representative, but it does not include a representative who is not acting in pursuit of profit with regard to those proceedings. A person is considered to be acting in pursuit of profit if he is acting on a conditional fee arrangement'.

Rule 48(5) provides that the order may not be made against a representative where that representative is an employee of a party.

The effect of these provisions is that the order may be made against any third party representing a party to the proceedings. Wasted costs orders cannot be made against in-house legal representatives, human resources managers or other employees who are conducting the proceedings on behalf of their employers. They can, however, be made against external representatives, including those who are not legally qualified such as employment consultants. 'In pursuit of a profit' is likely to be defined by the tribunal as acting for a fee, whether conditional or otherwise.

The provision that an order cannot be made against a representative who is not acting in pursuit of profit means that a lawyer acting *pro bono* or a CAB, Law Centre or similar adviser, or indeed a friend or relative of a party, appears not to be liable under these provisions. It would also appear to exclude trade unions since these are not profit making organisations and a trade union representative is arguably not acting for profit with regard to the proceedings in question. It has been suggested, however, that in relation to trade unions it might be argued that they are acting for profit, in so far as they only represent people who have paid their subscriptions. Guidance from EAT is awaited.

In favour of whom a wasted costs order may be made

[22.27] *Rule 48(5)* provides that the order may be made in favour of a party whether or not that party is legally represented. The same rule provides that the order may also be made in favour of the representative's own client.

The usual situation where a wasted costs order will be made is where the unreasonable, negligent or improper conduct of one party's representative causes the other party to incur additional legal costs.

It is difficult to envisage in what circumstances the order would be made in favour of a party when that party is not legally represented, since the wasted costs provisions provide for costs and expenses, but not, apparently, for preparation time to be recovered. However, the rule would clearly provide for a party to recover costs of non-legally-qualified representation.

The order may be made in favour of the representative's own client – this is because the costs which have been wasted by the representative's conduct may include that client's own costs of paying for the representative's services. An example would be where a representative prepares negligently for the hearing so that it cannot proceed and an adjournment is granted resulting in *both* parties having wasted the costs of attending the hearing. In that situation, the representative might be ordered to pay the costs of both parties (in respect of his own client either by the disallowance of the wasted costs, or by repayment of sums already paid).

The difficulty with an order being made in favour of the representative's client is of course that it makes the professional relationship between them very difficult. It is virtually inconceivable that a representative would himself apply for a wasted costs order to be made against himself and in favour of his client. Either the client must himself apply for the order, therefore, or the tribunal must make it of its own motion. In either case the representative and his client are likely to have a clear conflict of interests. It is clearly possible for such a situation to arise, particularly where there is unlikely to be any further relationship between the client and the representative. However, the most frequent use of the wasted costs provisions is likely to be to compensate the other party.

What costs may be ordered

[22.28] By virtue of *rule 48(2)*, the tribunal may in a wasted costs order:

- disallow, or order the representative or a party to meet, the whole or part of any wasted costs of any party, including an order that the representative repay to his client any costs which have already been paid; and
- order the representative to pay to the Secretary of State, in whole or in part, any allowances (other than those paid to members of tribunals) paid under *section 5(2)* or *(3)* of the *Employment Tribunals Act* to any person for the purposes of, or in connection with, that person's attendance at the tribunal by reason of the representative's conduct of the proceedings.

The procedure for making a wasted costs order

[22.29] Before making any wasted costs order, the tribunal is required to give the representative against whom the order is to be made a reasonable opportunity to make oral or written representations why the order should not be made (*rule 48(6)*). The tribunal is also required to have regard to the representative's ability to pay when considering whether to make an order or how much the order should be (*rule 48(6)*).

When an order is made, the amount to be paid or disallowed must be specified in the order.

Written reasons will be provided by the tribunal if a request is made within 14 days of the date of the wasted costs order, and will be sent to all parties in the proceedings (*rule 48(9)*). It is expressly provided that this time limit may *not* be extended under rule 10. It is therefore imperative for any person affected by the making or refusal to make a wasted costs order to apply immediately for written reasons as these will be important if any review or appeal is to be sought.

The Tribunal's Secretary will inform the representative's client in writing of any proceedings in respect of a wasted costs order or of any decision to award wasted costs made against the party's representative.

Do's and Don'ts

Do:

- Give written notice of intention of and reasons for applying for costs.
- Give all parties (including the tribunal) as much written notice as possible of the fact that, and reasons why, a postponement is needed.
- Seek guidance at an early stage from the tribunal as to when it wishes to be addressed on costs.
- Keep a schedule of costs identifying the hours worked (and by whom) on particular aspects of a case (ie for a particular hearing/application/aspect of the claim).
- Ask for a realistic figure of costs aimed at compensating you for the extra expense arising from the unreasonable/misconceived conduct.
- Provide documentary evidence of your costs.
- Try to avoid asking for hearings solely in relation to costs.
- Bear in mind the fact that the other party is unrepresented when considering whether it is reasonable to claim costs.
- Bear in mind the principles which the tribunal will apply in considering an application for costs, including the amount of the costs, the conduct which has led them to arise, and the paying party's means, and address your evidence and application to those issues.
- Be aware of the time limits for applying for costs and for seeking written reasons for any costs order.

Don't:

- 'Ambush' parties with costs applications.
- Delay in making an application.
- Make unreasonable, oppressive or multiple applications for small amounts of costs.
- Ask for costs to 'punish' the other side for its conduct.
- Seek to place undue reliance on previous case law, which may not be relevant under the rules.

Chapter 23

The decision

Introduction

[23.1] *Rule 28* of the *2004 Rules* distinguishes between:

- Judgments: which are final determinations of proceedings, or particular issue in proceedings, and which may include an award of compensation or other remedy, or an order for costs or preparation time; and
- Orders: which are interim directions requiring parties to carry out or refrain from carrying out specific things.

[23.2] Whilst *rule 28(1)* appears to suggest that tribunals may only make 'judgments' or 'orders' so defined, in reality tribunals routinely make 'orders' which do not 'require a person to do or not do something. See, for example *Onwuka v Spherion Technology UK Ltd* [2005] ICR 567, where the EAT held that a refusal of permission to amend a claim whist not an order under *rule 28* could nevertheless be an order for the purposes of *rule 10* (see also *Hart v English Heritage (Historic and Monuments Commission for England)* [2006] IRLR 915).

[23.3] Tribunals are required to give reasons (either oral or written) for all judgments (*rule 30(1)*). When a judgment is reserved tribunals are required to send a copy of the written judgment to all parties (*rule 29(1)* and *(2)*). There is, however, no automatic obligation on tribunals to provide written reasons for their judgments. Tribunals are only compelled to provide written reasons if one or other of the parties in response makes an appropriate request within the prescribed time limits (*rule 30(3)*). Such a request can be made either at the hearing where the oral judgment is given or within 14 days of the date when the judgment is sent to the parties (*rule 30(5)*).

[23.4] In rare circumstances the Employment Appeal Tribunal retains a residual power to request the production of written reasons for a judgment. Examples of judgments include:
- any determination of a party's right to bring or contest proceedings;
- striking out a claim or response under *rule 18(7)* or *13(1)(b)*;
- a default judgment (*rule 8(1)*).

When, after a pre-hearing review, an order is made for the payment of a deposit the grounds for making the order must be recorded in writing and a copy of the document sent to both parties (*rule 20(3)*).

[23.5] There is *no* requirement for a tribunal to give formal written reasons when making interim orders, for example in relation to the provision of further particulars, disclosure, postponement or directions for full Hearing. Having said this, however, they are required to give reasons (either oral or written) for an order, where they receive a request for reasons either before or at the hearing where the order is made (*rule 30(1)(b)*).

Historically, however, tribunals have not been expected or required to provide anything more than a brief summary of their reasons for interim orders. In practice this often means that all parties can expect to receive is a short summary of the grounds relied upon (which can have the effect of making an appeal difficult to sustain (see **chapter 26 – steps after the decision II – appeals**).

The characteristics of the formal written decision

[23.6] *Rule 30(6)* sets out a non-exhaustive list of the areas which the written reasons in a judgment should cover:
- the issues which were identified as being relevant to the claim;
- an explanation for why any of the above issues were not determined;
- findings of fact relevant to the issues which have to be determined;
- a concise statement of the applicable law;
- an explanation of how the relevant findings of fact and applicable law have been applied in order to determine the issues; and
- a table or other description of how any award of compensation or other order for payment has been calculated.

Other formal characteristics common to written decisions include the requirement that they be signed and dated by the relevant Employment

Judge (*rule 29(1)*) and that, thereafter, they be placed upon the public register rendering them available for public inspection (*rule 32*).

[23.7] The requirement to give reasons (whether orally or in writing) is a product of the common law principles of natural justice and finds further support in *Article 6* of the *European Convention on Human Rights* as the right to a fair trial. In the leading case on the duty to give reasons, *English v Emery Reimbold & Strick Ltd* [2002] EWCA Civ 605; [2002] 1 WLR 2409, the Court of Appeal gave guidance as to the need to give and sufficiency of reasons which supported a particular decision. For further guidance in the specific context of proceedings before employment tribunals, see *Meek v City of Birmingham Council* [1987] IRLR 250. The principles in both *Meek* and *English* find expression in *rule 30(6)* (see **23.16** below).

The significance of the formal written decision

[23.8] The formal written decision:

- provides the basis for any appeal;
- contains the reasons for the decision and the law that has been applied;
- constitutes the formal public record of what the tribunal has decided.

[23.9] Where a party wishes to appeal a judgment or order *rule 3(1)* of *Employment Appeal Tribunal Rules 1993* requires the party instituting the appeal to lodge with the EAT copies of the written record of the judgment, order and the written reasons for that judgment or order. Where they are not included the party must be explain why not (see, for example, *Kanapathiar v Harrow London Borough Council* [2003] IRLR 571).

Decisions announced orally on the day

[23.10] At the conclusion of a case a tribunal may:

- reserve its decision entirely, indicating to the parties that a formal written decision will follow;
- announce its decision orally on the day, giving brief reasons or even no reasons at all and indicating that a formal written decision will follow; or

- announce its decision with extended reasons on the day, with the Employment Judge speaking into a dictaphone, in which case the formal written decision sent to the parties will be a word-for-word, subject to normal editing requirements, report of what was said.

[23.11] Where a decision is announced orally on the day, the tribunal has an absolute obligation to send to the parties a formal written decision (*rule 29(1)* and *(2)*). As explained above, however, the tribunal is only required to provide written reasons for its judgment if it receives a request from one of the parties within the prescribed time limit (*rule 30(3)*). Although there is no statutory deadline for how soon after the hearing parties should receive their written decision, the Tribunals Service sets a target of (currently) 85% of decisions being issued within four weeks.

[23.12] The tribunal's written reasons should not conflict with any decision which has been given orally. To that extent, an oral decision by the tribunal still has the character of a 'final decision'. A tribunal should not change its mind in relation to a decision announced orally without, at the very least, giving the parties a further opportunity to address it. Where, however, this involves revisiting issues of fact which it had already properly decided, the practice is likely to be frowned upon by the EAT (*Lamont v Frys Metals Ltd* [1985] ICR 566 and *Arthur Guinness (Arthur) Son & Co (Great Britain) Ltd v Green* [1989] ICR 241. For cases emphasising the limited powers of recall, see *Spring Grove Services Group plc v Hickinbottom* [1990] ICR 111 and *Casella London Ltd v Banai* [1990] ICR 215).

Written reasons

[23.13] As stated at **23.9** above, in order institute an appeal before the EAT an appealing party is required to lodge a copy of the written judgment, order and reasons appealed against. However, the EAT does have a discretion, under *rule 39(2)* of the *Employment Appeal Tribunal Rules 1993*, to waive this requirement if in the interests of justice (i.e. to allow a party to appeal on the judgment alone). This power is exercised sparingly and a key factor is likely to be the completeness of any reasons included in the judgment (*Wolesley Centres Ltd v Simmons* [1994] ICR 503). In such circumstances it is also worth noting that the EAT has the power to require tribunals to provide written reasons for any judgment or order that it has made (*rule 30(3)(b)*).

[23.14] Written reasons must be requested either:

- at the conclusion of the hearing; or
- at the latest, within 14 days of the judgment being sent to the parties (*rule 30(5)*).

If the 14-day time period has expired, it is possible to make an application to an Employment Judge for reasons to be provided out of time. An Employment Judge will consider whether, in all the circumstances, it is just and equitable to extend time (*rule 30(5)*). Any application will also be considered with a view to giving effect to the overriding objective. As with any decision involving the exercise of discretion, appealing against a refusal can be difficult, and is only likely to succeed where it can be demonstrated that the Employment Judge's decision is one which was one which would no reasonable Employment Judge would have reached and/or was demonstrably contrary to the overriding objective.

[23.15] Where it is not possible for a judgment, order or reasons to be signed by the Employment Judge due to death, incapacity or absence, the document may be signed by the lay members of the tribunal or if the Employment Judge was sitting alone, by the Regional Employment Judge, the Vice President or President (*rule 31*).

What should the written reasons contain?

[23.16] The obligation to give reasons for a decision is a fundamental principle of natural justice. What, in tribunal proceedings, is the extent of that obligation? This issue has to a certain extent been clarified by *rule 30(6)*, which sets out the minimum information that parties can expect a judgment to contain (see **23.7** above). A tribunal must comply in both form and substance with rule 30(6) and a failure to do so will amount to an error of law (*Greenwood v NWF Retail Ltd* UKEAT/0409/09/JOJ). A judgment must demonstrate "substantial compliance" with rule 30(6) and to assist in determining whether this has happened tribunals should refer to the guidance provided by the Court of Appeal in *Meek v City of Birmingham District Council* [1987] IRLR 250.

[23.17] In broad terms the tribunal must set out its conclusions on all relevant issues of fact in the case. Unfortunately, there is some conflict in the case law as to the obligation to give reasons for those conclusions. The weight of case law suggests that there *is* an obligation to give sufficient basic reasons for important factual conclusions so as to enable the parties to understand why a particular conclusion has been reached (*Meek v City of Birmingham District Council* [1987] IRLR 250 suggests a slightly higher standard than the approach adopted in *British Gas plc v Sharma* [1991] ICR 19, [1991] IRLR 101). The most helpful guidance to parties is contained in the case of *Meek* where the Court of Appeal stated that a decision must contain:

- an outline of the story (or factual background) which has given rise to the complaint;
- a summary of the tribunal's basic factual conclusions;
- a statement of the reasons for those conclusions; and
- sufficient findings and reasons for the EAT to determine whether there has been an error of law and for the parties to understand why they have won or lost.

[23.18] In discrimination cases, the tribunal must set out the primary facts upon which it bases its inferences. The guidance given by the Court of Appeal in *Meek* has to be read in light of the specific requirements set out in *rule 30(6)* – in particular the requirement that written reasons contain an explanation of how the applicable law (which must be briefly set out in the judgment) has been applied in order to determine the issues which have identified as relevant.

Examples

Example one: The duty to give reasons in discrimination cases. The tribunal, in giving its reasons for finding in favour of the claimant on the ultimate issue, simply state that: 'we find that the employer discriminated against the claimant by not selecting her for promotion.' This, in itself, is insufficient. It probably would be sufficient, however, if it stated: 'We find, for the following reasons, that the claimant was the best qualified and most suitable candidate for the job [give reasons]. We reject, for those reasons, the assertion of the respondent that the reason for the promotion of the comparator was that she had better qualifications and experience than the claimant. Having rejected the respondent's explanation, and in the absence of any other explanation, we draw the inference that the reason for the claimant's non-promotion was her ethnic background and not the reason relied upon by the respondent. We therefore conclude that she was treated less favourably on grounds of race.'

Example two: The duty to give reasons in unfair dismissal cases. The tribunal summarise the factual basis of the claim and then state as follows: 'We find that there was a potentially fair reason under *section 98* for dismissal, namely misconduct in the form of theft, that the employer entertained an honest belief in that reason, further that he had reasonable grounds for that belief and that he carried out a sufficient investigation. We are overwhelmingly of the view that the dismissal was fair and within the range of reasonable responses open to the employer'. Those reasons are inadequate, because the factual basis for the conclusions is not set out. Now compare those with the following reasons in an identical context: 'The claimant has not disputed that the employer held an honest belief in the reason for dismissal, namely misconduct in the form of theft, and that that reason falls within one of the potentially fair reasons for dismissal in *section 98* of the *Employment Rights Act 1996*.'

'Applying the test in *British Home Stores Ltd v Burchell [1978] IRLR 379*, there are two further issues for the tribunal to decide. First, did the respondent hold that belief on reasonable grounds? Having regard to the evidence before the employer at the time [brief explanation of evidence] we find that it did. Second, was there a sufficient investigation? Whilst we are of the view that failing to give the claimant sufficient notice of the disciplinary hearing rendered that hearing unfair, we find that this defect was cured upon appeal, when the claimant was given more than sufficient notice of the allegation he had to meet, ample opportunity to put his case and had all relevant aspects of his case considered. We further find that dismissal for this type of misconduct, namely theft, was clearly within the range of reasonable responses open to the respondent…'. Those reasons *probably* are sufficient because they set out the basis upon which the tribunal has reached its conclusions.

[23.19] In addition, parties should note the following:

- A tribunal is required to consider all relevant evidence, but there is no requirement, provided the duty to give sufficient reasons is complied with, for them to set out all of the evidence in their reasons. Where the tribunal has failed to record some evidence, the

EAT will not assume that they have failed to consider it unless this is clear from the reasoning in the decision.

- The written reasons of a tribunal are not required to be akin to a judgment in a higher court of law (*Shamoon v Chief Constable of the Royal Ulster Constabulary* [2003] UKHL 11; [2003] ICR 337).
- The tribunal should set out its conclusions separately in respect of each head of claim that it considers, eg unfair dismissal, sex discrimination etc.
- In certain cases it may be appropriate for the tribunal to expressly refer to relevant statutory guidance and Codes of practice (see *Goodwin v Patent Office* [1999] IRLR 4 although compare with more recent cases which indicate a more relaxed approach, *Steel v Chief Constable of Thames Valley Police* UKEAT/0793/03).
- An award of compensation *must* be specified in a written decision, together with any award of interest, and the basis upon which interest is calculated (*rule 29(3)*).

[23.20] The extent of the duty will differ widely depending upon the facts and complexity of the individual case.

It is not possible to give definitive advice in a handbook such as this as to when, in a given situation, reasons will and will not be adequate, but simply to point the reader in the right direction. When in genuine doubt as to the adequacy of reasons, parties should consider taking specialist advice (see **chapter 3 – getting advice**).

Do's and Don'ts

Do:

- Consider asking for written reasons orally on the day of a hearing, even where you have not formed a view as to whether or not you intend to appeal the decision.
- Remember that written reasons are normally required for an appeal – so make sure that, if no oral request has been made, a written request is sent to the tribunal within 14 days of the date when the judgment has been sent (the date on the covering letter).

Don't:

- Appeal minor clerical errors and slips – ask for these to be corrected under *rule 37*.

Chapter 24

Remedies: calculating likely awards

Introduction

[24.1] This chapter discusses the basic essentials of how tribunal awards are calculated, with reference to the areas of unfair dismissal and discrimination. In part, the intention is to assist the reader in considering the issue of settlement. This chapter is not intended to provide the reader with a comprehensive account of the calculation of damages. For a comprehensive guide on remedies (including non-monetary orders such as reinstatement and re-engagement which are not covered in this chapter), the reader should consult a textbook on the substantive law of employment.

Early consideration of remedies is necessary:

- in order to judge what constitutes a reasonable settlement (see **chapter 16 – settlement of claims**); and
- to prepare effectively for the remedies hearing.

[24.2] An award in an unfair dismissal case usually comprises a *basic award* and a *compensatory award*. The basic award, which tends to be the smaller of the two, is not calculated according to the claimant's financial loss, but simply their age, years of service and weekly pay. By contrast, the compensatory award compensates the claimant for the financial loss they have sustained as a consequence of the dismissal. Depending on the extent of the claimant's economic loss the compensatory award may be nil or it may be a substantial sum. In addition, the tribunal has the power, in an unfair dismissal case, to order reinstatement or re-engagement. In a discrimination case, there is no basic award. The successful claimant is rewarded compensation for their loss and, in the case of direct discrimination, an additional sum to reflect 'injury to feelings'. It is now clear that injury to feelings awards are not available in straight unfair dismissal cases (*Dunachie v Kingston-Upon-Hull City Council* [2004] IRLR 727) although compensation may be awarded where the dismissal itself (as opposed to events preceding it) causes psychological injury which precludes the claimant from obtaining new employment (see *Dignity Funerals Ltd v Bruce* [2005] IRLR 189 and *Gab Robins (UK) Ltd v Triggs* [2008] IRLR 317.).

Schedules of loss

[24.3] A schedule of loss is a valuable tool which is now frequently the subject of a compulsory order by the tribunal. An example of a schedule is set out at the end of this chapter. The purpose of a schedule of loss is for the claimant to set out clearly all the losses which he claims that he has suffered because of the respondent's actions so that both parties and the tribunal can, at the appropriate stage, address their minds to the amount and nature of compensation which is sought. A well drafted schedule may also facilitate settlement.

[24.4] Increasingly, the tribunal will order the claimant to prepare a schedule of loss and serve it on the tribunal and the respondent (if this has not already been done) as one of the case management orders. In any event, claimants are now encouraged to give details of their losses in the claim form (ET1) and it is good practice to do so or to attach a schedule to that form. It should be borne in mind that a schedule can always be expressed on a rolling basis and updated later (eg giving details of loss of earnings to a fixed date and then stating 'and continuing at a rate of £ per week/month: an updated schedule will be supplied in advance of the Hearing').

[24.5] In addition (particularly in complex cases or cases where parts of the losses are disputed for legal or factual reasons and the respondent wishes to set out its case in relation to those losses) it is relatively common for a respondent to prepare and serve a counter-schedule in response to the claimant's schedule of loss. This can be useful in narrowing the issues between the parties and in assessing their respective cases for the purposes of settlement, as well as saving time by establishing which parts of the claimant's case on loss will require evidence and which are accepted (subject to the decision on liability).

Unfair dismissal: the basic award

[24.6] The basic award is calculated as follows (*sections 119* to *122* and *126* of the *Employment Rights Act 1996*):

(a) one week's pay for each year of employment (ending with the Effective Date of Termination (EDT) and up to a limit of £400 a week) in which the employee was between the ages of 22 and 40;
(b) one and a half weeks' pay for each year of employment in which the employee was not below the age of 41; and
(c) half a week's pay for any year of employment not falling into either of the above categories (ie when the employee was between the ages of 18 and 21).

A maximum of 20 years of employment will be taken into account.

[24.7] A week's pay means (in contrast to the compensatory award – see **24.5**) the *gross* weekly pay of the employee, up to a limit of, (as of 1 February 2011) of £400 (*Employment Rights Act 1996* (*ERA 1996*), *ss 220–229*).

[24.8] The limits on the amounts which a tribunal can be awarded are reviewed and revised in accordance with inflation. Hence, on 1 February 2011 the maximum week's pay was increased from £380 to £400. The maximum amount of the compensatory award is similarly revised (see **24.5**). The result is that as of 1 February 2011, the maximum basic award for unfair dismissal is £12,000 (ie 20 × 1.5 weeks × £400). Whilst there is generally no minimum basic award, in certain circumstances (eg union-related dismissals and dismissals associated with health and safety) claimants are entitled to a minimum award.

[24.9] The best way to calculate the award is to find the correct multiplier and then apply it to the weekly pay figure. A necessary prerequisite for doing so is to note down the claimant's date of birth, date of commencement of employment and EDT.

Example one

Date of birth: 5.4.1978

Employment commenced: 1.2.2004

EDT (effective date of termination): 9.5.2010 (aged 32)

Gross weekly pay: £500 (ie above the maximum level)

Category (a) above applies and the multiplier will therefore be 6.

TOTAL AWARD: 6 × 400 = £2,400.

> **Example two**
>
> Date of Birth: 1.2.1966
>
> Employment commenced: 16.12.1997
>
> EDT: 5.4.2010 (aged 44)
>
> Gross weekly pay: £600
>
> Categories (a) and (b) above apply.
>
> For 3 years of his employment (ie the final 3), the claimant was not less than 41 years of age (category (b)), entitling him to a multiplier of 1.5 in respect of each of those years = 4.5.
>
> For each of the remaining 9 complete years he was not below the age of 22, entitling him to a multiplier of 1 in respect of each of those years = 9.
>
> The total multiplier will therefore be 13.5 (9 + 4.5).
>
> TOTAL BASIC AWARD: 13.5 × 400 = £5,400.

Incomplete years

[24.10] An incomplete year of employment does not count. Where the claimant spans more than one age category, make sure you treat the incomplete year as being at the beginning of the employment rather than the end.

Reductions in the basic award

[24.11] There is not the same scope for reducing the basic award as exists with the compensatory award (see **24.5**). It may be reduced, however:

- where it would be just and equitable to do so (*ERA 1996, s 122(2)* (see **24.14**));
- where an ex gratia payment has been made by the employer sufficient to cover any basic and compensatory award which the tribunal might make; or

- where the employee has unreasonably refused an offer of reinstatement which would have restored them to the position as if they had never been dismissed (*ERA 1996, s 122(1)*).

Unfair dismissal: the compensatory award

[24.12] The maximum compensatory award available as from 1 February 2011 is £68,400. The compensatory award is calculated according to the loss sustained as a consequence of the dismissal (*ERA 1996, s 123*). Such loss may be minimal, for example where the claimant immediately takes up a new job, or substantial, for example where the claimant is out of work for long periods. All claimants are under a duty to mitigate their loss (**24.10**). Further, such awards are frequently reduced by tribunals to reflect either contributory fault by the claimant or the fact that, if the procedural unfairness had not arisen, the dismissal would have occurred in any event. The burden is on the claimant to prove the loss caused by the dismissal. In relation to failure to mitigate, the burden is on the respondent.

[24.13] The compensatory award is typically made up of all or some of the following heads of loss:

- past loss of earnings to the date of tribunal decision, subject to the duty to mitigate (see **24.6**);
- future loss of earnings for such period (if any) as the tribunal thinks reasonable (**24.7**);
- loss of benefits such as a company car, pension etc (see **24.8**);
- loss of statutory rights (usually a nominal figure of approximately £250).

[24.14] Deductions from the compensatory award can then be made to reflect:

- a failure to mitigate loss;
- payments received by the employer since the dismissal;
- contributory conduct by the claimant;
- the fact that a dismissal might have occurred in any event;
- what is just and equitable.

All of the above deductions, and the order in which they are made, are discussed below.

Heads of loss under the compensatory award

Past loss of earnings

[24.15] Where the claimant has been out of work from dismissal to the tribunal hearing he can claim, subject to the duty to mitigate, for his lost earnings during that period. The reference point for calculating such loss is usually what the claimant earned prior to dismissal in the way of:

- net pay;
- overtime; and
- bonuses and other financial rewards which he would have received such as a company car (see below), subsidised meals, medical insurance and free accommodation.

[24.16] There may, of course, be circumstances where this is not an accurate measure of the claimant loss, for example if it can be shown that the claimant was about to receive a pay increase. Such increases should be factored in to the assessment of loss. With overtime the tribunal, in assessing any loss, will usually have regard to the overtime earned by the claimant over a particular period before dismissal (usually 12 or 13 weeks), unless for any reason this is not an accurate measure. Loss of bonus will, likewise, be assessed on the evidence before the tribunal.

Future loss of earnings

[24.17] As with past loss of earnings, the award is capable of covering all relevant financial benefits and benefits in kind, not simply pay (eg bonuses, commission, travel concessions etc). Future loss will be calculated according to the length of time the tribunal consider it is reasonable for the claimant to be out of work or in work on lesser pay. Again, this is an area for the tribunal to make a finding of fact upon based on the evidence before it. Relevant factors are likely to include the availability of suitable alternative work on the job market and the extent to which the claimant has attempted to find alternative employment. If the tribunal finds that the claimant has found or is likely within a relatively short period to find alternative employment but at a lower rate of pay, the tribunal may award future loss based on the likely difference between the earnings with the respondent and those in the new job.

[24.18] The length for which compensation for future loss of earnings will be permitted to continue is likewise a matter for the tribunal to determine in the light of the available evidence. As a rule of thumb, however, it is relatively unusual for an award in respect of total loss of earnings to continue beyond two years from the date of the tribunal hearing unless there are good reasons to the contrary (such as that the claimant is approaching pension age and is unlikely ever to find suitable work before the age at which they would have retired in any event). Partial loss, however, might conceivably continue for a longer period.

[24.19] Where a claimant asserts that there will be substantial ongoing loss, for example because there is no demand in the market for a person with his profile/experience, consideration should be given to engaging an employment consultant who is able to provide an expert opinion on that matter.

Loss of benefits such as pension and company car

[24.20] Loss of pension rights is a recoverable head. The size of any award will be dependent upon a number of factors, including the size of contributions, the type of pension and the extent of pension provision in any future employment. With certain schemes, the loss can be calculated simply according to the total value of the lost contributions, although frequently this underestimates the loss, for example if there is a penalty for non-contribution in a given period.

[24.21] Claimants who need assistance in this frequently complex area should consider:

- contacting the trustees of the pension fund/s in question (who have a duty to give them accurate information) to assist in any calculation; and
- using the guidance booklet on pensions written by tribunal chairmen and the Government Actuary's Department *Compensation for Loss of Pension Rights*, published by TSO and available from the HM Courts and Tribunals Service website (www.justice.gov.uk).

[24.22] Loss of a company car for which a claimant was allowed personal use is a recoverable head. Valuing a car for a given period is problematic and parties are advised to adopt one of the following two courses:

- obtain from the AA the list of annual estimates which they publish for this purpose; and
- rely upon the taxable value of the car.

Loss of statutory rights

[24.23] The tribunal usually makes a small award to reflect the fact that the claimant will lose protection from unfair dismissal in the first year of new employment and/or will lose the benefit of an accrued statutory notice period. The award is usually in the region of £250.

Employer's failure to comply with the ACAS Code of Practice

[24.24] As discussed in **chapter 4: dispute resolution** for dismissals which occurred prior to 6 April 2009, a failure to complete the statutory dispute resolution procedures under the *Employment Act 2002* which was wholly or mainly attributable to failure by the employer to comply with a requirement of the procedure resulted in an increase in an award of between 10 – 50%. Under the new regime (ie for dismissals which occurred from 6 April 2009) a tribunal may, if it considers it just and equitable in all the circumstances to do so, increase any award it makes by up to 25% where an employer unreasonably fails to comply with the ACAS Code of Practice. Note, that the reverse is also true: where an employee unreasonably fails to comply with the Code the tribunal may reduce any award by up to 25% (see **24.32** below and **chapter 4**).

Factors which go towards reducing the compensatory award

Failure to mitigate

[24.25] Claimants are under a duty to mitigate their loss by making reasonable efforts to obtain alternative employment (*ERA 1996, s 123(4)*). Where a tribunal find they have not done so, the compensatory award will be reduced to reflect the loss which would have occurred if reasonable efforts had been made. The extent to which, if at all, a claimant is expected to accept lesser paid work will depend upon what, in the circumstances, a tribunal consider is reasonable. Tribunals will not generally expect claimants to accept work which is in a different category of skill and status to that which they have enjoyed before, at least not without re-training, for which in certain cases an award of compensation may be made. Where, however, the job is in the same bracket, they may be expected to accept the position if there is a decrease in pay. The circumstances are highly fact specific (see, for example, *Hardy v Polk (Leeds) Ltd* [2004] IRLR 420). As to a refusal to accept an offer of reinstatement, this might have the effect of disentitling the employee to a compensatory award if the offer would have been accepted by a reasonable employee uninfluenced by the prospect of recovering compensation: *Wilding v British Telecommunications plc* [2002] EWCA Civ 349, [2002] IRLR 524.

[24.26] What is reasonable will always depend upon the individual circumstances of the case including, for example, such matters as travel and working hours. The burden is on the employer to prove that a claimant has not made reasonable efforts to mitigate their loss. This means that an employer would be well advised, in advance of a remedies hearing, to request evidence from the claimant in the form of job application forms, responses etc which go to the issue of whether reasonable attempts have been made. In practice, a tribunal expects claimants to demonstrate what attempts they have made to secure alternative work.

A fair dismissal might have occurred in any event

[24.27] An award can be reduced by up to 100% to reflect the fact that a fair dismissal might have occurred in any event. The tribunal will decide this with reference to the hypothetical reasonable employer. This deduction is commonly known as a '*Polkey*' deduction (named after the case in which the principle was first introduced, namely *Polkey v AE Dayton Services Ltd* [1988] AC 344) and, unlike contributory fault (see **24.12**), is not limited to misconduct cases. It is generally, however, limited to the situation where the dismissal was unfair for some procedural reason rather than having been substantively unfair. Note that, in these circumstances, a tribunal should also make a finding as to when dismissal would have occurred. Examples of where reductions under this head might be made are:

- where the dismissal is procedurally unfair, but a fair procedure might still have resulted in dismissal; and
- where the claimant would have lost his job at a certain point in any event, for example because the respondent went out of business or the branch in which he was employed closed down and no staff were relocated.

Example

A tribunal decides that a dismissal for redundancy is unfair because there has been insufficient consultation with the employee but that, even if there had been sufficient consultation, there is a 70% chance that dismissal would have occurred in any event. The compensatory award will therefore be reduced by 70%.

Contributory fault by the claimant

[24.28] Tribunals are entitled to reduce any award by up to 100% to reflect the fact that the claimant caused or contributed to their own dismissal (*ERA 1996, s 123(6)*). Such findings, which are relatively common, are usually only appropriate in misconduct cases. They tend to occur where there is evidence of blameworthy conduct on the part of the employee justifying disciplinary sanctions, but the dismissal was unfair either because: (a) the employer failed to carry out a fair procedure; or (b) dismissal was an excessively harsh sanction. Note that in the case of (a), the employer might additionally benefit from a reduction under the *Polkey* head above. When assessing contribution, tribunals are limited to examining evidence in existence prior to dismissal. The extent of any finding of contribution will always depend upon the circumstances of the case. The tribunal will usually make its finding on contribution when it gives its decision on whether the dismissal was fair or unfair.

Arguing 'Polkey' or 'contributory fault'

[24.29] In both cases, tribunals usually decide whether to make a reduction at the same time as considering whether the dismissal was fair or unfair, as opposed to during the remedies hearing. So, in a misconduct case, a tribunal might find that the dismissal was unfair, but that the claimant contributed to his dismissal by 50%. For this reason, parties should address both issues at the substantive hearing of the dispute, not at the remedies hearing, unless the tribunal indicates otherwise. Note that whilst the finding on the appropriate percentage reduction is usually made when giving the decision on the fairness of the dismissal, the reduction is not then *applied* until the tribunal has assessed the extent (without any reduction) of the claimant's financial loss.

Just and equitable

[24.30]

The power to award compensatory damages in *ERA 1996, s 123(1)* expressly provides that 'the amount of the compensatory award shall be such amount as the tribunal considers just and equitable in all the circumstances…'. Tribunals enjoy a broad discretion which enables them to take into account a significant factor which makes it just and equitable to reduce the award (by up to 100%).

Examples

In deciding contribution, the tribunal is limited to assessing the evidence in existence prior to dismissal. If subsequent evidence comes to light (relating to events prior to dismissal) this could enable a just and equitable reduction to be made. So, if an employee, shortly after dismissal, is found to have stolen money from the employer, a total or partial reduction might be made.

Where, following a dismissal, an employee has chosen to retrain and carry out a completely different career for reasons unrelated to dismissal, they might not be entitled to an award which reflects the full extent of their financial loss. In other words, it could be said that part of the loss arises from a personal decision by the claimant (see, for example, *Simrad Ltd v Scott* [1997] IRLR 147).

Payments by the employer

[24.31] Where the employer has made payments to the employee, these will generally be taken into account and reduced from the award. So, if an employee is paid in lieu of notice, the loss will run from the end of the notice period. Similarly, an ex gratia payment may be taken into account. This can assist employers who have settled claims but failed to comply with the requirements of a compromise agreement (see **chapter 16**), meaning that the claimant is not prevented from pursuing the claim in the employment tribunal. In such circumstances, the tribunal is likely to deduct the sum paid in settlement from any award which it makes.

Employee's failure to comply with the ACAS Code of Practice

[24.32] Where an employee unreasonably fails to comply with the ACAS Code of Practice the tribunal may reduce any award by up to 25%. See **chapter 4** for more information on the current ACAS Code of Practice.

> **The order in which deductions should be made.**
> Following the case of *Digital Equipment v Clements (No 2)* [1998] IRLR 134, any deductions from the compensatory award should be made in the following order:
> - deduct any relevant payments made by the employer
> - make a *Polkey* reduction
> - make any deduction for failure to follow statutory procedures
> - make any reduction for contributory fault on the part of the employee
> - if applicable reduce the award to the statutory maximum.

Compensation in discrimination cases

[24.33] Where a tribunal finds that a claimant has been discriminated against it may:
- make a declaration as to the claimant's rights;
- order the respondent to pay compensation to the claimant for financial losses and / or injury to feelings;
- make a recommendation that within a specified period the respondent takes specified steps for the purpose of obviating or reducing the adverse effect of any matter to which the proceedings relate on the claimant or any other person (*Equality Act 2010, s 124*).

In addition, tribunals have the power to award interest in respect of awards of compensation. Unlike in claims for unfair dismissal, there is no statutory limit on the amount of compensation that can be awarded.

Compensation for financial loss

[24.34] The tribunal's power to award compensation is discretionary. The amount of compensation for financial loss in discrimination cases is assessed according to different principles from those applicable in unfair dismissal cases, but the outcome is often similar. The purpose of the compensation is to restore the claimant to the position he would have been in had the discrimination not occurred, subject to the claimant's duty to mitigate his loss (section 124(6); *Ministry of Defence v Wheeler* [1998] 1 WLR 637). Due to the fact that this process involves predicting the likelihood of future events, the tribunal will frequently apply a percentage figure in deciding this issue (*Ministry of Defence v Cannock* [1994] ICR 918 and *Ministry of Defence v Hunt* [1996] ICR 544).

Note that, with discriminatory dismissals, the tribunal will elect whether to calculate the loss according to unfair dismissal principles or on the tortious basis provided for in discrimination cases. Frequently, the outcome will be the same, particularly as the claimant cannot recover twice in respect of the same loss (ie be compensated for loss of earnings for unfair dismissal by a compensatory award and then be compensated for the same loss of earnings under tortious, 'just and equitable' principles).

It is important to remember, however, that unlike unfair dismissal awards, compensation for discrimination carries no statutory maximum.

Example one: discriminatory dismissal

[24.35] The tribunal find that the claimant, who earned £400 a week net, was unfairly dismissed for reasons relating to her pregnancy. The tribunal must seek to restore her to the position she would have been in had the discriminatory act not occurred, subject to the duty on the claimant to mitigate her loss. They calculate her loss as follows:

- Loss of pay prior to the time when she would have gone on maternity leave – eight weeks pay: £3,200.
- Loss of statutory maternity pay (18 weeks): £3,704.76 (as of April 2011, statutory maternity pay is calculated as 90% of net wages for the first six weeks and £128.73 for the remaining 33 weeks).
- The tribunal concludes that, on the evidence before it, there is a 60% chance that she would have returned to work at the conclusion of her maternity leave.

- It further finds that, applying the duty to mitigate her loss, she could be expected to find alternative work within four months of that date.
- In respect of the period after return to work, the claimant will therefore receive 60% of 14 weeks pay: 14 × £400 × 60% = £3,360.00.
- TOTAL AWARD FOR FINANCIAL LOSS: £10,264.76 (Note the claimant will, in addition, be entitled to an award for injury to feelings).

Note that it has been suggested by the EAT, in the case of a dismissal for a pregnancy related reason, that it will rarely be appropriate to award compensation for a period in excess of six months after the date when the claimant would have returned to work unless, as of that date, the claimant is actively engaged in looking for work (*Ministry of Defence v Cannock* [1994] ICR 918).

Example two: discriminatory non-selection

[24.36] The tribunal finds, in a race discrimination case, that the claimant, who was not selected for a more senior post, was discriminated against on the basis of his race. The claimant is still employed by the respondent in his original post which pays £10,000 a year less than the more senior post he was applying for. The tribunal must assess the likelihood of the claimant being selected for the post had the discriminatory act not occurred. The tribunal concludes that there is a 50% chance that the claimant would have obtained the post. The tribunal hearing takes place six months after the date when the claimant would have commenced the new position.

The tribunal concludes that the claimant is entitled, in respect of past loss, to 50% of the additional pay which he would have received, namely £2,500 (£5,000 × 50%). Applying the principle of mitigation of loss the tribunal conclude that the claimant could reasonably have been expected to obtain a position of equivalent seniority to that for which he was not selected within three months of the hearing. It therefore awards a further £2,500 in respect of future loss.

TOTAL AWARD IN RESPECT OF FINANCIAL LOSS: £5,000. (The claimant will in, addition, be entitled to an award for injury to feelings).

Compensation for non-financial loss

Injury to feelings

[24.37] As awards of compensation are intended to put the claimant in the position that he would have been in but for the discriminatory conduct, tribunals are entitled to make an award for distress, anxiety or humiliation occasioned by such behaviour. This principle is clearly articulated by the *Equality Act 2010, s 119(4)*. Awards for injury to feelings are an increasingly important component of compensation for discrimination. Whilst there is no statutory guidance on the size of these awards, they tend to range from £500 to a figure in excess of £25,000 in a truly exceptional case. The Court of Appeal in *Vento v Chief Constable of West Yorkshire Police* [2003] EWCA Civ 1871 gave guidance on the appropriate range of awards for injury to feelings. The amounts provided for by the Court of Appeal have recently been updated by the EAT in *Da'Bell v National Society for Prevention of Cruelty to Children* [2010] IRLR 19 to take inflation into account. Typically, the Court found that an award would fall in to one of three bands. The current rates are:

- A lower band of £750–£6,000 for 'less serious' cases where the act of discrimination is 'isolated or one-off'.
- A middle band of £6,000–£18,000 for cases which do not merit an award in the highest band.
- A top band of £18,000–£30,000 for the most serious cases, 'such as where there has been a lengthy campaign of discriminatory harassment on the ground of sex or race'.

The tribunal has a wide discretion in deciding what award to make, based upon the fact that it is in a position to hear the evidence and judge the extent of the injury first hand. Whilst tribunals should not apply the guidelines as if they were rules of law they enjoy considerable discretion meaning that the EAT and higher courts are unlikely to interfere in a tribunal's assessment of such damages unless it can be shown that there has been an error of law in the tribunal's decision.

The principles upon which the award will be assessed

[24.38] The leading case on assessing awards for injury to feelings is that of *Armitage, Johnson and HM Prison Service v Johnson* [1997] IRLR 162. In *Armitage* the EAT summarised the principles for deciding an award for hurt to feelings as follows:

- The aim of the award is to compensate the victim, not to punish the employer. It is hurt to the feelings of the victim, as opposed to indignation at the employer's conduct, which is the basis for assessing the award.
- The award should not be so low as to diminish respect for anti-discrimination legislation nor so high that it could be seen as a route to untaxed riches for the recipient.
- Awards should bear some broad similarity to the range of awards in personal injury cases.
- Tribunals should have regard to the value in everyday life of the sums they are awarding.
- Tribunals should have regard to the need for the public to have respect for the level of award which is made.

[24.39] In addition, it is submitted that the following instances may serve to increase the injury which has been suffered, and hence the award:

- Where the employee has been subject to victimisation or harassment.
- Where the employer has not taken a complaint seriously and failed to investigate it properly and sensitively.
- Where, as a consequence of the dismissal, the employee has lost the chance to pursue congenial employment – an example of this might be a police officer who was dismissed from the force and thereby prevented from pursuing a career which he was committed to and had spent many years training for (see, for example, *Orlando v Didcot Power Stations Sports and Social Club* [1996] IRLR 262).
- Where the act of discrimination is intentional.

Personal injury

[24.40] Tribunals have jurisdiction to make an award for personal injury caused by the act of discrimination. Indeed, where such an injury is alleged, it is essential that the employee includes it in their employment tribunal claim as they are likely to be precluded from subsequently doing so in the civil courts. In the majority of cases were such an award is appropriate, the personal injury suffered will be psychiatric in nature. If possible, medical evidence should be adduced in support of the proposition that an injury has been sustained just as it would be in civil proceedings for negligence or breach of statutory duty. In cases where there is the suggestion of a serious injury (psychiatric or otherwise), it is strongly advisable, both for employers and employees, to seek legal advice on the size of the likely award and any evidential steps which need to be taken to support or rebut the extent (or fact) of injury. Unlike 'pure' hurt to feelings awards, the personal injury element can usually be more precisely assessed and calculated with reference to existing tortious principles, case law and the Judicial Studies Board 'Guidelines for the Assessment of General Damages in Personal Injury Cases' (2010). The JSB Guidelines can be used to assist the quantification of damages for psychiatric injury (see *HM Prison Service v Salmon* [2001] IRLR 425). Tribunals are encouraged to include a personal injury award in any award for hurt to feelings.

Aggravated Damages

[24.41] The tribunal has the power to award aggravated damages where it considers that the employer, in committing an act of discrimination, has behaved in a high handed, malicious, oppressive or insulting manner (*Alexander v Home Office* [1988] ICR 685). In some instances, the award for aggravated damages will be included in the award for hurt to feelings, and in some instances expressed as an additional amount.

Exemplary Damages

[24.42] In cases where compensatory damages are considered to be insufficient to punish the party responsible for the discriminatory conduct, tribunals are permitted to make an award of exemplary damages (*Kuddus v Chief Constable of Leicestershire Constabulary* [2001] UKHL 29, [2002] 2 AC 122). Awards of exemplary damages are very rare and should only be awarded where there had been 'oppressive, arbitrary or unconstitutional action by servants of the government' or where the respondent's conduct had been calculated by him to make a profit for himself which might well exceed the compensation payable to the claimant.

Indirect discrimination

[24.43] In cases of indirect discrimination contrary to the *Equality Act 2010, s 19* a tribunal should not make an order for compensation if it is satisfied that the provision, criterion or practice was not applied with the intention of discriminating against the complainant, unless it first considers whether to make a declaration or recommendation (*s 124(4)*). This broadly reflects the position under the *Sex Discrimination Act 1975*.

Do's and Don'ts

Do:

- Remember that, in both unfair dismissal and discrimination cases, it is for the claimant to prove his loss, and for the employer to prove a failure to mitigate.
- The claimant should prepare a schedule of loss at the start of the proceedings and serve it with the claim form, and should then update it in advance of the Hearing.
- The employer should request full details in advance of attempts which the employee has made to mitigate their loss and make it clear that the claimant is required to prove all aspects of their claimed loss, giving details of information required.
- Respondents should consider whether it would assist matters to prepare a counter-schedule addressing the claimant's case on loss.
- In unfair dismissal cases consider any reductions in the compensatory award which might be made under the *Polkey* heading and/or for contributory fault.
- In discrimination cases consider: financial loss, injury to feelings (including, where appropriate, personal injury and aggravated damages) and interest.

Don't:

- Leave consideration of remedy until the last minute.
- Forget that income support and jobseeker's allowance will be recouped from any award made by the tribunal, providing an incentive to settle (as recoupment does not take place in the case of settlement) (see **chapter 16**).

Interest

[24.44] Interest starts to runs on most tribunal awards, including awards in unfair dismissal cases, 42 days from the date of decision (see *Employment Tribunals (Interest) Order 1990*). The rate payable is that defined in the Judgments Act 1838, currently standing at 8%. This occurs automatically, and should therefore be added by the claimant to any sum due when issuing county court proceedings.

[24.45] In discrimination cases there is a particular incentive for the respondent to pay quickly. If payment is made within 14 days, no interest of any kind becomes payable. If payment is not made within this period, interest will be awarded, in respect of a hurt to feelings or injuries award, from the date when the discriminatory act took place to the date of decision and, with other discrimination awards, from the 'midpoint date'. The midpoint date is the date half way between the commencement of the discriminatory act/s and the date of calculation by the tribunal of the award (see *Employment Tribunals (Interest on Awards in Discrimination Cases) Regulations 1996*). In addition, interest will accrue on the total award from the date of decision. The current rate of interest in discrimination cases is 0.5%.

Claimant's schedule of loss: unfair dismissal

[24.46] This example assumes a straightforward case of unfair dismissal. It assumes that the claimant is aged 45 (date of birth 1 September 1965) at the date of dismissal and was employed by the respondent for seven and a half years between start date (2 May 2003) and the effective date of termination (10 November 2010). It also assumes that the schedule is being prepared for a hearing that will take place nine months (39 weeks) after the effective date of termination (ie 10 August 2011) and that six months after the dismissal (9 May 2011), the claimant has started a new job which pays less than his employment with the respondent. It is assumed that his salary with the respondent was £365 gross or £290 net per week.

IN THE EMPLOYMENT TRIBUNALS Case number XXX

(ANYTOWN)

BETWEEN

MR AGGRIEVED

Claimant

– and –

THE DON'T BLAME US TRADING COMPANY

Respondent

CLAIMANT'S SCHEDULE OF LOSS

1.) Basic Award

The claimant earned £365 gross per week. The statutory maximum does not therefore apply.
He worked for 3 complete years aged not less than 22 (3 × 1 week).
He worked for 4 complete years aged not less than 41 (4 × 1.5 weeks).
Award is therefore 9 × £365 = £3,285.
Total *£1,980*

2.) Compensatory Award

a) *Loss of earnings to date of hearing* (for the purposes of this Schedule, accrued holiday pay has not been included. If at the time of dismissal the claimant has accrued holiday entitlement, most employers will resolve this issue by requiring the claimant to take the outstanding leave during the notice period. If the leave is in excess of the notice period, the employer does not adopt this course or the dismissal is without notice, advisors should be astute to the need to claim outstanding accrued holiday pay. However, this is arguably better achieved by claiming for unlawful deduction from wages and/or under the *Working Time Regulations 1998*).

(i) 11 November 2010 to 8 May 2011.
The claimant received no earnings during this period.
Net earnings prior to dismissal were £290 per week = £1,256.67 per month.
6 months × £1,256.67 = £7,540.02.
Total *£7,540.02*

(ii) 9 May 2011 to 10 August 2011.
On 9 May 2011 the claimant commenced employment on a part-time basis at a net salary of £170 per week = £736.67 per month.
His loss of earnings during this period is therefore £520 per month.
3 months × £520 = £1,560.
Total *£1,560*

b) *Future loss of earnings*
The claimant has been informed that on 11 October 2011 his salary in his current employment will increase to £1,500 net per month, ie there will be no ongoing loss after that date.
His future loss of earnings will therefore be £520 per month for a further two months, ie £780.
Total *£780*

c) *Loss of bonus*
The claimant would have received a bonus on [date] and on [date]. The amount of each bonus would have been [£XXX].
Total *£XXX*

d) *Loss of pension*
[Calculating the loss of pension entitlements is often a difficult process depending upon such factors as the type of pension involved, the length of service of the employee and their age. The majority of pension loss claims are assessed by the Tribunal according to the simplified approach where, broadly speaking, the employee recovers the loss of pension contributions, usually for a limited period. Where, however, there is an employee of longstanding service who is receiving a final salary scheme, the Tribunal may be more inclined to adopt the "substantial loss approach". This can result in a very large loss of pension award. Practitioners may wish to consult the Employment Tribunals' guidelines on 'Compensation for Loss of Pension Rights' (2003) which is available at www.justice.gov.uk.]
Total *£XXX*

e) *Loss of use of company car*
The claimant had use of a company car which was used for personal use.
The net value of the car, petrol and running costs is estimated at [£XXX] (annual estimates published by, for example the AA or RAC may be of assistance in assessing the loss).
Total *£XXX*

f) *Loss of private medical insurance policy*
The respondent paid for a private health insurance policy for the claimant. He no longer has this benefit in his new job.
[Include details]
Total £XXX

g) *Loss of other benefits in kind*
[Include details]
Total £XXX

h) *Cost of re-training*
The claimant had to undertake a [eg computer] course prior to obtaining alternative employment. This course cost £XXX.
Total £XXX

i) *Costs of seeking alternative employment* (this head may also include the situation where, for example, the claimant has to move house in order to start a new job.)
The claimant incurred costs in applying for jobs and travelling to interviews. These are as follows:
[Include details]
Total £XXX

j) *Loss of reputation* (these 'stigma' damages are only available in limited circumstances to compensate for difficulties in finding alternative employment as a result of the poor reputation of the employer at the time of the dismissal: (*Malik v BCCI* [1997] ICR 606). Note, however that a claimant is not entitled to damages for the stress or injury to feelings resulting from the manner of dismissal (*Dunnachie v Kingston-upon-Hull City Council* [2004] UKHL 36; [2005] 1 AC 226) A depressive reaction to a dismissal which renders the claimant unfit to work may sound in damages if just and equitable although there is considerable uncertainty surrounding this area – see [24.2] above.
[Include details]
Total £XXX

k) <u>Loss of statutory rights</u> (there is no hard and fast rule as to the amount which will be awarded under this head. However, a figure of around £250 is often used.)
Total £XXX

3.) TOTAL £XXX

Chapter 25

Steps after the decision I: Review

Introduction

[25.1] A tribunal may in certain circumstances review a judgment, decision or default judgment. Such a review may be initiated by one of the parties or may be of the tribunal's own motion. It will only do so, however, where it decides that specific criteria are met which need to be addressed in any application for a review. The same tribunal whose original decision is under scrutiny will usually consider the application and conduct any review, frequently at the same hearing. At the conclusion of the review it may affirm, vary or revoke the original decision and order a complete re-hearing. In the latter circumstance, the parties should be ready to make representations as to whether the re-hearing should be before the same or a differently constituted tribunal. For guidance on whether to apply for a review or appeal to the Employment Appeal Tribunal (EAT), see **25.13**.

What may be reviewed

[25.2] A tribunal may review the following:

- **Default judgments**: A party may apply under *rule 33* of the 2004 Rules to have a default judgment reviewed. The circumstances in which a tribunal may enter a default judgment are discussed in **chapter 7 – the employer's response** at **7.7**.
- **Judgments**: A judgment is defined by *rule 28(1)* of the *2004 Rules* as 'a final determination of the proceedings or of a particular issue in those proceedings' and may include an award of compensation, a declaration or recommendation, or an order for costs. Effectively, a 'judgment' is a final decision which has the effect of bringing the proceedings or part of them to an end.
- **Decisions**: A 'decision' for the purpose of a review includes a decision not to accept a claim, response or counterclaim (*rule 34(1)*).

[25.3] It is important to note that other decisions or orders not expressly mentioned cannot be reviewed under *rules 33–36*. Hence, what is *not* a decision and therefore not capable of review are interim or case management orders, for example in relation to orders for further particulars or disclosure. Where a party is unhappy with an interim order and does not wish to pursue an appeal to the Employment Appeal Tribunal, an interim order may be amenable to an application to vary or revoke within an Employment Judge's general power to vary or revoke under *rule 10(2)(n)*. The EAT has held that whilst there is a general prohibition against reviewing "other decisions or orders" within the rules, this means within *rules 33–36* and therefore it is not an exclusion for the purposes of the 2004 Rules as a whole (*Hart v English Heritage* [2006] ICR 655). Generally, however, such a power should only be exercised where there has been a change of circumstances from when the earlier decision or order was made (*Onwuka v Spherion Technology UK Ltd* [2005] ICR 567).

Review of default judgments

[25.3] The circumstances in which a tribunal may enter a default judgment are discussed in **chapter 7**. Where a default judgment has been entered a party may apply to have that judgment against or in favour of him reviewed (*rule 33(1)*). Where a party wishes to have a default judgment reviewed he must present an application in writing to the tribunal within 14 days of the date on which the default judgment was sent to the parties. The 14-day limit may be extended by an Employment Judge if he considers it just and equitable to do so. Where a party seeks an extension, they should state this clearly in the application and set out their grounds for seeking the extension and an explanation of why the application was not made sooner, as in the case of an application to extend time for presenting a response form (see **chapter 7**).

[25.4] The written application must state the reasons why the default judgment should be varied or revoked (*rule 33(2)*). When it is the respondent applying for the review the application must also include the following matters and documents:

- the proposed response to the claim itself;
- an application for an extension of time for presenting the response; and

- an explanation as to why the respondent did not comply with *rule 4(1)* and *(4)* (submitting a response within time containing all the relevant required information and applying in the proper manner before the expiry of the 28-day limitation period for an extension of time within which to respond).

An application for a review of a default judgment may be given preliminary consideration without the need to hold a hearing by an Employment Judge who may refuse the application if these requirements have not been met (*rule 33(2A)*).

[25.5] The review will be conducted by an Employment Judge in public unless all the parties to the proceedings consent in writing to the review without a hearing. Notice of the hearing along with a copy of the application shall be sent to all other parties.

[25.6] The Employment Judge will give a judgment on the application which will be notified to the parties in writing. The Employment Judge may:

- refuse the application for a review;
- vary the default judgment;
- revoke all or part of the default judgment; and/or
- confirm the default judgment.

[25.7] A default judgment *must* be revoked if (*rule 33(5)*):

- The whole of the claim was satisfied before the judgment was issued.
- The parties settled the proceedings (either by means of a compromise agreement or through ACAS) on or before the date on which the default judgment was issued.

Otherwise an Employment Judge has discretion as to whether default judgment should be varied or revoked. The default judgment may be revoked or varied in whole or part if the respondent has a reasonable prospect of successfully responding to the claim or a part of it (*rule 33(5)*). In considering the application for a review the Employment Judge must consider whether there was good reason for the response not being presented within the time limit (*rule 33(6)*).

[25.8] An application for a review of a default judgment should therefore address both of these factors (ie the respondent's prospects of success and the reason for the delay in presenting the response),

An application that does not address these issues is unlikely to be successful.

[25.9] If the Employment Judge decides to vary or revoke the default judgment and considers that the respondent should be allowed to respond to the claim, the response will be accepted and the case will proceed as normal (*rule 33(7)*).

[25.10] In addition to the parties being able to apply to review a default judgment, a tribunal or an Employment Judge may of its or his own initiative review a decision made by it or him on the following grounds:

- The decision was wrongly made as a result of an administrative error.
- A party did not receive notice of the proceedings leading to the decision.
- The interests of justice require such a review.

Review of judgments and decisions

[25.11] The procedure for reviewing other judgments and decisions is different from that in respect of default judgments. The relevant provisions are set out in *rules 34* to *36* of the *2004 Rules*. *Rule 34(1)* explains which decisions or judgments may be the subject of an application for review and makes it clear that no other decisions or orders may be reviewed under the rules (see **25.2** above). A party to the proceedings may apply to have a decision or judgment reviewed or a tribunal or Employment Judge may review a decision on its or his own initiative (*rule 34(5)*).

[25.12] Where the decision in question is one to reject a claim or response, only the party against whom the decision is made may apply for a review (*rule 34(2)*). Such a decision can only be reviewed on the basis that it was wrongly made as a result of an administrative error or that the interests of justice require such a review (*rule 34(4)*). The meaning of 'administrative error' and 'interests of justice' is discussed further below.

[25.13] A party can apply for a review of a decision or judgment (other than a default judgment but including an order for costs etc – see **25.2** above) where:

(a) the decision was wrongly made as a result of an administrative error;
(b) a party did not receive notice of the proceedings leading to the decision;
(c) the decision was made in the absence of a party;
(d) new evidence has become available since the conclusion of the hearing to which the decision relates, provided that its existence could not have been reasonably known of or foreseen at that time; or
(e) the interests of justice require such a review.

In addition, as with the exercise of all its procedural powers, the tribunal is required, in so far as it is practicable, to give effect to the overriding objective (see **chapter 8 – fairness: the overriding objective**) in deciding whether to conduct a review. In practice, this is likely to be most relevant in relation to ground E below.

Ground (a): administrative error

[25.14] Under the *2001 Rules*, this ground of review was expressed to be as an error 'on the part of the tribunal staff'. The *2004 Rules* widened the category of procedural errors such that errors on the part of the parties may found a basis for review (*Sodexho Ltd v Gibbons* [2005] ICR 1647). Hence, where a party fills in a claim form or response incorrectly (such as including the wrong postcode of their solicitors' offices) and this leads to a wrongly made decision, it may be possible to apply to review that decision. In practice reviews on this ground are most likely to arise in the context of the duties of the Tribunal Service's administrative staff. It is unlikely that errors on the part of Employment Judges or lay members could constitute 'administrative errors' for the purposes of *rule 34(3)(a)*, however in any event purely clerical mistakes in orders, judgments, decisions and reasons can usually be more efficiently corrected under the slip rule (see **25.40**).

[25.15] Note also that such an error will not, of itself, be sufficient to found a review unless it can be shown that the decision was 'wrongly made', ie the mistake is not purely technical in nature.

Ground (b): notice of proceedings not received

[25.16] A notice of hearing (or any other tribunal document) sent by post is deemed to have been received by the party to whom it was addressed unless the person applying for the review proves otherwise (see *rule 62(2)* of the *2004 Rules* and *section 7* of the *Interpretation Act 1978*). The effect of this provision is that a party who did not receive a notice must prove this fact before they can successfully rely upon this ground of review. If a relevant document is sent to the correct address of an organisation but it is lost internally, service is effective, emphasising the importance of efficient internal procedures for the processing of such information (see also *Migwain Ltd v Transport and General Workers Union* [1979] ICR 597 and *T and D Transport (Portsmouth) Ltd v Limburn* [1987] ICR 696).

Further, where a document is sent to the registered office of a limited company (even if not the office dealing with the matter in question), service will usually be deemed to have taken place (see *Migwain* above).

Ground (c): decision made in the absence of a party

[25.17] The party in question, when applying for the review, must show 'good cause' for their absence (*Morris v Griffiths* [1977] ICR 153). The tribunal will look both at the reason for non-attendance and whether the party asserting is telling the truth. The party seeking the review will be assisted by independent corroborative evidence in support of what they are saying, for example, a medical certificate.

Ground (d): new evidence

[25.18] The criteria for granting a review to hear new evidence are the same as the rules applicable on appeal to the EAT (*Wileman v Minilec Engineering Ltd* [1988] ICR 318). In addition to showing that the existence of the evidence could not have been reasonably known of or foreseen at the conclusion of the hearing to which the evidence relates, a party applying to review a decision on this basis must also establish:

- the evidence could not have been obtained with reasonable diligence for use at the trial;
- that the evidence would probably have an important influence on the result of the case; and
- the evidence must be apparently credible, though it need not be undisputed.

[25.19] Note that a review will not take place under this ground unless all three requirements are met, other than in the exceptional circumstances provided for under *rule 34(3)(e)*. The justification for this is the need for 'finality' in legal proceedings. Parties should note that there might be an overlap between the new evidence category, *rule 34(3)(d)*, and the interests of justice category, *rule 34(3)(e)* (see **25.21**).

[25.20] It is important to remember that a review is not a substitute for seeking an adjournment at the original hearing if one is necessary in order to adduce evidence to reply to a new allegation by the other side.

Ground (e): interests of justice

[25.21] The final ground of review is intended to confer on tribunals a wide discretion to ensure, in accordance with the overriding objective, that cases are dealt with justly. However the courts have been keen to emphasise the restricted circumstances in which this ground can be relied upon (see *Wileman v Minilec Engineering Ltd* [1988] ICR 318). Although it is no longer a requirement for an applicant to show "exceptional circumstances" (compare *Trimble v Supertravel Ltd* [1982] ICR 440 and *Williams v Ferrosan Ltd* [2004] IRLR 607), tribunals should have regard to the public interest in ensuring that there is finality in legal proceedings, and also to the prejudice which the other party may suffer if the review is allowed to proceed. In general terms, a party will not be able to rely upon *rule 34(3)(e)* simply where he has previously failed to persuade a tribunal that his case falls within *rules 34(3)(a)* to *(d)*. So where new evidence was available at the time of the original hearing, the party seeking to adduce it upon review will need to show that there were special mitigating circumstances why they failed to do so at the original hearing if they are to succeed under ground (e).

[25.22] A review under the interests of justice ground tends to fall into one of two categories. Firstly, where there has been a procedural mishap, and secondly where the tribunal's decision has been undermined by events taking place after the original decision was made.

Procedural mishap

[25.23] The type of 'procedural mishaps' which may merit an application to review a decision include the following instances:

(a) A party has not had a fair opportunity to respond to the other's case.

(b) There is an issue in relation to the jurisdiction of the tribunal to hear the case or the tribunal has made an obvious error of law which is better addressed by way of review than appeal.
(c) The claim has been dismissed without a hearing in circumstances which amount to a miscarriage of justice.
(d) The claim has been withdrawn after receiving erroneous legal guidance from the Employment Judge or due to a failure on the part of the respondent to disclose relevant documents.

[25.24] In relation to (a), a review will normally not be allowed where it was open to a party to apply for an adjournment at the original hearing in order to respond to a new allegation raised by the other side. The exception to this is where the party is unrepresented and the tribunal ought to have drawn their attention to the possibility of applying for an adjournment but failed to so. An example of where a review might be justified is where a tribunal decides the case on a point which it has thought of independently after retiring to consider the decision and upon which the parties have not had an opportunity to address it. This would fit in to category (a) above.

[25.25] In certain situations it may be more appropriate to correct straightforward errors of law by way of review rather than appeal, even in circumstances where the parties have had a fair opportunity to present their case at a hearing. The EAT has expressly approved this approach in circumstances where it would be more proportionate (and therefore in accordance with the overriding objective) to take the quicker and less expensive route by reviewing rather than appealing a decision (see *Williams v Ferrosan Ltd* [2004] IRLR 607 and *Sodexho Ltd v Gibbons* [2005] ICR 1647).

Events after the decision

[25.26] Sometimes events occurring after the tribunal's decision undermine its conclusions. There is a considerable overlap between this category and the 'new evidence' category, meaning that it is often sensible for a party to rely upon both grounds where significant new evidence emerges. Note, however, that if the evidence was available at the original hearing, the party seeking to adduce it will need to demonstrate that there were exceptional or special circumstances why it was not adduced at the original hearing. Similarly, if there is a significant piece of case law which existed at the time of the hearing but was not raised by the parties or considered by the tribunal, it may be possible to seek a review on the basis that the interests of justice require it, but it will normally be necessary to show a good reason why the case was not known to or raised by the parties at the hearing. A failure by a legal representative to raise a point at a hearing will not generally be sufficient to merit a review on this basis.

[25.27] An example of ground (e), review in the interests of justice because of events after the decision is where the applicant was unfairly dismissed for possession of cannabis (the employer, without carrying out a sufficient investigation, relied upon the fact that they had been charged by the police). Subsequently, the applicant was convicted of the offence in court. Evidence of the conviction was permitted upon review in relation to the issue of contribution to dismissal, which was found to be 100%.

Applying for a review – the procedure

[25.28] A review can be applied for orally on the day of the original hearing or, as is more common, in writing. *Rule 35* makes it clear that a written application must be made to the tribunal within 14 days of the date on which the decision was sent to the parties. Again, this time limit may be extended by an Employment Judge if he considers it just and equitable to do so, but where this is sought, an application to that effect should be made in clear terms in the written application for review, together with an explanation of why it was not possible to apply in time.

[25.29] The application must identify the grounds of the application in accordance with the various categories set out in *rule 34(3)*. As a matter of good practice, it should set out:

- the basis upon which the review is sought (with reference to the applicable grounds under *rule 34(3)*; and
- the relevance of this in terms of the original decision.

Parties should ensure that the written application is thorough, setting out all the facts upon which they rely. So in the case of non-attendance the party should give the reason for the non-attendance and, where it is available, submit documentary evidence in support. If a party is seeking to adduce new evidence, the application should:

- describe the new evidence and why it is credible;

- explain why it was not available at the original hearing and its existence not reasonably foreseen; and
- state why the original decision would or might have been different if the tribunal had seen the evidence in question.

[25.30] As with applications for the review of default judgments, an application under *rule 34* will normally be considered on the papers by way of a 'preliminary consideration' (*rule 35(3)*). This will be done by the Employment Judge of the tribunal which heard the case or, if that is not practicable, by a Regional Employment Judge or the Vice President, any chairman nominated by chairman Regional Employment Judge or the Vice President, or the President of the employment tribunals. If it is considered that there are no grounds for the decision to be revoked under *rule 34(3)* or that there is no reasonable prospect of the decision being varied or revoked, the application will be refused (*rule 35(3)*). In these circumstances the party making the application will be informed in writing of the refusal decision along with reasons (*rule 35(4)*).[25.31]

If the application is not refused on preliminary consideration, then the decision will be reviewed by the Employment Judge or tribunal who made the original decision or, where this is not practicable, by a different Employment Judge or tribunal appointed by a Regional Employment Judge, the Vice President or the President (*rule 36(1)*).

[25.32] Where the review is taking place on the initiative of the tribunal or Employment Judge, the review must be carried out by the same tribunal or Employment Judge who made the original decision and a notice must be sent to each party, before the expiry of 14 days from the date on which the original decision was sent to the parties, explaining in summary the grounds upon which it is proposed to review the decision and giving them the opportunity to give reasons why there should be no review.

[25.33] Whether the review is conducted on application by a party or on the initiative of the tribunal, the tribunal or Employment Judge carrying out the review may:

- Revoke the decision, in which case the tribunal or Employment Judge must order the decision to be taken again. If the original decision was taken by an Employment Judge without a hearing, the new decision may be taken without hearing the parties. If the original decision was taken at a hearing, a new hearing must be held.

- Vary the decision.
- Confirm the original decision.

Once a decision has been varied or revoked on review, any entry in the Register will be amended to reflect that and a copy of the amended entry will be sent to each of the parties (*rule 37(2)*).

The hearing

[25.34] If there is an oral hearing of an application for a review, both parties may attend and address the tribunal on whether the grounds for review are met and, if so, the consequences in terms of the original decision. This may involve calling witnesses, using witness statements and preparing a bundle of documentary evidence. So if, for example, seeking to demonstrate that there was a good reason for non-attendance, the party in question may need to give evidence as to why they were unable to attend. In relation to new evidence (ground (d)), it may be necessary to call a witness not only to adduce the new evidence but also to explain why it was unavailable at the original hearing, a matter which the party in question will have to prove if ground (c) is to be fulfilled. Submissions alone are likely to be appropriate only where there is a matter, for example in relation to jurisdiction, where the giving of evidence is unnecessary.

[25.35] Precisely how the review hearing is conducted is a matter for the tribunal and should always be clarified with the Employment Judge from the outset. In particular, parties should clarify whether the tribunal wishes to deal with the application for review separately, or whether the tribunal should be addressed both on the application and the outcome of any review. Often the latter is the more practical option. For example, if the tribunal concludes that there was, under ground (b), a good reason for non-attendance, it will invariably list the case for a full merits hearing. It is normal for the party seeking the review to open with submissions as to why the review is sought (with reference to the grounds in *rule 34(3)*) before proceeding to call relevant evidence. The opposing party will then have the opportunity to cross-examine and, if appropriate, call evidence of their own. Each party will then make closing submissions. The tribunal will then give its decision. Frequently, one decision will cover both: (a) whether the grounds for application for a review has been met; and (b) if so, the outcome of the review.

Review and appeal compared

[25.36] There are instances where it is more appropriate for a party to appeal a decision or judgment to the EAT or apply to review before the tribunal at first instance. There are also instances where it is legitimate for the party to pursue both options simultaneously.

- Where a point of law has already been argued at the original hearing, an appeal is the most appropriate forum.
- Where the grounds for review are *rules 34(3)(a), (b)* or *(c)*, a review, as opposed to an appeal, is the appropriate first avenue of recourse for the party concerned.
- Where the ground is seeking to adduce new evidence (whether under *rule 34(3)(d)* or *(e))* or a new point of law, a review is the appropriate first avenue of recourse. In certain circumstances a party may be penalised in costs if it seeks to adduce new evidence on appeal as opposed to review.
- Where the ground is an error of law (either in relation to jurisdiction or a procedural mishap) under *rule 34(3)(e)*, the party normally has a choice whether to pursue an appeal or a review which may involve tactical considerations, such as the likely effect of going back in front of the same tribunal. If the application for a review is successful and the tribunal decide to revoke the original decision and order a re-hearing, it is possible to apply for the case to be heard by a differently constituted tribunal.
- If the tribunal decide the case on a point which the parties did not have an opportunity to address it on at the hearing, consideration should be given to an application for review.
- Points relating to jurisdiction which have not been argued at the original hearing are appropriate for dealing with by way of review, with a further appeal if necessary.

[25.37] It is important to note that an appeal and a review are *not* mutually exclusive options. Parties should be aware that time limits for appeal still apply if a review has been applied for. It is possible, where appropriate, both to apply for a review and lodge an appeal. Both the tribunal and the EAT should be informed of this fact, and may stay of appeal pending hearing of the review. Paragraph 2.2 of the EAT's 2008 *Practice Direction* expressly provides that if the appellant has made an application to the tribunal for a review of its judgment or decision, a copy of such application should accompany the Notice of Appeal together with the judgment and written reasons of the tribunal in respect of that review application, or a statement, if such be the case, that a judgment is awaited. If any of these documents cannot be included, a written explanation must be given.

[25.38] A refusal to grant a review can itself be a ground for appeal.

Review on the tribunal's own initiative

[25.39] Under *rule 34(5)* the tribunal can, of its own motion, decide to review its decision, but it must give the parties notice of its intention in this respect, and an opportunity to respond to the issue of whether a review should take place (*rule 36(2)*). The grounds under which a tribunal may order a review are the same as that applicable to the parties.

The slip rule

[25.40] Under *rule 37(1)*, clerical mistakes in any order, judgment, decision or reasons, or errors arising in those documents from an accidental slip or omission, may be corrected at any time by certificate by the Employment Judge, Regional Employment Judge, Vice President or President. Any amendments of this type will also be made to any entry in the Register (*rule 37(2)*).

[25.41] Use of the slip rule is only appropriate where it is used to correct genuine slips or omissions. It should not be used in circumstances where the 'correction' amounts to a fresh decision.

Do's and Don'ts

Do:

- Ensure that an application for a review is effectively drafted with reference to the grounds upon which one may take place.
- Consider whether either a review and/or an appeal, is appropriate.
- Make any application for review within 14 days of the date the decision was sent to the parties.
- Prepare for the review hearing professionally, calling witnesses and preparing bundles as necessary.

Don't:

- Forget that applying for a review does not dispense with the need (where an appeal may be necessary) to comply with the time limits for the lodging of an appeal to the EAT.
- Apply for a review purely because you disagree with the decision of the tribunal – the ground/s need to be met.
- Apply for a review on issues which have already been properly argued before the tribunal – an appeal is the correct avenue in these circumstances.

Chapter 26

Steps after the decision II: Appeal

Introduction

[26.1] This chapter gives a broad outline of the basis upon which an appeal can be made to the Employment Appeal Tribunal (EAT) and the procedures which exist in that tribunal. Since this book is concerned primarily with employment tribunals, this chapter does not attempt to provide a comprehensive guide to practice and procedure in the EAT. In addition to reading the chapter, parties should have careful regard to the EAT's procedural rules, relevant practice direction and guidance notes (see **26.35**). They should also be careful to read the guidance sent to parties by the EAT, for which this chapter is not intended as a substitute. Specific rules apply in cases concerning national security; these provisions are outside the scope of this book.

Jurisdiction and procedure

[26.2] The EAT's jurisdiction is derived from statute (*Employment Tribunals Act 1996 (ETA 1996), s 21*). *Section 21* of the *ETA 1996* sets out an exhaustive list of those matters that the EAT has jurisdiction to hear. An appeal lies to the EAT 'on any question of law arising from any decision of, or arising in any proceedings before, an employment tribunal' under or by virtue of the following statutes or statutory instruments:

(a) *Trade Union and Labour Relations (Consolidation) Act 1992;*
(b) *Employment Rights Act 1996;*
(c) *Employment Tribunals Act 1996;*
(d) *National Minimum Wage Act 1998;*
(e) *Employment Relations Act 1999;*
(f) *Equality Act 2006;*
(g) *Pensions Act 2008;*

(h) *Equality Act 2010* (and where relevant, the statues and statutory instruments that this Act repealed and replaced such as *Equal Pay Act 1970, Sex Discrimination Act 1975, Disability Discrimination Act 1995* and *Employment Equality (Age) Regulations 2006*, etc);
(i) *Working Time Regulations 1998;*
(j) *Transnational Information and Consultation of Employees Regulations 1999;*
(k) *Part-time Workers (Prevention of Less Favourable Treatment) Regulations 2000;*
(l) *Fixed-term Employees (Prevention of Less Favourable Treatment) Regulations 2002;*
(m) *Merchant Shipping (Working Time: Inland Waterways) Regulations 2003;*
(n) *European Public Limited-Liability Company Regulations 2004;*
(o) *Fishing Vessels (Working Time: Sea-fishermen) Regulations 2004;*
(p) *Information and Consultation of Employees Regulations 2004;*
(q) *Schedule* to the *Occupational and Personal Pension Schemes (Consultation by Employers and Miscellaneous Amendment) Regulations 2006;*
(r) *European Cooperative Society (Involvement of Employees) Regulations 2006;*
(s) *Companies (Cross-Border Mergers) Regulations 2007;*
(t) *Cross-border Railway Services (Working Time) Regulations 2008;*
(u) *European Public Limited-Liability Company (Employee Involvement) (Great Britain) Regulations 2009;*
(v) *Employment Relations Act 1999 (Blacklists) Regulations 2010*; and
(w) *Agency Workers Regulations 2010.*

In addition, the EAT has certain limited jurisdictions as a court of first instance.

[26.3] The procedure in the EAT is derived from the *ETA 1996* and the *Employment Appeal Tribunal Rules 1993* (as amended by the *Employment Appeal Tribunal (Amendment) Rules 2001* and the *Employment Appeal Tribunal (Amendment) Rules 2004*) (*EAT Rules*). Subject to the EAT Rules, the EAT has the power to regulate its own procedure (*ETA 1996, s 30(3)*) and to this end it has adopted the *Practice Direction (Employment Appeal Tribunal – Procedure) 2008* ('the *EAT Practice Direction*') which came into force on 22 May 2008 and which replaced the previous *EAT Practice Direction*. Both the *EAT Rules* and *EAT Practice Direction* are available on the EAT's website (www.employmentappeals.gov.uk).

[26.4] Like employment tribunals below it, the EAT will seek to apply the overriding objective when it exercises any power given to it by the Rules or when it interprets any of the Rules. This mirrors the overriding objective provided by *regulation 3* of the *Employment Tribunals (Constitution and Rules of Procedure) Regulations 2004* (see **chapter 8 – fairness: the overriding objective**).

Composition of the EAT

[26.5] The composition of the EAT is very similar to that of employment tribunals. It consists of a lawyer sitting with two lay members (from employers' and employees' organisations) (*ETA 1996, s 22*). The principal difference is that the lawyer is either a high court judge or a senior circuit judge, and is described as the 'presiding judge' as opposed to the employment judge. The presiding judge will possess considerable legal experience. The extent of their experience of employment law will vary according to whether the judge sits permanently in the EAT. The President of the EAT (a High Court judge) sits permanently in addition to one other judge. The current President of the EAT is Underhill J.

Appealing to the EAT

[26.6] Parties sometimes feel a deep sense of grievance when they lose a case and are determined to appeal. They should be aware, however, that avenues of appeal to the EAT are limited. It is only possible to appeal where the tribunal has erred in law. In practice, this is likely to encompass six different scenarios:

- The tribunal has misapplied the law (ie case law, other than merely guideline authorities) or statute.
- The tribunal has improperly exercised the discretion derived from its procedural powers (including a breach of natural justice).
- The tribunal has reached a conclusion or made a finding of fact unsupported by any evidence.
- The tribunal has failed to make a finding of fact which it was required, on a proper application of the law, to make or has failed to give sufficient reasons.
- The tribunal has been guilty of bias in its decision making.
- The tribunal has reached a decision which is perverse – namely one which no reasonable tribunal could, on the evidence before it, have made.

All of these scenarios are deemed to be errors of law by the tribunal. Note that the same ground may engage one or more of them. Most grounds of appeal will, for example, involve a misapplication of case law or statute. The most common ground of appeal, perversity, is also generally one of the hardest to succeed upon. The higher courts are strong defenders of the rights of individual employment tribunals to decide issues of fact, something borne out by the 'industrial jury' label which both the EAT and the Court of Appeal have applied to them (*Williams v Compair Maxam Ltd* [1982] ICR 156).

Fresh evidence and new points of law

[26.7] All parties should note the general rule that it is not possible to raise a new point of law which was not raised at the tribunal or to withdraw a concession made before the tribunal. Although the EAT has a discretion to allow a new point to be raised this will only be exercised in exceptional circumstances and for compelling reasons, particularly where to allow the new point to be raised would result in the case being remitted to the tribunal for further evidence to be heard. Exceptional circumstances might include, for example, where a party has been prevented from arguing a point by deception on the part of the other party (*Kumchyk v Derby County Council* [1978] ICR 1116). Exceptional circumstances will not include lack of skill or experience on the part of an advocate, or a failure on the part of the tribunal to mention the point for consideration by the parties when neither party had raised that point (see eg *Glennie v Independent Magazines (UK) Ltd* [1999] IRLR 719; *Mensah v East Hertfordshire NHS Trust* [1998] IRLR 531).

[26.8] It has been held that the requirement for exceptional circumstances applies even where a case has been decided on the basis of law that is 'not merely arguably, but demonstrably, wrong by the time it reaches the appellate court' (see *Jones v Governing Body of Burden Coutts School* [1998] IRLR 521). In other words, even if the point on appeal is based on a decision of the Court of Appeal or the Supreme Court arising after the date of the tribunal case, it may be that it is not possible to appeal on this basis.

[26.9] In limited circumstances, however, the EAT may be prepared to exercise its discretion so as to permit a new point of law to be argued on appeal. These include situations where:

- the point goes to the jurisdiction (or right) of the tribunal to hear the case (although this discretion will only be exercised in very limited circumstances, and usually only where the issue raised 'is a discrete one of pure or hard-edged law requiring no or no further factual inquiry' or is an 'obvious knock-out point' (see *Glennie v Independent Magazines (UK) Ltd* [1999] IRLR 719); or
- the error of law is so basic that the tribunal ought to have considered it as a matter of course, although the circumstances in which this is likely to be the case are extremely limited (see *Langston v Cranfield University* [1998] IRLR 172); or
- the allegation is one of bias against the tribunal and the party could not reasonably have been expected to raise the complaint at the relevant time (see *Stransbury v Datapulse plc* [2003] EWCA Civ 1951; [2004] IRLR 466 and **26.11** below).

[26.9A] *Paragraph 8.1* of the *EAT Practice Direction* states:

> 'Where an application is made by a party to an appeal to put in, at the hearing of the appeal, any document which was not before the Employment Tribunal, and which has not been agreed in writing by the other parties, the application and a copy of the documents sought to be admitted should be lodged at the EAT with the Notice of Appeal or the respondent's Answer, as appropriate. The application and copy should be served on the other parties. The same principle applies to any oral evidence not given at the Employment Tribunal which is sought to be adduced on the appeal. The nature and substance of such evidence together with the date when the party first became aware of its existence must be disclosed in a document, where appropriate a witness statement from the relevant witness with signed statement of truth, which must be similarly lodged and served.'

If a respondent to an appeal intends to contend at the hearing of the appeal that the appellant has raised a new point of law (ie one which was not argued at the hearing below), paragraph 8.5 of the EAT Practice Direction requires the respondent to state this in writing within 14 days of receipt of the notice of appeal or in the Respondent's Answer (see **26.23**). If the parties are in dispute as to whether or not the point was raised below, the Employment Judge will be asked for his or her comments.

[26.9B] It is important to remember that the general rule is that points of law not taken at the tribunal hearing may not be raised before the EAT, and that the above discretion is limited to very narrow circumstances and exceptional cases. In relation to issues of fact, a party may not adduce evidence at the EAT which was not before the employment tribunal unless (see *paragraph 8.2* of the *EAT Practice Direction*):

- the evidence could not have been obtained with reasonable diligence for use at the employment tribunal hearing;
- it is relevant and would probably have had an important influence on the hearing; and
- it is apparently credible.

Parties should note that, in relation to new evidence, or indeed a new point of law in appropriate circumstances, it is usually best to pursue a review (see **chapter 25**) and they may be penalised in costs if they fail to do so.

Appealing interim orders

[26.9C] An interim order (eg as to disclosure, the provision of further particulars or other orders made under the tribunal's case management powers – see **chapter 10** and subsequent chapters) can be appealed in the same way as a final decision. Time starts to run from the date of the order, not the date of the final decision in the case. Usually, appealing an interim order will involve demonstrating that the tribunal has improperly exercised its discretion (see **26.8**). It has been said that there are three main issues for the EAT when considering whether an interim order was properly made (*Adams v West Sussex County Council* [1990] IRLR 215):

- whether the order was made within the tribunal's powers;
- whether the discretion was exercised within the legal principles laid down as guidance in the particular area (eg making a striking out order); and
- whether the way in which the discretion was exercised was wrong in law (see **26.10** below).

In practice, appeals against interim orders are rare and difficult to sustain. Parties should be aware that where an interim appeal is pursued without merit (and its only purpose is to delay proceedings), a costs award may be made.

Where an appeal is made against an interim order, the appeal may, where appropriate, be categorised by the EAT as a Fast Track Full

Hearing under *paragraph 9.20* of the *EAT Practice Direction*, and will be treated accordingly in terms of procedure (see **26.22** below). Parties should therefore note that the appeal is likely to be heard relatively quickly and that the procedural timetable may be compressed.

Grounds of appeal

Misapplication of the law

[26.10] Just as tribunals are bound by the decisions of the EAT (provided they have not been overturned by a higher court), so the EAT is bound by authorities in the Court of Appeal, the Supreme Court (formerly the House of Lords) and European Court of Justice.

On occasions, a tribunal will:

- fail to give any consideration to an authority or statute which is binding upon it;
- misconstrue (ie misinterpret) that case or statute; or
- fail to properly apply that statute – for example by omitting to make a finding of fact which, on a proper construction of the law, it was required to make.

In these circumstances, a party will need to demonstrate:

(a) the authority or statute which the tribunal misconstrued or failed to consider;
(b) that as a consequence of the omission or misconstruction it applied the law wrongly in making its decision; and
(c) that this may have affected the outcome – often called the 'would it have made any difference?' hurdle.

Note that (b) by no means follows as a consequence of (a), or (c) as a consequence of either. If a tribunal has omitted from or misdescribed in its reasons the applicable principle of case or statute law, it by no means follows that an appeal is bound to succeed. The decision will be upheld if it can be demonstrated that despite this error the tribunal followed the right approach in law to the evidence. It will even be upheld in a case where the tribunal has adopted the wrong approach if the circumstances disclosed by its findings of fact make it obvious that an application of the right approach would have been virtually certain to lead to the same conclusion.

Improper exercise of discretion

[26.11] 'Discretion' means any area where the law gives the tribunal a choice, according to the facts and nature of the dispute that is before it, as to how to proceed. The tribunal, within the confines of statute and case law, has a discretion in operating a wide range of its procedural powers. Examples include the conduct of the Hearing (including rulings on evidence, permissible questions to witnesses and the identification of issues), postponements, adjournments, striking out claims in default of an order, payments of a deposit under *rule 20(1)* of *Employment Tribunals (Constitution and Rules of Procedure) Regulations 2004*, and rulings on disclosure and the provision of further particulars. Where a party seeks to appeal an interim order by the tribunal then, more often that not, this will involve an exercise of the tribunal's discretion (see **26.5**).

[26.12] To found an appeal on the improper exercise of discretion it is necessary to show that the tribunal:

- has taken into account an improper consideration;
- has failed to take into account a proper consideration; or
- has exercised its discretion in a manner which is perverse (*Carter v Credit Change Ltd* [1979] IRLR 361).

In this context, an 'improper' consideration includes an irrelevant consideration. There can be an overlap between this category and the first (misapplying the law). For example, there are a number of cases governing how the tribunal should exercise its discretion with regard to such matters as the admissibility of evidence and postponements and orders for disclosure. Where the tribunal has failed to apply these cases, an appeal could lie both under improper exercise of discretion and, in the alternative, the first category of failing to apply a principle contained in statute or case law. Where the tribunal has failed to conduct proceedings in accordance with the principles of natural justice this will frequently engage both categories. It will be necessary to show that the alleged error of law is likely to have affected the outcome, ie that the same result would not in all probability have been reached even if the error had not occurred.

Finding of fact unsupported by any evidence

[26.13] To succeed on this ground, a party will need to demonstrate that there was no evidence at all for a particular conclusion reached by the tribunal, and that this might have had an effect on the outcome of the case. Usually, the Employment Judge's notes of evidence will be required in order to prove this ground (see **26.16**). Where there has been some evidence, however weak, upon which a finding is based, the only avenue of appeal is perversity (see, for example, *Eclipse Blinds Ltd v Wright* [1992] IRLR 133 and **26.12**).

There will be occasions when a tribunal has committed a simple, factual misunderstanding of the evidence. In these circumstances the best option is to appeal both under the 'no evidence' heading and (phrased in the alternative) the perversity heading (see **26.12**).

Failure to make a relevant finding of fact and/or give reasons for its decision

[26.14] The tribunal is required to make a finding of fact on all the relevant issues which are before it. It if fails to do so, this may found an appeal. Sometimes it is necessary for a tribunal to disclose the secondary findings of fact upon which its primary findings are based. So, for example, where a tribunal finds that an employee has contributed to their dismissal, it must set out the factual findings upon which this conclusion is based. If the tribunal fails to do so, this may amount to an error of law, although again it will be necessary to show that the error affected the outcome. For the extent to which the tribunal is obliged to give reasons for its decision (see **chapter 23 – the decision**).

Bias

[26.15] Bias means that one or more of the tribunal members might unfairly regard the case of a party with favour or disfavour. Both actual bias and the appearance of bias to a hypothetical reasonable person not involved in the case can give rise to an appeal, since an unbiased tribunal is a fundamental feature of a fair hearing. In considering whether there is bias, the court will first ascertain all the circumstances which have a bearing on the suggestion that the judge (or tribunal) was biased, and then ask whether those circumstances would lead a fair-minded and informed observer to conclude that there was a real possibility that the tribunal was biased (*Re Medicaments and Related Classes of Goods (No 2)* [2001] ICR 564, *Porter v Magill* [2002] UKHL 67; [2002] 2 AC 357).

[26.16] Bias can range from situations where a tribunal member has a direct interest in or association with one of the parties (or a third party with a direct interest in the outcome), to more mundane concerns such as a member failing to pay attention or falling asleep to the extent that one party may have been prejudiced (*Greenaway Harrison Ltd v Wiles* [1994] IRLR 380; *R v Gough* [1993] 2 All ER 724 and *R v Bow Street Metropolitan Stipendiary Magistrate, ex p Pinochet Ugarte (No 2)* [1999] 2 WLR 272).

[26.17] The appearance of bias may also be given where the Employment Judge makes remarks which would cause an impartial onlooker to perceive that he had formed a hostile view of one party's case before even hearing the evidence (*Peter Simpler & Co Ltd v Cooke* [1986] IRLR 19). A further example of the appearance of bias is where the tribunal fails to use moderate or temperate language in its questioning of the parties or the witnesses although, in practice, the higher courts have been reluctant to find an appearance of bias in these circumstances (*Kennedy v Metropolitan Police Commissioner* (1990) Times, 8 November, see also *Docherty v Strathkelvin District Council* 1994 SLT 1064). Other, if rare, examples have included an Employment Judge putting undue pressure on the parties, refusing to allow a party to cross-examine a witness and refusing to permit a party to make closing submissions. Generally, however, parties should not confuse the asking of difficult questions by a tribunal with bias. Many tribunals adopt the practice of expressing to a party during the course of proceedings particular concerns about their case in order to give them the opportunity to respond. Provided the tribunal makes it clear that the view is only preliminary and that it remains open to persuasion, such an approach can enhance rather than detract from the fairness of the hearing and will not usually be found to indicate bias (*Peter Simpler & Co Ltd v Cooke* [1986] IRLR 19; *Jiminez v Southwark London Borough Council* [2003] EWCA Civ 502; [2003] IRLR 477).

[26.18] The question of whether bias ought to be raised with the tribunal during the course of a hearing or can be argued for the first time upon appeal has recently been considered by the Court of Appeal *Stansbury v Datapulse plc* [2003] EWCA Civ 1951; [2004] IRLR 466. The test laid down in that case is whether the party ought reasonably to have made the complaint before the tribunal. The Court of Appeal acknowledged that, whilst it is desirable that the issue be raised before the tribunal, there may be circumstances where it is not reasonable to expect a party to do so, particularly where the party is still hoping for a favourable outcome from the tribunal. In the view of the authors, 'transient' bias, such as a member of the tribunal falling asleep, certainly ought to be raised before the tribunal. Other situations will require an exercise of judgment. The advantages of raising the allegation of appearance of bias at the relevant time are that: (a) the memory of the tribunal and the other party as to what was said is likely to be fresh; (b) it will (assuming the tribunal refuses to discharge itself from hearing the case) be apparent to the EAT that the remark was of real concern at the time when it was made and is not merely being seized upon after the event; and (c) there will be a reasoned decision by the tribunal which (provided it accurately sets out the basis for the bias allegation) may dispense with the need for notes of evidence and witness statements before the EAT (see below). Despite this, the Court of Appeal acknowledged, in the case of *Stansbury v Datapulse*, that it may be difficult for a party which is still hoping to win a case to make an allegation of bias and thus unreasonable to expect them to do so.

[26.19] Complaints of bias are subject to a special procedure in the EAT, set out in the *EAT Practice Direction* (*paragraph 11*). The procedure must be followed before such a complaint will be permitted to be raised or developed at the appeal hearing. The *EAT Practice Direction* expressly warns that tribunals have wide powers and duties of case management and duties in respect of the overriding objective and that appeals in respect of their conduct of tribunal proceedings pursuant to these provisions (ie in respect of case management decisions) are less likely to succeed (*paragraph 11.6.2*). The *EAT Practice Direction* further warns that the unsuccessful pursuit of an allegation of bias or improper conduct, particularly in respect of case management decisions, may give rise to an order for costs being made against the party concerned (*paragraph 11.6.3*). Essentially, the procedure which must be followed is:

- the appellant must give full particulars of any complaint of bias in the notice of appeal (*paragraph 11.1*);
- when the notice of appeal is received by the EAT, a judge or the Registrar may require the appellant or his representative to provide an affidavit setting out full particulars of the allegation of bias or misconduct and/or to indicate whether they intend to proceed with the allegation (*paragraph 11.2*);
- if the case proceeds to a hearing, the EAT may require any party or other person present at the hearing to make an affidavit or

witness statement giving their account of the events set out in the appellant's affidavit (*paragraph 11.3*);

- the EAT may further seek comments on all affidavits or witness statements from the Employment Judge and members of the tribunal;
- all documents so obtained will be supplied to all parties.

Perversity

[26.20] 'Perversity' is one of the more common grounds of appeal but is also one of the most difficult upon which to succeed. In order to establish that the tribunal's decision was perverse, the appellant will need to show that it was a decision that no reasonable tribunal, properly directed in law, could have made. As Mummery LJ put it in *Yeboah v Crofton* [2002] EWCA Civ 794; [2002] IRLR 634:

> 'Such an appeal ought only to succeed where an overwhelming case is made out that the employment tribunal reached a decision which no reasonable tribunal, on a proper appreciation of the evidence and the law, would have reached. Even in cases where the Appeal Tribunal has 'grave doubts' about the decision of the Employment Tribunal, it must proceed with 'great care': *British Telecommunications plc v Sheridan* [1990] IRLR 27 at paragraph 34.'

The test is emphatically not whether the EAT agree with the decision or whether they would, on the facts, have reached a different one, and indeed the EAT will not agree to turn the appeal into a rehearing of parts of the evidence. The EAT should only interfere with the tribunal's original decision where the conclusion of that tribunal on the evidence before it is 'irrational', 'offends reason', 'is certainly wrong' or 'is very clearly wrong' or 'must be wrong' or 'is plainly wrong' or 'is not a permissible option' or 'is fundamentally wrong' or 'is outrageous' or 'makes absolutely no sense' or 'flies in the face of properly informed logic' (*Stewart v Cleveland Guest (Engineering) Ltd* [1994] IRLR 440). It has been held that the decision must be so plainly wrong as not to have been a permissible option open to the tribunal, although this may be placing the test too highly (*Piggott Bros & Co Ltd v Jackson* [1991] IRLR 309).

[26.21] Examples of where a decision has been held to be perverse are:

- A decision that an employee was unfairly dismissed for a second instance of dishonesty shortly after a previous incident for which they received a warning (*United Distillers v Conlin* [1994] IRLR 169).
- A decision that a nurse was unfairly dismissed for making nuisance calls to other staff (*East Berkshire Health Authority v Matadeen* [1992] IRLR 336).

Examples are far more numerous of cases where the EAT has declined to interfere in decisions which are arguably perverse. Notable amongst them is a case where the EAT refused to interfere with a finding that displaying pictures of nude women in a male dominated work environment did not constitute less favourable treatment of women employees on grounds of their sex (*Stewart v Cleveland Guest (Engineering) Ltd* [1994] IRLR 440). In that case, the EAT was at pains to point out that individual tribunals will take a different view of such situations according to the factual context and that this was an area where there was room for legitimate variation in decision making. A tribunal's decision may, however, be found to be perverse where it has not properly appreciated what is 'currently regarded as fair industrial practice' (*Williams v Compair Maxam Ltd* [1982] ICR 156), although it should be emphasised that the circumstances in which this will be the case will be extremely rare.

[26.22] Where any allegation of perversity is made, full particulars must be given in the notice of appeal in order for the respondent to be able to meet it fully. *Paragraph 2.6* of the *EAT Practice Direction* provides:

> 'Perversity Appeals: an appellant may not state as a ground of appeal simply words to the effect that "the judgment or order was contrary to the evidence", or that "there was no evidence to support the judgment or order", or that "the judgment or order was one which no reasonable Tribunal could have reached and was perverse" unless the Notice of Appeal also sets out full particulars of the matters relied on in support of those general grounds.'

It is often necessary to secure the Employment Judge's note of evidence when instituting a perversity appeal (**26.16** below), although this is not always the case, for example where the tribunal's reasons set out in sufficient detail the evidence that was heard.

Common pitfalls when appealing

Appealing because of a failure to mention evidence in a decision

[26.23] Whilst a tribunal is obliged, in the exercise of its discretion, to apply its mind to all the relevant evidence in a case, the EAT will not assume that, simply because a tribunal has failed to mention a piece of evidence in its decision, that it has not considered it. The basic requirement (in terms of the written reasons) is simply that the tribunal should make findings of fact on all relevant issues before it and correctly apply the law. In practice, it is often difficult, other than in the most glaring circumstances, for a party to prove that a tribunal has not addressed its mind to certain evidence. For the requirement to give sufficient reasons, see **chapter 23 – the decision**.

Weight

[26.24] Often, a party will read a decision by a tribunal and conclude that it attached insufficient weight (ie importance) to one piece of evidence and too much weight to another aspect. This, of itself, cannot form the basis of an appeal, unless it can be shown that the decision was perverse (see **26.12**). Perversity apart, the weight to be attached to evidence is considered to be a matter for the tribunal, which is able to observe witnesses at first hand.

Appealing findings of fact: the Employment Judge's note of evidence and/or the transcript

[26.25] Where it is alleged that there was no evidence upon which the tribunal could base its finding, or that the tribunal misunderstood a piece of evidence, or that the decision was perverse, and in other circumstances where it is necessary for the EAT to examine a record of what happened at the hearing below, it is usually necessary to obtain the Employment Judge's notes of evidence (*Ministry of Defence v Wheeler* [1996] ICR 554). Tribunal proceedings are not ordinarily tape recorded, therefore the only official record of proceedings is likely to be the note taken by the Employment Judge. It is necessary to obtain an order from the EAT for the production of the Employment Judge's notes and/or a transcript where the tribunal had ordered its proceedings to be tape recorded.

[26.26] *Paragraph 7* of the *EAT Practice Direction* sets out the procedure to be followed where an appellant considers that the EAT will need to consider the evidence that was before the tribunal. *Paragraph 7.1* provides:

> 'An appellant who considers that a point of law raised in the Notice of Appeal cannot be argued without reference to evidence given (or not given) at the Employment Tribunal, the nature or substance of which does not, or does not sufficiently, appear from the written reasons, must ordinarily submit an application with the Notice of Appeal. The application is for the nature of such evidence (or lack of it) to be admitted, or if necessary for the relevant parts of the employment judge's notes of evidence to be produced.'

If such an application is not made, the request should be made in the skeleton submissions lodged prior to any preliminary hearing (PH) (see **26.22**) or, if there is no PH, in writing within 14 days of service of the order listing the matter for a full hearing (FH). Any application by the respondent to the appeal must, if not made earlier, accompany the respondent's Answer.

[26.27] The application must explain why the matter is considered necessary in order to argue the point of law, and must identify:
- the issue(s) in the Notice of Appeal or the respondent's Answer to which the matter is relevant;
- the names of the witnesses whose evidence is relevant or the nature of the evidence the absence of which is relevant;
- the part of the hearing when the evidence was given;
- the gist of the evidence (or lack of evidence); and
- if the party making the application has a record of the evidence, by whom and when it was made, or producing an extract from a witness statement (*paragraph 7.2*).

The application will be considered by the Registrar or judge either on the papers or at a PH as to whether the evidence in question may be necessary. Directions may be given for written representations, or for notice to be given to the other parties seeking their co-operation in agreeing a statement or note of the relevant evidence. If the evidence is considered necessary and there is no agreement between the parties as to the evidence, further directions may be given, or the EAT may request that the Employment Judge produce the notes of evidence in whole or part as required. If the notes are requested from the Employment

Judge, copies will be supplied to the parties by the EAT (*paragraphs 7.3–7.5*). The same procedure is applied where a transcript of the hearing is sought (*paragraph 7.6*).

[26.28] The EAT will not permit a request for notes of evidence to be used as a 'fishing expedition' by a party to establish grounds of appeal or because they have not kept their own notes of the evidence. If any application is found to have been unreasonably made, or any co-operation to agree the evidence to have been unreasonably withheld, there may be costs consequences (*paragraph 7.7*).

It is important to remember that if agreement can be obtained with the other parties informally as to the evidence at the hearing below, this will greatly assist and should dispense with the need to apply for an Employment Judge's notes at all. Even if the application is made, the EAT practice direction clearly requires the parties to co-operate, if at all possible, in agreeing a note of the evidence without the need for the notes to be produced.

Orders which the EAT can make

[26.29] The possible order which the EAT might make in the event of an appeal succeeding is an important consideration in deciding whether to appeal. For example, where the tribunal has misdirected itself in law but has made findings on the evidence which demonstrate the case to be a weak one, an appeal might not be regarded as worthwhile if the most likely outcome in the EAT would be an order remitting the case back to a tribunal for a rehearing.

[26.30] The EAT can:

(a) dismiss an appeal;

(b) allow an appeal and replace the tribunal's decision with one of its own (thereby finally resolving the issue in favour of the party who is appealing); or

(c) remit the case to a same or different tribunal either for a complete rehearing or for consideration to be given to a particular point (*ETA 1996, s 35*).

A broad summary of the criteria the EAT use for deciding which course to adopt is as follows. Where the tribunal has not erred in law (including not making a perverse decision) course (a) will be adopted. Course (a) may also, but only in an appropriate case, be adopted where there is a misdirection in law but nevertheless the decision is 'plainly and unarguably right' and should stand, or where the error is purely procedural and has not affected the substantive decision: in other words, where the misdirection would have made no difference. Where the decision of the tribunal is found to be perverse (but there is no misdirection in law), course (b) will normally be adopted. Course (b) may also be adopted where there has been a misdirection with the result that the decision is 'plainly and unarguably wrong' and the matter requires no further factual investigation. Where the tribunal has misdirected itself as to the law (ie misconstrued or failed to apply the law), the EAT will remit for a rehearing if, on a correct application of the law, it is still uncertain (or open to question) as to how the tribunal might, in the exercise of its fact finding function, determine the matter. The above powers should be seen in the context of the rule that that it is not for the EAT to usurp the fact finding function of the tribunal (*O'Kelly v Trusthouse Forte plc* [1983] IRLR 369. See also *Wilson v Post Office* [2000] IRLR 834).

[26.31] Despite the fact that the powers granted to the EAT under the *ETA 1996, s 35* to remit a case are 'for the purpose of disposing of an appeal', the EAT may also, in an appropriate case, remit a case to a tribunal simply for the tribunal to supply additional reasons, or specific reasons on a point where none had been given, for its decision in a case where the existing reasons are insufficient (*Burns v Consignia plc* [2004] IRLR 425 and *Barke v SEETEC Business Technology Centre Ltd* [2005] EWCA Civ 578; [2005] IRLR 633). The purpose of this is to avoid the time and expense of a full appeal and then a rehearing in a case where the tribunal may have had regard to appropriate considerations but this is unclear from its decision. The decision to remit for this purpose will usually be taken at a preliminary hearing, but may be taken at a final hearing, with an adjournment of that hearing pending the tribunal's response, if appropriate. *Paragraph 9.4* of the *EAT Practice Direction* expressly confirms the power to adjourn an appeal, usually for a period of 21 days, 'pending the making or the conclusion of an application by the appellant to the employment tribunal (if necessary out of time) for a review or pending the response by the tribunal to an invitation from the judge or Registrar to clarify, supplement or give its written reasons'.

Procedure for appealing

Time limits

[26.32] The time within which an appeal must be commenced depends on whether the appeal is against a judgment or against an order or decision of the tribunal (see **chapter 23 – the decision** for a discussion of the distinction). Rule 3(3) of the EAT Rules requires that an appeal must be instituted within the following time limits:

- If the appeal is against an order or decision, the appeal must be instituted within 42 days of the date of the order or decision (that is the date when the order or decision was sent to the parties).
- If the appeal is against a judgment, the appeal must be instituted within 42 days from the date on which the written record of the judgment was sent to the parties, unless:
  (a) written reasons were requested orally at the hearing before the tribunal;
  (b) written reasons were requested in writing within 14 days of the date on which the written record of the judgment was sent to the parties; or
  (c) the tribunal reserved its reasons and gave them subsequently in writing,

  in which case the time for appealing against the judgment will be 42 days from the date when the written reasons were sent to the parties.

[26.33] Time starts to run from the day after the date (recorded on the reasons) upon which the reasons were sent to the parties. So, if the relevant decision was sent on a Wednesday, the notice of appeal must be received at the EAT by 4pm on the Wednesday six weeks later. The distinction in the former tribunal rules between summary and extended reasons has now gone. All reasons, when given in writing, are now effectively extended reasons. However, it should be borne in mind that, under *rule 30(3)* of the *Employment Tribunals (Constitution and Rules of Procedure) Regulations 2004* (referred to in previous chapters as 'the *2004 rules*'), the tribunal is only required to give written reasons where one of the parties requests them within the time limits set out in *rule 30(5)* of the *2004 rules*. The tribunal is further required to give written reasons where these are requested by the EAT, but the latter might decline to exercise its discretion to do so. It is important not to confuse the tribunal's judgment (a brief document) with the written reasons, as normally only the latter will enable the EAT to form a view as to whether there was an error of law in the tribunal's decision. Under *rule 30(6)* of the *2004 rules*, written reasons are now expressly required to include the following information:

- the issues which the tribunal or Employment Judge identified as being relevant to the claim;
- if some of those issues were not determined, which ones and why;
- findings of fact relevant to the issues which have been determined;
- a concise statement of the applicable law;
- how the relevant findings of fact and applicable law have been applied in order to determine the issues; and
- a demonstration or description of how any amount or sum of any order for compensation has been calculated.

Written reasons must be requested, if the judgment is issued at a hearing, orally at the hearing, or if the judgment is sent in writing, within 14 days of it being so sent. These time limits may be extended by an Employment Judge where it is considered just and equitable so to do (*rule 30(5)*) Extension of time in which to lodge a notice of appeal

[26.34] The EAT has a discretion to extend the period of time in which a notice of appeal must be presented (*rule 37(1)* of *the EAT Rules*). In practice however, an appeal out of time will not normally be allowed unless there are exceptional circumstances (*United Arab Emirates v Abdelghafar* [1995] ICR 65; *Aziz v Bethnal Green City Challenge Co Ltd* [2000] IRLR 111). These criteria are strictly applied. Parties who leave the lodging of the notice of appeal to the last minute and then experience logistical difficulties may receive little sympathy from the EAT. Pressure of work is not considered to be an excuse. An example of just how strictly the time limits are enforced can be found In the case of *Mock v IRC* [1999] IRLR 785 (see also, *Jurkowska v HLMAD Ltd* [2008] EWCA Civ 231; [2008] IRLR 430). The notice of appeal was late due to last minute computer problems affecting counsel's computer. These circumstances were insufficient to warrant an extension of time. Furthermore, a represented party may have difficulty in obtaining an extension where it is asserted that the notice has been lost in the post and no attempt was made to check with the EAT that it had arrived (*Peters v Sat Katar Co Ltd* [2003] IRLR 574).

[26.35] The fact that an application for public funds is outstanding or that support is being sought from, but has not yet been obtained by, some other body, such as a trade union, employers' association or the Equality and Human Rights Commission will not usually constitute a good reason for delay (*paragraph 3.8* of the *EAT Practice Direction*). It is important, therefore, and this is emphasised by *paragraph 3.9* of the *EAT Practice Direction* itself, that in the case of any doubt or difficulty, a notice of appeal should be lodged in time and an application made to the Registrar for directions.

[26.36] Where necessary, a written application for an extension of time must be lodged with the notice of appeal, giving a clear and concise explanation for the delay. It should be borne in mind that, unlike the tribunal equivalent, it is not possible to apply for an extension of time until a notice of appeal has been lodged. The application will be considered at first instance by the Registrar (normally after inviting and considering representations from each side), with a right of appeal to a judge (such appeal must be lodged within five days of the Registrar's decision) (*paragraph 3.6* of the *EAT Practice Direction*). It is important to bear in mind that the time for appealing continues to run even where the appeal is against an interim order, or the issue of remedy has been adjourned by the tribunal, or there is an outstanding application for review.

Documents to be lodged

[26.37] When appealing, an appellant must, within the relevant time limit, lodge the following documentation at the EAT (*rule 3(1)* of the *EAT Rules*):

- the notice of appeal in the specified form or a notice of appeal in substantially the same format as the prescribed form (appeals from decisions of employment tribunals should use Form 1 which is attached to *EAT Rules* and annexed to the *EAT Practice Direction*);
- a copy of the judgment, decision or order which is the subject of the appeal;
- a copy of the tribunal's written reasons for the decision; and
- a copy of the claim (ET1) and response (ET3) from the tribunal proceedings.

If the appellant is unable to or otherwise does not provide any of these documents, he must also provide a written explanation. If the appellant has made an application to the employment tribunal for a review of its judgment or decision, a copy of this application should be attached to the notice of appeal together with the judgment and written reasons of the tribunal in respect of that review application, or if the judgment is awaited, a statement to that effect. If any of these documents cannot be included, a written explanation must be given. The appellant should also attach (where they are relevant to the appeal) copies of any orders including case management orders made by the tribunal.

[26.38] Where an appellant fails to lodge a notice of appeal and the necessary accompanying documents the EAT is likely to take a strict approach. The EAT Practice Direction is clear: 'A Notice of Appeal without such documentation will not be validly lodged'. The previous 'lax practice' of granting extensions of time was expressly disapproved of by Burton P in *Kanapathiar v Harrow London Borough Council* [2003] IRLR 571. In its Practice Statement of 3 February 2005 ([2005] ICR 660), Burton P confirmed that 'extensions of time are only exceptionally granted'. At paragraph 6 of the Practice Statement litigants and those representing them are warned:

> 'From the date of this Practice Statement, ignorance or misunderstanding of the requirements as to service of the documents required to make a Notice of Appeal within the 42 days valid will not be accepted by the Registrar as an excuse.'

Notice of appeal

[26.39] The notice of appeal provides space for inserting the grounds of appeal. Other than in straightforward cases, it is often best to attach a separate sheet containing the grounds of appeal.

Drafting grounds of appeal

[26.40] The importance of drafting effective grounds of appeal is underlined by the fact that all cases go through a sifting stage at which a judge or the Registrar will decide, inter alia, whether the claim is sufficiently meritorious to be allowed to proceed. Each ground of appeal must disclose a point of law, as defined above. This handbook (with its concentration on tribunals) is not intended to provide comprehensive guidance on the drafting of such grounds. Parties may wish, however, to bear in mind the following:

- The *EAT Practice Direction* itself provides (at *paragraph 2.4*) that 'the notice of appeal must clearly identify the point(s) of law which form(s) the ground(s) of appeal...It should also state the order which the appellant will ask the EAT to make at the hearing'.

- Consideration should be given to starting each ground with the words: 'The tribunal erred in law by…' or similar because unless the complaint relates to an error of law by the tribunal the EAT will be unlikely to accept jurisdiction (see **26.2**).
- Reference should then be made to one of the criteria outlined above: for example: 'The tribunal erred in law by misconstruing the provisions of *section 98(4)(a)* of the *Employment Rights Act 1996*'.
- The reasons for this assertion should then be given, for example: 'In paragraph 19 of its determination, the tribunal asserted that 'it did not consider the respondent behaved reasonably in dismissing the applicant'. In so doing the tribunal substituted its own view for that of the hypothetical, reasonable employer. The test the tribunal ought to have applied (as confirmed by the Court of Appeal in *Post Office v Foley* [2000] IRLR 827) was whether dismissal was within the range of reasonable responses open to the respondent.'
- Where there is an appeal on grounds of perversity, it is unacceptable to simply state 'the decision was one which no reasonable tribunal could have reached'. It is necessary to go on to give particulars as to why this was the case.

See **26.19** above in respect of bias appeals.

[26.41] In the past, appellants would sometimes reserve the right to amend the notice of appeal at a future date. This is expressly prohibited by the *EAT Practice Direction* (*paragraph 2.7*), which makes it clear that amendments can only be made following an order to that effect made on an interim application by the appellant. Any such application should be made as soon as the need for the amendment is known, and must include the text of the original document with any changes clearly marked and identifiable so that this can be considered by the EAT and other parties to the appeal (*paragraph 9.4*). Any application should also explain why the amendment is necessary and why it could not be included in the original notice of appeal. Sometimes an amendment will be permitted following a preliminary hearing in terms discussed during that hearing, particularly where the appellant was unrepresented at the time of the original notice of appeal but has subsequently secured legal representation (see **26.22** below).

[26.42] Where no response was entered by the respondent at the tribunal below, it should be noted that if the appellant was the respondent at the hearing at the tribunal and did not enter a response to the claim form or apply for an extension of time for doing so (or was refused an extension), the notice of appeal must include particulars directed to the issue of whether there is a good excuse for failing to enter a response and/or applying for an extension of time as well as showing that there is a reasonably arguable defence to the claim. In addition, the appellant must lodge a witness statement explaining in detail the circumstances in which there came to be a failure to serve a response or a request for an extension, the reason for that failure and the facts and matters relied upon for contesting the claim on the merits. All relevant documents, including a completed draft response form, should be exhibited to the witness statement (*paragraph 16* of the *EAT Practice Direction*).

Action upon receipt of the appeal: the sifting process

[26.43] Upon the appeal being lodged, it will first undergo a sifting process (*paragraph 9* of the *EAT Practice Direction*). The sifting process will be conducted by a judge or the Registrar so as to determine the most effective case management of the appeal where it will be allocated to one of four tracks. Those tracks are:
(a) Rule 3(7) cases;
(b) Preliminary Hearing ('PH') cases;
(c) Full Hearing ('FH') cases; and
(d) Fast Track Full Hearing ('FTFH') cases.

The purpose of the sifting process is to weed out those appeals which are, or may be, without merit. Appeals falling in to that category will be dealt with either through the *rule 3(7)* track or the PH track. By contrast, in cases where it is apparent that the grounds raise an arguable point, the case will either be placed in the FH track or, if the matter is urgent, the FTFH.

Rule 3(7) cases

[26.44] The term '*rule 3(7)* cases' is found within the *EAT Practice Direction* and refers to *rule 3(7)* of the *EAT Rules*. *Rule 3(7)* cases are those cases where it appears to the judge or Registrar that: (a) the notice of appeal discloses no reasonable grounds for bringing the appeal; or (b) that the appeal is an abuse of the EAT's process or is otherwise likely to obstruct the just disposal of the proceedings. Where this decision is taken, the judge or Registrar will give summary reasons which will be sent to the appellant. No further action will be taken on the case unless the appellant takes the appropriate steps under *rule 3(8)-(10)* of the *EAT Rules*. These are:

- To serve a fresh notice of appeal, within the original time limit or within 28 days from the notification of the *rule 3(7)* decision (whichever is longer). The fresh notice of appeal will then be considered by a judge or the Registrar in the normal way as though it were an original notice of appeal.
- If the appellant is dissatisfied with the reasons for the decision under *rule 3(7)*, to express that dissatisfaction in writing, again within 28 days from the notification of the *rule 3(7)* decision, he is entitled to have the matter heard before a judge. At that hearing the judge may confirm the earlier decision or order that the appeal proceeds to a Preliminary or Full Hearing.

Preliminary Hearing cases

[26.45] The previous practice of listing all cases for preliminary hearing has been abandoned. A preliminary hearing will now only be held in cases where it appears from the notice of appeal that there may not be an arguable point of law. The purpose of a PH is to determine whether the grounds of appeal raise a point of law which gives the appeal a reasonable prospect of success at a Full Hearing, or whether for some other compelling reason the appeal should be heard (eg to argue that a decision binding on the EAT should be considered by a higher court, or where the appellant seeks a declaration of incompatibility under the *Human Rights Act 1998*) (*paragraph 9.7* of the *EAT Practice Direction*).

[26.46] The procedure for the PH, which normally lasts no more than an hour, is as follows:

- Prior to the hearing the EAT will give automatic directions, including sending the notice of appeal to the respondent(s) and giving the respondent(s) the opportunity to lodge and serve, within 14 days of receiving it, concise written submissions in response to the notice of appeal, with the aim of showing that there is no reasonable prospect of the appeal succeeding. These submissions will be considered at the PH;
- If the respondent intends to serve a cross-appeal (see **26.24** below), this must be accompanied by written submissions and must be lodged and served within 14 days of receiving the notice of appeal,

and the respondent must state clearly whether it intends to advance the cross-appeal in any event, or only if the appellant succeeds. In either case, the respondent will then be entitled to attend the PH, which will also amount to a PH of the cross-appeal, and to make submissions;

- All parties will be notified of the date of the PH. Normally, only the appellant and/or a representative should attend to make submissions on the issues for consideration (usually whether there is a reasonable prospect of success). If the appellant does not attend, the hearing may nevertheless proceed on the basis of written submissions. Unless there is a cross-appeal or the EAT orders a hearing with all parties present, the respondent is not required to attend the PH and is not usually permitted to take any part, although written submissions will be considered as set out above;
- If the EAT considers that the appeal (and/or cross-appeal) should proceed to a Full Hearing on some or all of the grounds, the EAT will give directions (eg as to time estimate, applications for fresh evidence or the Employment Judge's notes, the exchange and lodging of skeleton arguments, chronologies and bundles of documents and authorities);
- Permission to amend the notice of appeal may be given at a PH if the proposed amendment is produced at the hearing, although if the amendment has not previously been notified to other parties, provision will usually be made for a formal amendment process and for the other party/parties to have the opportunity to apply as a result (see *paragraph 9.24* of the *EAT Practice Direction*);
- If not satisfied that the appeal, or part of it, should proceed to a Full Hearing, the EAT will dismiss the appeal, or part of it, giving a judgment in which reasons are set out. Reasons will not normally be given where the appeal is permitted to go forward;
- If the parties become aware that a similar point is being raised in other proceedings at a tribunal or the EAT, they should co-operate in bringing this to the attention of the Registrar so that consideration can be given to the most expedient way of dealing with the cases (eg by hearing two or more appeals together);
- If the appeal is permitted to go forward to a Full Hearing, it will be assigned to one of four listing categories:
  - P (recommended to be heard in the President's list);
  - A (complex and raising point(s) of law of public importance); and
  - B (any other cases).

Full Hearing cases

[26.47] Cases will normally be allocated to the FH track where it is apparent from the papers at the sifting stage that the appeal has a reasonable prospect of success. In such a case the Registrar of judge will list the case for a Full Hearing and consider appropriate directions (eg relating to amendment, further information, fresh evidence, Employment Judge's notes, allegations of bias, skeletons, chronology and bundles, time estimates and listing category).

Fast Track Full Hearing cases

[26.48] Whilst Full Hearing cases are normally heard in the order in which they are received by the EAT there will be times when it is appropriate to hear an appeal as soon as possible. Appeals allocated to the fast track will be subject to the same procedure as for Full Hearing cases but with a compressed timetable. Appeals placed in the fast track will normally fall into the following situations:

- cases where the parties have made a reasoned case for an expedited hearing;
- appeals against interim orders and directions of a tribunal which involve taking steps within a specified period (eg adjournments, disclosure, witness orders);
- appeals on the outcome of which other applications to the tribunal, EAT or civil courts depend;
- appeals in which a reference to the European Court of Justice or a declaration of incompatibility under the *Human Rights Act 1998* is sought; and
- appeals involving reinstatement, re-engagement, interim relief or a recommendation for action (in discrimination cases).

If a party wishes their appeal to be placed in the fast track they should state this in the relevant part of the notice of appeal.

The Respondent's answer

[26.49] If a decision is taken to permit the appeal to go forward to a FH, the EAT will send the notice of appeal (together with any amendments which have been permitted), and any submissions or skeleton argument lodged by the appellant, to all parties who are respondents to the appeal. Within 14 days of receiving these documents, any respondent must lodge at the EAT and serve on the other parties a respondent's answer (*rule 6(2)* of *the EAT Rules*). The *EAT Rules* direct that a respondent who wishes to resist an appeal should deliver to the EAT an answer 'in writing in, or substantially in, accordance with Form 3 … setting out the grounds on which he relies'. A copy of Form 3 is available on the EAT's website (www.employmentappeals.gov.uk).

[26.50] The answer is where the respondent sets out the basis upon which it resists the appellant's appeal, together with any cross-appeal of its own (see **26.24** below). If there is insufficient space on the form then, as with the notice of appeal, a separate sheet can be attached. Where the respondent simply wishes to rely upon the reasons given by the tribunal below, this should be stated in the answer. Generally it is sensible to give fuller grounds. As with the notice of appeal, a respondent cannot reserve a right to amend the answer: any amendment can only be made pursuant to an order made after an interim application, which must be made as soon as the need for amendment is known and must include the text of the proposed amendment. It would be sensible to include an explanation of why the amendment is necessary and could not have been made earlier. The provisions in respect of allegations of bias in the notice of appeal (see **26.11** above) also apply in respect of allegations of bias made by the respondent.

[26.51] Upon receiving these documents, the Registrar may, where necessary, invite applications from the parties in writing for directions and may give any appropriate directions on the papers or fix a day when the parties should attend an appointment (hearing) for directions.

[26.52] It is important to remember that a respondent who wishes to resist the appeal and/or to cross-appeal, but who has not delivered a respondent's answer in time, may be precluded from taking part in the appeal unless permission is granted to serve an answer out of time. Any application to extend time must accompany the answer. As with the notice of appeal, an extension will only be granted in exceptional circumstances (see **26.18** above).

[26.53] If the respondent includes a cross-appeal in a case which has already been assigned to the FH track without a PH, the respondent must immediately apply to the EAT in writing (on notice to the appellant) for directions to be given on the papers as to whether the EAT considers that there should be a PH in relation to the cross-appeal (*paragraph 9.12* of the *EAT Practice Direction*).

[26.54] If the respondent's answer contains a cross-appeal (see **26.24** below), the appellant must lodge with the EAT and serve a reply within 14 days of receiving the cross-appeal.

Meaning of cross appeal

[26.55] This is where the respondent also wishes to appeal the decision of the tribunal. Whilst this does not occur in the majority of cases, one example of where it might arise is where the employee brings a claim for constructive dismissal and race discrimination. The employment tribunal dismiss the claim for race discrimination but find that the applicant was constructively dismissed for reasons unrelated to race. The employee appeals the decision on race discrimination and the employer decides to cross appeal the decision on constructive dismissal. A further instance is where the tribunal could have found in a party's favour on an additional ground, but failed to do so due to an error in law. A cross-appeal may be unconditional (in other words, it will be pursued in any event), or conditional (where it will only be pursued if the appellant succeeds on the appeal), and the respondent's answer should make it clear which applies.

[26.56] If the appeal has been assigned to the PH track and the respondent intends to cross-appeal, then the cross-appeal will be considered at the PH (*paragraphs 9.9* and *9.10* of the *EAT Practice Direction* and **26.22** above). If the appeal has been assigned to the FH track, the respondent must apply to the EAT seeking its decision on whether a PH is necessary on the cross-appeal (*paragraph 9.12* of the *EAT Practice Direction* and **26.23** above). Where a respondent's answer contains a cross-appeal, the appellant must lodge and serve a reply within 14 days of receiving it.

[26.57] As with the notice of appeal, the rules provide (*rule 6(12)* of the *EAT Rules*) for a sifting by the Registrar or a judge such that no further action will be taken on cross-appeals which disclose no reasonable grounds for bringing the cross-appeal or where the cross-appeal is an abuse of the EAT's process or otherwise likely to obstruct the just disposal of the proceedings, unless the respondent takes certain steps (see **26.22** above – *rule 3(7)* cases).

Preparation: steps prior to the full hearing

[26.58] As with employment tribunals, the EAT has the power to give directions in relation to the conduct of any future hearing (*rule 25* of the *EAT Rules*). In addition, the parties should follow the *EAT Practice Direction* in relation to preparatory steps for that hearing.

Directions and interim applications

[26.59] The EAT has the power, either of its own motion or upon the application of one of the parties, to make directions relating to:

- the amendment of any notice, answer or other document;
- the admission of facts or documents;
- the mode in which evidence is given at the hearing;
- the consolidation of proceedings;
  - the date of hearing; and
  - other directions it thinks fit for the purpose of securing the just, expeditious and economical disposal of the proceedings (including ensuring that the parties avail themselves of opportunities for conciliation) (*rule 24(4) and 24(5)* of the *EAT rules*).

[26.60] Where a party considers that directions are necessary on any issue, they should make an interim application in writing. This will usually be disposed of on the papers by the Registrar or, where appropriate, a judge after consideration of the representations of all parties, however the EAT may refer the matter to an oral hearing where appropriate (*paragraph 4* of the *EAT Practice Direction*). If a PH or directions appointment is ordered, the parties should make any applications at that stage. Further, they should come to any such hearing equipped and prepared to deal with the issue of directions, including time estimates and issues such as whether there is a need for the Employment Judge's notes of evidence. If, due to an error, they fail to do so, thus necessitating a further directions hearing, there may be costs implications.

Listing

[26.61] It is important for parties to give an accurate and realistic time estimate for the hearing, and to notify the EAT if there is any change to the original estimate. This is because the lay members of the EAT sit part-time and attend only on pre-arranged dates, therefore if an appeal runs beyond its estimated length and has to be adjourned part-heard, there may be a substantial delay before the judge and members are available again. Time estimates should be given on the assumption that the EAT has read the papers in advance of the hearing. If the EAT considers that the hearing is likely to over-run, it may seek to avoid an adjournment by placing the parties under appropriate time limits in order to complete the presentation of the submissions within the estimated or available time.

[26.62] Listing is dealt with in *paragraph 12* of the *EAT Practice Direction*. Both PH and FH cases will be listed as soon as practicable. The EAT has a listing officer, who will normally consult the parties on dates. Reasonable requests will be accommodated if possible, although the listing officer is not bound to do so. Once the hearing has been fixed, it will be set down in the list. A party experiencing serious difficulties may apply to the listing officer for the date to be changed, but must notify all other parties of the application and provide reasons. On receipt of such an application, other parties should notify the listing officer of their views as soon as possible and in any event within seven days.

[26.63] Some cases, at the discretion of the listing officer, will be placed in a 'warned list' at the beginning of each calendar month. These will generally be short or expedited (fast track) cases (see **26.22** above). Parties or their representatives will be notified that the case has been included in the list. The case will normally remain in the warned list for one calendar month, and if it has not been heard by the end of that period it will be given a fixed date, although suitable cases may remain in the warned list at the discretion of the listing officer. The Registrar or judge may direct that a case be placed in the warned list, and the parties may apply for it. The parties may apply on notice to all other parties for a fixed date for a hearing.

[26.64] Other cases, even if they are not placed in the warned list, may be put in the list by the listing officer at shorter notice with the consent of the parties (for example, where other cases in the list have been settled or withdrawn or are likely to take less than their original time estimate). Parties who wish their cases to be taken as soon as possible and at short notice should notify the listing officer of this.

Each week an up-to-date list is prepared for the following week, including any changes and specifying which cases have been given fixed dates. This list can be viewed on the EAT website.

Preparation for the hearing

Documents

[26.65] It is the responsibility of the parties or their advisers to prepare a core bundle of papers for use at any hearing (including PH hearings), although the ultimate responsibility lies with the appellant, following consultation with the other parties. The contents of the bundle are prescribed in some detail in *paragraph 6* of the *EAT Practice Direction*. The bundle must include only those exhibits and documents used before the tribunal which are considered necessary for the appeal – in other words, it should not include every document used at the hearing below, regardless of relevance. The documents should be confined to those exhibits and documents (including witness statements) from the hearing below which are: (a) relevant to the point(s) of law raised in the appeal; and (b) likely to be referred to at the appeal hearing.

[26.66] The *EAT Practice Direction* provides for a core bundle of documents which should be included, if appropriate, in every case. The documents in the core bundle, and in any additional bundle, should be numbered by item and then paginated continuously and indexed. Furthermore, the *EAT Practice Direction* (*paragraph 6.2*) sets out an order in which the documents in the core bundle should be placed:

(1) Judgment, decision or order appealed from and the tribunal's written reasons;
(2) Sealed notice of appeal;
(3) Respondent's answer if a FH or the respondent's submissions if a PH;
(4) ET1 from the tribunal hearing (and any further particulars or written answers);
(5) ET3 from the tribunal hearing (and any further particulars or written answers);
(6) Questionnaires and replies;
(7) Relevant orders, judgments and written reasons of the tribunal;
(8) Relevant orders of the EAT (eg judgment from the PH, if any);
(9) Affidavits and tribunal comments (where ordered); and
(10) Any documents agreed or ordered pursuant to *paragraph 7* of the *EAT Practice Direction*.

In so far as other documents are concerned, these should follow at the end in the core bundle if they are limited in number or in a separate bundle if they are substantial. It should be noted that the *EAT Practice Direction* specifies that no bundle containing more than 100 pages should be agreed or lodged without the permission of the Registrar or the order of a judge: if permitted, the further pages should follow, with continuing pagination, in other bundles. All documents should be legible and unmarked.

[26.67] In PH cases, appeals from the Registrar's orders, *rule 3(10)* hearings and appointments for directions, the appellant should prepare and lodge four copies of the bundle as soon as possible after service of the notice of appeal and at least two weeks before the PH.

[26.68] In FH cases, the parties must co-operate in agreeing the bundle. The appellant is then responsible for ensuring that four copies of the agreed bundle is lodged no later than seven weeks before the FH. If there has been a PH, the EAT will not retain bundles and documents should be lodged again. If the parties cannot agree on the documents to be contained in the bundle, then an application should be made for directions to be given on the papers. Where there has been non cooperation by one side in the process of agreeing a bundle (for example, they have failed to respond to correspondence on the subject), it is sensible for the appellant to simply submit the bundle stating that it is not agreed. Where there is default on the part of the appellant, the prudent respondent will frequently prepare and submit a bundle of its own. If there is a dispute as to the contents of the bundle then it is sensible to prepare a separate bundle of the disputed documents so that the matter can be considered at the appeal hearing.

[26.69] In Warned List (**26.27** above) or FTFH cases, the bundles should be lodged as soon as possible and in any event within seven days after the parties have been notified that the case is expedited or is in the warned list.

Skeleton arguments

[26.70] Skeleton arguments are required in all hearings unless the EAT directs otherwise. In addition, there is no need to provide a skeleton argument if the notice of appeal or respondent's answer, as the case may be, contains the full legal argument, provided that the EAT is notified of this (*paragraph 13* of the *EAT Practice Direction*). The skeleton argument will be read in advance by the EAT and, if well-structured, will assist the EAT and the parties by focussing on the points of law to be decided, which will make the oral hearing more effective. A well-drafted skeleton argument will be concise and will identify and summarise the point(s) of law, the steps in the legal argument and the statutory provisions and authorities to be relied upon, identifying any authorities by name, page and paragraph and setting out the legal proposition sought to be derived from them. The skeleton argument, however, should not seek to argue the case on paper in detail. It is permissible in a skeleton argument to refer to the parties by name or as they appeared at the tribunal hearing, ie Claimant ('C') and Respondent ('R').

[26.71] The skeleton should include the form of order which the EAT will be asked to make at the hearing (eg to remit the case to the same or to a different tribunal or to substitute a different decision). Where possible, the skeleton should be prepared using the pagination in the index to the appeal bundle, and where the Employment Judge's notes have been obtained, should identify the parts of those notes to which the party wishes to refer. The appellant's skeleton must be accompanied by a chronology of events relevant to the appeal, which, if possible, should be agreed between the parties. This document will normally be regarded as uncontroversial unless corrected by another party or the EAT.

[26.72] Skeleton arguments may be lodged with the notice of appeal or the respondent's answer, as applicable, although this is not compulsory. They must, however, be lodged at the EAT and exchanged between the parties (where appropriate) no less than:

- 10 days before a PH, appeals from the Registrar's orders, *rule 3(10)* hearings and appointments for directions, unless the PH is fixed at less than seven days' notice, in which case as soon as possible after notification of the hearing date;
- 14 days before a FH;
- In warned list and FTFH cases, as soon as possible and (unless the hearing date is less than seven days later) in any event within seven days of notification that the case is expedited or in the warned list.

It is important to comply with these time limits. The fact that settlement negotiations are in process does not excuse delay. Failure to follow the procedure may lead to the adjournment of the appeal or to its dismissal for non-compliance, and to an award of costs. A defaulting party must immediately despatch any delayed skeleton to the EAT by hand, fax or e-mail and bring to the hearing sufficient copies (at least six) of the skeleton and any authorities referred to (*paragraph 13.10* of the *EAT Practice Direction*).

Chronologies

[26.73] The appellant's skeleton argument should be accompanied by a chronology, which if possible should be agreed between the parties (see **26.29** above).

Legal authorities

[26.74] Where the parties wish to rely upon legal authorities, *paragraph 14* of the *EAT Practice Direction* sets out the procedure for doing so. The main points are these:

- The parties should agree on which report (eg IRLR, ICR) will be used at the hearing, to avoid citation of the same case from different reports. Where the tribunal has cited a particular version, it is usually convenient to rely on that one;
- It is the responsibility of a party wishing to cite any authority to provide photocopies for the use of each member of the Tribunal and photocopies or at least a list for the other parties. All authorities should be indexed and incorporated in an agreed bundle.
- Where a party wishes to rely on unreported cases, cases not reported in the principal series of law reports, foreign cases, judgments of the ECJ and other international courts, proceedings of the Strasbourg institutions, *Hansard* or extracts from textbooks or journals, it is that party's responsibility to provide photocopies for the use of the EAT and the other parties. For ECJ decisions, the official report should be used wherever possible;
- Parties are advised not to cite an unnecessary number of authorities in the skeleton or in oral argument, and that it is rarely necessary to cite more than one case for a legal proposition – remember that it is quality, not quantity, which will be persuasive;
- If copies of the most important authorities are attached to the skeleton argument or included in a bundle, the passages relied upon should be highlighted or sidelined;
- There is no need to read the full case to the EAT in oral argument: the legal proposition for which the authority is cited should be stated and reference made to the relevant passages in the report. If the formulation of the legal proposition for which the authority

is cited is not in dispute, further examination of the authority will often be unnecessary;

- At a PH, three copies of any authority should be provided for the EAT (one copy if a judge is sitting alone), and copies provided for any other parties notified;
- At a FH, the parties must co-operate in agreeing a list of authorities and must jointly or severally lodge a list and a bundle of copies of such authorities not less than seven days before the FH.

The hearing

[26.75] The hearing involves legal arguments from both parties or their representatives. The appellant presents their case first. The old practice of addressing the presiding judge by their formal legal title (ie 'My Lord' or 'Your Honour') has been abandoned in the interests of accessibility. They should be addressed as sir or madam. In contrast to tribunal hearings, parties stand when they address the EAT.

[26.76] *Paragraph 18* of the *EAT Practice Direction* deals with the procedure for giving judgment. At the conclusion of the hearing judgment will normally be given orally. At a PH a transcript of a judgment dismissing all or part of the appeal is not normally produced unless either party applies to the EAT for one within 14 days of the oral hearing. At a FH a transcript of the judgment will not normally be produced unless either party applies for it within 14 days of the oral hearing or the EAT of its own motion directs that the judgment be transcribed (eg where a point of general importance arises or the matter is to be remitted to the tribunal).

However, in a complex case or where there is insufficient time, the EAT may reserve judgment to be handed down at a later date. The parties will be notified of the date when the judgment is ready to be handed down. It is not necessary for a party or representative to attend for the purposes of collecting the judgment unless it is intended to make an application, either for costs or permission to appeal from the decision. Copies of the judgment will be available to the parties or their representatives for collection on the morning on which it is handed down or, if so directed by a judge, earlier (subject to terms as to confidentially) on request by representatives of both parties made to the judge. The judgment will be pronounced by a judge on behalf of the EAT without being read aloud and a copy is provided to all parties and to recognised law reporters. The judge may deal with any application or may refer it to the judge and/or EAT who heard the appeal, to be dealt with on the papers or at a further oral hearing on notice. All FH judgments which are transcribed or handed down will be posted on the EAT website. Any other judgment may be posted onto the EAT website at the direction of the judge or the Registrar.

Disposal of appeals by consent

[26.77] An appellant may abandon or withdraw an appeal with permission from the EAT (*paragraph 15* of the *EAT Practice Direction*). If an appellant wishes to abandon or withdraw an appeal, the other parties and the EAT should be notified of this immediately. Similarly, if the parties reach settlement they should inform the EAT as soon as possible. The appellant should in these circumstances submit to an EAT a letter signed by or on behalf of the appellant and respondent, seeking permission to withdraw the appeal and asking the EAT to make a consent order in the form of an attached draft signed by or for both parties dismissing the appeal, together with any other agreed order (eg as to costs). If the other parties do not agree the proposed order the EAT should be informed and written submissions lodged at the EAT and served. Any outstanding issue may be resolved by the EAT on the papers, particularly if it relates to costs, or at an oral hearing to determine the outstanding matters in dispute.

[26.78] If the parties agree that the appeal should be allowed by consent and the tribunal's order reversed or varied or the matter remitted on the grounds that the decision contains an error of law, it will usually be necessary for the EAT to hold a hearing to determine whether there is good reason to make the proposed order. On notification by the parties of the proposed agreement, the EAT will decide whether the appeal can be dealt with on the papers or whether a hearing is necessary at which one or more of the parties or their representatives should attend to argue the case for allowing the appeal and making the order sought.

[26.79] If the application for permission to withdraw is made close to the hearing, the EAT may require the appellant and/or a representative to attend to explain the reasons for delay in making the decision not to pursue the appeal.

Costs

[26.80] The EAT has the power to award costs where it considers that proceedings were 'unnecessary, improper, vexatious or misconceived' or where there has been unreasonable delay or other unreasonable conduct in bringing or conducting of proceedings (*rule 34A(1)* of the *EAT Rules*). In addition to this general, catch all, provision, the rules entitle the making a costs order where a party has not complied with an EAT direction, has amended the notice of appeal, answer or cross-appeal, or has caused an adjournment of proceedings (*rule 34A(2)*). In these latter three circumstances costs are likely to be considerably easier to recover.

[26.81] Any application by a party for costs may be made at any time during the proceedings or within 14 days from the date when the order finally disposing of proceedings is sent to the parties (*rule 34(4)*). If the grounds for making the application arise before this date (for example if they are apparent at the hearing of the appeal) then a party would be wise to make the application promptly. The party seeking the order must state the legal ground on which the application is based, the facts upon which it is based, and must show (by schedule or otherwise) how the costs have been incurred. The EAT may resolve the application on the papers, provided that the opportunity is given to all relevant parties to make representations in writing, or the matter may be referred to an oral hearing. The sum awarded may be assessed on the papers or at an oral hearing, agreed by the parties, or referred for detailed assessment (*paragraph 19* of the *EAT Practice Direction*).

[26.82] The EAT also has the power to make a wasted costs order against a party's representative, having first given reasonable opportunity to make oral or written representations as to reasons why the order should not be made (*rule 34C* of the *EAT Rules*). A wasted costs order is one in respect of costs incurred by a party as a result of any improper, unreasonable or negligent act or omission on the part of any representative or which, in the light of any such act or omission occurring after the costs were incurred, the tribunal considers it reasonable to expect that party to pay (*rule 34C(3)*). Representatives not acting for profit are excluded from this provision, although those acting under a conditional fee agreement are not. The order will be made for a specified sum and written reasons for the decision will be given.

[26.83] *Rule 34D* of the *EAT Rules* provides for costs orders made in favour of a litigant in person. In those circumstances the nature of work and amount in respect of which costs may be ordered is set out by the provisions of the rule itself.

Review by the EAT

[26.84] The EAT may, either of its own motion or on an application by one of the parties, review any order made by it and on such review, revoke or vary that order on the grounds that:

(a) the order was wrongly made as the result of an error on the part of the Tribunal or its staff;
(b) a party did not receive proper notice of the proceedings leading to the order; or
(c) the interests of justice require such review.

Paragraph 20 of the *EAT Practice Direction* sets out the procedure by which an application for a review is made:

> 'Where an application is made for a review of a judgment or order of the EAT, it can be considered on paper by a judge who may, if he or she heard the original appeal or made the original order alone, without lay members, make such order, granting, refusing, adjourning or otherwise dealing with such application, as he or she may think fit. If the original judgment or order was made by the judge together with lay members, then the judge may, pursuant to Rule 33, consider and refuse such application for review on the papers. If the judge does not refuse such application, he or she may make any relevant further order, but would not grant such application without notice to the opposing party and reference to the lay members, for consideration with them, either on paper or in open court. A request to review a judgment or order of the EAT must be made within 14 days of the seal date of the order, or must include an application, with reasons for an extension of time copied to all parties.'

As to whether the EAT may 'reopen' a case after judgment has been given, see *Blockleys plc v Miller* [1992] ICR 749 and *Asda Stores Ltd v Thompson (No 2)* [2004] IRLR 598.

Appeal from the EAT

[26.85] An appeal may be made against the EAT's decision on a point of law. However, this may only be done with the permission either of the EAT itself or of the Court of Appeal (*ETA 1996, s 37(1)*). A party should approach the EAT first for leave. An application to the EAT for permission to appeal to the Court of Appeal must be made (unless the EAT otherwise orders) at the hearing or when a reserved judgment is handed down or in writing within seven days thereafter. If not made then, or if refused, or unless the EAT otherwise orders, any such applications must be made to the Court of Appeal within 21 days of the order being sealed. An application for an extension of time for permission to appeal may be entertained by the EAT where a case is made out to the satisfaction of a judge or Registrar that there is a need to delay until after a transcript is received (expedited if appropriate). Applications for an extension of time for permission to appeal should however normally be made to the Court of Appeal. The party seeking permission to appeal must state the point of law to be advanced and the grounds (*paragraph 19* of the *EAT Practice Direction*). If permission to appeal is given by the EAT, the appeal must be lodged with the Court of Appeal within 14 days of the date upon which the EAT's order was drawn up. Readers should refer to the Civil Procedure Rules (*Part 52*) for the detailed procedural provisions relating to appeal to the Court of Appeal.

Representation at the EAT

[26.86] As with tribunals, any person may appear in the EAT, and there is no requirement for that person to possess a legal qualification. Despite this, it is not surprising that, given the requirement to appeal on a point of law (and the somewhat daunting requirements relating to submission of skeleton arguments), parties do commonly instruct professional advocates to appear for them. Where a party does not have the resources to do so, they might consider the following alternatives (see also **chapter 2 – getting advice**):

- Applying for Community Legal Service funding (formerly legal aid) – a solicitor should be instructed to make the application. Funding will be subject to means and merits as with all CLS funding.
- The Bar Pro Bono Unit (consisting of barristers in independent practice who provide their services free).
- The Free Representation Unit (consisting of barristers and solicitors and those undergoing training).

- Citizens Advice Bureaux or Law Centres.

Where a party chooses to represent themselves, they should not feel daunted by the process. The EAT will strive to assist them to understand the proceedings and is likely to be more lenient in respect of non-compliance with certain procedural requirements, although this should not be taken for granted and is less likely to apply where there are stringent requirements, for example in respect of the time limits for bringing or responding to an appeal.

Contacting the EAT

[26.87] The EAT's address in England & Wales is Audit House, 58 Victoria Embankment, London EC4Y 0DS; Telephone 020 7273 1040; Fax 020 7273 1045; Email londoneat@tribunals.gsi.gov.uk.

The EAT's address in Scotland is 52 Melville Street, Edinburgh EH3 7HS; Telephone 0131 225 3963; Fax 0131 220 6694; Email edinburgheat@tribunals.gsi.gov.uk.

The EAT has a website, which is at www.employmentappeals.gov.uk.

Do's and Don'ts

Do:

- If you are thinking of appealing, request written reasons either at the conclusion of the full hearing or, at the latest, within 14 days of receipt of the written record of the decision.
- Consider taking specialist legal advice on the prospects of a successful appeal.
- Lodge your appeal within the 42-day time limit.
- Consider whether it is necessary to apply for the Employment Judge's note of evidence.
- Consider what directions you require before any PH or directions appointment.

Don't:

- Forget to read carefully the guidance notes sent to appellants and respondents by the EAT.
- Allow frustration with a tribunal's decision to cloud your judgment on the prospects of a successful appeal.

Appendix I

Claims a tribunal can hear

STATUTE	COMPLAINT	QUALIFYING EMPLOYMENT	TIME LIMIT
	Unfair Dismissal		
Transfer of Undertakings (Protection of Employment) Regulations 2006			
Regulation 7	Unfair dismissal arising from a transfer of an undertaking.	1 year	3 months from Effective Date of Termination (EDT) [1a]
Trade Union and Labour Relations (Consolidation) Act 1992			
	Unfair dismissal for:		
Section 152	reasons relating to union membership.	None	3 months from EDT [a]
Section 153	reasons underlying selection for redundancy relating to union membership.	None	3 months from EDT [a]
Section 161	Request for interim relief in *section 152* application (see above).	None	7 days from EDT [c]
Sections 238 and 238A	participating in official industrial action.	None	6 months from date of dismissal – this is either: i) date of employer's notice or ii) where no notice the EDT [a]
Schedule A1 paragraph 161	reasons arising from a claim for union recognition.	None	3 months from EDT [a]
Employment Rights Act 1996			
Section 92(1)	Written statement of reasons for dismissal.	1 year	3 months from EDT [a]

STATUTE	COMPLAINT	QUALIFYING EMPLOYMENT	TIME LIMIT
Section 94	Unfair dismissal.	1 year	3 months from EDT [a]
	Unfair dismissal for:		
Section 98ZG	reasons relating to retirement.	1 year	3 months from EDT [a]
Section 98B	reasons relating to jury service.	None	3 months from EDT [a]
Section 99	reasons relating to leave for family reasons (i.e. pregnancy, maternity and paternity leave etc).	None	3 months from EDT [a]
Section 100	health and safety reasons.	None	3 months from EDT [a]
Section 101	refusing to work on Sunday (applies to protected shop / betting workers).	None	3 months from EDT [a]
Section 101A	reasons arising from the *Working Time Regulations 1998*.	None	3 months from EDT [a]
Section 101B	participation in education or training.	None	3 months from EDT [a]
Section 102	carrying out the functions of occupational pension trustee.	None	3 months from EDT [a]
Section 103	carrying out the functions of an employee representative.	None	3 months from EDT [a]

STATUTE	COMPLAINT	QUALIFYING EMPLOYMENT	TIME LIMIT
Section 103A	whistle-blowing (making a protected disclosure).	None	3 months from EDT [a]
Section 104	asserting a statutory right.	None	3 months from EDT [a]
Section 104A	securing a right to the national minimum wage.	None	3 months from EDT [a]
Section 104B	securing the benefit of tax credits.	None	3 months from EDT [a]
Section 104C	reasons relating to flexible working.	None	3 months from EDT [a]
Section 104D	reasons relating to pension enrolment.	None	3 months from EDT [a]
Section 104E	reasons relating to study and training.	None	3 months from EDT [a]
Section 104F	reasons relating to a trade union blacklists (see *Employment Relations Act 1999 (Blacklists) Regulations 2010*).	None	3 months from EDT [a]
Section 105	selecting an employee for redundancy for an automatically unfair reason.	None	3 months from EDT [a]
Section 108(2)	reasons relating to treatment whilst on medical suspension (section 64(2)).	1 month	3 months from EDT [a]

STATUTE	COMPLAINT	QUALIFYING EMPLOYMENT	TIME LIMIT
Section 128	Request for interim relief in respect of certain dismissals relating to specific health and safety issues, employee representative and whistle-blowing cases etc.	None	7 days from EDT [2c]
Transnational Information and Consultation of Employees Regulations 1999			
Regulation 28	Unfair dismissal connected to establishment of / participation in European Works Council, or information / consultation procedure.	None	3 months from EDT [a]
Part-time Workers (Prevention of Less Favourable Treatment) Regulations 2000			
Regulation 7	Unfair dismissal relating to status as part-time worker.	None	3 months form EDT [a]
Fixed-Term Employees (Prevention of Less Favourable Treatment) Regulations 2002			
Regulation 6	Unfair dismissal relating to status as fixed-term worker.	None	3 months from EDT [3a]
Flexible Working (Procedural Requirements) Regulations 2002			
Regulation 16	Unfair dismissal relating to accompaniment in order to exercise rights to flexible working.	None	3 months from EDT [4a]

STATUTE	COMPLAINT	QUALIFYING EMPLOYMENT	TIME LIMIT
Wrongful Dismissal / Contract Claims			
Contract claims (pursuant to the **Employment Tribunals Extension of Jurisdiction (England and Wales) Order 1994**)	Employee complaint to employment tribunal.	None	3 months from EDT / last day that employee worked [a]
Contract claims (pursuant to the **Employment Tribunals Extension of Jurisdiction (England and Wales) Order 1994**)	Employer counterclaim to employment tribunal.	None	6 weeks from receipt of employee's claim [a]
Unlawful Deduction from Wages			
Employment Rights Act 1996			
Section 23	Unlawful deduction from wages or payment to employer.	None	3 months from date of deduction / final one in series [a]
Social Security Contributions and Benefits Act 1992			
Section 151	Right to Statutory Sick Pay.	None	3 months from date of deduction / final one in series [a]
Section 164	Right to Statutory Maternity Pay.	26 weeks	3 months from date of deduction / final one in series [a]
Section 171ZA and 171ZB	Right to Statutory Paternity Pay (birth and adoption).	26 weeks	3 months from date of deduction / final one in series [a]

STATUTE	COMPLAINT	QUALIFYING EMPLOYMENT	TIME LIMIT
Section 171ZL	Right to Statutory Adoption Pay.	26 weeks	3 months from date of deduction / final one in series [a]
Discrimination Claims			
Equal Pay Act 1970 (repealed from 1st October 2010)			
Section 2	Breach of equality clause.	None	6 months from end of employment
Sex Discrimination Act 1975 (repealed from 1st October 2010)			
Section 63	Discrimination on the grounds of sex, gender reassignment, marriage, pregnancy or maternity leave.	None	3 months from date of act complained of [5b]
Race Relations Act 1976 (repealed from 1st October 2010)			
Section 54	Discrimination on the grounds of race.	None	3 months from date of act complained of [b]
Disability Discrimination Act 1995 (repealed from 1st October 2010)			
Section 17A	Discrimination on the grounds of disability.	None	3 months from date of act complained of [b]
EC Treaty and Equal Pay Directive 75/117			
Articles 141 and Article 1	Equal pay / value claim under EC law.	None	3 - 6 months respectively from date of act complained of [1]

STATUTE	COMPLAINT	QUALIFYING EMPLOYMENT	TIME LIMIT
Employment Equality (Sexual Orientation) Regulations 2003 (repealed from 1st October 2010)			
Regulation 28	Discrimination on the grounds of sexual orientation.	None	3 months from date of act complained of [6b]
Employment Equality (Religion or Belief) Regulations 2003 (repealed from 1st October 2010)			
Regulation 28	Discrimination on the grounds of religion or belief.	None	3 months from date of act complained of [7b]
Employment Equality (Age) Regulations 2006 (repealed from 1st October 2010)			
Regulation 36	Discrimination on the grounds of age.	None	3 months from date of act complained of [8b]
Section 47 and Schedule 6	Rights relating to retirement.	None	3 months from date of act complained of [9b]
Equality Act 2006			
Section 21(5)	Appeal from an unlawful act notice issued by the Equality and Human Rights Commission.	None	6 weeks from the service of the notice
Equality Act 2010			
Section 120	Discrimination on the grounds of a protected characteristic, sex equality clause and maternity equality clause.	None	3 months from date of act complained of [10b 2]

STATUTE	COMPLAINT	QUALIFYING EMPLOYMENT	TIME LIMIT
Maternity / Parental Rights Claims			
Employment Rights Act 1996			
Section 48	Detriment sustained as a result of time off for family or domestic reasons (section 47C) or time off / payment for ante-natal care (sections 55 and 56).	None	3 months from date of act / failure to act [a]
Section 57	Failure to allow paid time off for ante-natal care.	None	3 months from date of refusal / failure to act [a]
Section 70	Failure to offer alternative work / pay remuneration during maternity suspension.	None	3 months from date of act / failure to act [a]
Section 71	Failure to allow ordinary maternity leave (currently 26 weeks) / to allow employee to return to same job etc.	None	3 months from date of act / failure to ac[t] a
Section 73	Failure to allow additional maternity leave (currently an additional 26 weeks).	1 year	3 months from date of act / failure to act [a]
Section 75A	Failure to allow ordinary adoption leave.	26 weeks	3 months from date of act / failure to act [a]
Section 75B	Failure to allow additional adoption leave.	26 weeks	3 months from date of act / failure to act [a]

STATUTE	COMPLAINT	QUALIFYING EMPLOYMENT	TIME LIMIT
Section 76	Failure to allow parental leave.	1 year	3 months from the date of act / failure to act
Section 77	Failure to accord rights during and after parental leave.	None (although in order to be entitled to parental leave 1 year's service is required)	3 months from date of act / failure to act [a]
Section 80	Failure to allow / unreasonable postponement of parental leave.	1 year	3 months from date of refusal / failure to act [a]
Section 80A	Failure to allow ordinary paternity leave: birth	26 weeks	3 months from date of act / failure to act [a]
Section 80AA	Failure to allow additional paternity leave: birth	26 weeks	3 months from date of act / failure to act [a]
Section 80B	Failure to allow ordinary paternity leave: adoption	26 weeks	3 months from date of act / failure to act [a]
Section 80BB	Failure to allow additional paternity leave: adoption	26 weeks	3 months from date of act / failure to act [a]
Section 80C	Failure to accord rights during and after paternity leave.	None (although in order to be entitled to parental leave 1 year's service is required)	3 months from date of act / failure to act [a]
Time off Work			
Safety Representatives and Safety Committees Regulations 1977			
Regulation 11	Failure to allow safety representative paid time off to perform his functions.	None	3 months from date of refusal / failure to act [a]

STATUTE	COMPLAINT	QUALIFYING EMPLOYMENT	TIME LIMIT
Trade Union and Labour Relations (Consolidation) Act 1992			
Sections 168, 168A, 169 and 170	Failure to allow time off for union activities or duties.	None	3 months from date of refusal / failure to act [a]
Employment Rights Act 1996			
Section 48	Detriment sustained as a result of jury service (section 43M), health and safety related reasons (section 44), Sunday working for shop and betting workers (section 45), reasons related to the Working Time Regulations 1998 (section 45A), being a trustee of an occupational pension scheme or an employee representative (sections 46 and 47), study or training (sections 47A, 47AA and 47F), family and domestic reasons (section 47C) and flexible working (section 47E).	None	3 months from date of act / failure to act [a]
Section 51	Failure to allow unpaid time off for public duties.	None	3 months from date of refusal / failure to act [a]
Section 54	Failure to allow paid time off to look for work to an employee who has been given notice of redundancy.	2 years	3 months from date of refusal / failure to act [a]
Section 57B	Failure to allow unpaid time off for dependant care.	None	3 months from date of refusal / failure to act [a]

STATUTE	COMPLAINT	QUALIFYING EMPLOYMENT	TIME LIMIT
Section 60	Failure to allow paid time off for a trustee of a pension scheme to perform their functions.	None	3 months from date of refusal / failure to act [a]
Section 63	Failure to allow paid time off for an employee representative to perform their functions.	None	3 months from date of refusal / failure to act [a]
Section 63C	Failure to allow paid time off for a young person to undertake training that will lead to a prescribed qualification.	None	3 months from date of act / date when time off should have been allowed [a]
Health and Safety (Consultation with Employees) Regulations 1996			
Regulation 11	Failure to allow paid time off for a safety representative to perform their functions / stand for election.	None	3 months from date of refusal / failure to act [a]
Working Time Regulations			
Employment Rights Act 1996			
Section 45A	Detriment sustained as a result of Working Time Regulations 1998.	None	3 months from date of act / failure to act [a]

STATUTE	COMPLAINT	QUALIFYING EMPLOYMENT	TIME LIMIT
Working Time Regulations 1998			
Regulation 10	Failure to allow statutory daily rest.	None	3 months from date right should have been allowed [a]
Regulation 11	Failure to allow statutory weekly rest.	None	3 months from date rest should have been allowed to begin [a]
Regulation 12	Failure to allow statutory rest breaks.	None	3 months from date right should have been allowed [a]
Regulation 13	Failure to allow annual leave to be taken.	None	3 months from date leave should have been allowed to begin [a]
Regulation 14	Failure to make payment in lieu of untaken holiday on termination of employment.	None	3 months from date payment should have been made [a]
Regulation 16	Failure to make payment for annual leave.	None	3 months from date payment should have been made [a]
Regulation 24	Failure to allow compensatory rest where collective agreement to work during rest period.	None	3 months from date right should have been allowed [a]
Regulation 24A	Failure to allow adequate rest for mobile workers.	None	3 months from date right should have been allowed [a]
Regulation 25	Failure to allow compensatory rest for young workers in the armed forces.	None	3 months from date right should have been allowed [a]

STATUTE	COMPLAINT	QUALIFYING EMPLOYMENT	TIME LIMIT
Regulation 27	Failure to allow compensatory rest for young workers in the event of a force majeure.	None	3 months from date right should have been allowed [a]
Regulation 27A	Failure to allow compensatory rest for young workers at night.	None	3 months from date right should have been allowed [a]
Other Trade Union Related Claims			
Trade Union and Labour Relations (Consolidation) Act 1992			
Section 66	Unjustifiable disciplining by the union.	None	3 months from date of union determination [11d]
Section 67	Compensation for unjustifiable disciplining by the union.	None	6 months but not before 4 weeks of the tribunal decision [c]
Section 68	Unauthorised deduction of union subscription.	None	3 months from date payment from which deduction made [a]
Section 137	Refusal of employment on grounds relating to union membership.	None	3 months from date of refusal / act complained of [a]
Section 138	Refusal of service employment agency on grounds relating to union membership.	None	3 months from date of refusal / act complained of [a]
Section 145A	Inducements relating to union membership or activities.	None	3 months from date of refusal / act complained of [a]

STATUTE	COMPLAINT	QUALIFYING EMPLOYMENT	TIME LIMIT
Section 145B	Inducements relating collective bargaining.	None	3 months from date of refusal / act complained of [a]
Section 146	Detriment sustained due to union membership or activities.	None	3 months from date of act / failure to act [a]
Section 174	Unlawful exclusion / expulsion from / by union.	None	6 months from date of expulsion [a]
Section 176	Compensation for unlawful exclusion / expulsion from / by union.	None	6 months but not before 4 weeks of the tribunal decision [c]
Schedule A1, paragraph 156	Detriment in relation to union recognition rights.	None	3 months from date of act / failure to act [12a]
TUPE / Redundancy Claims			
Transfer of Undertakings (Protection of Employment) Regulations 2006			
Regulation 13	Failure to inform or consult with employee representatives in relation to a transfer.	None	3 months from completion of transfer [a]
Regulation 14	Failure to act in respect of the election of employee representatives.	None	3 months from completion of transfer [a]
Trade Union and Labour Relations (Consolidation) Act 1992			
Section 188	Failure to consult with representatives in relation to redundancy.	None	3 months from date dismissal takes effect [a]

STATUTE	COMPLAINT	QUALIFYING EMPLOYMENT	TIME LIMIT
Section 188A	Failure to act in respect of the election of employee representatives.	None	3 months from date dismissal takes effect [a]
Section 190	Failure to pay remuneration due under protective award.	None	3 months from date of last day of failure to act [a]
Employment Rights Act 1996			
Section 135	Right to pay the whole / part of redundancy pay.	2 years	6 months from the 'relevant date' [d]
Section 166	Right to seek redundancy pay in respect of an insolvent employer against the Secretary of State.	2 years	None
Section 182	Right to seek payment of a debt in respect of an insolvent employer against the Secretary of State.	None	3 months from the date of communication of the Secretary of State's decision [a]
Other Claims			
Employment Rights Act 1996			
Section 11	Failure to provide written particulars of employment.	2 months	3 months from date on which employment ended [a]
Section 11	Failure to provide itemised pay statement employment.	None	3 months from date on which employment ended [a]
Section 34	Failure to pay the whole or part of guarantee payment.	1 month	3 months from date for which payment claimed [a]

STATUTE	COMPLAINT	QUALIFYING EMPLOYMENT	TIME LIMIT
Section 47B	Detriment for making a protected disclosure.	None	3 months from date of act / failure to act [13a]
Section 47D	Detriment for taking action to enforce or secure benefit of tax credit.	None	3 months from date of act / failure to act [14a]
Section 70	Failure to pay remuneration during medical suspension.	1 month	3 months from date refusal / failure to act [a]
Section 80F	Failure to properly deal with a request for flexible working.	26 weeks	3 months from date refusal / failure to act [a]
National Minimum Wage Act 1998			
Section 11	Failure of employer to produce relevant records / allow employee to inspect them where employee suspects that they are / have been paid less than NMW.	None	3 months from the date employer receives production notice from employee plus 14 days (unless a later time is agreed between the worker and employer)
Section 24	Detriment sustained where employer attempts to avoid provisions of NMW / penalty imposed.	None	3 months from date of act / failure to act [a]
Human Rights Act 1998			
Section 7	Public authority acts in a way that is incompatible with a Convention right.	None	1 year from date of act complained of – time limit may be extended for such period as is equitable having regard to all circumstances

STATUTE	COMPLAINT	QUALIFYING EMPLOYMENT	TIME LIMIT
Employment Relations Act 1999			
Section 11	Refusal / threatened refusal to allow an employee to be accompanied at a disciplinary hearing / postponement of a hearing to allow employee to be represented.	None	3 months from date of refusal / threat of refusal [a]
Transnational Information and Consultation of Employees Regulations 1999			
Regulation 32	Detriment relating to European Works Councils.	None	3 months from date of act / failure to act [15a]
Part-time Workers (Prevention of Less Favourable Treatment) Regulations 2000			
Regulation 5	Less favourable treatment arising due to status as a part-time worker.	None	3 months from act / failure to act complained of [b]
Regulation 7	Detriment relating to status as a part-time worker.	None	3 months from act / failure to act complained of [b]
Fixed-Term Employees (Prevention of Less Favourable Treatment) Regulations 2002			
Regulation 3	Less favourable treatment arising due to status as a fixed-term worker.	None	3 months from act / failure to act complained of [b]
Regulation 6	Detriment relating to status as a fixed-term employee.	None	3 months from act / failure to act complained of [16b]

STATUTE	COMPLAINT	QUALIFYING EMPLOYMENT	TIME LIMIT
Flexible Working (Procedural Requirements) Regulations 2002			
Regulation 15	Failure to comply with requirements as to accompaniment for purposes of exercising rights to flexible working.	None	3 months from date of failure or threatened failure [17a]
Regulation 16	Detriment relating to the exercise of rights to flexible working / accompaniment for purposes of exercising rights to flexible working.	None	3 months from act/failure to act complained of [18a]

a. The tribunal can extend the time limit where it considers that it was 'not reasonably practicable' to have presented the complaint in time.

b. The tribunal can extend time limit where it considers it 'just and equitable' to do so.

c. Time limit cannot be extended – save perhaps where there is evidence of fraud by the employer causing employee to miss time limit and giving rise to real injustice – see *Grimes v Sutton London Brought Council* [1973] ICR 240.

d. The time limit may be extended if it was 'not reasonably practicable' to present the complaint in time *or* where the delay arose due to reasonable attempt to pursue internal appeal etc.

1. There are no expressly stated time limits prescribed by EU law, however, it has repeatedly been held that time limits will be analogous to those under national law – see for example *Biggs v Somerset County Council* [1996] ICR 364.

2. An act or series of acts that extends over a period of time is treated as done at the end of the period (Equality Act 2010, section 123(3)).

Appendix II

The Equality Act 2010 – Discrimination and Other Prohibited Conduct

Questions and Answers Forms

These forms are in two parts;

Part 1: The complainant's questions (a questions form to be completed by the person with a discrimination or other prohibited conduct complaint)

Part 2: The respondent's answers (an answers form to be completed by the person/organisation the questions form is sent to)

There is accompanying guidance to the forms, called, *The Equality Act 2010: Obtaining Information – Discrimination and Other Prohibited Conduct – Guidance* which can be found on the Government Equalities Office (GEO) website www.equalities.gov.uk/news/equality_act_2010_forms_for_ob.aspx

These forms are to help someone obtain information under section 138 of the Equality Act 2010.

The questions form is for completion by someone who thinks they have been treated unlawfully under the Act ("the complainant") to help them get information from the person or organisation (the "respondent") he or she feels has discriminated against harassed or victimised him or her. The answers form is for completion by the respondent to reply to the complainant's questions.

The Equality Act 2010 makes it unlawful to discriminate against someone because of their age, disability, gender reassignment, marriage and civil partnership, pregnancy and maternity, race, religion or belief, sex and sexual orientation. It applies to work and (apart from in the case of age and marriage and civil partnership) to the provision of services, exercise of public functions, managing or letting premises, in education, in associations and private clubs.

There are separate questions and answers forms and supplementary guidance for equality of terms complaints (which used to be called an equal pay complaint) which are also on the GEO website www.equalities.gov.uk/news/equality_act_2010_forms_for_ob.aspx

Part 1: Complainant's questions form

- Part 1 is a questions form to be completed by the person with a discrimination or other prohibited conduct complaint.
- **Please read the instructions in this form and Parts 1 and 2 of the supplementary guidance *The Equality Act 2010: Obtaining Information – Discrimination and Other Prohibited Conduct – Guidance* before completing this form.** You may find it helpful to prepare what you want to say on a separate piece of paper.
- If you do not have enough space on the form then continue on an additional separate paper which should be attached to the form and sent to the respondent.

Section 1: This section is about the respondent (the person or organisation you think may have acted unlawfully against you and want to ask questions of)

1. *Enter the name of the person to be questioned (the respondent)*	**To**	
Enter the respondent's address	**of**	

Section 2: This section is about you (the complainant)

2. *Enter your name (you are the complainant)*	**I**	
Enter your address	**of**	

Section 3: This section is about the protected characteristic/s you (the complainant) have a dispute about

Please tick the appropriate box or boxes to indicate what protected characteristic you think your complaint relates to. A court or tribunal can consider complaints relating to more than one protected characteristic in the same case and you may tick more than one box if you think this applies to you.

Before you complete this section you may wish to read paragraph 2 of Part 2 of the supplementary guidance and you may want to seek professional advice to help complete this part of the form.

All of these terms are defined in the Equality and Human Rights Commission's guidance and Codes of Practice which you can get from www.equalityhumanrights.com

Age	☐
Disability	☐
Gender reassignment	☐
Marriage and civil partnership	☐
Pregnancy and maternity	☐
Race	☐
Religion or belief	☐
Sex	☐
Sexual orientation	☐

Section 4: This section is about the treatment which you (the complainant) thinks may have been unlawful

If you are able to, please tick the appropriate box or boxes to indicate what type of unlawful treatment you think you may have experienced. You may tick more than one box.

Before you complete this section you may wish to read paragraphs 3 – 4 of Part 2 of the supplementary guidance and you may want to seek professional advice to help complete this part of the form.

Direct discrimination	
Indirect discrimination	
Victimisation	
Harassment	
Discrimination arising from disability	
Failure to make reasonable adjustments (for disability only)	

Section 5: This section is about when the respondent might be responsible for what other people do

(If applicable) I think that you instructed, caused or induced or aided another person to treat me in a way which is unlawful under the Act as set out in section 3 and 4 above.

Before you complete this section you may wish to read paragraph 5 of Part 2 the supplementary guidance.

(Please continue on a separate sheet of paper if you run out of space here)

Section 6: This section is about what happened

Please give a brief factual description of the treatment, or the failure to make a reasonable adjustment to which your complaint relates and the circumstances leading up to that treatment or failure. You should give key factual details, such as the date, time, place and number of instances of the treatment or failure you are complaining about.

You should bear in mind that in section 8 of the questions form you will be asking whether the respondent agrees with what you say in this section.

(Please continue on a separate sheet of paper if you run out of space here)

I consider that this treatment may have been unlawful.

Section 7: This section lets you (the complainant) say why you think the treatment you experienced was unlawful

Please give the reasons why you think the treatment that you experienced was unlawful.

Before you complete this section you may wish read paragraphs 6 – 8 of Part 2 of the supplementary guidance.

Please continue on a separate sheet of paper if you run out of space here.

MY QUESTIONS

Section 8: In this section you should set out your questions to the respondent

Section 8 provides you (the complainant) with the opportunity to ask any other relevant questions you think may be important.

Please note there is a separate answers form which a respondent can use to answer these questions

Before you complete this section you may wish read paragraphs 9–14 of Part 2 of the supplementary guidance.	**Question 1:** Do you (the respondent) agree that the statement in section 6 above is an accurate description of what happened? If not, in what respect do you disagree or what is your version of what happened?
Please list and number the questions you would like to ask the respondent. We have included two standard questions here.	**Question 2:** Do you (the respondent) accept that your treatment of me was unlawful as I have set out in section 7 If not, why not? Why was I treated in the way I was? **Question 3**

Section 9: This section is about finalising your questions form

Please send your answers to the following address if different from my home address

Address ***(if appropriate)***

Insert the address you want the answers to be sent to if different from your home address in section 2.

This form must be signed and dated. If it is to be signed on behalf of (rather than by) the complainant, the person signing should:

- describe himself/herself e.g. 'solicitor acting for (name of complainant)'; and
- give their name and business address (or home address, if appropriate).

Signed	
Date	

The respondent does not have to answer your questions. But by virtue of section 138 of the Equality Act 2010, these questions and any answers are admissible as evidence in proceedings under the Act and a court or tribunal may draw an inference from a failure to reply within 8 weeks or from evasive or equivocal answer.

How to serve the questions

- We strongly advise you to keep a copy of the completed form in a safe place.
- Send the respondent your completed questions form and a blank answers forms (i.e. **whole** of this document) either to their usual last known residence or place of business or, if you know they are acting through a solicitor, to that address.
- You can either deliver the documents in person or send them by post, fax or e-mail. If you decide to send by post you are advised to use first class post. Alternatively, you can use the recorded delivery service, so that, if necessary, you can produce evidence that they were delivered.
- If you decide to send the documents by email or fax you are advised to do what you can to ensure the documents are delivered, for example, requesting a "read" receipt on emails or checking the fax delivery status.
- Whatever method you choose to send them, you should make clear that the forms may require action.
- Please read paragraphs 15 – 17 of Part 2 of the supplementary guidance for further information about serving the documents.

Part 2: Respondent's answers form

- Part 2 is an answers form to be completed by the respondent.
- **Please read the instructions in this form and Parts 1 and 3 of the supplementary guidance *The Equality Act 2010: Obtaining* Information – Discrimination and Other Prohibited Conduct – Guidance before completing the answers.** You may wish to prepare what you want to say on a separate piece of paper.
- If you do not have enough space on the answers form for what you want to say, continue on an additional piece of paper which should be attached to the answers form and sent to the complainant.

Section 1: This section is about the complainant

1. *Enter the name of the questioner (the complainant)*	**To**	
Enter the complainant's address	**of**	

Section 2: This section is about you (the respondent)

2. *Enter your name (you are the respondent)*	**I**		
Enter your organisation's name and address	**of**		
		acknowledge receipt of the questions form signed by you and dated	
		which was served on me on (date)	

Section 3: This section is about what happened

Please indicate whether you agree or disagree that the complainant's statement in section 6 of the questions form is an accurate description of what happened and tick the appropriate box.

Please tick the appropriate box

**delete as required.*

☐ **I agree with the statement in full or in part ***

☐ **I disagree with the statement in full or in part***

If you ***agree with the statement only in part or you do not agree*** *with the statement in full or in part please say why.*

If appropriate, include your own version of what happened.

Before you complete this section you may wish to read paragraphs 3–4 of Part 3 of the supplementary guidance.

I do not agree that the statement is an accurate description of what happened for the following reason(s).

Section 4: This section is about whether the treatment was unlawful

Please *indicate whether you agree or disagree that the treatment or failure experienced by the complainant as set out in section 7 of the questions form was unlawful.* *Please tick the appropriate box* **delete as required.*	☐ **I agree with the statement in full or in part*** ☐ **I disagree with the statement in full or in part***
If you **do not agree** *that treatment complained of by the claimant was unlawful please say why.* *Include any reasons which in your view explain or justify the treatment experienced by the complainant.* *Before you complete this section you may wish to read paragraphs 5–9 of Part 3 of the supplementary guidance.*	**I do not agree that the treatment complained of was unlawful for the following reason(s).**

Section 5: In this section you should give answers to the other questions the complainant has asked

Please include here the answers to the other questions the complainant has asked in section 8 of the questions form.

Before you complete this section you may wish to read paragraphs 10 – 14 of Part 3 of the supplementary guidance.

Section 6: In this section you should indicate which questions you are not answering and why

You do not have to complete this section if you have answered all the questions in the complainant's questions form

I have not answered the questions identified in the box below because I am
☐ unable
☐ unwilling
to do so for the reasons given.

***But**, if you are unable or unwilling to answer some or all of the questions, please tick the appropriate box, identify the unanswered questions and give your reasons for not answering them.*

Before you complete this section you may wish to read paragraph 2 and paragraphs 12–14 of Part 3 of the supplementary guidance.

Section 7: This section is about finalising your answers form

The answers form must be signed and dated. If it is to be signed on behalf of (rather than by) the respondent, the person signing should:

Signed

Date

- *describe himself/herself e.g. 'solicitor acting for (name of employer)' or 'personnel manager of (name of firm, government department etc)'; and*
- *give their name and business address (or home address if appropriate).*

Name/description

Address (if appropriate)

Please note:

You (the respondent) do not have to answer the complainant's questions. However, if you do not answer within 8 weeks, or answer in an evasive or equivocal way a court or tribunal may draw an inference from this.

How to serve the answers form on the complainant

- If you wish to reply to the question form, you should do so within **8 weeks**.
- You should retain, and keep in a safe place, the questions sent to you and a copy of your reply.
- You can serve the answers form either by delivering it in person to the complainant or by sending it by post.
- If you decide to send by post you are advised to use first class post. Alternatively, you can use the recorded delivery service, so that, if necessary, you can produce evidence that the answers were delivered.
- You should send the answers form to the address indicated in section 9 of the complainant's question form.
- If you decide to send the documents by email or fax you are advised to do what you can to ensure the documents are delivered, for example, requesting a "read" receipt on emails or checking the fax delivery status.
- Please read paragraphs 15 – 16 of Part 3 of the supplementary guidance for further information about serving the documents.

Appendix III

Employment Tribunals Claim Form

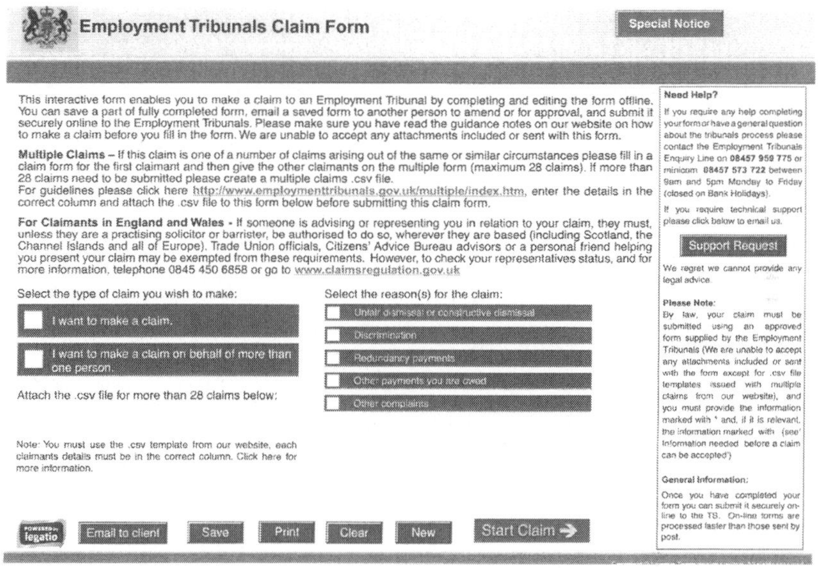

Employment Tribunals Claim Form

Special Notice

This interactive form enables you to make a claim to an Employment Tribunal by completing and editing the form offline. You can save a part of fully completed form, email a saved form to another person to amend or for approval, and submit it securely online to the Employment Tribunals. Please make sure you have read the guidance notes on our website on how to make a claim before you fill in the form. We are unable to accept any attachments included or sent with this form.

Multiple Claims – If this claim is one of a number of claims arising out of the same or similar circumstances please fill in a claim form for the first claimant and then give the other claimants on the multiple form (maximum 28 claims). If more than 28 claims need to be submitted please create a multiple claims .csv file.
For guidelines please click here http://www.employmenttribunals.gov.uk/multiple/index.htm, enter the details in the correct column and attach the .csv file to this form below before submitting this claim form.

For Claimants in England and Wales - If someone is advising or representing you in relation to your claim, they must, unless they are a practising solicitor or barrister, be authorised to do so, wherever they are based (including Scotland, the Channel Islands and all of Europe). Trade Union officials, Citizens' Advice Bureau advisors or a personal friend helping you present your claim may be exempted from these requirements. However, to check your representatives status, and for more information, telephone 0845 450 6858 or go to www.claimsregulation.gov.uk

Select the type of claim you wish to make:

- I want to make a claim.
- I want to make a claim on behalf of more than one person.

Attach the .csv file for more than 28 claims below:

Note: You must use the .csv template from our website, each claimants details must be in the correct column. Click here for more information.

Select the reason(s) for the claim:

- Unfair dismissal or constructive dismissal
- Discrimination
- Redundancy payments
- Other payments you are owed
- Other complaints

Email to client | Save | Print | Clear | New | Start Claim →

Need Help?

If you require any help completing your form or have a general question about the tribunals process please contact the Employment Tribunals Enquiry Line on **08457 959 775** or minicom **08457 573 722** between 9am and 5pm Monday to Friday (closed on Bank Holidays).

If you require technical support please click below to email us.

Support Request

We regret we cannot provide any legal advice.

Please Note:
By law, your claim must be submitted using an approved form supplied by the Employment Tribunals (We are unable to accept any attachments included or sent with the form except for .csv file templates issued with multiple claims from our website), and you must provide the information marked with * and, if it is relevant, the information marked with (see' Information needed before a claim can be accepted')

General Information:

Once you have completed your form you can submit it securely on-line to the TS. On-line forms are processed faster than those sent by post.

1 Your details

1.1 Title: Mr Mrs Miss Ms Other

1.2* First name (or names):

1.3* Surname or family name:

1.4 Date of birth (date/month/year): Are you: male? female?

1.5* Address: Number or Name
Street
+ Town/City
County
Postcode

1.6 Phone number including area code **(where we can contact you in the day time)**:
Mobile number **(if different)**:

1.7 How would you prefer us to communicate with you? E-mail Post
(Please tick only one box)

E-mail address:

2 Respondent's details

2.1* Give the name of your employer or the organisation you are claiming against.

2.2* Address: Number or Name
Street
+ Town/City
County
Postcode

Phone number:

2.3● If you worked at a different address from the one you have given at 2.2, please give the full address and postcode.

Postcode

Phone number:

If there are other respondents please complete **Section 11.**

3 Employment details

3.1 Please give the following information if possible.

When did your employment start?

Is your employment continuing? Yes No

If your employment has ceased, or you are in a period of notice, when did it, or will it, end?

3.2 Please say what job you do or did.

4 Earnings and benefits

4.1 How many hours on average do, or did, you work each week? hours each week

4.2 How much are, or were, you paid?

Pay before tax £ .00

Normal take-home pay (including overtime, commission, bonuses and so on) £ .00

Hourly
Weekly
Monthly
Yearly

4.3 If your employment has ended, did you work (or were you paid for) a period of notice? Yes No

If 'Yes', how many weeks' or months' notice did you work, or were you paid for? weeks months

4.4 Were you in your employer's pension scheme? Yes No

Please answer 4.5 to 4.9 if your claim, or part of it, is about unfair or constructive dismissal.

4.5 If you received any other benefits, e.g. company car, medical insurance, etc, from your employer, please give details.

4.6 Since leaving your employment have you got another job? Yes No
If 'No', please now go straight to section 4.9.

4.7 Please say when you started (or will start) work.

4.8 Please say how much you are now earning (or will earn). £ .00 each

4.9 Please tick the box to say what you want if your case is successful:

a To get your old job back and compensation (reinstatement)

b To get another job with the same employer and compensation (re-engagement)

c Compensation only

5 Your claim

5.1* Please tick one or more of the boxes below. In the space provided, describe the event, or series of events, that have caused you to make this claim:

a I was unfairly dismissed (including constructive dismissal)

b I was discriminated against on the grounds of

Sex (including equal pay)	Race
Disability	Religion or belief
Sexual orientation	Age

c I am claiming a redundancy payment

d I am owed
- notice pay
- holiday pay
- arrears of pay
- other payments

e Other complaints

5.2* Please set out the background and details of your claim in the space below.
The details of your claim should include **the date when the event(s) you are complaining about happened;** for example, if your claim relates to discrimination give the dates of all the incidents you are complaining about, or at least the date of the last incident. If your complaint is about payments you are owed please give the dates of the period covered.
Please use the blank sheet at the end of the form if needed.

5.3 If your claim consists of, or includes, a claim that you are making a protected disclosure under the Employment Rights Act 1996 (otherwise known as a 'whistleblowing' claim), please tick the box below if you wish a copy of this form, or information from it, to be forwarded on your behalf to a relevant regulator (known as a 'prescribed person' under the relevant legislation) by the Tribunals Service.

6 What compensation or remedy are you seeking?

6.1 Completion of this section is optional, but may help if you state what compensation or remedy you are seeking from your employer as a result of this complaint. If you specify an amount, please explain how you have calculated that figure.

7 Other information

7.1 Please do not send a covering letter with this form. You should add any extra information you want us to know here. Please use the blank sheet at the end of the form if needed.

8 Your representative

Please fill in this section only if you have appointed a representative. If you do fill in this section, we will in future only send correspondence to your representative and not to you.

8.1 Representative's name:

8.2 Name of the representative's organisation:

8.3 Address: Number or Name

Street

+ Town/City

County

Postcode

8.4 Phone number **(including area code):**

Mobile number **(if different):**

8.5 Reference:

8.6 How would they prefer us to communicate with them? (Please tick only one box) E-mail Post

E-mail address:

9 Disability

9.1 Please tick this box if you consider you have a disability Yes

Please say what this disability is and tell us what assistance, if any, you will need as your claim progresses through the system, including for any hearings that may need to be held at Tribunal Service premises.

10 Multiple cases

10.1 To your knowledge, is your claim one of a number of claims against the same employer arising from the same, or similar, circumstances? Yes No

11 Details of Additional Respondents

- Name of your employer or the organisation you are claiming against.
- Address: Number or Name
  Street
  + Town/City
  County
  Postcode

  Phone number:

- Name of your employer or the organisation you are claiming against.
- Address: Number or Name
  Street
  + Town/City
  County
  Postcode

  Phone number:

- Name of your employer or the organisation you are claiming against.
- Address: Number or Name
  Street
  + Town/City
  County
  Postcode

  Phone number:

Please read the form and check you have entered all the relevant information.
Once you are satisfied, please tick this box.

Data Protection Act 1998. We will send a copy of this form to the respondent(s) and Acas. We will, if your claim consists of, or includes, a claim that you have made a protected disclosure under the Employment Rights Act 1996 (and you have given your consent that we should do so) send a copy of the form, or extracts from it, to the relevant regulator. We will put the information you give us on this form onto a computer. This helps us to monitor progress and produce statistics. Information provided on this form is passed to the Department for Business, Innovation and Skills to assist research into the use and effectiveness of employment tribunals.

Additional information for sections 5.2 and 7.

Additional information for sections 5.2 and 7.

Additional information for sections 5.2 and 7.

Equal Opportunities Monitoring Form

You are not obliged to fill in this section but, if you do so, it will enable us to monitor our processes and ensure that we provide equality of opportunity to all. The information you give here will be treated in strict confidence and this page will not form part of your case. It will be used only for monitoring and research purposes without identifying you.

1. What is your country of birth?

England
Wales
Scotland
Northern Ireland
Republic of Ireland
Elsewhere, *please write in the present name of the country*

2. What is your ethnic group? Choose ONE section from A to E, then ✓ the appropriate box to indicate your cultural background.

A White

British
Irish
Any other White background *please write in*

B Mixed

White and Black Caribbean
White and Black African
White and Asian
Any other Mixed background *please write in*

C Asian or Asian British

Indian
Pakistani
Bangladeshi
Any other Asian background *please write in*

D: Black or Black British

Caribbean
African
Any other Black background *please write in*

E Chinese or other ethnic group

Chinese
Any other, *please write in*

3. What is your religion?
✓ box only

None
Christian (including Church of England, Catholic, Protestant and all other Christian denominations)
Buddhist
Hindu
Jewish
Muslim
Sikh
Any other religion, *please write in*

4. Sexual orientation

Which of these best describes you?
✓ box only

Heterosexual
Gay or lesbian or homosexual
Bisexual
Other

5. Disability

Do you have any health problems or disabilities that you expect will last for more than a year?
✓ box only

Yes
No

Click Here to return to the Home page when you have finished completing the form

Copy 1

Employment Tribunals - Multiple Claim Form

Please use this form if you wish to present two or more claims which arise from the same set of facts. Use additional sheets if necessary.

The following claimants are represented by ______ (if applicable) and the relevant required information for all the additional claimants is the same as stated in the main claim of

______ V

______

______

Title ______
First name (or names) ______
Surname or family name ______
Date of birth ______
Number or Name ______
Street ______
Town/City ______
County ______
Postcode ______

Title ______
First name (or names) ______
Surname or family name ______
Date of birth ______
Number or Name ______
Street ______
Town/City ______
County ______
Postcode ______

Title ______
First name (or names) ______
Surname or family name ______
Date of birth ______
Number or Name ______
Street ______
Town/City ______
County ______
Postcode ______

ET1a v01

Copy 1

Title
First name (or names)
Surname or family name
Date of birth
Number or Name
Street
Town/City
County
Postcode

Title
First name (or names)
Surname or family name
Date of birth
Number or Name
Street
Town/City
County
Postcode

Title
First name (or names)
Surname or family name
Date of birth
Number or Name
Street
Town/City
County
Postcode

Title
First name (or names)
Surname or family name
Date of birth
Number or Name
Street
Town/City
County
Postcode

Employment Tribunals check list and cover sheet

You have completed stage one of your application and opted to print and post your form. We would like to remind you that applications submitted on-line are processed much faster than ones posted to us. If you wish to submit on-line please go back to the form and click the submit button, otherwise follow the Check list before you post the completed applications to the relevant office address.

A list of our office's contact details can be found at the hearing centre page of our website at - http://www.employmenttribunals.gov.uk/ ; if you are still unsure about which office to contact please call our national enquiry line on 0845 7959775 (Mon - Fri, 9am-5pm) or Mincom 0845 757 3772; they can also provide general procedural information about the employment tribunals.

Please check the following:

1) Read your application to ensure the information entered is correct and truthful, and that you have not omitted any information, which you feel, may be relevant to your claim.

2) You must not attach a covering letter to your form. If you have any further relevant information please enter it in the 'Additional Information' space provided in the form.

3) The completed form should be returned to the relevant office address. If you are using a window envelope you may insert this page with your claim form. Please do not clip or staple this page to your claim form.

4) Keep a copy of your claim form.

Once your application has been received, you should receive confirmation form the office dealing with your claim within 5 working days. If you have not heard from them within five days, please contact that office directly.

Appendix IV

Employment Tribunals Response Form

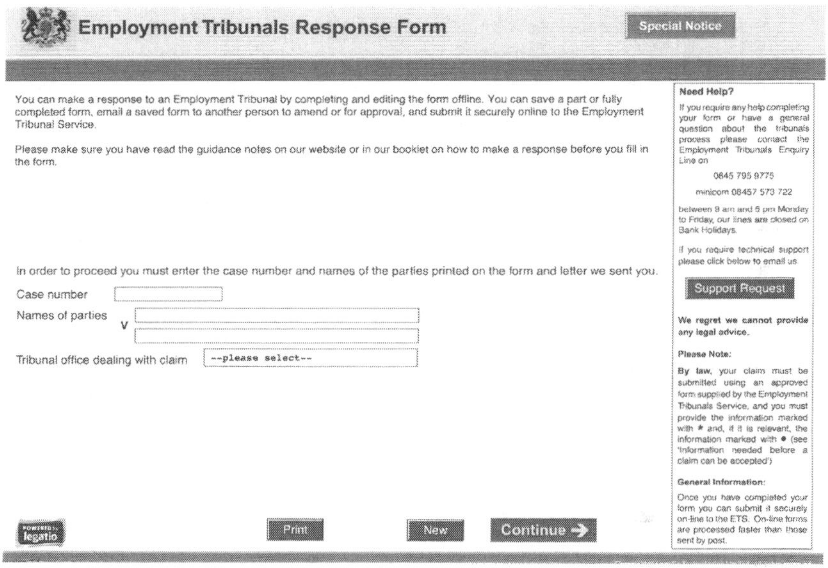

Employment Tribunals Response Form

Special Notice

You can make a response to an Employment Tribunal by completing and editing the form offline. You can save a part or fully completed form, email a saved form to another person to amend or for approval, and submit it securely online to the Employment Tribunal Service.

Please make sure you have read the guidance notes on our website or in our booklet on how to make a response before you fill in the form.

In order to proceed you must enter the case number and names of the parties printed on the form and letter we sent you.

Case number

Names of parties v

Tribunal office dealing with claim --please select--

Print New Continue

Need Help?

If you require any help completing your form or have a general question about the tribunals process please contact the Employment Tribunals Enquiry Line on

0845 795 9775

minicom 08457 573 722

between 9 am and 5 pm Monday to Friday, our lines are closed on Bank Holidays.

If you require technical support please click below to email us

Support Request

We regret we cannot provide any legal advice.

Please Note:

By law, your claim must be submitted using an approved form supplied by the Employment Tribunals Service, and you must provide the information marked with * and, if it is relevant, the information marked with ● (see 'Information needed before a claim can be accepted')

General Information:

Once you have completed your form you can submit it securely on-line to the ETS. On-line forms are processed faster than those sent by post.

Case number:

1 Claimant's name

1.1 Claimant's name:

2 Respondent's details

2.1* Name of Individual, Company or Organisation

Contact name:

2.2* Address: Number or Name

Street

+ Town/City

County

Postcode

2.3 Phone number including area code **(where we can contact you in the day time):**

Mobile number **(if different):**

2.4 How would you prefer us to communicate with you? (Please tick only one box) E-mail Post

E-mail address:

2.5 What does this organisation mainly make or do?

2.6 How many people does this organisation employ in Great Britain?

2.7 Does this organisation have more than one site in Great Britain? Yes No

2.8 If 'Yes', how many people are employed at the place where the claimant worked?

3 Employment details

3.1 Are the dates of employment given by the claimant correct? Yes No
If 'Yes', please now go straight to section 3.3.

3.2 If 'No', please give dates and say why you disagree with the dates given by the claimant.

When their employment started

When their employment ended or will end

3 Employment details (continued)

Is their employment continuing? Yes No
I disagree with the dates for the following reasons.

3.3 Is the claimant's description of their job or job title correct? Yes No
If 'Yes', please now go straight to section 4

3.4 If 'No', please give the details you believe to be correct below.

4 Earnings and benefits

4.1 Are the claimant's hours of work correct? Yes No

If 'No', please enter the details you believe to be correct. [ ] hours each week

4.2 Are the earnings details given by the claimant correct? Yes No
If 'Yes', please now go straight to section 4.3

If 'No', please give the details you believe to be correct below.

Pay before tax £ [ ] .00

Normal take-home pay (including overtime, commission, bonuses and so on) £ [ ] .00

Hourly
Weekly
Monthly
Yearly

4.3 Is the information given by the claimant correct about being paid for, or working, a period of notice? Yes No
If 'Yes', please now go straight to section 4.4

If 'No', please give the details you believe to be correct below. If you gave them no notice or didn't pay them instead of letting them work their notice, please explain what happened and why.

4.4 Are the details about pension and other benefits, e.g. company car, medical insurance, etc, given by the claimant correct? Yes No
If 'Yes', please now go straight to section 5.

If 'No', please give the details you believe to be correct below.

5 Response

5.1* Do you resist the claim? Yes No
If 'No', please now go straight to section 6.

5.2● If 'Yes', please set out in full the grounds on which you resist the claim.

ET3 v03 003

6 Other information

6.1 Please do not send a covering letter with this form. You should add any extra information you want us to know here.

7 Your representative

If you have a representative, please fill in the following.

7.1 Representative's name:

7.2 Name of the representative's organisation:

7.3 Address: Number or Name

Street

+ Town/City

County

Postcode

7.4 Phone number:

7.5 Reference:

7.6 How would you prefer us to communicate with them? E-mail Post
(Please tick only one box)

E-mail address:

Please read the form and check you have entered all the relevant information.
Once you are satisfied, please tick this box.

Data Protection Act 1998. We will send a copy of this form to the claimant and Acas. We will put the information you give us on this form onto a computer. This helps us to monitor progress and produce statistics. Information provided on this form is passed to the Department for Business, Enterprise and Regulatory Reform to assist research into the use and effectiveness of employment tribunals. (URN 05/874)

Additional space for notes.

Additional space for notes.

Additional space for notes.

Employment Tribunals check list and cover sheet

You have completed stage one of your application and opted to print and post your form. We would like to remind you that applications submitted on-line are processed much faster than ones posted to us. If you wish to submit on-line please go back to the form and click the submit button, otherwise follow the Check list before you post the completed applications to the relevant office address.

A list of our office's contact details can be found at the hearing centre page of our website at - http://www.employmenttribunals.gov.uk/ ; if you are still unsure about which office to contact please call our national enquiry line on 0845 7959775 (Mon - Fri, 9am-5pm) or Mincom 0845 757 3772; they can also provide general procedural information about the employment tribunals.

Please check the following:

1) Read your application to ensure the information entered is correct and truthful, and that you have not omitted any information, which you feel, may be relevant to your claim.

2) You must not attach a covering letter to your form. If you have any further relevant information please enter it in the 'Additional Information' space provided in the form.

3) The completed form should be returned to the relevant office address. If you are using a window envelope you may insert this page with your claim form. Please do not clip or staple this page to your claim form.

4) Keep a copy of your claim form.

Once your application has been received, you should receive confirmation form the office dealing with your claim within 5 working days. If you have not heard from them within five days, please contact that office directly.

Appendix V

Case Study

Faultless v Trouble Likes Us Limited

This case study provides examples of a number of documents in the context of a fictional case. The claim is brought by a female employee (Felicity Faultless) who has been dismissed by her employers (Trouble Likes Us Ltd) following an incident of fighting at work. She is claiming unfair dismissal and sex discrimination.

The examples are intended to give the reader a broad idea of how to draft documents of this nature by placing them in a specific context.

Taken together, they are *not* intended to constitute a comprehensive survey of a case from beginning to end. Readers will notice, for example, that there is no pre-claim correspondence or questionnaire and many steps which might arise in a case like this, such as applications for a witness order, are also not included. Further, witness statements have only been produced for two witnesses, rather than the total number that would be needed in this kind of scenario.

On the Respondent's side, witnesses would normally include at least the dismissing manager and the appeals manager. With the Claimant, you would expect her to adduce corroborative evidence, if possible, in relation to the assertions she has made about the Respondent. Evidence would not normally be adduced as to whether or not the fighting incident itself happened (i.e. as to the Claimant's guilt or otherwise of the disciplinary charges), unless this was in some way relevant to the sex discrimination complaint.

Readers might also note that the grounds of complaint (section 5.2 of the ET1) and the response (section 5.2 of the ET3) are fairly comprehensive. It may not always be possible or desirable to provide this much information. Care should be taken not to create hostages to fortune, or make assertions at such an early stage which are abandoned later on.

It is assumed for the purposes of this example that the employer had and used a disciplinary procedure which included provision for the allegation to be set out in writing, for a disciplinary meeting, for the employee to be informed in writing of the outcome and her right of appeal, for an appeal hearing, and for the outcome of the appeal to be notified in writing. The disciplinary procedure therefore met the requirements of the ACAS Code of Practice on Discipline and Grievance. It is also assumed that before bringing the claim, the Claimant sent a written grievance to the employer setting out her allegations of sex discrimination and that the employer sent her a written response to that document.

IN THE FICTITIOUS EMPLOYMENT TRIBUNAL **Case No. [ ]**

BETWEEN:

Felicity Faultless

Claimant

- and -

Trouble Likes Us Limited

Respondent

GROUNDS OF COMPLAINT

---

1. The Claimant's claim is for unfair dismissal and sex discrimination. On 25 October 2010, the Claimant was engaged in an altercation with her supervisor, Anne Beattie, in which the Claimant is alleged to have pushed Ms Beattie and been threatening towards her. The Respondent dismissed the Claimant on 17 November 2010. The reason given for dismissal was gross misconduct.

UNFAIR DISMISSAL

2. The Claimant will contend that the Respondent acted unreasonably in treating the Claimant's conduct as a reason for dismissal[1]. The Claimant contends that there was both an insufficient investigation by the Respondent and that the decision to dismiss fell outside the range of reasonable responses open to the Respondent.

Sufficiency of the investigation

3. The Respondent failed to carry out a sufficient investigation into the issue of whether the Claimant was the first to make physical contact or whether, as the Claimant alleges, she pushed Ms Beattie away in self-defence after the latter grabbed the Claimant by her collar. There were four eyewitnesses to the altercation which took place between the Claimant and Ms Beattie. The Respondent only

1 Author's note: on the facts of this particular case the reason for dismissal, i.e. conduct, is not in dispute.

interviewed three of them stating that the fourth, Peter Sleep, was away sick during the course of the investigation and could not be interviewed. The Claimant will contend that the Respondent made no effort to contact Mr Sleep to obtain his account despite an express request from the Claimant. The Claimant will rely upon the fact that, of the three witnesses they interviewed, only one, Marjorie Gossforth, stated that she saw the Claimant make physical contact first. The Claimant will further contend that the Respondent failed to investigate her claim during the disciplinary hearing that she had been victimized by Ms Beattie over a period of two years.

Reasonableness of the sanction of dismissal

4. The Claimant will contend that, as she acted in self-defence, the decision to dismiss must have been outside the range of reasonable responses open to the Respondent. She will further contend that, even on the version of events which the Respondent acted upon, dismissal was not within the range of reasonable responses. In this respect the Claimant will rely, amongst other things, upon: (a) her immaculate conduct record during the twelve years of her employment; (b) the fact that the altercation between herself and Ms Beattie was provoked by the unreasonable behaviour of the latter; (c) Ms Beattie had victimized her over a period of time, a matter which had been the subject of a number of informal complaints; and (d) that the Respondent treated her differently (and less favourably) than two male employees who, the previous month, were involved in a serious incident of fighting at work, but who merely received a formal warning (see sex discrimination below).

<u>SEX DISCRIMINATION</u>

5. The Claimant will allege that, in deciding to dismiss the applicant, the Respondent treated the Claimant less favourably on grounds of her sex. The Claimant alleges that, if a male employee had been involved in a similar incident, he would not have been dismissed. In or about September 2010, John Striker and Michael Ram, two male employees of the Respondent, were involved in a serious incident of fighting at work in which both sustained injuries. Despite this, each escaped dismissal and received a written warning. Further, the Claimant knows of numerous other incidents in which fights have resulted in nothing more severe than a warning.
6. The Claimant will contend that there was a culture in place in the Respondent's organisation in which fighting was tolerated amongst men but not amongst women.

7. The Claimant will claim compensation for unfair dismissal and sex discrimination including, in the case of the latter, an award for the injury to her feelings.
8. The Claimant raised her complaint of sex discrimination by way of a written grievance sent to her employer on 23 December 2010. The Respondent responded to that grievance on 29 January 2011.

IN THE FICTITIOUS EMPLOYMENT TRIBUNAL **Case No. [ ]**

B E T W E E N:

Felicity Faultless

Claimant

- and -

Trouble Likes Us Limited

Respondent

GROUNDS OF RESISTANCE

---

1. The Respondent denies that it unfairly dismissed the Claimant or treated her less favourably on grounds of her sex.
2. The Claimant was summarily dismissed for gross misconduct on 17 November 2010. The conduct in question was violent and threatening behaviour, constituting gross misconduct under the Respondent's disciplinary procedure.
3. The Respondent will assert that it had reasonable grounds for believing that the Claimant was guilty of the misconduct in question, that it carried out a sufficient investigation and that dismissal was within the range of reasonable responses open to it.
4. Sufficiency of investigation: On 25 October 2010 the Respondent's level one supervisor, Anne Beattie, reported to her line manager, John Weary, that she had been the victim of an assault by the Claimant, a member of the team of whom Ms Beattie had charge. Mr Weary decided that, in view of the seriousness of the allegation, he would suspend the Claimant on full pay pending further investigation, in accordance with the provisions of the Respondent's disciplinary procedure.
5. After enquires, Mr Weary established that there were four eyewitnesses to the incident. Three of those were interviewed. The fourth, Peter Sleep, could not be interviewed because he was unwell at the time when the interviews were carried out. The Respondent will contend that it had sufficient information to proceed without his evidence.

6. Of the three witnesses interviewed, Marjorie Gossforth (a worker at the same grade as the Claimant) stated that she saw the entire incident and that the Claimant pushed Mrs Beattie in the face aggressively. She also stated that she never observed Ms Beattie make physical contact with the Claimant. The other two eyewitnesses, Betty Chatter and Sharon Stonewall, did not observe the assault itself, but turned around after hearing Ms Beattie shout out in pain and further heard Ms Beattie say 'she's just hit me'. Finally, Ms Beattie herself was interviewed. She stated that the Claimant, after being told to carry out a reasonable instruction, had become rude and aggressive and had hit her in the face. The Claimant was asked to attend a disciplinary hearing on 14 November 2010. She was informed of the allegations against her, and maintained that she had pushed Ms Beattie away in self-defence after being grabbed by her collar. On this particular occasion, the Claimant was angry because Ms Beattie had asked her to clear up a spillage on the floor.
7. The Respondent's manager reached the conclusion, on the evidence before him, that the Claimant had physically pushed away Ms Beattie in a violent and threatening manner. He did not believe the Claimant when she stated that she was assaulted first by Ms Beattie. Whilst he accepted that the Claimant was, at the time of the assault, angry about the instruction she had received, he did not believe that she was subjected to any provocation. If, which he did not accept, there was any problem with the behaviour of Ms Beattie towards the Claimant, he considered the correct course was for the Claimant to make a formal complaint through the grievance procedure. He also considered the Claimant's clean conduct record. However, having come to the conclusion that the Claimant had carried out an unprovoked assault upon a supervisor who was simply carrying out her duties, he considered that the right sanction was dismissal.
8. The Claimant exercised a right of appeal and a full rehearing was conducted by John Judge, the Respondent's chief line manager, on 2 December 2010. The decision to dismiss was confirmed.
9. The reasonableness of the sanction of dismissal: The Respondent will rely upon the fact that fighting is a serious offence of gross misconduct. It will further rely upon the fact that the assault was carried out upon a senior member of staff who was simply trying to carry out her duties. Further, the Claimant showed no remorse for what had taken place. The Respondent denies, for the reasons set out below, that there was any disparate treatment between the Claimant and two male colleagues.

10. The Respondent confirms that it has a written disciplinary procedure which was followed in this case. This procedure conforms to all relevant ACAS guidance. It is the Respondent's contention that the dismissal was procedurally as well as substantively fair.
11. Sex discrimination: The allegation of sex discrimination has only recently been made for the first time and has taken the Respondent by surprise. Although the Claimant raised the matters she relies upon in a written grievance dated 23 December 2010 and received on 7 January 2011, she had never previously raised any of these matters with the Respondent, whether in the course of the disciplinary proceedings, by way of an internal grievance or otherwise. The Respondent denies that it views fighting amongst female employees more seriously than amongst men, or that there is any culture in place in the workplace to that effect. It denies that there was less favourable treatment of the Claimant on account of her sex.
12. The Respondent accepts that two male employees, John Striker and Michael Ram, were involved in an incident of fighting at work during the week prior to the Claimant's dismissal, and received a formal warning. The circumstances of that case were different, and the decision not to dismiss was unrelated to the sex of those involved. The Respondent will rely upon the fact that, in relation to that incident: (a) both employees admitted their involvement in the fight from the outset and expressed remorse for what had occurred; (b) the fight was not related to the giving of a work instruction by a manager; and (c) both employees had since resolved their difficulties and were prepared to work together as part of a team. If, which is denied, any employee of the Respondent is found to have acted unreasonably, the Respondent will assert that it carried out all reasonable steps to prevent such an act taking place, including thorough equal opportunities training.

IN THE FICTITIOUS EMPLOYMENT TRIBUNAL **Case No. [ ]**

B E T W E E N:

Felicity Faultless

Claimant

- and -

Trouble Likes Us Limited

Respondent

CLAIMANT'S REQUEST FOR FURTHER PARTICULARS OF THE GROUNDS OF RESISTANCE

---

1. Of 'The fourth, Peter Sleep, could not be interviewed because he was unwell at the time…'.
   Request:
   Please state: (a) the date when Peter Sleep went sick; (b) the date when he returned; (c) all attempts that were made to communicate with Peter Sleep about the incident which led to the Claimant's dismissal. In relation to each such attempt: (i) the date when the communication took place; (ii) whether the communication was oral or in writing; and (iii) the contents of the communication in question.
2. Of 'If, which he did not accept, there was any problem with the behaviour of Ms Beattie towards the Claimant, he considered the correct course was for the Claimant to make a formal complaint through the grievance procedure.'
   Request:
   Please state whether it is the Respondent's case that the Claimant was aware of the Respondent's grievance procedure. If it is so claimed, please state the basis upon which it is so claimed, including the date, place and means by which she was informed about the procedure.

3. Of 'The Respondent will assert that it carried out all reasonable steps to prevent such an act taking place, including thorough equal opportunities training.'
   Request:
   Please give full details of the training which was carried out, including dates and the nature of the training in question.

IN THE FICTITIOUS EMPLOYMENT TRIBUNAL **Case No. [ ]**

B E T W E E N:

Felicity Faultless

Claimant

- and -

Trouble Likes Us Limited

Respondent

RESPONDENT'S REQUEST FOR FURTHER PARTICULARS OF THE GROUNDS OF COMPLAINT

---

1. Of 'Ms Beattie had victimized her over a period of time, a matter which had been the subject of a number of informal complaints…'.
   Request:
   Please state the date (or approximate date) when the alleged complaints were made and the person/s to whom the complaint/s were made.
2. Of 'Further, the applicant knows of numerous other incidents in which fights have resulted in nothing more severe than a warning.'
   Request:
   Please give details of each such incident, including the date when it occurred and who was involved.

IN THE FICTITIOUS EMPLOYMENT TRIBUNAL Case No. [ ]

B E T W E E N:

Felicity Faultless

Claimant

- and -

Trouble Likes Us Limited

Respondent

CLAIMANT'S APPLICATION FOR DISCLOSURE

The order sought:

The Claimant requests an order for disclosure of all documents in the possession of the Respondent relating to the incident between John Striker and Michael Ram, including, but not limited to:

- the notes of any formal investigation that took place, including interview notes;
- the notes of any disciplinary hearing which took place;
- any letters sent out informing the parties of the outcome of the investigation and/or the sanction which was to be imposed upon them.

The reasons for the application:

The Respondent has refused a voluntary request for the provision of the information, stating that it is irrelevant, and that disclosure of the information would be disproportionate to the complexity of the issues the tribunal has to decide.

The information sought is of fundamental importance to the Claimant's case both in relation to unfair dismissal and sex discrimination. The Claimant has alleged from the outset of the claim that two other male employees were treated more favourably than her in comparable circumstances. The Respondent has denied this, stating that the circumstances are different. The Claimant has no means of proving her case except by reference to the documents sought. It is not accepted that disclosure would be disproportionate to the complexity of the issues before the tribunal. The documentation sought is limited in nature.

IN THE FICTITIOUS EMPLOYMENT TRIBUNAL **Case No. [ ]**

B E T W E E N:

Felicity Faultless

Claimant

- and -

Trouble Likes Us Limited

Respondent

WITNESS STATEMENT OF JOHN WEARY

---

1. I, John Weary, am the Respondent's senior shift manager. The Respondent is an organisation which manufactures furniture. I have worked for the Respondent for a total of 15 years and have held the post of senior shift manager since 2005. In that capacity, I have responsibility for approximately 100 staff, including the Claimant. I have attended, in my position as manager, a number of seminars relating to equal opportunities. I have also given equal opportunities briefings to the staff under my supervision, including the Claimant. I am the manager responsible for taking decisions in relation to formal warnings and dismissals under the disciplinary procedure. A copy of the procedure currently in place can be found at page 20 in the bundle. I would refer the tribunal in particular to page 24, the section entitled 'Gross Misconduct.'
2. I have known the Claimant since I started my current post in 2005. Prior to that date, I was engaged in a different part of the factory. I have not, since 2005, had a great deal of contact with the Claimant. We did, however, exchange pleasantries from time to time and I like to think that, had there been any difficulty, the Claimant could have approached me.
3. On 25 October 2010, Ms Anne Beattie, the Claimant's supervisor, walked into my office on the first floor. She was in tears and said to me: 'I have just been assaulted by Felicity'. I told her to sit down and confirmed that this is a matter that I would take seriously. I

did not ask her in detail about the incident as I knew I would be carrying out a formal interview with her at a later stage. I did ask her for the names of other people who witnessed the incident. I was given the names of four individuals.

4. I decided that the matter was potentially one of gross misconduct. As such, it fell to be dealt with under the Respondent's disciplinary procedure. I further concluded that the matter was sufficiently serious to warrant suspension of the Claimant on full pay pending the outcome of the investigation. The right to suspend in these circumstances is referred to both in the disciplinary procedure at page 23 and also the Claimant's contract of employment (page 18 of the bundle of documents). I called the Claimant in to my office and informed her of her suspension, also giving her a letter to that effect (page 35 of the bundle).
5. I next began the process of interviewing the witnesses to the incident. I planned the questions that I would ask to each witness. They were as follows: (a) were you present at the altercation between Felicity Faultless and Anne Beattie on 25 October 2010; and (b) describe what you saw. Depending upon the answers, I would then ask a number of follow up questions. During each interview, my secretary made a contemporaneous note of what was said. Notes of all of the interviews can be found at pages 36–40 in the bundle.
6. The first witness to be interviewed, Marjorie Gossforth, said she saw the entire incident. She was an employee at the same level as the Claimant. She stated that she was standing about ten yards away. Anne Beattie had asked the Claimant to clear up a spillage on the floor. The Claimant had become extremely annoyed and refused to do so. The Claimant 'squared up' to Ms Beattie and then pushed her away aggressively.
7. No other third parties witnessed the incident from beginning to end although two, Betty Chatter and Sharon Stonewall, said they turned around at the point when they heard Ms Beattie cry out and heard her say of the Claimant: 'she hit me'.
8. I next interviewed Ms Beattie, the complainant. She informed me that she had asked the Claimant to clean a spillage on the floor. The Claimant became very angry, claiming that she had not caused the spillage. Ms Beattie was attempting to explain the reason for the request when the Claimant aggressively squared up to her as if about to start fighting. The Claimant then put her hand on Ms Beattie's face and pushed her away so that Ms Beattie almost fell to the floor.

9. There was a fourth eyewitness to the incident, Peter Sleep, who was off sick on the day when the interviews were being carried out. I considered that I had sufficient information to call the Claimant to attend a disciplinary hearing without interviewing Mr Sleep. I should add that I am an extremely busy manager with many other duties. I had set aside a specific time to carry out interviews in relation to this matter during which Mr Sleep was not available. I concluded, on the information before me, that I had sufficient information upon which to proceed to a disciplinary hearing.
10. On 5 November 2010 I wrote to the Claimant setting out the charge and requesting that she attend a disciplinary hearing on 14 November 2004. The notes of that hearing, typed up from a contemporaneous note made by my secretary, are contained at pages 43–48 in the bundle. The Claimant told me that she did not want a representative present. At the hearing, I informed the Claimant that there was evidence before me that she had assaulted a manager, but that I certainly had not made up my mind on the issue and that this was her opportunity to tell me her side of the story. I asked the Claimant whether she had assaulted Anne Beattie. The Claimant replied that she had not. She admitted pushing Ms Beattie but only after Ms Beattie had grabbed her by the collar. The Claimant stated that she was very upset and that Ms Beattie had been victimising her for the entire year they had been working together. On this occasion, the Claimant was asked to clear up a mess on the floor she had not created. At the conclusion of the hearing, which lasted approximately 40 minutes, I told the Claimant that I would consider all of the evidence in the case, including what she had told me, and reach my decision. I also, at the conclusion of the hearing, summarised her case as she had told it to me, and asked her to confirm that this was an accurate summary, which she duly did.
11. Prior to making my decision, there was one matter that I decided required further investigation. I asked Marjorie Gossforth whether she saw Anne Beattie make physical contact with the Claimant at any stage. Ms Gossforth replied that she did not. I recorded this conversation in a written memorandum, which is at page 41 in the bundle.
12. I next came to consider my decision. I formed the view that the Claimant had committed an assault and should be dismissed. My reasons for so concluding are set out in a memorandum written at the time, to be found at page 49. It can be seen from

the memorandum that I did not believe the Claimant's account of what had taken place. It was contradicted by that of Anne Beattie, a supervisor whose judgement and integrity I had come to respect, and by Marjorie Gossforth, an independent witness. I also considered that the other witnesses' accounts were consistent with the version given by Ms Beattie. I had little doubt that the Claimant had assaulted Ms Beattie. I next considered the issue of the appropriate sanction. I took into account the Claimant's previous good conduct, but concluded that unprovoked assaults on managers in the workplace could not be tolerated. I formed the view that the Ms Beattie was simply trying to do her job and needed to be protected in doing so. If, which I was doubtful of, there was any truth in the suggestion that the Claimant had been victimised, I consider that the correct course would have been for the Claimant to pursue a complaint through the grievance procedure, or to at least mention her concerns to me. The first mention of it was at her disciplinary hearing. I further considered that the Claimant had shown no remorse for what took place.

13. I informed the Claimant of the outcome of her hearing by letter, which can be found at page 50 in the bundle. I also informed her that she had the right to appeal against the decision, a right which the Claimant chose to exercise. I enclosed the typed notes of the disciplinary hearing and asked the Claimant to sign in the space at the bottom to confirm their accuracy and return the notes to me. This she duly did. I had no further involvement with the case. The outcome of the appeal, which I understand took the form of a complete rehearing, is for the Respondent's chief line manager to give evidence upon.
14. I have been informed of the allegation by the Claimant that I treated her differently from two male employees involved in fighting a month or so before. I further understand that the Claimant is claiming that this constituted sex discrimination. I can confirm that two male employees, John Striker and Michael Ram, had been involved in a fight the previous week for which both had received a formal warning from myself. The circumstances were, however, different. Both informed me that they had fallen out over a personal matter unrelated to work. They were both sorry for what had occurred and had since made up. In those circumstances, I considered that a formal warning was merited. The circumstances of the Claimant's case were different. She carried out an unprovoked assault on a manager who was simply trying to carry out her duties. I refute the suggestion

> that there is any 'culture' in place in our workplace whereby violence is tolerated amongst men and not women. Any violence at work is treated extremely seriously, regardless of the sex of those involved. On a personal level, I find the allegation of sex discrimination to be grossly unfair.

I confirm that the contents of this statement are true.

Signed:

Dated:

IN THE FICTITIOUS EMPLOYMENT TRIBUNAL **Case No. [ ]**

B E T W E E N:

Felicity Faultless

Claimant

- and -

Trouble Likes Us Limited

Respondent

WITNESS STATEMENT OF FELICITY FAULTLESS

---

1. I, Felicity Faultless, am the Claimant in these proceedings. I was employed by the Respondent from 24 April 1998 until my dismissal on 17 November 2010. I had an immaculate conduct record and was an extremely hard working employee. I had carried out the same job on the production line, that of production assistant, for all of the twelve and a half years I had been at the company. Approximately one year before my dismissal, Anne Beattie became my supervisor. I had previously enjoyed a good relationship with all of the supervisors with whom I had worked.
2. For some reason Anne Beattie took a strong dislike to me from the moment she started in the job. On one occasion, shortly after she started, she told me that I was too 'stuck in my ways' and that I would need to change. I got the strong impression that she felt insecure about the fact that I was older than her. Whenever there was an unpleasant task that needed doing, she would always pick me out to do it. This was very upsetting, as I considered I was being bullied. I never made a formal complaint, but I did mention to Mr Weary on a number of occasions that I was not happy in my team and that I wanted to move. He asked me why this was and I stated that I did not get on with my supervisor.
3. On 25 October 2004, I was asked by Anne Beattie to clean up a spillage on the floor which a member of another team had caused. I could not believe it. There was a special cleaning unit in the factory who could have been asked to come down. Ms Beattie said that it

needed cleaning immediately. I said: 'in that case, why don't you do it'. At this point, Ms Beattie grabbed me by my collar. I panicked and pushed her away, whereupon she cried out 'she hit me'. I don't think that more than two people saw the incident. One of those was Marjorie Gossforth and the other was Peter Sleep. Each was standing to my left about ten yards away. I am very surprised that Marjorie Gossforth states that she did not see Anne Beattie grab me by the collar. That said, the whole thing happened very quickly and she could easily have missed it. Peter Sleep also witnessed the incident. He is not part of my team and works in a different part of the factory. I am amazed that the Respondent has not interviewed him. I told John Weary at the disciplinary hearing that he also saw the incident and that they should ask him for his account. The whole incident happened very quickly and it is perfectly possible that Marjorie Gossforth simply got it wrong.

4. I now understand that the Respondent is saying that Peter Sleep was off sick on the day that interviews were being held. I cannot understand why he was not interviewed after his return. I notice that, after my disciplinary hearing, Mr Weary carried out another interview with Marjorie Gossforth. It would have been easy for him to do the same thing with Mr Sleep. I also cannot understand why Mr Judge, the chief line manager who conducted the appeal hearing, relied solely upon Mr Weary's interview records and did not, at the very least, interview Mr Sleep. Given the importance of the matter, and the draconian nature of the penalty they were considering, I think this was both necessary and fair.
5. I am both angry and upset that Mr Weary and Mr Judge did not investigate my complaint that I had been victimised by Ms Beattie over a period of approximately two years. This was obviously a relevant factor.
6. I was never, during the course of my employment, made aware that there was a grievance procedure which I could use. Mr Weary must have known that I had been a loyal and hardworking employee and that there might be more to the incident that Anne Beattie had led him to believe. I really believe that, had he taken the trouble to look into the issue, other members of the team would have told him about the unfair treatment I had received. I am also surprised that he did not speak to my previous supervisors, who would have told him that I was a calm and hardworking employee.
7. I worked in a section of the factory where the majority of employees were women. In the warehouse section, however, the vast majority of employees were men. It is a well-known fact that fights break out

in that section of the factory on a fairly frequent basis. The fights are usually overlooked completely. Shortly before the incident that led to my dismissal, a serious fight broke out between two men in that section. It is my understanding that one of them suffered from a broken jaw. Despite this, both received a written warning and were not dismissed. It is quite obvious that this was a much more serious incident than the one that I was involved in. I do not believe that anything can justify the different way in which I was treated. I firmly believe that the Respondent had a different attitude towards fights amongst women than amongst men, and that I was treated less favourably as a result.

Signed:

Dated:

IN THE FICTITIOUS EMPLOYMENT TRIBUNAL **Case No. [ ]**

B E T W E E N:

Felicity Faultless

Claimant

- and -

Trouble Likes Us Limited

Respondent

DOCUMENTS BUNDLE: INDEX

Claimant's Notice of Appeal	Page 51
Notes of Appeal Hearing	Page 52
Letter dismissing appeal	Page 59
DIVIDER D: Incident between John Striker and Michael Ram	
Notes of disciplinary hearing	Page 60
Formal warning	Page 64

IN THE FICTITIOUS EMPLOYMENT TRIBUNAL **Case No. [ ]**

B E T W E E N:

Felicity Faultless

Claimant

- and -

Trouble Likes Us Limited

Respondent

CAST LIST

Felicity Faultless (Claimant)	Production Assistant
Anne Beattie	Supervisor
Betty Chatter	Production Assistant
Marjorie Gossforth	Production Assistant
John Judge	Chief Line Manager
Michael Ram	Warehouse Assistant
Peter Sleep	General Assistant
Sharon Stonewall	Production Assistant
John Striker	Warehouse Assistant
John Weary	Senior Shift Manager

IN THE FICTITIOUS EMPLOYMENT TRIBUNAL Case No. [ ]

B E T W E E N:

Felicity Faultless

Claimant

- and -

Trouble Likes Us Limited

Respondent

CLAIMANT'S SKELETON ARGUMENT

THE LAW

1.1 Unfair dismissal

1.2 Statute

1.3 The relevant statutory provisions are sections 98(1), (2) (4) of the Employment Rights Act 1996 (ERA 1996)).

1.4 Relevant case law

1.5 *British Home Stores v Burchell [1978] IRLR 379*:

1.6 In a case where misconduct is relied upon as the reason for dismissal, the tribunal should address itself to the following questions:

- Did the employer have a genuine belief in the reason for dismissal?
- Was that belief held on reasonable grounds?
- At the final stage when the belief was held, had the employer carried out such investigation as was reasonable in the circumstances?

1.7 In addition to applying the test in *Burchell* cited above, the tribunal should have regard to the global issue of whether the decision of the employer fell within the range of reasonable responses available to it (*Iceland Frozen Foods v Jones [1983] ICR 17*).

2. Sex discrimination

2.1 A person (A) discriminates against another if, because of a protected characteristic (i.e. sex), A treats B less favourably than A treats or would treat others (i.e. a man) (Equality Act 2010, s.13).

2.2 The Claimant relies, as comparators, upon John Striker and Michael Ram, whom it is alleged were treated more favourably in comparable circumstances.

2.3 In the alternative if, which is denied, those circumstances are held not to be comparable, the Claimant relies upon the case of a hypothetical male comparator whom she alleges would have been treated more favourably than herself.

THE LAW APPLIED TO THE FACTS OF THIS CASE

3. Unfair dismissal

3.1 Applying the three-fold test set out in *Burchell.*

3.2 Did the employer have a genuine belief in the reason for dismissal?

3.3 This is not disputed by the Claimant[2].

3.4 Was this belief held on reasonable grounds?

3.5 It is asserted, for the following reasons that, this was not so:

(a) There was no interview by either the dismissing manager or the appeals manager with a crucial witness to the incident, Peter Sleep, who might have corroborated the Claimant's account that she has been assaulted by Ms Beattie.

(b) There was no investigation by either the dismissing manager or the appeals manager of the Claimant's claim that she had been victimized by the alleged victim, Anne Beattie. This was central to the issue of whose account was credible and to the issue of provocation.

3.6 Did the employer carry out an investigation which was reasonable in the circumstances?

3.7 For the reasons given in 3.5(a) and (b) above, the Claimant contends that this was not so, particularly in view of the size and resources of the Respondent's organisation.

3.8 Was the decision within the range of reasonable responses?

3.9 The Claimant will contend that the decision was outside the range of reasonable responses open to the Respondent because:

- the Claimant had worked for the Respondent for twelve years with an immaculate conduct record;
- even on the version accepted by the Respondent, the incident was relatively minor;
- there was disparate treatment between the Claimant and two male employees who had received a formal warning the week before for a more severe incident.

2 Author's note: this limb is commonly conceded, since to do otherwise necessitates an allegation of bad faith against the employer something, which, on the facts of this case, is not part of the Claimant's case.

4. Sex Discrimination

4.1 The Claimant will contend that, in being dismissed by the Respondent, she was treated less favourably by them on grounds of her sex and that a male employee would have received a lesser sanction.

4.2 The Claimant relies, as comparators, upon two male employees – John Striker and Michael Ram – who were treated more favourably in comparable circumstances. In that case, the only material difference was that the altercation was much more serious, resulting in injuries, yet both escaped with formal warnings.

4.3 If, which is denied, the above case is held not to be comparable the Claimant relies, in the alternative, upon a hypothetical comparator as proof of less favourable treatment. In support of the proposition that such a comparator would be treated more favourably the Claimant relies upon: (a) the fact that fights between men at the factory were, in general, tolerated, but not amongst women; and (b) the incident between John Striker and Michael Ram cited above.

IN THE FICTITIOUS EMPLOYMENT TRIBUNAL **Case No. [ ]**

B E T W E E N:

Felicity Faultless

Claimant

- and -

Trouble Likes Us Limited

Respondent

SKELETON ARGUMENT ON BEHALF OF THE RESPONDENT

---

1. THE LAW

Unfair dismissal

1.1 The relevant legislative framework is provided for by s.98 of the Employment Rights Act 1996.

1.2 The relevant case law can be found in the cases of *British Home Stores v Burchell [1978] IRLR 379*. The tribunal should ask the following questions:

- Did the employer have a genuine belief in the reason for dismissal?
- Was that belief held on reasonable grounds?
- At the final stage when the belief was held, had the employer carried out such investigation as was reasonable in the circumstances?

1.3 The tribunal should have regard to the issue of whether or not the employer's decision was one that fell within the range of reasonable responses available to it (*Iceland Frozen Foods v Jones [1983] ICR 17*).

Sex discrimination

1.4 A person discriminates against a woman if, on the ground of her sex, they treats her less favourably than they would treat a man (Equality Act 2010, s.13).

1.5 S.23(1) of the Equality Act 2010 provides that "On a comparison of cases for the purposes of section 13, 14 or 19 there must be no material difference between the circumstances relating to each case".

1.6 The burden of proving less favourable treatment than a comparator, either actual or hypothetical, lies on the Claimant. Only if less favourable treatment is proved does the burden then shift to the

Respondent to prove that this was not on grounds of sex (Equality Act 2010, s.136).

2. SUBMISSIONS: UNFAIR DISMISSAL

Did the employer have a genuine belief in the reason for dismissal?

2.1 This is not disputed by the Claimant[3].

Was this belief held on reasonable grounds?

2.2 The Respondent relies on the following:
   (a) the evidence of the victim as to what had occurred;
   (b) the evidence of Marjorie Gossforth that the Claimant assaulted Ms Beattie and was not assaulted first;
   (c) the accounts of Betty Chatter and Sharon Stonewall which did nothing to contradict the victim's account;
   (d) the fact that the Claimant was given a full opportunity to give her account of what took place, both at her disciplinary hearing and at the appeal hearing;
   (e) the fact that Ms Beattie was a respected senior employee who was thought to be unlikely to fabricate her account.

Did the employer carry out an investigation which was reasonable in the circumstances?

2.3 The Respondent relies on 2.2(a) to (e) in support of the fact that it carried out a reasonable investigation. Interviews were carried out with all of the eyewitnesses to the event, except for one witness who was away sick. Given the information gathered from those interviews, the Respondent could not reasonably be expected to delay its investigation pending the return to work of Peter Sleep.

2.4 The Respondent denies that it was under a duty, as part of a reasonable investigation, to investigate the allegation of victimization levelled against Ms Beattie by the Claimant. The Claimant had the right to pursue a formal grievance in relation to this but at no time did so. The Claimant's main 'defence' was, in any event, that she was not the aggressor in the incident and acted in self defence. It was this that the Respondent was under a duty to investigate, a duty it fulfilled.

Was dismissal within the range of reasonable responses?

2.5 The assault committed by the Claimant constituted gross misconduct under the Respondent's disciplinary procedure, rendering the Claimant liable to dismissal.

2.6 Full consideration was given to applying another sanction but, for the following reasons, the Respondent's managers, both at

3 Author's note: this should be clear from the grounds of complaint but, if not, it should be established before the start of the case.

first instance and at appeal, considered that dismissal was the appropriate response:

- this was an assault on a manager who was simply attempting to carry out her duties;
- the Respondent had a duty to protect its staff in such circumstances;
- the Claimant had shown no remorse for what had taken place;
- the Respondent further contends that, as the incident constituted gross misconduct under the disciplinary procedure, the issue of what sanction to apply was a matter for the discretion of the Respondent's managers, a discretion which should only be interfered with on the basis that the choice they made was not open to them.

3. SUBMISSIONS: SEX DISCRIMINATION

3.1 The Respondent denies that it treated the Claimant less favourably on grounds of a protected characteristic, namely her sex. Each episode of fighting at the workplace is considered separately on its own merits. The manager with responsibility for taking the decision has a discretion whether to dismiss or not.

3.2 The Respondent denies that the Claimant is entitled to rely upon John Striker and Michael Ram as comparators. The circumstances in relation to that case were materially different:

- the cause of their dispute was unrelated to work and, in particular, did not relate to the giving of a reasonable instruction by a manager to an employee;
- both had shown genuine remorse and regret for the incident, and expressed a determination that it would not happen again;
- the Respondent contends that it was plainly open to their management to take the different views they did of the two incidents and that the views which they did hold were unrelated to sex. The issue of sanction was a matter within their discretion, a discretion which was exercised reasonably. It is denied that the Claimant was treated less favourably than a male comparator, either actual or hypothetical.
- the Respondent disputes that fights break out on a regular basis amongst men at its factory. The Claimant has been unable to single out specific incidents to support this assertion. The Respondent denies that there is a culture in place where fighting is tolerated amongst men. Fighting amongst both men and women is deemed to constitute gross misconduct and treated equally seriously in both cases.

IN THE FICTITIOUS EMPLOYMENT TRIBUNAL **Case No. [ ]**

B E T W E E N:

Felicity Faultless

Claimant

- and -

Trouble Likes Us Limited

Respondent

CHRONOLOGY

24 April 1998	The Claimant commences employment with the Respondent as a production assistant.
18 September 2010	An incident takes place of fighting at work between two other employees, John Striker and Michael Ram.
25 October 2010	The incident of alleged fighting between the Claimant and Ms Beattie.
25 October 2010	The Claimant is suspended at work by the production manager, John Weary.
27 October 2010	John Weary carries out interviews with witnesses to the event.
5 November 2010	The Claimant is invited to attend a disciplinary hearing.
14 November 2010	A disciplinary hearing takes place.
17 November 2010	The Claimant is told of her dismissal.
2 December 2010	An appeal hearing takes place.
12 December 2010	The decision to dismiss confirmed.
24 February 2011	The Claimant lodges her claim with the employment tribunal.

Appendix VI

Compromise agreement

[Agreement to refrain from instituting or continuing with proceedings before an employment tribunal][1]

This Agreement is made between [AB of (*address*) (hereafter referred to as 'the Employee')] and [XYZ Ltd of (*address*) (hereafter referred to as 'the Company')]

It is agreed between the parties as follows:

1. The Company will pay to the Employee the sum of [£15,000] within [7 days], and the Employee will accept the said sum, in full and final settlement of [the proceedings currently before the employment tribunal under Case No (*specify and briefly describe the nature and statutory basis of the claim*)] [and/*or* all claims (other than any claim for damages for personal injury or any claim arising under the Company's pension scheme, *or as the case may be*) which the Claimant has or may have against the Company arising out of his contract of employment or the termination thereof, whether at common law or under the statutory provisions set out in paragraph 2 below, being provisions in respect of which an employment tribunal has jurisdiction].[2]
2. The statutory provisions mentioned in paragraph 1 above are: (*eg*)
   (i) Employment Rights Act 1996 s 23(1) (unlawful deduction of wages), and/*or* s 48(1) (detriment in respect of leave for family and domestic reasons under s 47C) and/*or* s 48(1A) (detriment relating to protected disclosures), and/*or* s 80 (parental leave), s 80H (flexible working); and/*or* s 111 (unfair dismissal), and/*or* s 163 (redundancy payments); and/*or*
   (ii) Working Time Regulations 1998, reg 30(1); and/*or*
   (iii) Part-Time Workers (Prevention of Less Favourable Treatment) Regulations 2000, reg 8(1); and/*or*
   (iv) Fixed-Term Employees (Prevention of Less Favourable Treatment) Regulations 2002, reg 7(1); and/*or*
   (v) Equality Act 2010 Pt 2 (discrimination, whether direct or

indirect, on grounds of (*specify* those which are appropriate) age, disability, gender reassignment, marriage and civil partnership, pregnancy and maternity, race, religion or belief, sex or sexual orientation) and/or Pt 5 (equality of terms).

3. Upon the signing of this Agreement the Employee will [forthwith withdraw his claim against the Company under Case No (*specify*)] [and/*or* refrain from instituting any claim against the Company before an employment tribunal in respect of any claim under the statutory provisions set out in paragraph 2 above].
4. The Employee acknowledges that, before signing this Agreement, he received independent legal advice from (*name of adviser*) as to the terms and effect of this Agreement and in particular its effect on his ability to pursue his rights before an employment tribunal. The said adviser is a [qualified lawyer (*specify whether barrister, solicitor or advocate*) *or* certified trade union official *or* certified advice centre worker, *or* fellow of the Institute of Legal Executives][3] in respect of whom there is in force a contract of insurance or a professional indemnity insurance covering the risk of a claim by the Employee in respect of loss arising in consequence of the advice.
5. The conditions regulating compromise agreements under the [Employment Rights Act 1996 and/*or* Equality Act 2010 and/*or* Working Time Regulations 1998 (*or as the case may be*)] are satisfied in relation to this Agreement.[4]

(Signed)

(Employee): Date:

(For the Company): Date

1 See, for example, ERA 1996 s 203(2)(*f*), (3)–(5); TULR(C)A 1992 s 288(2A)–(5); EqA 2010 s 144(4)(b), s 147. For a full list of statutory claims which may be contracted out by means of a compromise agreement, see PI [727]; and for compromise agreements generally, see PI [726]–[730.06].

2 It is to be noted that a compromise agreement, to be effective in precluding an employee or worker from instituting or continuing claims in employment tribunals, must relate to 'the particular complaint' or the 'particular proceedings' (see, for example, ERA 1996 s 203(3)(*b*) ('particular proceedings')). This means that, unlike the position where a settlement is negotiated under the auspices of ACAS, a blanket exclusion in a compromise agreement of all statutory rights will be ineffective as a means of excluding particular rights: see *Hinton v University of East London [2005] IRLR 552, CA.*

3 The categories of persons who can give independent legal advice in relation to compromise agreements are defined in the relevant statutory provisions (see, for example, ERA 1996 s 203(3A)–(4), as amended by ERDRA 1998), and can be extended by order of the Secretary of State (see ERA 1996 s 3A(*d*)). By virtue of the Compromise

Agreements (Description of Person) Order 2004 SI 2004/754, as amended by SI 2004/2515, a Fellow of the Institute of Legal Executives may also give such advice provided he is employed by a solicitor's practice. It is a requirement that the adviser be identified in the agreement (see, for example, ERA 1996 s 203(3)(e)).

4 Such a statement must be made in the agreement (see, for example, ERA 1996 s 203(3)(f)). Where complaints are made under more than one statute, it is important to state in the agreement that the conditions regulating compromise agreements have been satisfied in relation to each statute (see *Lunt v Merseyside TEC Ltd [1999] IRLR 458, [1999] ICR 17, EAT*).

Index

[all references are to paragraph number]

D